INTRODUCTION TO MANAGEMENT IN THE HOSPITALITY INDUSTRY

WILEY SERVICE MANAGEMENT SERIES
TOM POWERS, Series Editor

Introduction to Management In The Hospitality Industry, Third Edition
Tom Powers

Basics of Quantity Food Production
Jo Marie Powers

The Management of Maintenance and engineering systems in the Hospitality Industry, Second Edition
Frank D. Borsenik

Food Service Operations: Planning and Control
Tom Powers/Jo Marie Powers

The BAR and Beverage Book: Basics of Profitable Management
Costas Katsigris/Mary Porter

Purchasing: Selection and Procurement for the Hospitality Industry, Second Edition
John M. Stefanelli

Introduction to the Hospitality Industry
Tom Powers

Supervision in the Hospitality Industry
Jack E. Miller/Mary Porter

INTRODUCTION TO MANAGEMENT IN THE HOSPITALITY INDUSTRY

THIRD EDITION

TOM POWERS
School of Hotel and Food Administration
University of Guelph

JOHN WILEY & SONS
New York
Chichester
Brisbane
Toronto
Singapore

Library of Congress Cataloging in Publication Data:

Powers, Thomas F.
   Introduction to management in the hospitality industry / Thomas F.
   Powers.—3rd ed.
   p.   cm.—(Wiley service management series)
   Bibliography: p.
   ISBN 0-471-83933-7
   1. Hotel management.   2. Food service management.   3. Restaurant
management.   I. Title.   II. Series.
TX911.3.M27P68   1988   87-34529
647′.94′068—dc19   87-34529
                                                                                        CIP

ISBN 0-471-83933-7
ISBN 0-471-62957-X (pbk)

Printed in the United States of America

10 9 8 7 6 5 4 3 2 1

Production supervised by Laura McCormick
Cover and text design by Carolyn Joseph
Cover photo by Robert Phillips/The Image Bank

With affection to my father, the late F. Urban Powers, a pioneer in the application of modern management techniques to the hospitality industry, who taught me to understand the relationship between the particular and the general and to guide practice with theory.
1898—1980

PREFACE

The hospitality industry and its fast-paced rate of change makes life difficult for authors revising textbooks. A simple updating of facts and statistics—although that is provided here, where appropriate—is just not enough. The question really is, "Which facts are relevant in analyzing today's industry?" Large parts of this book are new, including entire new chapters concerned with franchising, technology and computers, as well as new developments in lodging, tourism, and food services. Moreover, within chapters retained from the earlier edition, there are numerous new sections.

Perhaps we should pause here, however, to emphasize that the text's basic commitments have remained the same. The student still needs to be able to see hospitality as a single, interrelated industry. The emphasis on problem solving *tools* rather than answers and on understanding industry-wide *trends* rather then simple facts and figures remains central. This is not a "how to" book. The commitment in the first edition to the importance of field experience and personal observation still comes through loud and clear in Chapter 1 and, I hope, throughout the rest of the text. Finally and most fundamentally, the student is challenged throughout to realize that in building a career in hospitality he or she is building a business and a way of life as well. For all that, however, there is much here that is new.

In the chapters on food service, the improved availability of information on consumer trends and preferences makes addition of those topics possible. The food service chapters have also been reorganized to accommodate new material on the consumer's view of service, nutrition and alcoholic beverages. New or expanded services make discussion of topics such as mobile units, popular-priced operations outside fast food, and the growing impact of competition from commerical operations on institutional operations essential.

There are new chapters on lodging. The first of these deals with the growing importance of computers and technology in lodging, where well over half of front offices are computerized and the property management system is becoming the norm. We look ahead, too, to the increasing adoption of automation in the "smart hotel room." Chapter 9, which is also new, discusses the forces behind the expansion in the number of hotel rooms available and the segmentation of amenities and services. The role of management companies and real estate developers, and the interaction between the two, is also discussed there.

We have added new chapters on tourism, in recognition of the importance of changing demand factors and travel motives, as well as the favorable and unfavorable impacts of tourism. There is new material on casinos in tourism as well as other smaller scale attractions like waterfront developments, shopping centers, museums, and zoos. The discussion of campgrounds is strengthened by a broader understanding of the motives of campers.

The new chapter on franchising discusses its economic significance and details the services provided by franchisors while assessing the franchise relationship and its advantages and disadvantages for both parties.

Throughout the text there is major attention to assessing the impact of North America's rapidly changing demographics and the accompanying changes in life styles. Very few factors are likely to be as important in hospitality in the next ten years. In the last chapter, we consider the outlook for the hospitality industry in the first half of the 1990's and the years ahead.

The dynamic and everchanging hospitality industry is a hard task master for all of us who work in this business. But it is exciting, and I can only hope that students will take some of the pleasure in reading this text which I found in writing it.

I am indebted to many people for help with this text. First and foremost among them is my wife, Jo Marie, who prepared the instructor's manual and the test bank, to say nothing of bearing with the confusion and annoyances that are a part of any writing project.

In regard to the research for the section on gaming, I am indebted to Dean James Healy and Professor Richard Wisch at Fairleigh Dickinson University and Dean Francis X. Brown and Professor Richard Gill at Widener University for arranging the contacts without which that research could not have been accomplished. Professor Steven Rosenbey of Fairleigh Dickinson and James Kilby, Boyd Professor of Casino Management and Operations at the University of Nevada at Las Vegas read the section of the manuscript pertaining to casinos and gaming and made numerous helpful suggestions. Dean Jerome Vallen of the University of Nevada at Las Vegas was also most helpful in the research related to this section of the text. Dr. Kenneth Hornbach, Director of Research for the National Parks Service, suggested publications I should consult and made several of them available to me for the chapters on tourism. Finally, my colleague at Guelph, Professor Michael Haywood was generous in directing my attention to material related to fairs and festivals and, generally, in identifying appropriate information on tourism's impacts.

This text has also benefited from the many suggestions of colleagues who have used the text. In addition, this revision has been reviewed by 14 reviewers. The thoughtful comments of these HRI educators resulted in numerous improvements in the final manuscript and I am grateful for their interest. It is a pleasure to list them here.

Earl R. Arrowood, Bucks County Community College; V. Chandrasekar, University of Central Florida; H.A. Divine, Pennsylvania State University; Jill Dybus, Oakton Community College; Evan Enowitz, Grossmont College; Stephenson W. Fletcher, University of Massachusetts; James B. Healy, Fairleigh-Dickinson University; Lenka Hospodka, Widener College; Carol Kizer, Columbus Technical Institute; Joseph Van Kornfeld, University of Nevada; Cynthia Nelson, Cuyohoga Community College; Karen O'Brien, Hunter College; Teresa M. Schultz, University of Wisconsin, Stout; Andrew Schwartz, Sullivan County Community College.

In spite of all the help I have had, there still remain errors and deficiencies in this text for which, of course, the author must accept the responsibility.

Tom Powers
Moon River, Ontario
August, 1987

CONTENTS

CHAPTER 20   FRANCHISE SYSTEMS IN THE HOSPITALITY INDUSTRY ... 516

INTRODUCTION TO MANAGEMENT IN THE HOSPITALITY INDUSTRY

P A R T 1

A LOOK
AT YOU
IN THE
HOSPITALITY
INDUSTRY

Chapter 1 looks at some of the ways you and the hospitality industry fit together. We will cover topics such as career planning; how employment in the industry fits into your education; and employment at graduation. The chapter concludes with a brief look at the prospects for people interested in working in hospitality management.

C H A P T E R 1

Courtesy of The Plaza.

THE HOSPITALITY INDUSTRY
AND YOU

THE PURPOSE OF THIS CHAPTER

Your own career choice is probably the most important *management decision* you'll ever make—at least from your point of view. This chapter has been designed, therefore, to help you analyze a career in the hospitality industry and correlate that analysis with your field experiences while in school. It will also help prepare you for the first career decision you make just before or after you graduate. This chapter, in short, discusses the career decisions ahead of you over the next three to five years.

THIS CHAPTER SHOULD HELP YOU

1. Know what kind of businesses (and other establishments) make up the hospitality industry.
2. Know why people study in hospitality management programs—and what advantages these academic programs may have for you.
3. Think of your career decision in terms of a life's work, not just a job.
4. Start planning your field experiences—again, not just as jobs, but as crucial parts of your education.
5. Relate your education—both class and field experiences—to your employment goals at graduation.
6. Evaluate the employment outlook in the various sectors of the hospitality industry, and learn where the "hot spots" and "soft spots" are.

WHAT IS HOSPITALITY MANAGEMENT?

When we think of the *hospitality industry,* we usually think of hotels and restaurants. But the term has a much broader meaning. According to the *Oxford English Dictionary,* hospitality means "the reception and entertainment of guests, visitors or strangers with liberality and good will." The word *hospitality* is derived from *hospice,* a medieval "house of rest" for travelers and pilgrims. A hospice was also an early form of what we now call a nursing home, and the word is clearly related to *hospital.*

Hospitality, then, includes hotels and restaurants. But it also refers to other kinds of institutions that offer shelter or food or both to people away from their homes. Moreover, these institutions have more than a common historical heritage. They also share the management problems of providing food and shelter—problems that include erecting a building; providing heat, light, and power; cleaning and maintaining the premises; and preparing and serving food in a way that pleases the guests. Of course, we expect all of this to be done "with liberality and good will" when we stay in a hotel or dine in a restaurant, but we can also rightfully expect the same treatment from the dietary department in a health-care facility or from a school lunch program.

The hospitality professions are among the oldest of the humane professions, and they involve making a guest, client, or resident welcome and comfortable. But there is a more important reason that people interested in a career in these industries should think of them collectively. Today, managers and supervisors, as well as skilled employees, find that opportunities for advancement often mean moving from one part of the hospitality industry to another. For example, a hospitality graduate may begin as a management trainee with a restaurant company, complete the necessary training, and in a short time take a job as an assistant innkeeper in a motor hotel. The next job offer could come from a hospitality conglomerate, such as ARA Services. ARA provides food service operations not only in plant and office food services, but also in such varied areas as recreation centers, college campuses, health-care facilities, airline food services, community nutrition centers, and gourmet restaurants. Another such conglomerate is Marriott, which some people think of as a hotel company (which it is) or a restaurant company (which it is). But Marriott is also one of the largest airline food service companies in the world and one of the largest institutional food service companies in the United States. Likewise, Holiday Inns, as everybody knows, is in the motor hotel business, but it is also one of the largest food service companies in the United States.

The point, of course, is that the hospitality industry is tied together as a clearly recognizable unit by more than just a common heritage and a commitment to "liberality and good will." Careers in the industry are such that your big break may come in a part of the industry entirely different from the

Saga Food Service, a Marriott subsidiary, provides food service on the ferries that serve travelers commuting to Seattle through one of North America's most beautiful waterways, Puget Sound.

one you expected. Hospitality management is one of the few remaining places in our specialized world of work that calls for a broadly gauged generalist—and the student who understands this principle increases the opportunity for a rewarding career in one of the hospitality industries.

THE MANAGER'S ROLE IN THE HOSPITALITY INDUSTRY

As a successful manager in the hospitality industry, you must exhibit many skills and command much specialized knowledge, but for now, let's discuss three general kinds of hospitality objectives:

1. *A manager wants to make the guest welcome personally.* This requires both a friendly manner on your part toward the guest and an atmosphere of "liberality and good will" among the people who work with you in serving the guests. That almost always means an organization in which workers get along well with one another.

2. *A manager wants to make things work for the guest.* Food has to be savory and hot or cold according to design—and on time. Beds must be made and rooms cleaned. A hospitality system requires a lot of work, and the manager must see that it is done.

3.   *A manager wants to make sure the operation will continue providing service and making a profit.*   When we speak of "liberality and good will," we don't mean giving the whole place away! In a restaurant or hotel operated for profit, portion sizes are related to cost, and so menu and room prices must be related to building and operating costs. This enables the establishment to recover the cost of its operation and to make enough additional income to pay back any money borrowed, as well as to provide a return to the owner who risked a good deal of money—and time—to build the establishment. (This situation is surprisingly similar to subsidized operations such as school lunch or health-care food services. Here the problem is not to make a profit but to achieve either a break-even or zero-profit operation, or a controlled but negative profit—that is, a loss covered by a subsidy from another source. The key lies in achieving a controlled profit, loss, or break-even operation. A good term to describe this management concern is "conformance to budget.")

Managers, then, must be able to relate successfully to employees and guests, direct the work of their operation, and achieve operating goals within a budget.

WHY STUDY IN A HOSPITALITY MANAGEMENT PROGRAM?

One way to learn the hospitality business is actually to go to work in it and acquire the necessary skills to operate the business. The trouble with this approach, however, is that the skills that accompany the various work stations (cook, waitress, and so forth) are not the same as those needed by hospitality managers. In earlier times of small operations in a slowly changing society, hospitality education was basically skill centered. Most hospitality managers learned their work through apprenticeship. The old crafts built on apprenticeships assumed that knowledge—and work—were unchanging. But for reasons that later chapters will make clear, this assumption no longer holds true. As Peter Drucker, a noted management consultant, pointed out, "Today the center [of our society's productivity] is the knowledge worker, the man or woman who applies to productive work ideas, concepts, and information."[1] In other words, *studying* is a necessary part of your preparation for a career as a supervisor or manager.

Of course, many people argue that the liberal arts provide excellent preparation not only for work but also for life. They're quite right. What we've found, however, is that many students just aren't interested in the liberal arts subject matter. Because they are not interested, they are not

[1]Peter F. Drucker, *The Age of Discontinuity* (New York: Harper & Row, 1968), p. 264.

Luxury food service is vital to the success of first-class resort hotels—a fact that underscores the importance of regarding hospitality (hotels and restaurants) as one industry. (Photo courtesy of Resorts International.)

eager to learn. On the other hand, these same people become hard-working students in a career-oriented program that interests them. Besides, there's no reason for educational preparation for work to be separate from preparation for life. We spend at least half our waking hours at work. As we will learn shortly, work lies at the heart of a person's life and can lead directly to "self-discovery."

Business administration offers a logical route to management preparation. Indeed, many hospitality managers have prepared for their careers in this field. But business administration is principally concerned with the manufacturing and marketing of a physical product in a national market. By contrast, the hospitality industry is a service industry, and the management of a service institution *is* different. Food is, of course, a restaurant's product, but most of the "manufacturing" (often all of it) is done right in the place that offers the service. The market is local, and the emphasis is on face-to-face contact with the guest. Hospitality operations are also smaller; so the problems of the large bureaucracy are not as significant as are the problems of face-to-face relationships with employees and guests.

Our point is not that there is something wrong with the liberal arts or with business administration. The point is that hospitality management programs are usually made up of students who are interested in what they're studying and that there is a difference between the hospitality service system and the typical manufacturing company.

Now, why might anyone want to study in a hospitality management program? Perhaps the best answer is the reasons that students before you have chosen to study there. Their reasons fall into three categories: their experience, their interests, and their ambitions. Figure 1.1 lists the various reasons

---

EXPERIENCE
   Personal work experience
   Family background in the industry
   Contact with other students and faculty in hospitality management programs
INTERESTS
   Enjoy working with people
   Enjoy working with food
   Enjoy dining out, travel, variety
AMBITION
   Opportunity for employment and advancement
   Desire to operate own business
   Desire to be independent

FIGURE 1.1   The reasons that students select hospitality management programs.

that students cite, in order of frequency. As you can see, many students become interested in hospitality because a job they once had proved particularly attractive. Others learn of the industry through family or friends working in the field.

One important consideration for many students is that they like and are interested in people. As we just saw, working well with people is a crucial part of a manager's job in our industry. Many students, too, have a natural interest in food, and some are attracted by the natural glamour of the hospitality industry.

In addition, the employment outlook (as we'll see later in this chapter) is excellent in most segments of the hospitality industry, particularly for managers. Many people are attracted to a field in which they are reasonably sure they can secure employment. Others feel that in a job market with more opportunities than applicants, they will enjoy a good measure of independence, whether in their own businesses or as company employees. Many students are drawn to the hospitality industry because they want to get into their own business. One way to do that is through franchised operations, discussed in Chapter 20. Others, with good reason, suspect there are opportunities for innovation off the beaten track of the franchise organizations. And there are many examples of success.

Many young entrepreneurs have chosen catering as a low-investment field that offers opportunities to people with a flair for foods and careful service. Catering, perhaps the fastest-growing segment of food service, according to the National Restaurant Association,[2] is also a business that students sometimes try while in school, through either a student organization or groups of students setting up a small catering operation.

In the lodging area, one enterprising young couple expanded in an ingenious way the services of a small country firm. Once they and their tiny inn had been established in the community, they arranged to represent a large number of rental-unit owners in the area, offering marketing services to the owners and providing "front office" and housekeeping services for their guests in some 50 units, ranging from one-bedroom condominiums to larger condos and even houses.[3] The magazine *Restaurant Business* described this "new breed of independents" as follows:

> They practice modern management techniques rather than seat of the pants management, and they understand the importance of personnel policies, marketing and promotion, well-defined business strategies, and staying abreast of the industry. . .."[4]

[2]*NRA News*, February 1985, p. 17.
[3]*Lodging*, September 1984, pp. 68–71.
[4]*Restaurant Business*, January 20, 1986, p. 96.

Marriott In-Flite Services, the world's largest and oldest independent airline caterer, serves over 100 U.S. and foreign carriers in 50 major cities. Today the company also caters for railroads and health-care institutions from flight kitchens.

There are many other opportunities as well—for instance, people with chef's training may open their own business, especially if they feel that they have a sufficient management background. In the health-care area, home-care organizations are expanding in response to the needs of our growing senior citizen population and offer a wide range of opportunities to entrepreneurs. This interest in independent operations reinforces the need for studying hospitality management.

Whether you're studying hospitality management because you want to start a business of your own or because you found your past work experience in the business especially interesting—or perhaps just because the continuing growth in the area makes the job prospects especially attractive—management studies are an important preparation for budding entrepreneurs. Hospitality management students tend to be highly motivated, lively people who take pride in their future in a career of service.

PLANNING A CAREER

WHY DO WE WORK?

We all have several motives for going to work. Of course, we work to live—to provide food, clothing, and shelter. Psychologists and sociologists tell us, however, that our work also provides a sense of who we are and binds us to the community in which we live. The ancient Greeks, who had slaves to do menial tasks, saw work as a curse. Their Hebrew contemporaries saw it as punishment. Early Christians, too, saw work for profit as offensive. But by the time of the Middle Ages, work began to be accepted as a vocation, that is, as a calling from God. Gradually, as working conditions improved and work became something that all social classes did, it became a necessary part of maturation and self-fulfillment in our society.

Today, workers at all levels demand more than just a job. Indeed, work has been defined as "an activity that produces something of value for other people."[5] This definition puts work into a social context. That is, it implies there is a social purpose to work as well as the crude purpose of survival. It is an important achievement in human history that the majority of Americans can define their own approach to a life of work as something more than mere survival.

Work contributes to our self-esteem in two ways. First, by doing our work well, we prove our own competence to ourselves. Psychologists tell us that this is essential to a healthy life, as this information gives us a sense of control over both ourselves and our environment. Second, by working we contribute to others—others come to depend on us. Human beings, as social animals, need this sense of participation. For these reasons, what happens at work becomes a large part of our sense of self-worth.

Education for such a significant part of life is clearly important. The next section explores career planning in regard to employment decisions that you must make while you are still in school. We also will discuss selecting your first employer when you leave school. If you've chosen the hospitality industry as your career, this section will help you map out your job plans. If you are still undecided, the section should help you think about this field in a more concrete way and give you some ideas about exploring your career through part-time employment.

It's hard to overstate the importance of career planning. Young people, particularly in high school, find that their career plans change constantly. But by the time they've graduated from high school, their career plans have begun to take definite shape. But there still may be more changes. For example, people who start out studying for a career in the hotel business may find the opportunities they want in food service. Others may begin preparations for the restaurant industry only to find they prefer the hours offered in industrial food service. This kind of change in plans will be easier to cope with if you have a plan that can guide you until your experience enables you to judge the "fit" between yourself and the available opportunities. As a prospective manager, give at least as much time and attention to planning for decisions that affect your career as you expect to give to decisions you will be making for your employer. Remember that no matter who you work for, you're always in business for yourself, because it's *your* life.

[5]*Work in America* (Cambridge, Mass.: MIT Press, n.d.), p. 3.

EMPLOYMENT AS AN IMPORTANT PART OF YOUR EDUCATION

Profit in a business is treated in two different ways. Some is paid out to the owner or shareholders as dividends (returns on their investment). Some of the profit, however, is retained by the business to provide funds for future growth. This portion of profit that is not paid out is called *retained earnings*. WE NEED A CONCEPT OF RETAINED EARNINGS TO CONSIDER THE REAL PLACE OF WORK EXPERIENCE IN CAREER DEVELOPMENT.

PROFITING FROM WORK EXPERIENCE

The most obvious profit we earn from work is the income paid to us by an employer. But in the early years of your career, there are other kinds of benefits that are at least as important as is income. The key to understanding this statement is the idea of a lifetime income. You'll obviously need income over your entire life span, but giving up some income now may gain you income (and, we ought to note, enjoyment, a sense of satisfaction, and independence) just a few years later. There is, then, a *job benefit mix* made up of both money and knowledge to be gained from any job. Knowledge gained today can be traded with an employer for income tomorrow: a better salary for a better-qualified person. The decision to take a job that will add to your knowledge is thus a decision for retained earnings and for acquiring knowledge that you can use later.

Every job, therefore, has to be weighed according to its benefit mix, not just in terms of the dollar income it provides. A part-time job as a supermarket stock boy (well, it is a "food-related" job in a way) might seem attractive because it pays more than a bus boy's job does. But if you think about the learning portion of the benefit mix and your *total* income, including what you learn, your decision may—and probably should—be for the job that will add to your professional education.

There is another important point to consider about retained earnings and the benefit mix. Very often, the only part-time job in the industry available to students is an unskilled one. Many people find these jobs dull, and they often pay poorly. But if you think about these jobs in terms of their total income, you may change your perspective. The work of a bus boy or a dishwasher won't take you very long to learn. But, you can improve your total profits from such a job by resolving to learn all you can *about the operation*. In this way you can build your retained earnings—the bank of skills and knowledge that nobody can ever take away from you.

Learning Strategies for Work Experience

When you go to work, regardless of the position you take, you can learn a good deal through careful observation. Look first at how the operation is organized. More specifically, look at both its managerial organization and its physical organization.

Managerial Organization.   In chapter 15, we will consider briefly some of the typical organizational forms of hotels and restaurants. Even now, however, you can begin to think about this problem. Who is the boss? Who reports to (or works directly with) him or her? Is the work divided into definite departments or sections? Is one person responsible for each department? To whom do the department staff members report? If you can answer these questions, you will have figured out the *formal organization* of the operation. Indeed, most large companies will have an organization chart that you can look at. If your employer doesn't have such a chart, ask him or her to explain the organization to you. You'll be surprised at how helpful to hospitality management students most employers and supervisors are.

While you're thinking about organization, it is also important to notice the "informal organization" or the "social organization" of the group you are working with. Which of the workers are influential? Who seem to be the informal leaders, and why? Most work groups are made up of cliques with informal leaders. After you identify this informal structure, ask yourself how management deals with it. Remember that someday, the management of these "informal organizations" will be *your* problem; in time, you will be helping to plan the organization, and you will need their cooperation. In the meantime, this first-hand experience will help you both in your studies and in sizing up the real world of work.

The Physical Plant.   You can learn a great deal about a physical plant by making a simple drawing of your workplace, like the one shown in Figure 1.2. On this drawing, identify the main work areas and major pieces of equipment. Then begin to note on it where you see problems resulting from cross traffic or bottlenecks. For example, if you're working in the *"back of the house,"* you can chart the flow of products from the back door (receiver) to storage and from there to preparation. You should also trace the flow of dishes. Dirty dishes come to the dishroom window and go to the clean-supply area after washing. How are they transported to the cooler or to the pantry people for use in service? If you are working in the back of the house, you will be looking mostly at the flow of kitchen workers and dishes from the viewpoint of the kitchen, dishroom, or pantry. A similar flow analysis of guests and servers (and plates) can also be made from the *front of the house* (that is, the dining room).

A study of guest flow in a hotel lobby can be equally enlightening. Trace the flow of room guests, restaurant guests, banquet department guests, and service employees arriving through the lobby. Then note where you observe congestion.

These simple charting activities will give you some practical experience that will be useful for later courses in layout and design and in food service operations and analysis.

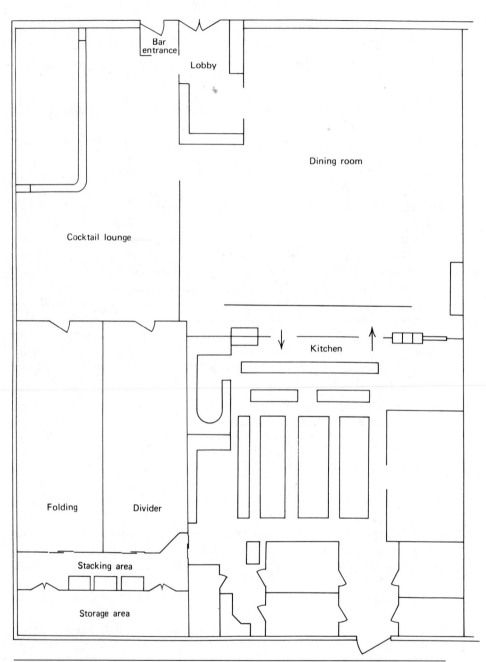

FIGURE 1.2   A sample layout (not to scale).

Atlanta's Peachtree Center offers a most dramatic and beautiful "front of the house."
(Photo by Alexandre Georges.)

Dining and food service is an important part of any luxury hotel. The room pictured here is Appley's in the Sheraton Boston. (Photo courtesy of Fay's Photos.)

Learning from the Back of the House

Things to look for in the back of the house include how quality is assured in preparation, menu planning, recipes, cooking methods, supervision, and food holding. (How is lunch prepared in advance? How is it kept hot or cold? How long can food be held?) How are food costs controlled? For instance, are food portions standardized? Are they measured? How? How is access to storerooms controlled? These all are points you'll consider a great deal in later courses. But from the very beginning you can collect information that is invaluable to your studies and your career.

Learning from the Front of the House

If you are working as a bus boy, waitress, or a server on a cafeteria line, you can learn a great deal about the operation from observing the guests or clients. Who are the customers, and what do they value? Peter Drucker called these the two central questions in determining what a business is and what it should be doing.[6] Are the guests or clients satisfied? What in particular seems to please them?

[6]Peter F. Drucker, *Management: Tasks, Responsibilities, Practices* (New York: Harper & Row, 1974), pp. 80–86.

Employees in the hospitality industry derive personal satisfaction from pleasing the guests. So be sure to find out whether or not your job will allow you this satisfaction. Would you change things? How?

In any job you take, your future work lies in managing others and serving people. Wherever you work and whatever you do, you can observe critically the management and guest or client relations of others. Ask yourself, "How would I have handled that problem? Is this an effective management style? In what other ways have I seen this problem handled?" Your development as a manager also means the development of a management style that suits you, and that is a job that will depend in large part on your personal experience.

GETTING A JOB

Hospitality jobs can be obtained from several sources. For example, your college may maintain a placement office. Many hospitality management programs receive direct requests for part-time help. Some programs maintain a job bulletin board or file, and some even work with industry to provide internships. The "help wanted" pages of your newspaper also may offer leads, as may your local employment service office. Sometimes personal contacts established through your fellow students, your instructor, or your family or neighborhood will pay off. Or you may find it necessary to "pound the pavement," making personal applications in places where you would like to work.

Some employers may even arrange for hospitality management students to rotate through more than one position and even to assume some supervisory responsibility.

Getting in the Door

But it is not enough just to ask for a job. Careful attention to your appearance is important too. For an interview, this probably means a coat and tie for men, a conservative dress for women. Neatness and cleanliness are the absolute minimum. (Neatness and cleanliness are, after all, major aspects of the hospitality product.) When you apply for or have an interview for a job, if you can, find out who the manager is; then, if the operation is not a large one, ask for him or her by name. In a larger organization, however, you'll deal with a personnel manager. The same basic rules of appearance apply, regardless of the organization's size.

Don't be afraid to check up on the status of your application. Here's an old but worthwhile adage from personal selling: It takes three calls to make a sale. The number *three* isn't magic, but a certain persistence—letting an employer know that you are interested—often will land you a job. Be sure to identify yourself as a hospitality management student, because this tells an employer that you will be interested in your work.

Learning from a Job

Let's look at some ideas about learning on the job. One key is your attitude. If you are really interested and eager to learn, you will, in fact, learn a great deal more, because you will naturally extend yourself, ask questions, and observe what's going on around you.

Many hospitality managers report that they gained the most useful knowledge on the job *on their own time*. Let's suppose you're working as a dishwasher in the summer and your operation has a person assigned to meat cutting. You may be allowed to observe and then perhaps help out—as long as you do it on your own time. Your "profit" in such a situation is in the "retained earnings" of increased knowledge. Many job skills can be learned through observation and some unpaid practice: bartending (by a waitress or waiter), clerking on a front desk (by a bellman), and even some cooking (by a dishwasher or cook's helper). With this kind of experience behind you, it may be possible to win the skilled job part time during the year or even for the following summer.

One of the best student jobs, from a learning standpoint, is a relief job, either day-off relief or vacation relief. The training for this fill-in work can teach you a good deal about every skill in your operation. Although these skills differ from the skills a manager uses, they are important for a manager to know. This is because the structure of the hospitality industry keeps most managers close to the operating level. Knowledge of necessary skills gives them credibility among their subordinates, facilitates communication, and equips them to deal confidently with skilled employees. In fact, a good manager ought to be able to pitch in when employees get stuck.[7] For these reasons, one phrase that should never pass your lips is "that's not my job."

Other Ways of Profiting from a Job

In addition to income and knowledge, after-school part-time employment has other advantages. For example, your employer might have a career for you upon graduation. This is particularly likely if your employer happens to be a fairly large firm or if you want to remain close to the area of your schooling.

In addition, you may choose to take off a term or two from school to pursue a particular interest or just to clarify your longer-term job goals. This does have the advantage of giving you more than "just a summer job" on your résumé—but be sure you don't let the work experience get in the way of acquiring the basic educational requirements for progress into management.

Wherever—and for however long—you work, remember that through your employment you may make contacts that will help you after gradua-

---

[7]If they get stuck too often, of course, management must find out why and correct the problem. If a manager has to pitch in frequently, it can be a sign of inadequate organization.

tion. People with whom you have worked may be able to tell you of interesting opportunities or recommend you for a job.

Don't underestimate a recommendation. Even if your summer employer doesn't have a career opportunity for you, a favorable recommendation can give your career a big boost when you graduate. In addition, many employers may have contacts they will make available to you—perhaps friends of theirs who can offer interesting opportunities. The lesson here is that the record you make on the job now can help shape your career later.

EMPLOYMENT AT GRADUATION

Graduation probably seems a long way off right now, but you should already be considering strategies for finding a job when you finish your formal education. Clear goals formed now will direct your work experience plans and, to a lesser degree, the courses you take and the topics you emphasize within those courses. If you have not yet decided on a specific goal, then this question deserves prompt but careful consideration as you move through your education. You still have plenty of time.

The rest of this section offers a kind of "dry-run" postgraduation placement procedure. From this distance, you can view the process objectively. When you come closer to graduation, you may find the subject a tense one: People worry about placement as graduation nears, even if they're quite sure of finding a job.

GOALS AND OBJECTIVES: THE STRATEGY OF JOB PLACEMENT

Most hospitality management students have three concerns. First, many students are interested in such income issues as starting salary and the possibility of raises and bonuses.

Second, students are concerned with personal satisfaction. They wonder about opportunities for self-expression, creativity, initiative, and independence. Although few starting jobs offer a great deal of independence, some types of work (for example, employment with a franchising company) can lead quite rapidly to independent ownership. Students also want to know about the number of hours they'll be investing in their work. Many companies expect long hours, especially from junior management people. But other sectors, especially the institutional operations, make more modest demands (and generally offer more modest prospects for advancement).

Third, many students, particularly in health-care food service, want to achieve such professional goals as competence as a dietitian or a dietetic technician. Although professional goals in the commercial sector don't lead to formal certification, they are clearly associated with developing a top-flight reputation as an operator. These three sets of interests are obviously related; for example, most personal goals include the elements of income, satisfaction, and professional status. Our point is that although it may be too early to set definite goals, it it not too early to begin evaluating these elements. From the three concerns we've just discussed, the following are five elements for your consideration:

1. *Income.*   The place to begin your analysis is with the issue of survival. How much will you require to meet your financial needs? For example, your needs will be greater if you plan to support a family than if you need to support only yourself. If your income needs are modest, you may decide to forgo luxuries to take a lower-paying job that offers superior training. Thus, you would make an investment in retained earnings—the knowledge you hope someday to trade for more income, security, and job satisfaction.

2. *Professional Status.*   Whether your goal is professional certification (as a dietitian, for example) or a reputation as a top-flight hotelier or restaurateur, you should consider the job's benefit mix. In this case, you may choose to accept a lower income (but, of course, one on which you can live and in line with what such jobs pay in your region). Although you shouldn't be indifferent to income, you'll want to focus principally on what the job can teach you.

3. *Evaluating an Employer.*   Students who make snap judgments about a company and act aggressively in an interview often offend potential employers, who, after all, see the interview as an occasion to evaluate the student crop. Nevertheless, in a quiet way, you should learn about the company's commitment to training. Does it have a training program? If not, how does it translate its entry jobs into learning experiences? (Inquiries directed to your acquaintances and the younger management people can help you determine how the company really scores in these areas.) Because training beyond the entry-level basics requires responsibility and access to promotion, you will want to know about the opportunities for advancement. Finally, you need to evaluate the company's operations. Are they quality operations? Can you be proud to work there? If the quality of food or service is consistently poor, can you help improve things? Or will you be misled into learning the wrong way to do things?

4. *Determining Potential Job Satisfaction.*   Some students study hospitality management only to discover that their real love is food preparation. Such students may decide, late in their student careers, to seek a job that provides skill training in food preparation. Other students may decide they need a high income immediately (to pay off debts or to do some traveling, for example). These students may decide to trade the skills they have acquired in their work experiences to gain a high income for a year or two as a waitress or waiter in a top-flight operation. Such a goal is highly personal but perfectly reasonable. The key is to form a

goal and keep moving toward it. The student who wants eventually to own an operation will probably have to postpone his or her goal while developing the management skills and reputation necessary to attract the needed financial backing.

5. *Accepting Skilled Jobs.*   Students sometimes accept skilled jobs rather than management jobs because that is all they can find. This happens, sometimes, during a period of recession. Younger students, too, are prone to suffer from this problem for a year or two, as are students who choose to locate in small communities. The concept of retained earnings provides the key to riding out these periods. Learn as much as you can and don't abandon your goals, because (as the next section will make clear) the prospects for people with management aspirations remain bright.

THE OUTLOOK FOR HOSPITALITY MANAGEMENT

The factors that underlie the changes that the hospitality industry faces are so important that we will refer to them repeatedly throughout the text and discuss them again in Chapter 21. These forces are bound to affect your career, and so it is useful to look at a few of them here. In general, we can expect a dramatic increase in the peak age groups that use hospitality services, and this growth will extend until the turn of the century. Accompanying this growth will be a general labor shortage brought on by a reduction in a key labor market for the hospitality industry: young people.

DEMAND FOR HOSPITALITY SERVICES

People under 35 years of age are starting their careers and often their families. Family formation means large outlays for the purchase of a home, furniture, and appliances and the costs of having children. Thus, to roughly age 35, the combination of still relatively moderate income and heavy financial outlays limits new families' discretionary spending on such things as travel and dining out. But in middle age, average incomes increase. People 35 to 44 years of age are those most inclined to travel, whereas people 45 to 54 years of age spend the most on food away from home. The middle years, then, ages 35 to 54, are the peak years for spending on hospitality services.

Figures 1.3 and 1.4 give a 50-year perspective on the number of U.S. consumers in these two middle-aged population groups. After a period of modest growth or even modest decline, since 1980 the number of middle-aged people has begun to increase rapidly. The 35-to-44-year-old group started first, and the 45-to-54-year-old group began to accelerate in 1985. These trends will continue to the year 2000, fueling the demand for services such as hotel rooms and meals away from home.

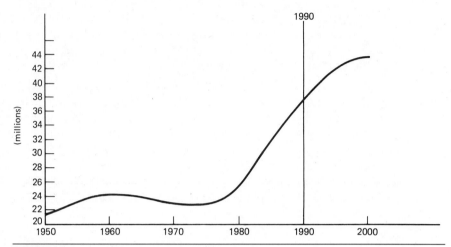

FIGURE 1.3   People 33 to 44 years old, 1950–2000. [Adapted from Peter K. Franchese, "Consumer Perspectives," *Proceedings: Chain Operators Exchange, 1985* (Chicago: International Foodservice Manufacturers Association, 1985).]

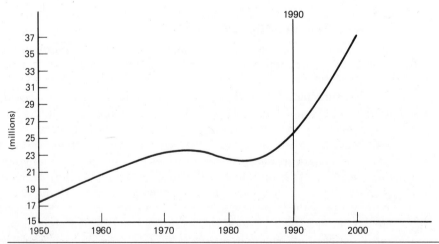

FIGURE 1.4   People 45 to 54 years old, 1950–2000. [Adapted from Peter K. Franchese, "Consumer Perspectives," *Proceedings: Chain Operators Exchange, 1985* (Chicago: International Foodservice Manufacturers Association, 1985).]

HOSPITALITY LABOR SUPPLY

Although people of all ages work in the hospitality industry, younger workers are the source of both part-time and full-time workers. Figures 1.5 and 1.6 demonstrate why in the second half of the 1980s there have been serious labor shortages in some U.S. markets. Differing regional age distributions have softened the shortage in some markets. But in the Northeast, for instance, Friendly's (a chain that combines ice-cream specialties with family dining) reported an increase in 1985 in sales, but *no* increase in profit, and it attributed its poor relative performance to the labor shortage in its markets.[8]

In Boston, Wendy's Restaurants were reportedly busing employees an hour or so from nearby towns where more teenagers were available, and paying them for their transportation time. Indeed, Wendy's even went so far as to insert a brief employee recruiting message in its TV commercials in Boston.[9]

As Figures 1.5 and 1.6 indicate, the shortage of teenagers will begin to ease around 1990, and not surprisingly, the shortage of college-age people will begin to moderate about five years later. It seems likely, however, that there will continue to be a serious shortage of entry-level workers throughout much of this decade. This means that getting a *first* job should be rela-

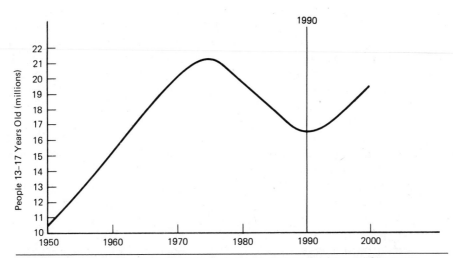

FIGURE 1.5   Teenagers, 1950–2000. [Adapted from Peter K. Franchese, "Consumer Perspectives," *Proceedings: Chain Operators Exchange, 1985* (Chicago: International Foodservice Manufacturers Association, 1985).]

[8]*Nation's Restaurant News,* October 21, 1985, p. 19.
[9]*Nation's Restaurant News,* October 10, 1985, p. 3.

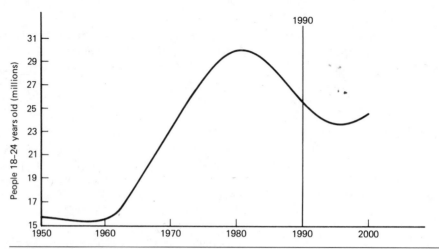

FIGURE 1.6   College-age people, 1950–2000. [Adapted from Peter K. Franchese, "Consumer Perspectives," *Proceedings: Chain Operators Exchange, 1985* (Chicago: International Foodservice Manufacturers Association, 1985).]

tively easy. A closer look at population trends, however, underlines the importance of preparing yourself aggressively for competition in the management market of the 1990s. Another way of looking at the growth of the middle-aged market is noting that this means that a lot of people in the U.S. work force are competing for middle-level jobs. Figure 1.7 reinforces this picture, showing the rapid and continuing buildup of people 25 to 34 years old, a buildup that began in the early 1970s and will extend into the early 1990s.

The first job may be easy to get, but as *Restaurant Institutions* observed: "Baby boomers—the largest and best educated generation in the U.S. history—crowd the next rung of the career ladder."[10] Younger managers will thus need to be ready for stiff competition if they want to rise above junior management positions. People entering the hospitality industry's management and supervisory ranks will have some advantages: a current shortage of qualified managers at all levels *and* continuing growth in the industry. For instance, industry leaders questioned in a National Restaurant Association study of problems likely to face the industry in 1990 were "unanimous in the belief that well-trained, seasoned managers will be scarce."[11] Getting a place on the management ladder, in these circum-

[10]*Restaurant Institutions*, August 7, 1985, p. 62.
[11]*The Restaurant Industry in 1990* (Washington, D.C.: National Restaurant Association, n.d.), p. 11 (L3–5).

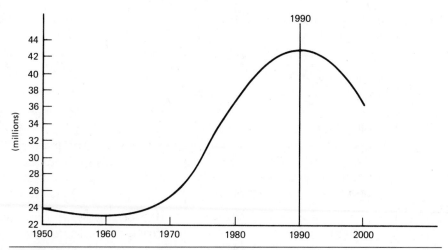

FIGURE 1.7   People 25 to 34 years old, 1950–2000. [Adapted from Peter K. Franchese, "Consumer Perspectives," *Proceedings: Chain Operators Exchange, 1985* (Chicago: International Foodservice Manufacturers Association, 1985).]

stances, will probably not be difficult, but competing against the rest of the "best educated generation in U.S. history" makes a solid educational background a sensible investment.

Industry Conditions

Industry trends toward more competition, discussed in Chapters 3 and 7, mean that there will be more operations striving to serve the growing markets for hospitality services, and those operations will naturally need more managers and supervisors. Because of the projected expansion in the industry into the 1990s in the face of a serious shortage of management positions already, the outlook is for faster promotion in the hospitality industry than in many other areas of employment that are not expanding and that do not face the hospitality industry's current management shortage.

Beyond the growth in traditional hospitality operations, another factor favoring people with hospitality management education and experience is what might be called the "spread" of the industry. Convenience stores, for instance, and other retailers have begun to expand their food service operations. Because food service away from home is increasingly a necessity for families in which both spouses are employed, the number of nontraditional food service sites will probably continue to grow, expanding further the need for food service workers, managers, and supervisors.

Your prospects in management are bright indeed, as the changing nature of the industry makes hospitality a "management-intensive" industry in all of its aspects. Welcome, then, to your hospitality studies, and good luck in a promising career! Now let's see how much of this first chapter you can recall.

SUMMARY

The hospitality industry includes hotels, restaurants, and other institutions that offer shelter and/or food to people away from home. A manager in the hospitality industry, therefore, must have the following three objectives: (1) making the guest welcome personally, (2) making things work for the guest, and (3) making sure that the operation will continue providing service and meeting its budget.

There are many reasons for studying in a hospitality program, among them being a good past experience working in the field, interests in the field, and ambitions in the field.

We also discussed why people work and how to get the most from a job, including weighing both retained earnings and the job benefit mix. We pointed out that in the hospitality industry, you can learn a lot from the physical plant and from the front and the back of the house.

We then turned to ways to get a job—including preparing for an interview—and how to gain the most from whatever job you do find. We also talked about what you should consider in regard to a more permanent job: income, professional status, your employer, potential job satisfaction, and accepting an interm, less-skilled job.

Finally, we began our book-long discussion of the outlook for the hospitality industry, which we found to be bright.

KEY WORDS AND CONCEPTS

To help you review this chapter, keep in mind the following:

Hospitality	Job benefit mix
Hospitality industry	Back of the house
Retained earnings	Front of the house

REVIEW QUESTIONS

1. What kinds of institutions or establishments does the hospitality industry include?

2. What is the role of a manager in the hospitality industry?

3. Why study in a hospitality management program?

4. What are some of the reasons that people work?

5. What is retained earnings?

6. What is a job benefit mix?

7. What are some things to learn from the front of the house? The back of the house?

8. What kinds of things can you learn from a part-time or summer job that are not strictly part of the job?

9. What are three principal concerns in regard to a job after graduation?

P A R T 2

FOOD
SERVICE

Food service is by far the largest element in the hospitality industry. The next four chapters are devoted to it.

Chapter 2 describes the various types of restaurants and the principal functions—and markets—they serve. The chapter concludes with a brief discussion of the major food service operating ratios and the terms related to them.

Chapter 3 looks first at the growing significance of chains but also at the still vital role played by independents, identifying strengths and weaknesses of each. Our attention will then shift to the guest and the issues that are on the minds of contemporary consumers.[1]

In Chapter 4 we will examine topics that affect what the restaurant business will look like tomorrow. Topics such as food service equipment, energy costs, competition, and employment trends are all of vital interest to everyone who plans a career in hospitality.

Chapter 5 turns our attention to institutional food service. We will examine the major segments of institutional food service and the trends affecting them.

Courtesy of the Greater New Orleans Tourist and Convention Commission.

THE RESTAURANT
BUSINESS

THE PURPOSE OF THIS CHAPTER

At this beginning point in your hospitality industry career, you should gain some perspective of the scope of the hospitality field. Chapter 2 is, then, the first of several chapters describing the major segments of the hospitality industry. This chapter provides a brief overview of the entire food service industry and describes in some detail the principal components of the restaurant business in the United States today.

Within the food service field, the operating styles and the managerial challenges and rewards differ widely. We will be looking at the commercial restaurant business in just a moment. Combined with your own field experiences and those of other students, this chapter should help you consider—and eventually shape—your career decisions. As you learn about important segments of the industry, you will take important steps toward developing yourself as a professional who knows what is going on in the field.

In this chapter we describe some restaurant categories designed to help you visualize in an orderly way the variety of commercial food service operations currently doing business. First, we consider *full-service restaurants* (operations that feature extensive menus, prepare most of their food on the premises, and offer table service). Full-service restaurants can be contrasted to *specialty restaurants* (which offer limited menus and often feature self-service). The specialty restaurant category includes operations such as fast-food and take-out shops, family restaurants, budget steak houses, and pizza parlors.

Restaurants can also be categorized according to the markets they serve. In the section of this chapter that makes these comparisons, we will contrast the "dining market" (served by the haute cuisine and theme restaurants) to the "eating market" (served by specialty restaurants). Another section of this chapter discusses restaurants that are parts of other larger retail enterprises, such as the dining rooms located in department stores. The chapter concludes with a brief introduction to and explanation of what professionals call "food service operating ratios."

THIS CHAPTER SHOULD HELP YOU

1. Estimate the relative and absolute size of the major components of the food service field.

2. Describe and contrast the major kinds of restaurant operations.

3. Define the key *operating ratios* for restaurants and learn to use them as performance measures.

THE VARIED FIELD OF FOOD SERVICE

Commercial firms make up by far the largest sector of the food service industry. According to the National Restaurant Association (NRA), about 69 percent of the food purchased away from home is sold in restaurants, cafeterias, and taverns. Hotel, motel, and motor-inn restaurants account for another 5.6 percent. Sales in restaurants located in other retail establishments, such as department drugstores, account for over 3 percent of the market for food consumed away from home. Contractors and caterers (who serve food under contract in settings such as industrial plants and office buildings, health-care facilities, and schools and colleges) generate 6.2 percent of food sales, and 2.6 percent of sales are made through vending machines. These estimates are summarized in Table 2.1.

The market for food away from home applies to 97 percent of Americans, up from 85 percent in 1960. On the average, food service customers eat out three to four times a week. In 1970, guests spent about 27 percent of their food expenditures away from home, and by 1985 that proportion had risen to just over 30 percent. Not surprisingly, food service is a growth industry.[1] For the first half of the 1980s, food service sales increased 1.3 percent faster than did the U.S. economy as a whole, and their continued growth seems likely.

---

[1]John J. Rohs, *The Restaurant Industry* (New York: Wertheim and Co., April 1985), pp. 8–12.

TABLE 2.1   Commercial and Institutional Food Service Sales, 1984

Restaurants, cafeterias, and fast-food bars and taverns	$111,437,097	68.3%
Food service in hotels, motels, and motor hotels	9,164,681	5.6
Food sales in retail stores	5,394,529	3.3
Vending and nonstore retailers	4,256,258	2.6
Contractors and caterers	10,147,530	6.2
Recreation and sports	1,905,961	1.2
Institutions operating own food service	20,861,063	12.8
	$163,167,118	100.0%

Source: NRA News, June–July 1986.

THE RESTAURANT BUSINESS

One problem in describing the restaurant business is that it changes so fast that today's description may well be outdated tomorrow. Moreover, restaurants have so many forms that it is almost impossible to devise a model to fit all operations. Nevertheless, to describe the field even generally, we need some basic terminology. Two obvious (and descriptive) terms are the *full-service restaurant* and the *specialty restaurant.*

THE FULL-SERVICE RESTAURANTS

The term *full service* refers to the *style of service* in the dining room, to the *menu,* and to the *style of preparation.* A traditional full-service restaurant offers a wide variety of menu choices, and most full-service restaurants prepare most of their food "from scratch" (that is, from fresh or raw ingredients). Waitresses and waiters serve the food. Some chains operate full-service restaurants, but most such restaurants are "independents." These are single operations, privately owned and not affiliated with any other food service organization.

There are really three kinds of full service restaurants: first, the independent luxury restaurants specializing in haute cuisine[2] and second, such lower-priced operations as neighborhood restaurants with simple and inexpensive fare, usually prepared "from scratch" and served by waitresses. These operations are sometimes called mom-and-pop restaurants, because they are often family concerns in which one spouse supervises the cooking while the other looks after the front of the house. Mom-and-pop restaurants are increasingly threatened by franchised and chain fast-food and coffee

[2]Loosely translated, the term means "elegant dining," or food prepared in the manner of the classic French (or European) chefs.

shops and budget steak house operations, which offer competitive prices in more modern surroundings.

The third kind of full-service restaurant grew up during the 1930s and 1940s. These restaurants are usually from three to five times the size of the first two, and they use semiskilled cooks working under close supervision in a recipe kitchen, in which the cooks follow recipes exactly, weighing and measuring each ingredient. The recipes and the supervision replace, to a large degree, the skills of the chef. The meals are moderately priced.

For convenience, we will refer to the classic, "from scratch" full-service restaurants as *haute cuisine restaurants*. Haute cuisine restaurants remain popular, but they are usually found only in heavily populated areas that can supply enough customers who can afford the relatively high prices—as much as $50 to $100 or more per meal, including wines. Haute cuisine restaurants must charge these high prices to recover their costs and earn enough profit to pay their highly skilled employees and repay the owners for their efforts and capital risks. Because of their high food standards, haute cuisine operations tend to be quite small. At the other end of the scale is the *neighborhood restaurant*, denoting the mom-and-pop firm that offers a full-service menu at decidedly lower prices.

Many, though by no means all, full-service restaurants are currently experiencing financial difficulties because they are labor intensive, which means that they require a large number of employee hours per guest served. As the proprietors of the neighborhood establishments reach retirement age, their operations often close, because no one wants to work the long hours it takes to keep them profitable. Similarly, companies, such as Stouffer's and Marriott Hot Shoppes, that run moderately priced, full-service restaurants—our third category—have found those operations unprofitable and are either closing them or converting them into other styles of operation.

Fine dining is "the little giant of full service," according to *Restaurant & Institutions*. Though often beset by high costs and labor problems, luxury restaurants can remain profitable if they can maintain the quality of their food and service. Indeed, in 1984 the full-service restaurant's share of total food service sales actually expanded for the first time in several years, growing from nearly 27 percent to just over 29 percent.[3]

SPECIALTY RESTAURANTS

A wide variety of restaurants can be called *specialty restaurants*, and here, too, it is difficult to establish neat categories. All of the specialty operations tend to simplify their production processes, and most of them use at least some self-service. The result is a drastic reduction in the labor in both the front and the back of the house, as Table 2.2 shows. Because specialty restaurants require less labor, they can pass on their savings to the guests in

---

[3]*Restaurants & Institutions,* March 15, 1985, p. 136.

TABLE 2.2 Productivity in Food
Service Establishments

Food Service Type	Direct Labor Hours per 100 Guests
Luxury restaurants	72.3
Family restaurants	20.7
Cafeterias	18.3
Fast food	10.5

Source: Agricultural Research Service.

the form of lower prices. Furthermore, these operations, even with their lower prices, generally earn profits substantially higher than those in other operations. Although not all specialty restaurants are affiliated with chains or franchise groups, most of them are. A few exceptions will be discussed later in this chapter. Specialty restaurants may look different from one another. But to a surprising degree, they all are modeled on one pattern, dictated by the fast-food concept.

Fast Food

Fast food is the largest single type of specialty restaurant, and probably the fastest growing in terms of both sales and numbers of units. *Restaurants & Institutions* magazine estimated that in 1986 there were 140,700 fast-food units in operation, employing 1,960,000 food service workers.[4] The most popular menu item is still the hamburger. Table 2.3 shows the relative popularity of the major fast-food formats in 1984, as reflected in the 100 largest food service companies in the United States.

Automation is the key to the modern fast-food restaurant. When we think of automation, a factory, a lot of machinery, and repetitive tasks usually come to mind. But as Peter Drucker pointed out, "automation is not 'technical' in character. Like every technology, it is primarily a system of concepts, and its technical aspects are results rather than causes."[5] Fast-food restaurants are not automated in the sense of depending on new, automatic machinery. Some new variations of the traditional food service equipment are found in these operations, but it is really the customer who has been automated!

The *automating concept* in the fast-food operation means a reduction in menu choices, a sharp limitation on customer service, and different customer behavior. Through self-service, the customer replaces the entire front

[4]*Restaurants & Institutions,* January 8, 1986, p. 133.
[5]Peter Drucker, *The Practice of Management* (New York: Harper & Row, 1954), p. 19.

TABLE 2.3   Relative Popularity of Fast-Food Categories in 1984, Top 100 Chains

Fast-Food Category	Number of Chains	Number of Units	Sales (millions of $)	
Hamburger	18	19,516	$18,290	61.2%
Chicken	11	8,089	3,891	13.0
Ice cream	7	8,996	2,228	7.4
Mexican	5	2,659	1,262	4.2
Roast beef	2	1,862	1,232	4.1
Seafood	3	1,890	885	3.1
Pizza	2	2,523	853	2.8
Donuts	3	2,609	802	2.6
Limited menu	5	1,335	448	1.5
Bakery	3	99	23	.1
			$29,885	100.0%

Source: Technomic Consultants, *Dynamics of the Chain Restaurant Market* (Chicago: International Foodservice Manufacturers Association, 1985).

of the house staff, even to the point of cleaning up. There may be some choice in regard to cleaning up, but absolutely no choice in regard to self-service. Moreover, because fast-food operations offer a simple menu, very specialized, highly efficient kitchens can be built around this limited food choice.

The fast-food operation is, in many ways, more like a manufacturing enterprise than the traditional restaurant is. One management scholar put it this way:

> McDonald's has created a highly sophisticated piece of service technology by applying the manufacturing mode of managerial thought to a labor-intensive service situation. If a machine is a piece of equipment with the capability of producing a predictably standardized, customer-satisfying output while minimizing the operating discretion of its attendant, that is what a McDonald's outlet is. It produces, with the help of totally unskilled machine tenders, a fairly sophisticated, reliable product at great speed and low cost.

> McDonald's represents the industrialization of service—applying, through management, the same systematic modes of analysis, design, organization, and control that are commonplace in manufacturing. These more than anything account for its success.[6]

[6]Theodore Levitt, "Management and the Post-Industrial State," *The Public Interest*, Summer 1976, p. 89.

New Products in Fast Food.   Another way of contrasting fast-food operations with the more traditional restaurant is to observe how they introduce a new product. In a traditional operation, a new item can be introduced on the menu quite easily, because of the flexibility of a traditional kitchen. If the item succeeds, it will be continued; if not, it can easily be dropped. But introducing a new product in fast food is more complicated, because the fast-food restaurant itself is a highly specialized kind of machine. The process begins in the product development lab, a relatively new unit for the restaurant industry. Wendy's, for instance, reportedly had no people working in that area in 1979 but by early 1984 had a staff of 42.[7] The next stage is trying out the product in a few markets, where the product's appeal is tested and its compatibility with the production process is gauged. If the product passes these early tests, it will be tested in wider and wider markets until all the wrinkles have been ironed out. Finally, it will be adopted systemwide.

Nation's Restaurant News (NRN) traced the introduction of breakfast items at McDonald's. The Egg McMuffin was introduced in 1973, hot cakes in 1974, and scrambled eggs and sausage in 1975. During the test period, McDonald's determined the specific operating procedures and equipment required for each new product. Once this equipment was perfected, the company's chief supplier prepared a standard adaptation kit for the entire system.

Packaging was another technical problem that McDonald's encountered. Paper packaging, which was tried first, did not hold heat efficiently. "This hurt our breakfast image," a McDonald's spokesperson explained to *NRN,* "because it meant slow service. People coming into our restaurant were expecting our normal fast service, which we just couldn't provide if we had to make each item only as it was ordered.[8] Consequently, McDonald's designed a new insulated package that for up to 10 minutes retains product quality in a warming bin.

Once its new products—and the system to match them—were perfected, McDonald's launched a major advertising campaign to support the "rollout," or the systemwide introduction of its new product, using television, radio, and the other media.

Likewise, in 1984, when Taco Bell decided to introduce "Pizzaz Pizza," it followed the same general pattern: product development, test marketing, and then a rollout supported by a 12-week broadcast and print advertising campaign. An equipment package costing $10,000 to $15,000 per store had to be in place in each unit to support the rollout. In one franchise group participating in the market test, store sales rose by 15 percent.[9]

[7]*Wall Street Journal,* January 1, 1984, p. 21.
[8]*Nation's Restaurant News,* August 4, 1975, p. 77.
[9]*Restaurant Institutions,* June 26, 1985, p. 70.

The physical limits of the existing equipment became clear in the case of Arby's. The company wanted to develop a ⅓-lb burger to broaden its product line so as to offset the limited market penetration of its signature product, roast beef. Although this new product had good consumer acceptance, *Nation's Restaurant News* reported that "roll out is not likely to occur in the near future because most of Arby's system remains unequipped for grilling or broiling."[10]

The problems that can develop in a *systemwide* introduction of a product are illustrated in the rollout of a new catfish dinner by Church's Fried Chicken. In April 1985, the company spent $5 million to introduce the new product, but then operational problems cropped up. Plans were made to increase the portion size from 1 to 1.75 oz so that the product would cook better, be less subject to breakage, and help speed service. Church's proposed to spend an additional $1 million to introduce the change but then had to stop the test for a period because the manufacturers were unable to procure the new portions of fish or guarantee their delivery.[11] The product did improve sales, but the purchasing and production problems had to be worked out under operational conditions.

The logistics of a systemwide distribution of key ingredients is not simple. When Wendy's introduced baked potatoes—a product ordered 600,000 times *daily* in 1985—the potato market was disrupted, with prices rising significantly.[12] When McDonald's rolled out Chicken McNuggets, it had to arrange to have a total of 5 million pounds of chicken delivered each week to its 6,200 restaurants across the United States. In a final example, according to the *Wall Street Journal* a decision by Burger King to put three strips of bacon on a cheeseburger increased the national demand for bacon so much that it had a noticeable effect on the national commodity market.[13]

It is generally recognized that new products serve the following marketing purposes:

1. They broaden the restaurant's appeal. That is, if two people in a party of three want hamburgers, but one wants chicken or fish, all of the party will be satisfied with, for instance, McDonald's menu. Or, as another example, Wendy's used new products—salad bars and baked potatoes—to attract more women to its restaurants.

2. New products match changing consumer tastes. For instance, salad bars and "lite" menu items fit in with the current interest in health food.

---

[10]*Nation's Restaurant News*, August 12, 1985, p. F18.

[11]*Nation's Restaurant News*, August 19, 1985, p. 100.

[12]Michael Culp, "Wendy's International Company Report," *Prudential Bache Securities*, March 8, 1985, pp. 8–9.

[13]*Wall Street Journal*, January 5, 1984, p. 21.

3.   When salads and desserts are added, they enable the unit to offer a full meal, which helps fast food compete better with the fuller-menu family restaurants. The full meal, in turn, helps build higher average sales per guest.

4.   Some new products help spread business throughout the day, such as items that attract guests for snacks or a meal period such as breakfast.

5.   Some products are added "defensively." For example, several chicken restaurants are reported to have added chicken-nugget products largely because they were losing customers to McDonald's, which, with its introduction of Chicken McNuggets, became the second-largest "chicken restaurant chain" in the world.

The point is that when a fast-food operation introduces a new product, it spends much more time studying it than a full-service restaurant would, and its reasons for doing so usually extend well beyond a mere increase in variety. In short, when a full-service restaurant introduces a new menu item, it is a minor change—just one item among several. But when a fast-food restaurant makes such a decision, the item introduced is seen as a "new product" that requires adjustments in both its production procedures and its marketing strategies.

It is fashionable in some circles to look down on fast-food operations, either because they don't seem to be "real restaurants" or because their food supposedly lacks nutritional value. But the customers are the best people to define what a restaurant really is, and they have clearly voted with their feet. Moreover, a study conducted by one fast-food chain indicated that a customer who orders a specialty hamburger sandwich, french fries, and a milkshake receives approximately one-third of the recommended dietary allowance (RDA), or about the same nutritional value found in the typical school lunch.

As we'll see in the next chapter, such a meal *does* have more salt and fat than would be sensible if that meal were eaten every day, but the facts just don't warrant disdain of fast food on nutritional grounds.

The management of a fast-food operation is more demanding than it appears. The preparation of the products has to be planned so that the food will be available almost the minute it is ordered (this is *fast* food, don't forget). In fact, most products must be thrown out if they are held for more than 10 or 20 minutes. To minimize waste, therefore, management must devise a sales-forecasting system based on operating experience, often keyed to 10-minute time segments throughout the operating day.

It is important to realize that a single fast-food unit of a chain or franchise system is, itself, a part of a complex "machine" (*system* is technically the more accurate word) that produces a standard, reliable product in every such unit. The achievement of these systems, then, is not measured just by the output of a single unit but also by the overall effect on a national (or regional) market of a standard product and service. The reputation of a system is valuable to all the franchisees, and in this sense, the *product* that McDonald's has developed is not just a hamburger, but the entire McDonald's franchise as well. Therefore, to preserve the value of the franchise for all, each franchisee must meet the same high standards.

Although the product may be simple, the demands for precision in performance, tight cost controls, and exemplary sanitation procedures make unit operations a demanding entry-level job for new managers. But because fast food is a growing field and highly "management intensive," it also offers entry-level managers many attractive opportunities. This is because most fast-food operations are part of a chain, and so there also are opportunities for advancement into multi-operational management posts.

The Outlook for Fast Food.   The baby boom generation fueled the explosion of fast food in the 1960s and 1970s, but the recession of the early 1980s hurt all restaurants, and it took until 1984 to regain the customer counts of 1978.[14] The number of restaurant units, however, continued to grow. During the first half of the 1980s, the increase in the number of restaurant units was five times the rate of the population growth,[15] with the lion's share of the growth going to fast food.

Furthermore, the growing number of young people in the 1960s and 1970s supported the development of fast food. But these same people in the 1970s and 1980s are now 25 to 34 years old, a group that eats out frequently and is relatively prosperous. Their growing number, therefore, has led to the upscaling of fast food to larger portions and more sophisticated decor, marked by the rapid growth of chains such as Wendy's and, more recently, "gourmet" hamburger chains such as Fuddrucker's. Some analysts feel, however, that fast food—with 40 percent of restaurant sales—may have passed its time of fastest growth and that fast food's proportionate share of restaurant sales may begin to decline.[16] As a case in point, George Rice, the leading authority on eating out trends in the United States, indicated that in early 1986, many consumers decided not to eat the dinner meal—which he calls a crucial competitive battleground—at a fast-food restaurant.[17] But lunch is still an established well-served, and highly competitive market in which fast-food restaurants must fight with other kinds of restaurants for its

[14]George D. Rice, "Foodservice Perspective & Implications," *Proceedings of the 12th Annual Chain Operators Exchange,* Miami, February 17–20, 1985.

[15]Charles Lynch, "Leadership in the Toughest Environment Ever," *Proceedings of the 13th Annual Chain Operators Exchange,* Las Vegas, February 23, 1986.

[16]Rohs, *The Restaurant Industry,* p. 12.

[17]George D. Rice, "Year in Review and a Look Ahead at the Opportunity for '86," *Proceedings of the 13th Annual Chain Operators Exchange,* op. cit.

market share. And fast food's outlook for continuing growth in breakfast sales as a whole is also bright.

Even though the growth rate of fast food will probably eventually slow, this does not mean that employment opportunities will shrink. Indeed, with so many units in operation, even a low growth rate—in percentage—still means a large total number of units. Note, too, that some kinds of restaurants, such as Mexican and Asian, are likely to grow faster than is the entire segment. Furthermore, because of the shortage of qualified management personnel and the high turnover, there will continue to be many opportunities for employment in the fast-food industry. And although the number of fast-track opportunities that have characterized this segment of the industry is likely to fall in the future, this segment is likely to continue to give significant responsibility to new managers, along with generous compensation to those who can deliver results.

Other Specialty Restaurants

Although other specialty restaurants may not look like fast-food operations, the heart of the operating system closely resembles that successful format. Their "back of the house" production system has been simplified by a specialized menu that reduces skill levels, thus holding down wage costs and speeding service. Specialty restaurants might therefore be called "moderately fast food," for although the guests in these operations are prepared to wait a bit longer for food, they will not have to wait much longer. We will discuss three examples of specialty restaurants: family restaurants, budget steak houses, and pizza parlors.

Family Restaurants.   Family restaurants, sometimes referred to as coffee shops, depart quite a bit from the fast-food format in that they offer waiter or waitress service, as well as self-service, in the form of salad bars, breakfast bars, and dessert bars. Specialty restaurants usually offer breakfast, lunch, and dinner. Another similarity to full-service restaurants is the extensive menu variety they appear to offer.

This resemblance to full service can, however, be deceiving. First, the preparation staff is limited to one or more short-order cooks. Almost everything is prepared to order, sometimes from scratch (as with the sandwiches and breakfast items that give the menu much of its variety) and sometimes from frozen prepared foods that are reconstituted to order. The production process is really almost as simple as the fast-food process.

Furthermore, the service the customers receive is anything but elaborate. Place settings usually consist of paper place mats and a minimum of china and silver. Most meals consist only of the main course and perhaps a dessert. This reduction in courses also simplifies service. *Nation's Restaurant News* surveys show, for instance, that in 1985, four out of ten sales dollars came from platters, salads, sandwiches, and dinners. Breakfast sales accounted for another third of sales.[18] Taken together, nearly three-quarters of the family restaurants' volume came from these main meal items. Given their relatively straightforward operating format, the cost of training new service employees remains minimal. And the flexible menu permits operations to drop menu choices when their food costs advance too rapidly and to substitute less costly items.

The guests who visit a family restaurant want to be waited on, and in choosing a family restaurant, they are opting for an informal, simple, relatively inexpensive style of service. These operations generally offer a pleasant, modern restaurant located near dense pedestrian or vehicular traffic and convenient to shoppers and suburban family diners.

Michael Culp, security analyst at Prudential Bache Securities, estimates that 85 to 90 percent of coffee shops are independently operated,[19] whereas *Nation's Restaurant News* puts that range at 80 to 85 percent. On the other hand some of America's best-known national and regional chains, such as Marriott's Big Boy, Howard Johnsons, Denny's, Shoney's, and Friendly Ice Cream, operate in this market. Population trends are certainly on the side of family restaurant whose most loyal customers base is mature adults.

Family restaurants face competition not only from budget steak and pizza restaurants but also from upscaled fast-food restaurants in both menu and decor. Fast food's share of the breakfast market has been growing, too, largely "at the expense of independently owned coffee shops while chain owned family restaurants barely held their own."[20] In fact, in the United States, McDonald's alone accounts for one-quarter of all breakfasts eaten away from home.

Although the family restaurant segment faces competition in all its markets, consumer expectations in 1985 give some additional encouragement on top of the trend toward a growing middle-aged population. Although U.S. diners' intentions were to eat dinner out less often in fast-food and upscaled restaurants, according to George Rice, they planned to eat more often in mid-scale operations such as family restaurants.[21]

Budget Steak Houses. Before 1974, budget steak houses grew rapidly. However, they relied on one main product, steak, and when the price of beef began to soar, they felt serious cost pressures. Moreover, they relied principally on the evening meal for most of their sales. Finally, their main target market in the 1970s was the blue-collar family. During the recession of the early 1980s, therefore, many of these operations turned to other formats,

[18]*Nation's Restaurant News,* August 19, 1985, p. F6.
[19]*Nation's Restaurant News,* August 19, 1985, p. F6.
[20]*Nation's Restaurant News,* February 18, 1985, p. 1.
[21]Rice, "Year in Review."

recognizing that the blue-collar work force was not growing as fast as was white-collar employment—and their vulnerability to blue-collar unemployment in a recession became painfully apparent. Their experience offers an interesting example of a common food service strategy much in use in the late 1970s and early 1980s—that of repositioning, or changing, the operating format and image in the customer's mind.

One of the largest chains, Bonanza, developed an upgrading concept called Freshtastick's, which featured decor upgrading and all-you-can-eat food bars offering salads, cheeses, breads, fresh vegetables, fruits, and desserts. Operations that used the new format also switched to a higher grade of beef. The new concept helped improve the company's luncheon volume, attracted new customers, and increased unit volume. Family steak houses have continued to diversify their menus by adding chicken and fish entrees, sandwiches, and elaborate salad bars. In an effort to widen their market, some have also added breakfast bars, thus expanding into another mealtime. Today's budget steak house has thus broadened its concept and thereby offers an interesting example, too, of the way in which the competitive restaurant industry responds to changing customer preferences. In 1970, the budget steak house was a major growth concept. By the mid-1970s the concept was in trouble, and in the 1980s the "budget steaker" has, to a large degree, become something else, offering a wider menu and upscaled decor.

Pizza Restaurants. Pizza restaurants, like budget steak houses, once depended almost exclusively on a single item. But in recent years, pizza restaurants have extended their product line so as to appeal to more customers. For instance, in 1984, Pizza Hut rolled out "Priazzo," a two-crusted Italian pie stuffed with a variety of foods such as pepperoni, cheese, and tomato sauce or a quichelike mixture of spinach, ham, and cheese. The product was targeted to customers who had not typically been tempted by more traditional pizza products.[22] Earlier, deep-dish "Chicago style" pizza had added menu variety, and then personal pan pizzas were added to speed service and as a competitively priced product for the lunch market. Domino's Pizza has even been reported to be testing a breakfast product called "Domino's Bake Ups," which are a kind of breakfast pie made from pizza dough with fruit, ham and cheese, bacon and tomato, or western omelet toppings.[23] The major development in the pizza segment, however, has been the surge in home delivery and in drive-through service, which require new systems for making pizza faster.[24] But despite all their menu and service expansion, they are still principally pizza restaurants. The cost of their food product itself is relatively low, and these operations also have low labor costs. Pizza's continuing

[22]*Restaurant Business,* August 10, 1985, p. 145.
[23]*Restaurants & Institutions,* November 13, 1985, p. 115.
[24]*Nation's Restaurant News,* August 2, 1985, p. F22.

popularity with consumers ensures its remaining in the front ranks of growth concepts. Another noteworthy aspect of the pizza business is that it is a stronghold for independents.

There are, of course, numerous other specialty restaurants, featuring, for instance, chicken, seafood, ice cream, Mexican food, and Asian food. They generally fit the pattern already described: limited menus, highly efficient productivity based on an "automated customer," and a product characterized by a relatively low food cost. Figure 2.1 summarizes schematically our discussion to this point. It rates various types of operations on the scale from left to right according to whether they are full service (at the far left) or specialty restaurants (at the far right). In turn, their typical price range is measured from lowest to highest on the scale at left.

THE DINING MARKET AND THE EATING MARKET

One of the twentieth century's most innovative restauranteurs, Joe Baum, summed up the challenge of food service in this way:

> A restaurant takes a basic drive—the simplest act of eating—and transforms it into a civilized ritual; a ritual involving hospitality and imagination and satisfaction and graciousness and warmth.[25]

Restaurants serve both our social and our biological needs. In order to try to see the restaurant business from both of these perspectives, we will divide restaurants into those serving predominantly our social needs—the *dining market*—and those serving our biological needs—the *eating market*. Of course, nearly all meals eaten in public have a social dimension, just as the most formal state dinner has its biological aspect. The main purpose, however, is usually clear.

The specialty restaurants we have been discussing are more or less part of the eating market. Although many of them seem to emphasize decor and service, they really concentrate on economy and speed. The dining market, serving our social and recreational needs, emphasizes the service ritual, food excellence, and often entertainment.

DINING WELL

From research by the National Restaurant Association, we have some clues to the motives of diners: to escape from boredom, to socialize, to avoid drudgery, to be waited on, to have foods different from those served at home. Finally, panelists in focus groups sponsored by NRA said that dining out was convenient.[26]

Because dining (as opposed to eating) is predominantly a social event, service rituals are important. Another set of focus groups whose discussions centered on what consumers valued in *service* were held under the auspices

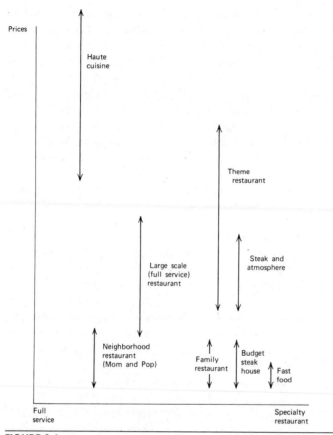

FIGURE 2.1   The range of restaurants compared on the basis of service type and relative price.

of the International Food Manufacturers Association.[27] The role of the server is, therefore, ideally much more than a mechanical one. The server in a good restaurant is expected to anticipate the guests' needs and to be attentive, but not disruptive. At lunch, but to a lesser degree at dinner, guests value promptness and efficiency. At dinner, the service needs to be both timely (no long waits) and well timed ("when I'm ready"). The servers are expected to be friendly, as signified by a warm smile, and to be accurate.

In the expensive restaurants serving the dining market, the operation that falls short on significant measures of service is therefore, likely to lose customers quickly. The demographics of such customers are, again, impor-

[25]*Restaurants & Institutions,* February 5, 1986, p. 16.

[26]*NRA News,* January 1986, p. 39.

[27]Ron Dimbert, "An Evaluation of Service Requirements," *Proceedings of the 12th Annual Chain Operators Exchange,* op. cit.

tant. The older consumer who dines in a fine restaurant is well educated, has a higher-than-average income, and is accustomed to dining out and to traveling. As Don Smith, Westin Distinguished Professor at Washington State University, put it recently, "We're dealing with an aging, more experienced society".[28]

The importance of service was illustrated in a Gallup survey which indicated that service strongly influences whether guests will return and whether they will recommend the operation to others. "It's incredible how much diners will put up with if they are treated properly. Mediocre food, too much noise, cramped tables all appear to be accepted as long as people are greeted with a welcoming smile and are made to feel that the management cares about them."[29] In the dining market, sometimes food is the primary consideration—and sometimes service is.

Haute Cuisine Restaurants

Most full-service haute cuisine establishments are small, independent operations, some seating fewer than 100 guests. Despite their modest capacities, these restaurants succeed because of their excellent quality. Many are staffed by European chefs who have brought with them a craft tradition that dates back to the Middle Ages and, incidentally, to a time when wage costs were relatively lower and labor intensity was more practical. Many haute cuisine operations, however, provide excellent food prepared by American staffs who are often less formally trained.

Excellence is the absolute prerequisite in these operations, because the prices they must charge are high. An operator may do everything possible to make the restaurant efficient, but the guests still expect careful, personal service: food prepared to order by highly skilled chefs and served by expert waiters or waitresses. Because this service is, quite literally, manual labor, only marginal improvements in productivity are possible. For example, a waitress can move only so much faster before she reaches the limits of human performance. Thus, only moderate savings are possible through improved efficiency, which makes an escalation in prices inevitable. (It is an axiom of economics that as prices rise, consumers become more discriminating.) Thus the clientele of the haute cuisine restaurant expects, demands, and is willing to pay for excellence.

These distinguished operations generally require a "critical mass" of three different kinds. First, because of the high prices they must charge, most are located in or near major population centers that have a sufficiently large proportion of people with adequate incomes to ensure a satisfactory sales volume. Second, haute cuisine restaurants require chefs and service personnel with highly polished skills. It is, of course, difficult to find such

[28]*NRA News,* March 1986, p. 14.
[29]*NRA News,* March 1986, p. 14.

workers anywhere, but they are most likely to be found in big cities. Third, and most important, successful haute cuisine restaurants require a special devotion from their key operating personnel, especially their owners. The hours tend to be long, and the owners, although amply compensated, often devote their lives to their work.

The haute cuisine field requires a person to invest in long training periods to achieve competency. On the other hand, for those attracted to this kind of operation, the satisfactions go far beyond monetary compensation. To be sure, key people in haute cuisine restaurants earn comfortable livings, but their principal reward comes with the professional satisfaction and respect found only in the achievement of excellence.

Casual Dinner Houses

The variety of forms of the casual dinner house is suggested by *Nation's Restaurant News*'s list of nine leading dinner house chains (see Table 2.4). These operations appear to be restaurants who have taken to heart the advice of William Rice, the food editor of the *Washington Post* and a restaurant consultant:

> The single-minded visions of the restaurant as a temple of gastronomy is too narrow today. The restaurant is becoming an urban recreation center. Customers want crowds, noise and distraction. Cooking should be free form. Dining should be fun. Informality is the rule. Uniform is out. Menu language is casual. Creature comforts are few but the energy level is high. No longer in this country is "restaurant" a French word. Today's restaurants are being designed to *accommodate* customers.[30]

TABLE 2.4 Nine Leading Dinner House Chains

Chain	Specialty
Red Lobster	Seafood
Chi Chi's	Mexican food
Bennigans	Full menu
TGI Fridays	Full menu
El Torite	Mexican food
Stuart Anderson's	Steak
Steak and Ale	Steak and seafood
Ground Round	American food
Brown Derby	American food

Source: Nation's Restaurant News.

[30]*Nation's Restaurant News,* November 4, 1985, p. 14.

Casual dinner houses are changing with the times as their customers age. Several are "expanding their menus, dropping prices, bolstering their marketing program and adding more staff to reduce serving time." Those who survive the changing market will be "those chains that shift their image from 'fern bars' packed with young singles bumping their heads on hanging kayaks to restaurants serving families whose major draws are convenience and extensive, low cost menus."[31] One problem with these operations is that "everyone who opens up a neighborhood bar makes it look like Friday's. The casual restaurant used to be unique and that was what attracted people to them in the 70's."[32] In fact, most communities of any size have their own casual themers and this, too, is an area in which there is a great deal of activity by independents and small, regional chains that have caught the particular local taste.

Theme Restaurants

The haute cuisine restaurants and casual dinner houses we have been discussing are clearly full-service operations. *Theme restaurants,* on the other hand, are almost invariably specialty restaurants serving a limited menu. Some are chain restaurants; many are independents. They rely on creating, through decor and setting, an atmosphere that will entertain. Diners who flock to these operations seek a "total experience," not just a meal, and they are apparently willing to accept a smaller menu selection to get it:

> Most theme restaurants succeed by lavishing attention on the decor. The food often sounds clever on the menu—but usually the fare is unimaginative and bland, although restaurant-goers don't seem to mind. . .. "The food is not the best in the world but there are so many rooms here I guess it stops you from getting bored," said a businessman after lunching at New York's Auto Pub, which is divided into sections like the Pit Stop, Lover's Lane, and The Drive-In Movie.[33]

Car themes are used in many of the popular fifties-concept operations, as is suggested by some of their names: Caddy's, Studebaker, Cadillac Jacks, Chevy's, Packards, and T Bird. Other fifties themers use music as a unifying idea: Juke Box Saturday Night, Hard Rock Cafe, and the Philadelphia Bandstand. Ed Debevics, which operates on the West Coast and in Chicago, is built around a fictional 1950s character of that name, whose bowling trophies are hung on the wall. Its staff are trained to maintain the fiction that Ed Debevic is a real person who has just temporarily stepped out.

Studebaker's, like most 1950s themes, features entertainment as a major part of its offering. Waitresses are dressed in bobby socks and poodle skirts.

[31]*Nation's Restaurant News,* November 11, 1985, p. 1.
[32]*Nation's Restaurant News,* November 11, 1985, p. 151.
[33]*Newsweek,* February 3, 1975, p. 58.

The record library features two thousand "mega hits of the 50's". Chevy's puts more emphasis on food, but here too the waitresses' costumes feature bobby socks and cheerleader's jumpers. Juke Box Saturday Night, according to *Restaurant Business*, bears more resemblance to an amusement park than to a typical night club. "We're entertainment oriented," according to Steve Schussler, a cofounder.[34]

Another popular motif is the rejuvenated American diner. These new diners offer lower prices than do the dinner houses, but the atmosphere is more stylish than that of family restaurants. The combination has worked to produce a sales volume of over $2 million a year per unit. Many of the new diners are small chains or independents bent on becoming chains.[35] The older, established diners operate with low profit margins. They are usually 24-hour operations that are managed mainly by family members. Diners typically offer extensive menus and scratch preparation, as well as good location, familiarity, and low prices.

The success of many theme restaurants rests on showmanship and gimmickry. This can lead to some surprising, even bizarre tasks—waitresses on roller skates and singing bartenders, to name two of the more wholesome examples. *Nation's Restaurant News* reported a new restaurant opening in a converted mausoleum. Its slogan: "Thomas Powell's Funeral Parlor— We'll dig you later." According to *NRN*, "Decor includes various funeral parlor fixtures and attachments like dark curtains, caskets, and plenty of flowers, anything 'if it can be done in good taste.'" Even fast food has its entry in the theme area—with a topless doughnut shop reported in Fort Lauderdale, Florida.[36]

Most theme restaurants try to establish charming atmospheres—old mills, early American (often authentic) history, palatial elegance reminiscent of earlier European times—something that catches the guests' interest without being outlandish. Nautical and railroad themes are particularly popular. A number of abandoned railroad stations have, in fact, been converted into restaurants, and one theme restaurant is actually on board a moving train. The Star Clipper operates on the Cedar Valley Railroad, taking a 56-mile round trip out of Cedar Rapids, Iowa, at 12 miles per hour. It departs at 7:30 P.M. and returns at 10 P.M., and charges $35 for the trip and dinner. The Star Clipper is booked months in advance, and the owner is reportedly establishing another, similar operation.[37]

Theme restaurants seem to be limited only by their owners' imaginations. And themes rise and fall in popularity. In the 1960s and 1970s, Polynesian was an "in" theme; currently, it is the 1950s and diners. It will be

[34]*Restaurant Business*, July 20, 1985, pp. 124–134.

[35]*Nation's Restaurant News*, January 27, 1986, p. 1.

[36]*Nation's Restaurant News*, February 3, 1975, p. 52.

[37]*Nation's Restaurant News*, September 30, 1985, p. 86.

Theme restaurants offer an atmosphere that will entertain. Shown above is Baby Doe's Matchless Mine, a hilltop restaurant in Monterey Park, California, and on the opposite page is Crawdaddy's Restaurant, on the Tampa Bay Waterfront in Florida. Both represent concepts operated in a number of locations by Specialty Restaurants Corp., which also operates the 94th Aero Squadron restaurants and other themed operations. (Photos courtesy of Specialty Restaurant Corp.)

interesting to see what the future brings. One company, McFadden Ventures, has developed a new building design that places all the equipment at the back of the building and uses hollow floors and ceilings to accommodate changes in wiring or plumbing. This design allows quick concept makeovers. Indeed, one of this company's units has used four concepts in only eight years—from "Elain" to "Cowboys" to "Confetti" to "Rialto."[38] The current physical design accepts, in effect, the fact that the unit is really a stage setting.

Theme restaurants are designed for the middle-class mass market. They typically offer a few popular dishes. The significance of a limited selection

[38]*Nation's Restaurant News,* November 4, 1985, p. 13.

was dramatized by a study of leading U.S. restaurants, in which restaurants offering more than 20 entrees on the menu spent 29 percent of their sales dollars on payroll. Those offering between 8 and 20 entrees spent 28 percent of sales on payroll, and operations with fewer than 8 entrees reported spending only 24 percent of sales on payroll. In a business in which net profit commonly runs below 5 percent, this difference is substantial.[39]

Ethnic Restaurants

The increasingly well traveled and sophisticated consumer seeks not only a meal but also a miniadventure, or at least "a different experience" in both the atmosphere and the more distinctive ethnic foods in specialty restaurants. Chi Chi's, for instance, is a chain of Mexican dinner houses. Most ethnic restaurants are independents, frequently run by people whose families come from the ethnic region of the restaurant. Many ethnic foods offer the consumer, besides "different" foods and an exotic ambience, a health

[39]*Hospitality,* July 1976, pp. 14–17.

Benihana of Tokyo offers adventure by recreating the atmosphere of a Japanese country inn. All foods are cooked at a "hibachi table" in front of the guest, providing entertainment while the meal is being prepared. (Photo courtesy of Benihana of Tokyo.)

appeal—less fat and less cholesterol. And because of the lower food costs of most ethnic restaurants, they can also offer very competitive prices. Ethnic restaurants have also entered the eating market as well the dining market. For example, Mexican restaurants have been among the fastest-growing fast-food segments in recent years.

SIGNIFICANT ENTRIES IN THE EATING MARKET

The most significant of the eating market's "refueling stops" is the fast-food operation we've already considered. Close behind are the other lower-price specialty units such as family and pizza restaurants. But not all units in the eating market are specialty restaurants.

Cafeterias

In cafeterias, customers choose their food from visual inspection as well as from a menu board. Cafeteria service is also used in many budget steak houses and other operations, but the distinctive features of the cafeteria, in addition to self-service, is menu variety. Because of the space requirements of an extensive kitchen and the cafeteria line, cafeterias require a larger building than do most other food service concepts, and so they are often located in suburban areas where land costs are lower than in a city's central business district.

The price/value perception is a key selling point for cafeterias. A family of four can spend almost the same amount at a fast-food restaurant as they would at a cafeteria, but they have a much wider variety of food to choose from, and with a "home style" appeal. Most cafeterias average about $4 per customer, not much higher than fast food.

As with so many other segments, cafeterias are moving toward more "lite" selections—baked and broiled fish and chicken and less beef. Cafeterias also appeal to older consumers, and the growth in that population group (which will be discussed in more detail in Chapter 5), together with cafeteria's superior price/value perception, makes them a segment to watch during the "middle aging" of America, as this value-conscious group becomes the population's largest segment.[40]

Country Cooking

"Country" chains such as Po Folks, Cracker Barrel, and Southern Cooker have a somewhat more limited menu than do cafeterias, but they offer more service. With the average check ranging from $3.50 to $4.50, as well as generous portions of food, these operations appeal to value-conscious, price-sensitive customers.[41] With corny jokes, a lot of "down home" spelling on the menu, and a country decor, these operations offer some of the entertainment value of the more-upscale theme restaurants.

"Gourmet" Hamburgers

The "gourmet" hamburger restaurant offers large portions, a price range of $5 to $6, and the fast service associated with fast-food or family restaurants. Some units are entirely self-service, whereas others offer table service. These operations, unlike fast-food restaurants, do serve alcoholic beverages. Their decor is generally either more upscale, like that of dinner houses, or "trendy," using art deco to give a stylish look. Such hamburger restaurants show solid growth prospects because of their good price/value relationship as well as their competitiveness with the more expensive casual dinner houses and the less distinctive family restaurants.[42] After 1990, however, population trends may work against them, as the population group they serve begins to shrink.

[40]*Nation's Restaurant News*, August 12, 1985, p. F52.
[41]Rohs, *The Restaurant Industry*, p. 32.
[42]This discussion also draws in part on Rohs, *The Restaurant Industry*.

Fuddruckers, an early leader in the gourmet hamburger segment, merchandises a sense of plenty with its self-service condiments and trimmings bar. Because the meat is ground on the premises in the butcher shop (shown in the background), customers are convinced that they are receiving fresh, all-beef hamburgers. (Photo courtesy of Fuddruckers, Inc.)

Takeout and Delivery

According to the National Restaurant Association, over than 85 percent of Americans use take-out food services. Two-thirds of food service consumers buy take-out food at least three times a month, and half of them do so at least weekly. In a busy society, convenience has become an important buying motive: the principal customers are singles; families with children, particularly those with working mothers; and people 18 to 34 years old.[43]

   Fast-food operators provide 58 percent of take-out sales, and family restaurants provide 7 percent, according to a Gallup survey.[44] Throughout the 1980s, take-out food service has grown substantially faster than has the industry as a whole; indeed 39.5 percent of all restaurant traffic is for take-out food.[45] Takeout serves the at-home and the on-the-go markets: 46 percent of take-out food is consumed at home, and of the rest, 21 percent is

[43]*NRA News*, December 1985, p. 14.
[44]*Nation's Restaurant News*, March 10, 1986, p. 143.
[45]Rohs, *The Restaurant Industry*, p. 30.

consumed in the car and 15 percent at work, with 18 percent of consumption attributed to "other" places.[46]

Surprisingly, haute cuisine is a growth area for takeout, as well. New York City's Quilted Giraffe, for instance, where the average bill for lunch is $115, offers take-out service with an average take-out sale of $15. In fact, its take-out volume is so good that a commissary is planned to supply three different Quilted Giraffe take-out units in New York. In Boston, the Creative Gourmet offers cold items to go for lunch, as does Mr. B's in New Orleans.[47] Takeout offers several advantages to operators of all kinds. Most obviously, it offers add-on sales in a new service format, but it also attracts customers who, if satisfied, are likely to return, for a sit-down meal, and it generally enhances the restaurant's image. Because take-out food increases the restaurant's volume, it also reduces its food and payroll costs.[48]

Delivery. The delivery of prepared food is in its infancy with pizza, the only food product that is commonly delivered to the home. The delivery of food products, including pizza, is also a business different from that of the regular restaurants from which most deliveries are made. In fact, Pizza Hut is setting up independent units devoted to delivery, so as to avoid overcrowding its parking lots which are essential to its on-premise business. Domino's, the largest pizza deliverer, relies almost exclusively on delivery and generally does not even offer seating in its stores. The cost structure for the delivery business includes both the labor for the delivery and the transportation costs. These added costs lower margins and support the notion that delivery is a different business.

The delivery of fast food is still in the experimental stage. Two students at Indiana University are among the field's pioneers. Based on an in-depth study of student needs, which indicated a demand for the delivery of Mexican food and hamburgers, they began a delivery service which eventually joined Taco Bell and McDonald's, increasing those companies' unit volumes by 20 percent.[49]

Home delivery is also growing in the gourmet market. One Chicago company offers "mobile maitre d's who give customers verbal and written heating instructions" for the gourmet foods they deliver. Another Chicago operator advertises entrees such as bass poached in white wine and pears ($10.95) or chicken vesuvio ($8.95).[50] In addition to delivering to the home, many fast-food services are constructing mobile units that will take the food

[46]George D. Rice, "Retargeting Consumers—Segmentation on Attitudes and Behavior," *Proceedings of the 11th Annual Chain Operators Exchange* (Chicago, International Foodservice Manufacturers Association, 1984), p. 7.

[47]*Nation's Restaurant News,* November 11, 1986, p. 10.

[48]*Nation's Restaurant News,* November 11, 1986, p. 10.

[49]*Wall Street Journal,* December 7, 1984, p. 27.

[50]*Nation's Restaurant News,* November 4, 1985, p. 10.

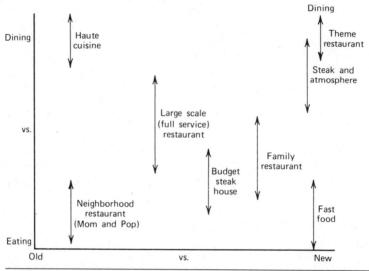

FIGURE 2.2   The range of restaurants compared according to relative novelty and role in the eating or dining markets.

where the business is—to college campuses, seasonal resorts, construction sites, and military bases.[51] Other companies are experimenting with delivery units, some of them equipped for cooking and others just for holding hot food.

Figure 2.2 contrasts the older forms of restaurant operations with the newer ones (from left to right). It also shows the relative position of restaurant types with regard to the eating and the dining markets. Remember, though, that all public dining is partly a social activity and that even the most formal, highly social dinner fulfills the biological function of feeding people.

RESTAURANTS AS A PART OF A LARGER BUSINESS

Thus far, this chapter has examined freestanding restaurants—separate and distinct operations. A substantial part of the food service industry is, however, made up of operations that are the service arms of larger organizations. These operations are often hard to classify, because the broader goals of the large organization may impinge on the food service operation. Thus, the restaurants in hotels, as we will learn in Chapter 6, often open earlier and close later than their volume of food service sales would justify. They do

[51]*Nation's Restaurant News,* September 23, 1985, p. 13.

Morrison's Cafeterias aim to expand their share of the eating market with "Home Cooking to Go" take-out centers which feature both a pickup counter and a drive-through. (Photo courtesy of Morrison Incorporated.)

this as a convenience to hotel guests and as a means of inducing people to choose this particular place for a night's stay. Similarly, Chapter 5, which discusses institutional food service, will demonstrate the importance of the special diet to health-care food service, quite apart from its cost effectiveness. In this chapter, however, we will briefly examine restaurants in retailing establishments such as department stores, drugstores, truck stops, theaters, sports complexes, and convention centers. It is interesting to see how trends in these eating establishments match those in the restaurant business elsewhere.

RESTAURANTS IN RETAILING

Restaurants in department stores and drugstores were originally built as store services: A shopper who had to leave the store for lunch might resume shopping in some other store. The restaurants, therefore, helped keep the shoppers in the store and often helped attract them there in the first place. Increasingly, in-store restaurants are becoming in themselves worthwhile businesses that often generate higher profit margins than do the store's other retail sales. In fact, if properly merchandised, the stores can *bring* shoppers into the store, not just *keep* them in.

Demonstrating that in-store restaurants have become big business, Wal-

The truck stop restaurant is generally a part of a larger roadside service center. (Photo courtesy of Truck Stops of America.)

Food service in retail stores has increasingly adopted a fast-food format. (Photo courtesy of Walgreen's Corp.)

green's food service operations recently topped $125 million. And the giant Federated Department Store chain, according to *Nation's Restaurant News*, now rates its food service division as one of its five major business areas, and that division operates some 300 restaurants. A number of retailers have also opened restaurants outside their stores. Walgreen's operates a chain of freestanding restaurants called Wags; Federated has its own fast-food chain; and Carson Pirie Scott (a Chicago department store with a large food service operation) operates the restaurants at O'Hare Airport.

Today's truck stop restaurant has a coffee shop style of operation, with a cheerful and comfortable interior. (Photo courtesy of Truck Stops of America.)

The economics of restaurant operations that gave rise to the specialty restaurant are now at work in retailing. Retailer-housed restaurants are being pressed to adopt specialty restaurant (especially fast food) service patterns to hold costs in line and to meet the guests' demand for speed.

Restaurant operations in truck stops generally feature a family restaurant or a coffee shop style of operation that offers travelers a break in their journey—a chance to eat and to sit for a few minutes in a comfortable atmosphere. In addition, these operations usually provide special sections for truckers who need superquick service. *Nation's Restaurant News* puts truck stop food service volume at over $1 billion. Many of these twenty-four-hour units do over $2 million per year. As this segment of the business develops, theme truck stop restaurants are on the increase, with a steamboat theme operation in Fulton, Minnesota, American colonial in Connecticut, and a Warfside Restaurant in Warren, Indiana.

The truck stop restaurant is almost always part of a larger service package, which includes gas and diesel fuel, truck repair facilities, gift and sundry shops, and often a motel. Originally intended as an ancillary service, truck stop restaurants now do about a tenth of the dollar volume of all truck stop business.

Although we will discuss vending in more detail later, we note here the growing role of vending in the restaurant picture. In office buildings, factories, and other work settings, vending machines offer menus sometimes as extensive as those of a family restaurant. In some areas, in fact, they actually are replacing restaurant facilities. In a vending operation, one or two on-site employees together with workers at a remote commissary can replace an entire crew of food service employees.

OPERATING RATIOS

Elsewhere in your hospitality curriculum you will undoubtedly study the subject of control. As a part of your introduction to the hospitality field, this section will therefore only briefly define some key food service control terms.

COST OF SALES

The *cost of sales* refers to the cost of a product used by the guest in the process of operations. The principal product costs include:

Food costs.   The cost of food prepared for and consumed by guests.

Beverage or bar costs.   The cost of alcoholic beverages and other ingredients, such as juices, carbonated water, or fruit, used to make drinks for guests.

Note that these (and all other) costs are customarily stated as a percentage of sales. For example, if your food cost is $25,000 and your food sales are $75,000, then the food cost percent will be $25,000 ÷ $75,000, or 33.3 percent. Although dollar costs are essential to the accounting system, the percentage of the cost (that is, its size relative to sales level) is more significant to managers, because the percentages for one month (or for some other period) can readily be compared with those of the other months, with a budget, and with industry averages.

CONTROLLABLE EXPENSES

Controllable expenses are costs that may be expected to vary to some degree and over which operating management can exercise some direct control.

Payroll Costs.   Payroll costs are the wages and salaries paid to employees.

Employee Benefits.   Employee benefits include social security taxes; such social insurance as workers' compensation, pension payments, and hospitalization; and other benefit expenses such as those for education and sports activities.

Direct Operating Expenses.   Direct operating expenses usually vary, reflecting the volume of sales. The principal direct operating expenses include those for uniforms, laundry, linen, china, glass and silver, guest and cleaning supplies, and menus.

Other Operating Expenses.   Most other operating expenses are fixed (some basic minimum amount of money essential to staying in business). But they can and sometimes do vary. One group, sometimes called *mixed costs,* includes a base minimum charge or an irreducible minimum cost, to which are then added costs according to usage, such as the costs for utilities, administration, and repairs and maintenance. Other costs in this group result from policy decisions by management regarding such activities as advertising and sales promotion, music, and entertainment. They need not vary with sales volume, but they do vary with the management's decisions.

CAPITAL COSTS

Capital costs are mainly determined when the operation is established. They include rent, insurance, depreciation, interest, and taxes.

By categorizing cost information in this way, we focus attention on the operation's key variables. The cost percentages also reflect the efficiency of various segments of an operation. Food costs reflect management pricing and the kitchen crew's efficiency. Labor costs reflect efficiency in employee scheduling and the adequacy of sales volume in proportion to the operation's needs. They can be improved by either reducing employee hours or increasing sales.

This discussion brings us to yet another pair of terms: *covers* and *check averages*. The number of covers refers to the number of guests. (*Guest count* is the alternative term.) The *check average* is what it sounds like—the total sales for a period divided by the number of parties (that is, the number of checks). Because parties (a group of guests seated together) vary in size, the check average is usually quoted as the average sale per guest. This figure is found by dividing total dollar sales by the number of guests served during the period and is sometimes referred to as the *average cover*.

Clearly, there are two ways to increase total sales: to increase the number of covers served by bringing in more guests or to increase the check averages by selling more to the guests who do come. In comparing check averages, it is important to note whether the figure represents food only or both food and beverages. The best way to collect and report these data is to show separately a food-only and a beverage check average and then to lump the two in a combined check average.

Figure 2.3 shows an example of a restaurant statement of income and

SALES		
Food	$ 534,000	74.6%
Beverage	182,000	25.4
Total sales	$ 716,000	100.0%
COST OF SALES		
Food	$ 230,700	43.2%
Beverage	52,000	28.6
Total cost of sales	$ 282,700	39.5%
CONTROLLABLE EXPENSES		
Payroll	$ 185,400	25.9%
Employee benefits	20,800	2.9
Direct operating expenses	38,700	5.4
Music and entertainment	4,300	.6
Advertising and promotion	11,400	1.6
Utilities	16,500	2.3
Administrative and general	28,700	4.0
Repairs and maintenance	10,000	1.4
Total controllable expenses	$ 315,800	44.1%
INCOME BEFORE CAPITAL COSTS	$ 117,500	16.4%
CAPITAL COSTS		
Rent, property taxes, and insurance	$ 42,900	6.0%
Interest and depreciation	40,000	5.6
Total capital costs	$ 82,900	11.6%
NET PROFIT BEFORE INCOME TAXES	$ 34,600	4.8%
Number of covers served	74,918	
Food check average	7.128	
Beverage check average	2.429	
Total check average	9.557	

FIGURE 2.3   Statement of income and expenses, Suburban Restaurant (year ending December 31, 19XX).

expenses (also called an operating statement or a profit-and-loss statement). This statement shows the relationship of the costs we just discussed and also how the check averages are computed.

As a final way to compare and contrast differing restaurants, Table 2.5 presents selected *average operating ratios* for the typical operations of the kinds of restaurants we have been describing in this chapter. The similarities and distinctions among the types are not accidental but reflect some major differences in profit potential. The family restaurants and fast-food chains have a somewhat lower *prime cost* (products and labor cost), and that limited advantage passes right down to pretax profit. Although food costs are

TABLE 2.5 Comparison of U.S. Restaurant Operating Statistics, 1980

	Hamburger Chain	Family Restaurants	Suburban Table Service Restaurants
Food cost	35.5	35.1	41.0
Beverage cost[a]			
Disposable cost	4.1	3.1	29.0
Product cost[b]	39.6	38.2	39.0
Payroll and related[c]	26.4	29.5	30.4
Prime cost[d]	66.0	67.7	69.4
Other operating costs	15.6	16.1	18.0
Occupancy and capital costs	12.5	12.0	10.0
Pretax profit	5.9	4.2	4.4

Source: Estimates are based on *Nation's Restaurant News,* and *Restaurant Industry Operations Report,* prepared by the National Restaurant Association and Laventhol & Horwath.
[a]Beverage cost as percentage of beverage sales.
[b]Total food and beverage cost as percentage of total food and beverage sales.
[c]Includes employee benefits.
[d]Total of product cost and labor cost.

higher for suburban restaurants than for the other two groups, their overall *product costs* are roughly comparable, because of the lower percentage product cost for liquor. On the other hand, the extremely high food cost for budget steak operations has forced those operations to experiment with more diversified menus.

Payroll costs are, not surprisingly, highest in the most labor intensive operations—the family restaurant and the suburban restaurant—both of which offer table service. On the other hand, the higher disposable costs for the two quick-service operations has, in a way, "purchased" lower wage costs by eliminating labor. Disposables also have the effect of reducing the space required for dishwashing and thus reducing investment and the capital cost of depreciation.

SUMMARY

We began our discussion of the restaurant business by differentiating the various types of restaurants. First are the full-service restaurants, the full service referring to the style of service, the menu, and the style of preparation. Such restaurants run from haute cuisine restaurants, at the top end, to neighborhood or mom-and-pop restaurants, at the bottom end. Second are specialty restaurants, ranging from fast-food operations to family restaurants to budget steak houses to pizza restaurants. We also describe how a large fast-food chain introduces a new menu item, as compared with how an independent restaurant does this.

We then distinguished the dining market from the eating market. The dining market serves mainly our social needs, and the eating market serves mainly our biological needs, although of course, the two do overlap. The dining market refers to haute cuisine restaurants, casual dinner houses, theme restaurants, and ethnic restaurants. The eating market encompasses fast-food operations and family and pizza restaurants, as well as cafeterias, "country" chains, "gourmet" hamburgers, and takeout and delivery.

Next we talked about restaurants as part of a larger business, such as restaurants in department stores, drugstores, and truck stops that are meant both to attract customers and to keep them.

Last, we touched on the subject of restaurants' operating ratios, or their income versus their expenses. These expenses are cost of sales (food and beverage costs), controllable expenses (payroll costs, employee benefits, direct operating expenses, and other operating expenses), and, finally, capital or fixed costs.

KEY WORDS AND CONCEPTS

To help you review this chapter, keep in mind the following.

Full-service restaurants	Theme restaurants
Specialty restaurants	Food costs
Haute cuisine restaurants	Beverage costs
Neighborhood restaurants	Payroll costs
Fast food	Direct operating costs
The eating market	Check averages
The dining market	Covers

REVIEW QUESTIONS

1. What are the three elements of a full-service restaurant?
2. What kinds of restaurants are defined as full-service restaurants?
3. What are the characteristics of a specialty restaurant?

4. What kinds of restaurants are defined as specialty restaurants?

5. Describe the process of introducing a new menu item in a fast-food restaurant.

6. How do the dining market and the eating market differ?

7. What kinds of restaurants are included in each market?

8. What are some of the new trends in the restaurant business?

9. What larger businesses do restaurants serve?

10. List the principal expenses of a restaurant.

Courtesy of W. R. Grace.

ISSUES FACING FOOD SERVICE

THE PURPOSE OF THIS CHAPTER

Knowing who you are and who your customer is answers two really fundamental questions. In the first part of this chapter, we will look at *who the restaurateur is:* part of a chain, a franchisee, or an independent. Understanding the choices to be made in terms of affiliation should help you to think about your own future—as a trainee, employee, and, some day, as an operator.

In the second part of the chapter, the focus shifts to our customer. The industry's customers are growing older; their tastes are changing as are their needs. The successful restaurateur (or the hotel operator with a restaurant as a major part of the property) needs this information to prosper and grow.

THIS CHAPTER SHOULD HELP YOU

1.   Describe the competitive strengths of the chain operator and the independent.
2.   Become familiar with the changing size of restaurant chains and the continuing vital role of the independent.
3.   Know the significance of today's key markets—in terms of age, income and lifestyle—for the restaurant business.
4.   Understand the key consumer *concerns* shaping menu trends.

5. Evaluate the role of the consumer movement as it effects the restaurant business.

6. Identify and examine the principle consumer issues facing food service.

ORGANIZATIONAL FORM: CHAIN, INDEPENDENT, OR FRANCHISE?

Even though we sometimes hear that the day of the independent is past and the chains will soon gobble up the entire food service market, nothing could be further from the truth. Chains do have enormous advantages in some markets, but in others they have disadvantages. It is useful, therefore, to examine the competitive advantages of both the independents and the chains and franchisees. In our discussion, we will treat franchised restaurants much like chains. If there are important differences, we will point them out.

CHAIN SPECIALTY RESTAURANTS

Chains have six strengths: (1) brand recognition or preference, (2) site selection expertise, (3) access to capital, (4) purchasing economies, (5) centrally administered control and information systems, and (6) personnel program development. All of these strengths represent *economies of scale:* the savings come, in one way or another, from the spreading of a centralized activity over a large number of units so that each absorbs only a small portion of the cost but all have the benefit of specialized expertise or buying power when they need it.

Brand Recognition

More young children in America recognize Santa Claus than any other public figure. Ronald McDonald comes second! Because McDonald's and its franchisees spend well over a half-billion dollars (in 1985, $686 million) on advertising, it's no wonder more children recognize Ronald than, say, Mickey Mouse, Donald Duck, or the Easter Bunny. Indeed, "McDonald's has taken the hamburger to the American public and created a generic item—the Big Mac. The company has done for the hamburger what Coke did for cola, Avon for cosmetics, and Kodak for film." The reasons for this success are threefold: simplicity of message, enormous spending, and the additive effect.

The *message* of modern advertising is affected by the form in which it is offered: 10-, 30-, or 60-second television commercials, for instance. Even in the printed media, the message must be kept simple, because an advertisement in a newspaper or magazine has to compete with other ads and news or feature stories for the consumer's casual attention. The message of the specialty restaurant resembles its menu. It boils down to a simple state-

One of the big advantages of a major franchise is a well-known brand name. (Photo courtesy of McDonald's Corp.)

ment or a catch phrase. In fact, marketing people generally try to design a "tag line" that summarizes the benefits they want an advertising campaign to tell the consumer. Not long ago, Wendy's Restaurants used the slogan, "Ain't no reason to go anyplace else." Although this slogan set off a letter-writing campaign complaining about the grammar, (apparently organized by high school English teachers), Wendy's officials judged it effective in "breaking through the clutter." Classic tag lines of the past are still memorable:

"We do it all for you."
"You deserve a break today."
"Finger lickin' good."

TABLE 3.1   Advertising Expenditures by Type of Restaurant

	Advertising As a Percentage of Sales
Independent restaurants	1.9%
Hamburger chains	4.6%
Family restaurants	3.6%

Source: Nation's Restaurant News and NRA Restaurant Industry Operations Report.

Moreover, the *level of spending* for chain specialty restaurant advertising is higher. Chains spend more on advertising because their efficient, routinized operating procedures yield profits generous enough to make such expensive advertising feasible. Table 3.1 shows that the two most effective chain specialty restaurant groups spend proportionately between 80 and 100 percent more of their sales dollar on advertising than independents do.

The *additive effect* of belonging to a chain or franchise group permits units to pool the budgets of many stores. Thus, the total advertising budget available enables them to use the expensive medium of television—and not just in a local market but in regional and national markets as well.

Of course, all this advertising will be effective only if the consumers get exactly what they expect. Therefore, some of the chains' most effective controls are aimed at ensuring the consistency of quality and service. The customer does know exactly what to expect in each McDonald's, and in an increasingly mobile society, that is important. For people on the go as tourists, shoppers, or businesspersons, what is more natural than to stop at a familiar sign? If that experience is pleasant, it will reinforce the desire to return to that sign in the local market or wherever else it appears.

Site Selection Expertise

The success of most specialty restaurants is also enhanced by a location near the heart of major traffic patterns. The technique for analyzing location potential requires a special kind of knowledge, and the chains alone can afford real estate departments that possess that expertise.

Access to Capital

Most bankers and other money lenders have traditionally treated restaurants as risky businesses. So an independent operator who wants to open a res-

A site convenient to local auto traffic and with adequate parking is essential to success in fast foods. (Photo courtesy of McDonald's Corp.)

taurant (or even remodel or expand an existing operation) may find it difficult to borrow the needed capital. But the bankers' willingness to lend increases with the size of the company: if one unit should falter, the banker knows that the franchise will want to protect its credit record. To do so, it can divert funds from successful operations to "carry" one in trouble until the problems can be worked out. Thus, the banks not only make capital available to units of larger companies. but they also lower the interest rates on these loans, sometimes substantially.

Purchasing Economies

Chains can centralize their purchasing either by buying centrally in their own commissary or by negotiating centrally with suppliers who then deliver the products, made according to rigid specifications, from their own warehouses and processing plants. Chains obviously purchase in great quantity, and they can use this bargaining leverage to negotiate the best possible prices and terms. Chains can also afford their own research and development departments for testing products and developing new equipment.

Control and Information Systems

Economies of scale is the important concept here. Chains can spend large sums on developing accounting procedures and procedures for collecting market information. They can devise costly computer programs and purchase or lease expensive computer equipment, again spreading the cost over a large number of operations. Moreover, in most chains, an expert staff dispatched from central headquarters reviews the units' efficiency. Unit managers may not always enjoy these inspections, but they make them stay on their toes.

Personnel Program Development

Some restaurant chains have established sophisticated training programs for hourly employees, using audiovisual techniques such as films, tapes, and slide shows to demonstrate the proper ways of performing food service operations. These standardized procedures in turn lower the cost of training and improve its effectiveness. This economy is especially important in semi-skilled and unskilled jobs, which traditionally experience high turnover rates and, therefore, waste considerable training time.

Management training also is important, and the chains can usually afford the cost of thorough entry-level management training programs. ARA, for instance, estimates the first-year training direct costs for a management trainee fresh out of college at $12,400, including the trainee's salary and fringe benefits, with an additional $1,200 estimated as the cost of managers' time to provide on-the-job training. In effect, this company spends as much as or more than a year of college costs on their trainees, a truly valuable education for the person who receives it.

Because of their multiple operations, moreover, chains can instill in beginning managers an incentive to work hard, by offering gradual increases in responsibility and compensation. In addition, a district and regional management organization monitors the managers' progress. Early in a manager's career, he or she begins to receive performance bonuses tied to the unit's operating results. These bonuses and the success they represent obviously are powerful motivators.

Performance of the Top 100 Restaurant Companies

The advantages of the chains have helped the largest of them increase their share of the food service market. The 100 largest restaurant companies, which operate 179 separate chains, were tracked by Technomic Consultants in an annual study, from which the data in this section are taken.[1] These companies operated 70,984 units in the United States and had total sales of $47,588 billion. As Figure 3.1 shows, the 100 largest companies' food service

[1]Technomic Consultants, *Dynamics of the Chain Restaurant Market 1985* (Chicago: International Foodservice Manufacturers Association, 1985).

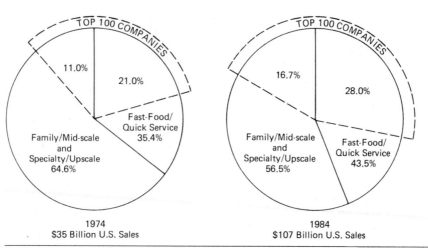

FIGURE 3.1   Top 100 companies' share of sales volume of U.S. separate eating places by type of operation. (International Foodservice Manufacturing Association.)

dollar sales increased by nearly 50 percent in the past decade, from a 31-percent share in 1974 to nearly a 45-percent share in 1984. The 100 largest companies also owned 30 percent of all the units in operation. The larger share of the dollar sales, compared with the proportion of units in operation, reflects these chains' substantially higher-than-average unit sales.

Table 3.2 shows the growth in sales, adjusted for inflation, for the top 100 restaurant companies and for all other U.S. restaurants. From 1974 to 1979, the growth rate for smaller chains and independents was at least within hailing distance of that of the larger chains. During the recession from 1980 to 1983, however, the top 100's staying power was clear, as shown in the increase in sales of 36.3 percent, whereas sales for all other restaurants declined by nearly 2 percent. From 1983 to 1984, the large chains grew nearly five times as fast as did the smaller chains and independents. In the same period, the smaller companies and the independents grew by only 27 percent, but the top 100 more than doubled.

OPERATING ADVANTAGES OF THE INDEPENDENT

Although chains undeniably have advantages in the competitive battle for the consumer's dollar, the independents also enjoy advantages that ensure them a continuing place in the market, a different place from that of the chains, perhaps, but a significant place nevertheless.

We can follow the same method we used for the chain specialty restaurants to analyze the strengths of the independents. Just as the advantages of the large organization relate to economies of scale, the independent's operating advantages share their attributes as well. The independent's flexibility,

TABLE 3.2   Growth in Sales: Top 100 Companies and Smaller Chains
and Independents

	Growth Rate	
Period	Top 100 Companies	Smaller Chains and Independents
1974–1979	44.0%	26.6%
1979–1983	36.3	− 1.9
1983–1984	10.8	2.4
1974–1984	117.8	27.2

Source: Technomic Consultants, *Dynamics of the Chain Restaurant Market, 1985* (Chicago: International Foodservice Manufacturers Association, 1985); *Statistical Abstract of the United States, 1985* (Washington, D.C.: U.S. Government Printing Office, 1985).

the motivation of its owner, and the owner's closeness to the operation all affect its success.

Although the following analysis does not deal directly with the issue, we should note that economies of scale also are important in the independent restaurant. The small operation—the mom-and-pop restaurant—finds itself increasingly pressed by rising costs. We cannot specify a minimum volume requirement for success, but the *Restaurant Industry Operating Report '85* showed that urban and suburban restaurants had median sales of about $4,445 per seat. Rural restaurants, on the other hand, had median sales of only $2,365, suggesting that they have a more cyclical sales pattern, which dips very low off day and off season. Simpler operations can undoubtedly make a profit with substantially lower sales, but the problem of fixing the minimum economic size is a real one.

Brand Recognition

Ronald McDonald may be a popular figure, but he is not a real person. The successful restaurant proprietor, however, is real. In fact, successful restaurateurs often become well known, are involved in community affairs, and establish strong ties of friendship with many of their customers. This local celebrity can be especially effective "standing at the door," greeting guests by name as they arrive, moving through the dining room, recognizing friends or acquaintances, dealing graciously with complaints, and expressing gratitude for praise. "Thanks and come back again" has an especially pleasant ring when it comes from the boss—the owner whose status in the town isn't subject to corporate whim or sudden transfer.

Although the chain may have advantages among transients, the operator of a high-quality operation enjoys an almost-unique advantage in the local

market. Moreover, word-of-mouth advertising may spread his or her reputation to an even larger area. The key to recognition for the independent is
more than just personality; it is, first and foremost, quality. To build a reputation, the operation must be different from others and noticeably better
than the ordinary restaurant. This is hard to achieve with a "hamburger and
chicken" menu. Hamburgers and chicken can be good, but not so distinc-
tively better as to make a difference.

Site Selection

The chain operation continually faces the problem of selecting the right site
as it seeks new locations for expansion. The established operator, however,
gives location less attention. True, over the long term, an independent operator must adjust to changing urban patterns and real-estate values, perhaps by moving. Not long ago, the finest independent restaurants were located in the city's center, whereas fast-food operations chose the suburbs.
But now in the large cities and even in some medium-sized cities, the downtown area has begun to decay, and reports of crime and violence make these
areas unattractive, particularly for the evening meal. When a center city
location has not decayed, rising land values sometimes escalate rentals to
the point that full-service restaurants often can no longer afford them. In the
past few years, fast-food restaurants—with their high seating density and
higher operating margin on a high volume—have moved into the big-city
downtown market, whereas the independent has joined the fast-food operator out in the suburbs, near the new shopping centers and office complexes
and adjacent to the affluent residential areas. When contemplating such a
move, a local operator can supplement his or her own knowledge of the area
by hiring a consulting firm to conduct a location study. It's an expensive
service but valuable if it is needed.

Access to Capital

In most cases, the chain will have the most ready access to capital. Nevertheless, the successful operator can often establish contacts with local financial institutions and investors.

Purchasing Economies

Once again, the chain enjoys substantial advantages in its purchasing economies. But the independent's problem may differ somewhat from the
chain's. Because of the importance of quality in the independent operation,
the price advantages in centralized purchasing may not be as important as
is an ability to find top-quality products consistently. Thus, long-standing
personal friendships with local purveyors can be an advantage for the independent.

Control and Information Systems

Because of its simple menu, the chain specialty restaurant can take advantage of the sort of information on marketing and sales patterns produced by computerized routines. This practice is, in fact, essential to companies operating many units in a national market. But the complex menu of the single, independent, full-service restaurant lends itself to the operator's subjective interpretation, impressions, and "hunches" about the changing preferences of the guests. Moreover, the independent operator can easily analyze some simple data (such as menu popularity counts) without paying for programming or computer time.

Improved control systems have recently become available to the independent with the advent of electronic cash registers (ECR) and point-of-sales (POS) register systems controlled by a minicomputer. A fairly wide variety of hardware and programming options has enabled the independent to obtain daily reports detailing sales as well as payroll and product costs.[2]

Cost-control procedures may be more stringent in the chain operation, but if an owner keeps an eye on everything from preparation to portion sizes to the garbage can (the amount of food left on a plate is often a good clue to the overportioning), very effective cost control can be achieved even when an ECR/POS system to fit the operator's needs is not available or when the cost of such a system seems prohibitive. By using the uniform system of accounts and professional advice available from restaurant accounting specialists, independents can readily develop control systems adequate to their needs.

This description of the independent operator suggests what has become a food service axiom: Anyone who cannot operate successfully without the corporate brass looking over his or her shoulder will probably be out of business as an independent in less than a year.

Personnel

The independent proprietor can and usually does develop close personal ties with the employees, a practice that can help reduce turnover. But even though "old hand" employees can act as trainers, the cost of training new workers tends to be higher for the independent, because of the complex operation and because he or she lacks the economies of a centralized training program.

Although advancement incentives are not as abundant in independent operations as in the chains, many successful independents hire young people, train them over a period of several years to become effective supervisors, and then help them move on to a larger operation. Often, too the independent finds key employees whose life goals are satisfied by their

---

[2]For a fuller discussion of the subject, see Thomas F. and Jo Marie Powers, *Food Service Operations: Planning and Control* (New York: Wiley, 1983), especially chap. 3.

positions as chef, host or hostess, or head bartender. These employees often receive bonus plans similar to those offered by the chains.

The Independent's Extra: Flexibility

One strength that the independent boasts is the flexibility inherent in having only one boss or a small partnership. Fast decision making permits the independent to adapt to changing market conditions. And because there is no need to maintain a standard chain image, an independent is free to develop menus that take advantage of local tastes. Finally, there are many "one of a kind" niches in the marketplace, special situations that don't repeat themselves often enough to make them interesting to chains. Yet these situations may be ideally suited to the strengths of independents. Can you see a chain mass-marketing delicate meals featuring freshly gathered wild mushrooms in the way that a fancy little independent operation in Reading, Pennsylvania, does?

Between Independent and Chain

Between the independent and the chain lie at least two other possibilities. First, some independent operations are so successful that they open additional units, without, however, becoming so large as to lose the "hands-on" management of the owner-operator. *Nation's Restaurant News* refers to these as *independent group operators:*

> Perhaps the best illustration of the independent's greatest plus, flexibility, is found in a new group of restaurants which are not exactly chains but which because of their success are no longer single unit operators"[3]

A Second Possibility is a Franchise

Franchisees operate under the name and with the concept of a franchising organization but own their own businesses and have much greater freedom of action than do managers of chain-owned units. The franchisees' proportion of restaurant sales has doubled since 1974 and currently accounts for over 40 percent of all restaurant sales. Franchising in the hospitality industry is discussed at greater length in Chapter 20.

RESTAURANT SIZE

Independents own half of all restaurants and will certainly continue to occupy a large share of the market. Furthermore, the majority of independent restaurants are operated by two or more members of the same family, which gives them some advantages in flexibility of scheduling and costs.[4] Nonetheless, the smaller units' sales have declined, as shown in Table 3.3 (Because

---

[3]*Nation's Restaurant News,* May 20, 1985, p. 22.
[4]*NRA News,* August 1985, p. 28.

Fast-food restaurants do offer fast service, but they also provide a relaxing, pleasant place to eat. (Photo courtesy of McDonald's Corp.)

the 1982 dollar was worth only about 65 cents in 1977 dollars, the table is somewhat distorted by inflation.) Units with sales of less than half a million dollars accounted for only a quarter of the market, down from 40 percent in 1977. For the same period, units with over a million dollars in sales (only 28.4 percent of all units) accounted for three-quarters of the market. Nearly as much business was done in the 12 percent of total units doing over $50 million as was done in the much larger number (62.5 percent of all units) doing under $500,000.

THE CONSUMERS: KEY TO THE FUTURE

Jeffrey Campbell, chairman and chief executive officer of Burger King, remarked, "The competitive pressures are so great in this industry that you can't afford to go 18 to 24 months without consciously articulating to people what your overall purpose is."[5]

Competitive action—a subject we'll discuss in the next chapter—is only

[5]*Nation's Restaurant News,* October 21, 1985 p. 161.

TABLE 3.3 Eating Place[a] Size, 1977 and 1982

	Percentage of Units		Percentage of Sales	
	1977	1982	1977	1982
Under $500,000	77.4%	62.5%	40.7%	25.8%
$1,000,000–$999,999	5.5	9.1	14.8	14.5
$5,000,000–$4,999,999	5.1	9.4	16.4	22.4
$10,000,000–$49,999,999	2.4	4.2	5.8	8.0
$50,000,000 and over	8.2	12.5	18.7	24.4

Source: Bureau of the Census and National Restaurant Association.
[a]Includes restaurants, lunchrooms, and fast food.

one source of this pressure. Equally fundamental is the massive shift in consumer needs and preferences in our fast-changing society. Indeed, they—and these changes—are as important to food service companies as competition from other companies is. Consequently, before a company can decide on its position and how it must change, it must determine the needs of its consumers. In this section we will look at the forces shaping consumer demand today, at just who the consumers are and then at what their concerns are.

CONSUMER DEMAND

Recall our discussion of the baby boom and the changing age distribution of North America's population in Chapter 1. Accordingly, Table 3.4 shows us some spending patterns by age group: The *proportion* of food dollars spent by younger consumers is higher than average, but the *absolute dollar amount* spent rises with age up to the age of 55. This says that younger consumers are very good customers, indeed, that although their number will be declining, they will remain an active and significant group in terms of consumer demand. Older consumers, however, are even better customers in terms of total dollars spent.

Table 3.5 views consumer behavior from a different perspective, that of income. It indicates that as incomes rise, the amount of money spent on food away from home increases in both absolute amount and proportion. That is certainly encouraging news in the light of current income trends. Unfortunately, compiling and publishing government statistics require a lot of time, and so the most recent figures available are for 1983. The trends represented in these figures, however, have been relatively stable over the past 10 years. A U.S. Department of Commerce Bureau of Economic Analysis study predicts that in 1990, income per capita will increase 17.6 percent in "real," inflation-adjusted dollars over that in 1983, an annual increase of

TABLE 3.4   Weekly Away-from-Home Expenditures by Age Group, 1982–1983

	Amount	Proportion
Under 25	$15.34	47.4%
25–34	21.03	38.8
35–44	25.26	35.4
45–54	25.70	34.5
55–64	20.31	34.1
65 and over	10.37	27.4
All Households	$19.60	35.6%

Source: U.S. Bureau of Labor Statistics and National Restaurant Association.

TABLE 3.5   Weekly Away-from-Home Food Expenditures by Household and by Income Level, 1982–1983

Household Income	Amount	Proportion
Less than $5,000	$8.92	34.9%
$ 5,000–$9,999	9.26	26.1
$10,000–14,999	13.50	29.1
$15,000–19,999	17.73	33.5
$20,000–29,999	23.17	35.3
$30,000–39,999	28.56	38.0
$40,000 and over	40.65	42.7

Source: Bureau of Labor Statistics and National Restaurant Association.

2.3 percent. And by the year 2000, another 14 percent increase is expected.[6] The 1983 per-capita income was approximately $13,900. Thus, according to these projections, by 1990 this will have risen to roughly $16,400 and by 2000 to $18,800 (in inflation-adjusted, 1983 dollars).

Table 3.6 shows the impact of family size on eating out. Singles—a group that has been growing in recent years—are clearly excellent customers, and so it is hardly surprising that the industry has spent so much effort wooing them. Two-person households are nearly as good customers.

[6]*NRA News,* September 1985, pp. 36–37.

TABLE 3.6   Weekly Away-from-Home Food Expenditures by Household Size, 1982–1983

Household Size	Household Expenditures	Per-Person Expenditures	Proportion
One	$14.14	$14.14	50.3%
Two	20.20	10.10	37.6
Three	19.53	6.51	31.4
Four	27.31	6.83	33.4
Five	24.58	4.92	28.0
Six or more	21.14	3.25[a]	22.8

Source: Bureau of Labor Statistics and National Restaurant Association.
[a]Estimate assuming average household of 6.5 persons in this category.

On the other hand, families with five and six members spend less than average, both in total dollars and as a proportion of their income.

Families in which both spouses work are prime restaurant customers, for two reasons. First, they have a higher household income. Second, and just as important, they have a greater need to eat out because of the time pressures such families experience. Female-headed households, however, are generally not as good customers because of their significantly lower income, but when, as in most cases, the single parent is employed, they have the same or even greater time pressures as those of two-income families.

CONSUMER CONCERNS

The baby-boom generation is generally affluent, well educated, and discriminating and wants an active, pleasurable, and very long life. Not surprisingly, therefore, they are concerned about their health, nutrition, and fitness as means both to stay alive and feel more alive and vigorous. Consumerists and government officials have probably heightened consumer interest in several areas, including truth in dining, sanitation, food ingredients, and labeling. Because of the time pressures of our fast-paced life-style, convenience is a prime consumer concern as well. We will next examine each of these consumer interests and concerns.

Health

Although nutrition and diet are very much on the consumer's mind, they are a part of a larger concern regarding overall health and fitness. Drive down a residential street in the early morning or late afternoon and count the joggers, if you doubt it. This interest in health, in turn, has affected restaurants beyond their menus. For example, in 1984, over 40 percent of consumers polled for a *Restaurants & Institutions* study of consumer preferences com-

Heightened consumer concerns about nutrition and fried food are giving impetus to operations like El Pollo Loco (in Spanish, "the crazy chicken") that broil rather than fry their chicken. (Photo Courtesy of El Pollo Loco.)

plained about smoking in restaurants, and the study suggested that smoking sections are likely to become a standard design feature. The biggest impact of health concerns for us, however, is on menus.

Nutrition

Statistics cited by the *Wall Street Journal* suggest that everyone is at least conscious of diet, and so the proportion of nondieters who use diet products is surprisingly high: 83 percent of those who drink light beer are nondieters; 65 percent for light margarine; 61 percent for diet soft drinks; and 59 percent for sugar substitutes.[7] Clearly, "weight consciousness" is more prevalent than dieting. Restrictive dieters, in fact, account for only 20 percent of consumers. Research in 1984[8] and 1985[9] shows a fairly stable set of consumer preferences with regard to food. The market segments resulting from these consumer attitudes are shown in Table 3.7.

"Health food" leads the list in popularity for those who eat out, according to a two-year study by CREST. (CREST is the acronym for Consumer Reports in Eating Out Share Trends, a series of market research studies based on diaries that consumers keep for the researchers.) In fact, 4 out of 10 consumers have changed their eating habits because of nutrition concerns, thereby reducing their intake of sugar, fats, cholesterol, and caffeine and consequently choosing more frequently fruits, juices, and salads. Table 3.8 shows the 10 menu items that were selected most often from 1982 to 1984.[10]

In addition to a concern with fats, consumers have become interested in the fiber content of various foods, as fiber has been shown to reduce cholesterol levels and the incidence of heart disease.[11] It is also widely thought to lower the risk of cancer of the bowel and colon. Fiber includes all those components of foods that are not broken down in the digestive tract and absorbed into the bloodstream. The desirable levels of fiber intake—25 to 50 grams per day—is as much as 2.5 times most people's current levels of consumption. Common servings of fruits, vegetables, and whole grain breads and cereals contain about 2 to 4 grams of dietary fiber.

Dietary Schizophrenia

Despite their avowed concerns, however, consumers are not necessarily consistent in their responses to health, fitness, and nutrition consciousness. For instance, Steve's Ice Cream, specializing in ultrarich, high-butterfat ice cream, was asked to put an outlet in a major fitness center! When they expressed surprise, "We were told that 'people want to reward themselves for all that work.'"[12] And when companies developed low-salt soups to respond to people's widely expressed concerns about sodium in their diet, they were

[7]*Wall Street Journal,* December 11, 1985, p. 3.

[8]George D. Rice, "Retargeting Consumers—Segmentation on Attitudes and Behavior," *Proceedings of the 11th Annual Chain Operators Exchange* (Chicago, International Foodservice Manufacturers Association, 1984).

[9]Harry Bolger, "The Conscious Consumer—Eating Right and Eating Light," *Proceedings of the 12th Annual Chain Operators Exchange* (Chicago, International Foodservice Manufacturers Association, 1985).

[10]*NRA News,* September 1985, p. 43.

[11]*Restaurants & Institutions,* May 29, 1985, p. 76.

[12]*Restaurant Business,* May 20, 1985, p. 135.

[13]*Wall Street Journal,* February 3, 1985, p. 19.

TABLE 3.7 Major Food Service Segments by Nutritional Attitude

Segment	Description	Percentage of Consumers	Income Level	Typical Occupation of Husband	Education	Occupation of Spouse	Number of Householders
Nutritionally fit	Most concerned with nutrition and health; less concerned with taste, convenience, or calories	30%	$25,000 and over	White collar	Well educated	Working wife	21 million
Conventional	Rates taste more important in selecting food than nutrition, convenience, or calories.	26%	$15,000 and under	Blue collar	Less educated	Homemaker wife	17 million
Busy urbanite: Convenience cook	Hates to cook; rates convenience as the most important item in selecting food items	24%	$25,000 and over	White collar	Well educated	Working wife	14 million
Restrictive dieter	Conventional tastes, older	20%	$25,000 and under	Blue collar; retired	Less educated	Homemaker wife	13 million

Source: George D. Rice, *Proceedings of the 11th Annual Chain Operator's Exchange* (Chicago: International Foodservice Manufacturers Association, 1984); Harry Balzer, *Proceedings of the 12th Annual Chain Operator's Exchange* (Chicago: International Foodservice Manufacturers Association, 1985).

TABLE 3.8   Fastest-Growing Menu Items, 1982–1984

Item	Growth Rate
Decaffeinated coffee	57%
Fruit	48
Breakfast sandwiches	39
Diet cola	39
Mexican food items	36
Main dish salads	31
Rice	29
Pizza	21
French toast	17
Cheeseburgers	17

Source: CREST Household Report; *NRA News,* September 1984, pp. 43–44.

surprised when the product didn't sell well. Apparently people aren't as prepared to give up the taste of salt as they are to talk about it.[13]

Industry Response

But menus have been changing to respond to consumers' positive nutritional concerns. In 1985, Mrs. Warner's became the first major fast-food chain to introduce baked, as opposed to fried, chicken.[14] Fish restaurants, too, are changing their methods of preparation. Long John Silver's, famous for its fried fish, is introducing broiled and baked dinners which Warren Rosenthol, the company's chairman, called "the wave of the future."[15] The company has also reformulated its fish breading to make it lighter and less greasy.[16] From the other end of the price spectrum, *Restaurants & Institutions* reported that Ben's Steak House in Tampa, Florida, one of the country's best-known steakhouses and famous for its charbroiled steak, now offers an all-vegetable plate on its dinner menu.[17]

Industry is playing both sides of the "dietary schizophrenia." Bakeries and snack chains, that is, doughnuts and ice-cream specialty shops, are growing rapidly at the same time many of the health-conscious restaurants

[14]*Restaurants & Institutions,* September 18, 1985, p. 184.
[15]*Nation's Restaurant News,* October 28, 1985, p. 2.
[16]*Restaurants & Institutions,* May 15, 1985, p. 38.
[17]*Restaurants & Institutions,* June 12, 1985, p. 190.

growing rapidly at the same time many of the health-conscious restaurants concepts have experienced problems. Bakeries are another dessert-oriented speciality restaurant that have been growing rapidly. Hardee's recently shifted from cooking its hamburgers on broilers—associated with a lower fat content—to grills because "consumer research tells us thickness and juiciness are what people want in a burger."[18] Thus, it seems that consumers are concerned about nutrition and health but want to reward themselves from time to time or have the best of both worlds: a salad with lots of rich dressings; a feeling of virtue *and* a full stomach. The industry, quite naturally, is responding to both sides of the consumer's personality.

CONSUMERISM

Many of the concerns of individual consumers, such as health, fitness, and nutrition, are shared by lots of consumers. On the other hand some of these concerns have been selected by organized interest groups as important to consumer education, to raise the consumer's consciousness: this is *consumerism*. Dr. Robert Blomstrom, of Michigan State University's School of Hotel, Restaurant, and Institutional Management pointed out that although some industry leaders regard the consumer movement as a fad, many others "believe that it is here to stay and that, if unheeded, it may lead to consequences which the hospitality industry will not be happy to accept." Blomstrom observed that American consumerism has been around since the mid-nineteenth century, and he defined it as follows:

> Consumerism is, first of all, a social movement. It is a movement by which society, through representative groups and individuals, seeks social change. Consumerism has as its specific objective to achieve a balance of power between buyers and sellers. It is an effort to equalize the rights of buyers with the rights of sellers.[19]

In view of its increasing size and visibility, the hospitality industry has begun to attract the attention of consumer groups. A sampling of hospitality issues typically raised by consumers may lead to a better understanding of how consumerism can affect the food service field. Our discussion will include complaints about junk food, labeling and truth in dining, problems related to sanitation, and the question of food additives.

[18]*Nation's Restaurant News,* May 6, 1985, p. 1.
[19]Robert L. Blomstrom, "The Hospitality Industry and the Consumer Movement," *The Institute Journal,* April 1973, p. 9.

JUNK FOOD AND A HECTIC PACE

One of the principal indictments by consumerists against food service (and especially against fast food and vending) is that it purveys nutritionless "junk food." Although fast food does pose some nutritional problems, the junk-food charge is just not true. Regarding mechanical vendors, the charge may comment more tellingly on American food habits than on the nutritional adequacy of the food itself.

A study by the Warf Institute, commissioned by McDonald's, indicates that a typical meal at McDonald's—a hamburger, french fries, and a milk-shake—provides nearly one-third of the recommended dietary allowance (RDA), or the equivalent of what a Type A school lunch provides, with, however, a deficiency in vitamins A and C. (The deficiency in these two vitamins can be remedied somewhat if the customer switches from a hamburger to a Big Mac, which contains the necessary lettuce and tomato slices.)

The continuing call for mandatory nutritional labeling may, if it is accepted, actually help the industry's image in this area, as the information about the realities of nutritional value becomes more widely understood. Some voluntary nutritional labeling has already appeared. But nutritional labeling cannot solve all our problems; moreover, many of the fast-food critics just don't seem to like the look of the restaurants or the taste of the food. These criticisms are perhaps typified by the remarks of Dr. Leonard Bachman, Pennsylvania's secretary of health, quoted by *Nation's Restaurant News*. After charging that "fast foods with their abundance of useless calories and sugar" (the junk-food charge) are a part of the problem of Americans' poor diet, Bachman continued,

> Meals should be taken in a leisurely way, with personal interaction . . . [people who opt for fast foods are being] dehumanized—they are becoming more like automobiles driving up to a gas station and being refilled. . . . The ubiquitous multimillion dollar advertising campaigns, particularly the millions spent on television advertising, has greatly influenced the public in the direction of fast foods.[20]

Two problems here go beyond the junk-food issue. Critics such as Bachman believe they know what is good for people (which, in a medical sense, they may), and they resent the fact that people choose to disregard their expert advice. Bachman's main criticism, however, is really of Americans' poor eating habits, notably "the quick pace inherent in our society."

Whatever else is true, the duty of the American restaurant industry in a market economy is to serve consumers, not to reform them. But it is difficult for hospitality to deal with this kind of criticism, in which the industry

[20]*Nation's Restaurant News*, November 10, 1974, p. 4.

becomes a scapegoat for the annoyance that some feel at a simple economic reality: the food service within the reach of most pocketbooks uses food service systems that are not (and cannot be) labor intensive.

The second problem that Bachman raises is that of the effect of advertising on consumer behavior. His remarks here reflect an old and complex debate in the general field of marketing. From our earlier explanation of the procedure for introducing a new product, perhaps you remember that restaurants are interested in only offering what the guests want, not in forcing something on them. For example, notice that the decor and atmosphere in specialty restaurants have been growing warmer and friendlier to meet earlier criticisms of coldness and austerity. And salad bars were added because that is what consumers wanted. That is, the weight of consumer opinion is usually felt in the marketplace. Change in business institutions does, of course, come more slowly than consumerists would like, but particularly in competitive industries such as food service, change does come when it is clear the consumer wants it.

The junk-food criticism will not just go away, however. Studies conducted at Pennsylvania State University and elsewhere suggest that many guests do not follow the Big Mac–fries–milkshake meal profile referred to earlier. For instance, to save money or suit their tastes, many customers replace the milkshake with a soft drink, and the result is distinctly less than one-third the RDA.

Michael F. Jacobsen, executive director of the Center for Science in the Public Interest (C.S.P.I.), asked some hard questions of the industry. Why not, for example, replace beef fat, palm oil, and other saturated fats used as frying agents in fast food? A Whopper with cheese, a milkshake, and fries have 2 oz. of fat, and Chicken McNuggets and Filet of Fish—supposedly "lite" foods—contain twice as much fat as a hamburger does. Another fast-food menu problem is sodium. A Kentucky Fried Chicken dinner can easily account for 1500 mg. of sodium, and three pieces of fish plus fries at Long John Silvers provide 2000 mg. These amounts of fat and sodium are at or above the daily limits recommended by the National Academy of Sciences for a 10-year-old.[21] And because fast food is often targeted to young people, it is significant that one fast-food meal can provide a full day's sensible use of potentially hazardous food ingredient. Under the circumstances, then, we shouldn't be surprised if the call for labeling is answered in the near future. Fast food isn't just empty calories, but as a steady diet, it can pose some nutritional problems, depending on the choices consumers make.

NUTRITIONAL LABELING

Mr. Jacobsen and the C.S.P.I. have filed a false advertising charge against McDonald's, claiming as "false and misleading" the company's statement

---

[21]*Nation's Restaurant News,* January 27, 1986, p. F7.

that "only tender, juicy chunks of breast and thigh meat" are used in Chicken McNuggets, that McNuggets also contain chicken skin, sodium phosphate, and beef fat (as a frying agent). McDonald's replied that the proportion of skin in McNuggets is lower than on a chicken bought in a grocery store, but that doesn't deal with the question of sodium phosphate. Some fast-food companies have stopped using beef fat as a frying agent, except for french fries, to which it is essential for flavor.

In regard to the nutritional labeling of fast food, the National Restaurant Association (NRA) has contended that the costs of such a move could outweigh any real benefit. The U.S. Department of Agriculture has ruled out labeling, largely because of the enormous cost of enforcing it.[22] The city of San Francisco did pass a nutritional labeling act, however, and to avoid such statewide bills in California and Texas, several fast-food chains have reached "voluntary" product-labeling agreements with the attorneys general in those states.[23]

TRUTH IN MENU

The increasing use of convenience foods, frozen prepared foods, and foods prepared in remote commissaries has created an issue closely related to the nutritional labeling issue. The food service industry, in fact, has long advocated honest dealings with the consumers but individual operators have frequently strayed from full candor.[24] Included in one's "right to know," consumer groups insist, is a right to know where and how restaurant food was prepared. Laws requiring menus to state who prepared the food and when, where, and how it was prepared have already been proposed.

The use of frozen food is certainly widespread. *Restaurants & Institutions* indicated that 90 percent of all operations use frozen food. Twenty percent of Denny's menu is purchased frozen, and Bonanza buys virtually all its entrees frozen.[25] Many operators feel it is their special method of preparation rather than the food's state before cooking that imparts quality. Most operators would like to think that "fresh" means prepared to order, whether or not the raw products are frozen and that "natural" means unadulterated and not necessarily anything more. But the fact is that frozen products, because of "field-side" or "on-board" freezing, are often of higher quality—that is, possessing more of the characteristics of the fresh—than does a "fresh" product that has worked its way through the channels of distribution, deteriorating gradually in unfrozen storage. For example, several fast-food companies purchasing Icelandic cod deal with packers who have on-

---

[22]*Nation's Restaurant News,* January 20, 1986, p. 1.

[23]*Nation's Restaurant News,* September 1, 1986, p. 1.

[24]John J. Bilan, "Taking Another Look at Accuracy in Menus," *Cornell Hotel and Restaurant Administration Quarterly,* November 1979, p. 8.

[25]*Restaurants & Institutions,* October 2, 1985, p. 106.

board processing capabilities. Similarly, large frozen vegetable processors have equipment that follows the harvesters, processing the vegetables and freezing them immediately after they are picked. The term *fresh frozen,* then, is not really a contradiction in terms.

It is, of course, possible to cook top-quality food in one place, freeze or chill it, transport it, reconstitute it, and serve a tasty, attractive product in another place. The problem is not the technology but a culture that changes more slowly than does its own technical capacities. Someday, commissaries and other centralized production systems may make genuine haute cuisine available to the mass market at prices that that market can afford. Before this happens, food service marketing techniques will be needed to complement (that is, to fulfill) the technology that already exists. Finally, when such a feat becomes possible, a consumer willing to accept gourmet food reconstituted from the chilled or frozen state will have to be waiting for it—and that is a marketing problem.

In the meantime, if the industry resists truth in menu because of the disruptions it clearly will cause, it might study the experience of grocery chains and retailers, who have learned not only to accept reasonable consumer demands but also to incorporate them in their marketing programs and to turn compliance to their advantage as well.

Some segments of the restaurant business have already become *service-intensive* retail establishments that give the final processing to products prepared elsewhere. The first person to show guests an advantage in choosing to accept remotely prepared food will have made an important marketing breakthrough. In the meantime, there are some signs that consumers are gradually beginning to accept remotely prepared foods.

Peter Drucker called consumerism "the shame of marketing." Consumerism, he feels, reflects business's almost exclusive emphasis on selling (which begins with "our product" and how to sell it) instead of on "marketing," which begins with the consumers' needs and expectations and moves toward supplying products that meet those needs.

> Consumerism is also the opportunity of marketing. It will force business to become market focused in their actions as well as their pronouncements. Developing a positive response to consumerist sentiment is probably more effective than resentment and resistance. There is truth in the old adage, "If you can't fight 'em, join 'em."[26]

SANITATION

As with so many consumer issues, sanitation involves government regulations—in this case, as embodied in public-health officers and inspectors.

---

[26]Peter F. Drucker, *Management: Tasks, Responsibilities, Practices* (New York: Harper & Row, 1974), p. 64.

With the increasing use of off-premise, prepared foods, the incidence of food poisoning in public accommodations has been rising steeply. The kinds of sanitary precautions associated with traditional food service operations are inadequate for food service systems that prepare food, freeze or chill it, and then transport it elsewhere. First, the risks of thawing and spoilage are high. Second, the food is handled by more people. Some operators resist the increased emphasis on sanitation, but most have accepted—many enthusiastically—the need to upgrade sanitation practices and to establish and enforce high sanitation standards. Although the National Restaurant Association has resisted legislation demanding the testing of food service managers' and food handlers' knowledge of sanitation as impractical and too costly, the association's affiliate, the National Institute for the Foodservice Industry (NIFI), has pioneered in the development of sanitation educational materials and programs. It is quite clear that for the most part, the industry and those calling for the highest standards of sanitation are, in principle, in the same camp.

ADDITIVES

The practice of adding preservatives, coloring agents, and flavor enhancers to food is as old as salt, paprika, and cloves. Recently, however, the practice has spread and intensified. There is no real consensus on the desirability of using additives extensively. Some food scientists insist on the advantages of additives, whereas some nutritionists and consumerists adamantly oppose nearly all use of additives.

Solutions to the additive issue emerge case by case and generally involve balancing the benefits against the risks. When the benefit of preserving food against spoilage (as with the calcium propionate in bread) is matched by little if any risk to health, the use of additives is accepted by nearly everyone. On the other hand, when the effect is purely cosmetic and some health danger appears to be present (as with the coloring in some presweetened breakfast foods), the consumerist's ire will continue, and with increasing effect.

One food preservation practice that has been condemned is using sulfiting agents. These are used commonly to freshen raw vegetables and fruits on salad bars and also are used in many processed foods, including dried potatoes, canned vegetables, dried fruits, corn syrup, sugar, some starches, soft drinks, and instant tea.[27] The National Restaurant Association recommended that restaurants stop using sulfites, and many operators have complied. The reason for the prohibition is that the ingestion of sulfites is hazardous to some asthmatics and has even contributed to several deaths. Unfortunately, sulfites are still used by some food manufacturers, but op-

[27]*Restaurants & Institutions,* December 5, 1984, p. 30.

erators can limit the problem by avoiding the use of "vegetable fresheners" and "potato whiteners."[28]

Many additives, however, are perfectly harmless natural substances, such as the carotin used to give margarine its yellow color. On the other hand, the nitrites used to preserve ham, bacon, and other smoked meats, although they have a cosmetic effect (without them the meat would be gray) and reduce the risk of botulism, are also carcinogens; that is, they have been shown to cause cancer. It isn't as if we have to choose between botulism and cancer; neither event is very likely. But we do have to weigh the risk against the benefit.

The decision on food additives lies, of course, primarily with the food manufacturers. But as a hospitality manager, you can expect questions from your guests about the subject. Probably the best response to these questions as well as to other issues related to consumerism is simply to be well informed, open, and responsive rather than resentful. The guests who raise consumerist issues are not cranks. Rather, they are a part of one of the great mass movements of the twentieth century, and they tend to be intelligent and well educated. Their concern is not likely to vanish.

ALCOHOL AND DINING

The many fatal accidents attributed to driving under the influence of alcohol has handed to the hospitality industry a wide-ranging set of problems. On the one hand, in many jurisdictions, restaurants and bars that sell drinks to people who are later involved in accidents are now being held legally responsible for damages. The result has been, among other things, a great rise in liability insurance rates. Laws have been proposed—and in many jurisdictions passed—making illegal the "happy hours" and other advertised price reductions on the sale of drinks. In addition, in a less strictly legal sense, operators have been concerned about the image of their operations and the industry in general.

The industry's response has generally been swift and positive. One idea is "designated driver" programs. For instance, at Maggie's Lounges, part of a chain based in Maryland, one customer in a party signs a "Declaration of Non-Inebriation." The designated driver is identified with a large button and receives $5.00 worth of "Maggie's Money" good at the time of his or her next visit—when somebody else takes a turn as the designated driver.[29] Some operations also give the designated driver all the soft drinks he or she wants, at no charge. Alcoholic awareness training—teaching bartenders and servers how to tell when people have had too much to drink and how to deal with them—is also becoming more common. Studebaker's waitresses, for instance, receive 18 hours of alcohol awareness training during their first year on the job.

[28]*Restaurants & Institutions,* January 23, 1985, p. 252.
[29]*Restaurants & Institutions,* August 8, 1985, p. 19.

CONVENIENCE

We have spoken of consumer concerns, some represented by consumerist professionals and others just by consumer choices in the market. Another of these consumer choices is not related to health and fitness; some might even argue it pulls in the other direction because it reflects the hectic pace of life in much of North America. This is the concern for convenience, reflecting what has been called the "poverty of time." With the majority of families finding it necessary to have both spouses working—and with all the tasks and duties of the home remaining to be done—we live in a prosperous but unusually harried time.

As with consumers' interest in health and fitness, the industry has responded with products and services that fit the time pressures of our hurried lifestyles. In shopping centers, "food courts" bring together a number of different kinds of units to facilitate "grazing," a pattern of "grabbing a bite on the run," eating on impulse: perhaps a gyro from one shop, french fries from another, a cookie from a third, and a cup of "gourmet coffee" to top it off. Grazing, too, is related to a desire to eat less and to choose only those foods that please the individual. Later we will discuss other responses to consumers' needs to save time: 24-hour convenience stores, drive-throughs, and conveniently located take-out units; in short, fast food faster.

SUMMARY

We first considered the organizational forms of restaurants—chain, independent, and franchise. Chain specialty restaurants have six strengths: (1) brand recognition or preference, (2) site selection expertise, (3) access to capital, (4) purchasing economies, (5) centrally administered control and information systems, and (6) personal program development.

We also analyzed independent restaurants using the same six factors and pointed out the independent restaurants' advantages of flexibility, the owner's motivation, and the owner's closeness to the operation.

Franchised restaurants fall somewhere between the chains and the independents, having greater freedom of action than the chains do but also having access to expertise and capital that the independents do not.

Next we discussed consumers, from the perspective of age, income, and size of household. We then turned to the consumers' concerns, particularly health and nutrition and their impact on restaurants' menus. But even though restaurants have responded to consumers' demands by changing their menu items as well as their methods of cooking, the restaurants have often found consumers' convictions and desires to be contradictory. Such a contradiction may be, for example, a low-calorie dinner topped off by a rich dessert.

Finally, we looked at consumerism, or consumers' concerns translated into organized interest groups. The most widely discussed concerns are junk food, nutritional labeling, truth in menu, sanitation, additives, and alcohol. We examined the arguments of both the consumerists and the restaurant industry and the actions of each. We ended with another consumer concern, convenience, which has become an issue in our busy lives, and we talked about how the industry has responded.

KEY WORDS AND CONCEPTS

To help you review this chapter, keep in mind the following:

Chain	Consumerism
Independent	Junk food
Franchise	Nutritional labeling
Economies of scale	Truth in menu
Additive effect	Convenience

REVIEW QUESTIONS

1. What advantages do chain restaurants have?

2. What extra advantage do independent restaurants have?

3. What are the characteristics of franchise restaurants?

4. Explain why people are having more meals away from home. What kinds of people eat out most often? Why?

5. What are consumers' main concerns in regard to food?

6. Is health food always the consumer's first choice? Explain.

7. What is consumerism?

8. What are consumerists' principal concerns?

C H A P T E R

Courtesy of W. R. Grace.

THE FUTURE OF THE RESTAURANT BUSINESS

THE PURPOSE OF THIS CHAPTER

This chapter will help you build on your understanding of the components of the food service industry by examining the factors likely to affect its future.

We will look inside the industry at equipment changes, at their effects on operations, and how the new equipment meets the needs of guests. We will review the impact of energy costs on operations.

Next we turn our attention to the ever-escalating competition for the restaurant consumer's patronage within the industry. We have to look, too, at competition from other businesses like the convenience store. Increasingly stiff competition comes, too, from grocery stores and from home entertainment. The chapter closes with a look at the problems and opportunities posed by the looming labor shortage.

By identifying the forces that are shaping food service, we can better plan our personal strategy for personal and professional development.

THIS CHAPTER SHOULD HELP YOU

1. Understand further the different kinds of restaurant systems and compare them to one another.
2. Discuss critically the kinds of equipment changes likely to occur in the industry.

3.   Assess the impact of energy costs in the food service industry.

4.   Understand the competitive environment of the restaurant business and the major competitive strategies firms have developed.

5.   Become familiar with the labor outlook for the industry and consider what it might mean for your career.

6.   Assess your own prospects in the industry in terms of your personal goals and in the light of the overall employment outlook.

THE RESTAURANT INDUSTRY: A VIEW OF WHERE WE'RE GOING

The restaurant industry of today is much like the restaurant industry of 15 years ago. All the elements present now were present then; only the proportion of those elements has changed. In the next 10 or 15 years a similar kind of evolution will probably have taken place. To the question, "What will the restaurant industry be like tomorrow?" the answer is, "Like it is today—only more so."

Figure 4.1 presents a frame of reference for considering the major elements of the restaurant industry. The chart can help you visualize today's restaurant industry and how it is likely to look tomorrow. (This chart refers only to restaurants and does not attempt to address the many other elements

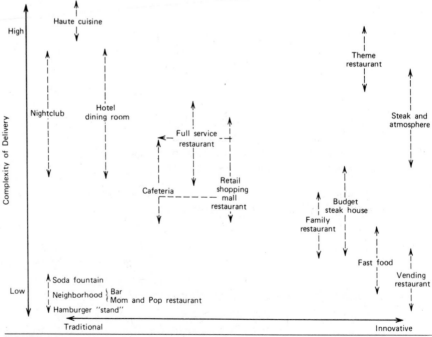

FIGURE 4.1   A restaurant typology.

of the food service industry, such as in-plant feeding, college feeding, or government food service. These elements will be considered later.)

In Figure 4.1, the vertical axis rates restaurants on a scale from low to high in terms of complexity of delivery, the haute cuisine restaurant having the most complex delivery system. A restaurant with a complex delivery system is characterized by high-quality food, a variety of menu choices, high prices, and a high-status ambience. On the other hand, a fast-food restaurant (although the quality of the product may be excellent as far as it goes) offers relatively simple, inexpensive fare. It is no reflection on McDonald's to say that a hamburger can be only so good. The prices in these restaurants tend to be lower, and (in the sense that one would not take the boss out to dinner there) their status association is relatively low.

On the horizontal axis, we move along a scale from the traditional establishments at the left to the innovative operations at the right. There are three general kinds of vertical groupings in the figure, suggesting that there are three different "time-dimensioned" kinds of establishments represented at most price levels. First, we see the traditional restaurant, imported from Europe or in operation in this country for many, many years. Second, in the middle of the chart we find a grouping of restaurants representing typically American systems that grew up in the 1930s and 1940s and generally hit their peak in the 1950s. These tend to be more service intensive and to use a complex system of delivery. Finally, at the right we see a group of restaurants that have come on the scene mostly since the early 1960s, although earlier prototypes probably existed.

The restaurants classified in Figure 4.1 as relatively more traditional are in the decline stage of the product's life cycle. Their number, in short, is diminishing. Between 1970 and 1985, fast-food sales increased about seven and a half times, whereas all sales of food consumed away from home increased five times. Thus, fast-food sales are growing roughly half again as fast as are all restaurant sales. Clearly, the growth potential in the restaurant industry lies with those operations that are less labor intensive and hence can offer guests reasonably priced dining out.

Traditional restaurants will not disappear. At the upper end of the complexity of delivery scale we see that a strong demand remains for haute cuisine establishments. Moreover, there will always be the special niche in the marketplace that only the independents can fill, and this is likely to become more significant as the middle aging of North America raises the demand for innovation and variety. Increasingly, however, growth is in the mass-market specialty restaurants of the type clustered at the right of Figure 4.1. Thus, the restaurant industry of the next 10 years will contain all of the same elements it does today, but the proportionate sizes of the three groups will change.

We probably should note here that this is a view of what the industry will look like from the outside. Inside the industry and its operations that

Traditional table service restaurants are labor intensive, and as long as services are maintained, it is difficult to make great improvements in productivity. There is an absolute limit, for instance, to how fast this waitress can move.

make it up, however, we will not find this kind of continuity of the 1970s and the early 1980s. The changing ages and incomes of the population and the resulting changes in consumer tastes are likely to accelerate growth in some areas and delay it in others. Equally significant is the growth in competition both inside and outside the restaurant business. Finally, a growing labor shortage is bound to affect services and prices. We will begin our examination with a look at the "nuts and bolts," equipment and technology.

THE FOOD SERVICE EQUIPMENT OF THE FUTURE

In 1975, a researcher looked into the future of food service, and this is what he saw:

> The restaurant of 1986 will be automated. One individual will be capable of running a 10,000-meal-a-day commissary. Computer-controlled, automated equipment will run the food processing operation from storeroom to cleanup as well as take care of inventory control and the reordering process. In addition, the computer will handle all records, write all necessary business reports (including the annual report), forecast requirements, and perform all cost accounting duties.

Customers will dine in a computer-manipulated environment of aromatic and visual stimuli. They will stand before lighted menus picturing various entrees and punch out selections at order stations. Within 2½ minutes, they will be served the meal via conveyor belt running with the wall and stopping at the proper table. Dish busing commences upon the customer arising from the seat. Dirty dishes move onto a conveyor belt within an adjacent wall. The dishwashing process is completely automated. A 200-seat restaurant will require four employees and a manager.[1]

If technology can put an astronaut on the moon, it can surely bus tables. But it's not what is technically possible that counts; it's what makes economic sense. In the foreseeable future, even in the face of steeply rising wages, the 10,000-meal-a-day commissaries that come into use will require a good many more people than one, because it will make economic sense. Although a computer-operated food production, storage, and cleanup system is theoretically possible, it would be like using a computer just to add up a grocery bill. Less expensive methods are available.

The impatience with impersonal behavior patterns expressed by customers in vending restaurants suggests that the time when lines form "to punch out selections at order stations" may be pretty far off. Here again, the problem is cost effectiveness and guest acceptance rather than technological capabilities.

In fact, the Food Institute reported, "An international burger chain has commissioned Hughes International to supply a six-armed robot that takes orders, cooks the food, serves it, takes the money, clears tables and sweeps the floor for $100,000."[2] But the big problems are not essentially technical; they are economic and human. First, if this six-armed fellow replaced three full-time workers, it would take five years for the savings to pay for the investment—if the repair bills were not too high. Moreover, how will people feel about giving their order to something out of a science fiction film, taking their food from it, and having it clean up after them? As a novelty, it sounds interesting, but for a steady diet, people may need quite a lot of time to get used to it, much less like it.

The revolution in information processing has had an important impact on food service record keeping, and computerized report preparation has been a fact of life for some time. But as applied to the management information environment in other industries, the computer hasn't displaced people as much as it has increased management's ability to control costs and regulate quality. The available evidence suggests that the same will be true in food service.

Surprisingly enough, amid all this talk of technology and computers, there are few varieties of new equipment designed for use in the individual

---

[1] *Institutions/Volume Feeding*, October 1975, p. 47.
[2] *Restaurants & Institutions*, June 12, 1985, p. 70.

Decor designed to meet special customer interests helps make eating out a pleasant experience. The merry-go-round motif in this McDonald's dining room is aimed at young customers. (Photo courtesy of McDonald's Corp.)

food service operation. The only "revolutionary" invention is the microwave oven, and even it has been around for some 30 years. What is revolutionary, though, is the increasing acceptance of the microwave ovens after so many years of availability. The delay in acceptance suggests that it takes technical innovations a long time to be accepted and used. Another recent equipment innovation that is likely to affect fast food is the clamshell grill which was initially tested by McDonald's in 1984. This grill, which is fired to cook on *both* sides, cuts cooking time by up to 60 percent. This speeds service to hurried consumers, particularly in drive-through operations in which time is especially important. McDonald's is also using a radio headset that relays the orders to the cook and manager, thus speeding service.[3]

Other food service innovations can currently be found in food preprocessing and the development of centralized food service systems, and in the development of electronic cash registers (ECRs) and point-of-sales (POS) systems. The ECR/POS revolution is making possible much closer attention to daily, and even shift by shift, detail in regard to both food and labor cost. Centralized systems employ central production and/or storage units linked

[3]*Nation's Restaurant News,* December 2, 1985, p. 32.

by transportation networks. In these systems, delivery trucks are dispatched and routed by computers to minimize transportation costs. The "system" links a group of service-intensive retail outlets (call them restaurants).

Although centralized production facilities (call them commissaries) have not been uniformly successful, the evidence suggests that such systems have failed because of one of three problems: (1) management was unable to change from traditional restaurant thinking to the "factory thinking" that commissaries require in operation; (2) management did not think through how the entire company (units and central office as well as commissary) had to change to adapt to a new system of operation; or (3) a successful commissary became unsuccessful when the company outgrew it.

Mr. Spock and Captain Kirk may well interrupt their trek to come to dinner. But the restaurant they'd choose in the year 2000 will look a good deal like the restaurant of today. If there is a "revolution," it will be the invisible revolution resulting from the way the already-existing elements in the system are rearranged.

SCALED-DOWN AND MOBILE UNITS

A good example of the kind of "creeping revolution" that food service has been experiencing for the last 30 years can be found in the development of new kinds of units. Cost pressures as well as consumer demands for more convenience are encouraging the construction of scaled-down units in locations that wouldn't have been considered earlier. For example, a smaller unit being tested by Pizza Hut features a limited menu designed for fast service which is backed up by a new conveyorized oven that reduces cooking time.[4] Moreover, mobile units are being used not only to deliver food but also to operate from temporary sites where there is a short-term demand. A mobile unit costing $70,000 is reportedly often able to do essentially the same volume of sales as can a regular unit costing over $900,000 to build, with obvious advantages in the return on investment.[5] The technology of smaller units is not as colorful as flashing order panels and six-armed robots, but it is more firmly grounded in consumers' needs and preferences and in economic reality.

ENERGY COSTS AND FOOD SERVICE

Energy costs accounted for 10 percent of the operating costs of food service in 1985, up from 8.4 percent in 1982 and 7.8 percent in 1980.[6] Approximately

[4]*Nation's Restaurant News,* August 12, 1985, p. 1.

[5]*Nation's Restaurant News,* February 10, 1985, p. 80.

[6]Julie G. Woodman, *The IFMA Encyclopedia of the Foodservice Industry,* 5th ed. (Chicago: International Foodservice Manufacturers Association, 1985), p. 13.

Mobile fast-food units are an equipment innovation that broadens the market for fast food by providing greater location convenience for consumers. (Photo courtesy of Burger King Corp.)

76 percent of U.S. energy comes from petroleum and natural gas. We can expect these scarce and expensive fuels to have a major impact on at least three aspects of the food service industry: transportation systems, food processing, and the use of what the industry calls *disposables*.

ENERGY AND THE TRANSPORTATION SYSTEM

At least until the internal combustion engine gives way to some other device, gasoline-powered cars will carry guests to their restaurants, hotels, and resorts. But even though auto transportation is expensive, barring a catastrophe, energy supplies seem reasonably secure. Costs will surely fluctuate, but the explosion in gasoline prices is probably behind us. There is no guarantee prices will not begin to rise again, but adequate supplies seem sure, barring a major political crisis.

ENERGY AND FOOD PROCESSING

Freezing foods entails chilling the product to well below freezing and then holding it and the environment around it at that temperature. Thus, fresh or canned products save energy costs, an advantage that may overcome the labor costs and quality considerations that have, up until now, given frozen products some advantages.

Frozen prepared products have traditionally been used in restaurants to reduce labor costs. Freezing, however, is energy intensive: it requires energy first to reduce temperature and then, during reconstitution, to return the product to serving temperature. Moreover, freezing has drawbacks relating to product quality. The formation of ice crystals, a part of freezing, cuts tissue, which changes the consistency of some products and, upon reconstitution, results in the loss of flavor-filled juices.

Chilled foods, however, were found to taste better than did frozen products, in tests conducted by the U.S. Army's Nattick Laboratories, but those tests relied on conventional refrigeration, and the maximum safe holding time was found to be 72 hours. Recent innovations in refrigeration offer a promising new approach to chilled foods using what is called latent zone temperature storage. The latent zone lies just below the freezing point, at 28° to 30° Fahrenheit or − 1° to − 2° Celsius. In this temperature range, holding characteristics, in terms of both flavor and microbiological quality, remain at the level of the fresh product's quality. It appears possible that holding times may be extended to three weeks or more without quality loss for some prepared products, and at a lower energy cost.

If our experience with the microwave oven is any guide, operators will adopt this technological innovation only very slowly, despite its advantages. Moreover, prepared products will be available only to operations large enough to do their own central production and maintain their own refrigerated storage. It is unlikely that chilled rather than frozen prepared foods will be available from conventional suppliers in the foreseeable future. Nevertheless, the laborsaving advantage usually associated with frozen foods is now available to large institutions, and even to innovative operators in smaller units, in a form that is also less wasteful of energy.

One fact seems likely to remain true: The increase in the cost of labor, as well as its magnitude relative to energy cost, makes it likely that timesaving processing steps such as freezing will continue to be used as long as they result in significant labor savings, even though they consume energy. Labor is likely to remain the more important cost for the foreseeable future.

ENERGY AND DISPOSABLES

Because many disposable plastic products derive from petroleum, the cost advantages associated with discarding these products after use is related to the cost of petroleum. Because disposables have commonly been used even when petroleum prices have been higher than they are currently, the role of disposables appears secure at any foreseeable price level.

ENERGY AND THE GENERAL HOSPITALITY ENVIRONMENT

The almost-universal use of air conditioning in American food service imposes a heavy tax on guests in the form of energy costs passed on in the food prices. It seems unlikely, however, that energy prices could rise to a point that guests would tolerate the elimination of air conditioning. Newly constructed units, moreover, generally incorporate energy savings into all facets of their design.

COMPETITION

Earlier we said that the restaurant industry of the future will look much like today's industry—from the outside. That is, the same kinds of operations will be offered to consumers, although there will be gradual changes in the market share of the various types of units. The competitive forces at work, however, suggest that developments inside the industry will be quite different in the 1980s and 1990s from what they were in the 1960s and 1970s. During the earlier 20-year period, increases in the consumption of food away from home were driven by the increasing number of working women and dramatically rising incomes. Expanding "new" kinds of restaurants—fast-food and family restaurants—took advantage of this market growth.

Of equal importance, the competition available to meet the growth of the new restaurants was outmoded. Fast food drove many a mom-and-pop operation out of business, just as numerous traditional full-service operations were driven to the wall by specialty and family restaurants. The "new" offered numerous advantages, including self-service; menus that limited variety, and hence the skills and the payroll cost required; lower prices related both to the latter advantages and to high volume; a more modern look; careful location planning; and vastly more sophisticated marketing. Thus, the new restaurants advanced strongly and largely unchallenged into a market that was waiting for them. From time to time, there was talk of market saturation, and each downturn in the economy produced a shakeout, eliminating the weak, loosely planned, or poorly marketed operations. Nevertheless, in the 25 years from 1960 to 1984, the number of fast-food units grew from approximately 16,000, with roughly 6 percent of restaurant sales, to about 137,200 units, with an estimated 45 percent of restaurant sales.[7]

The conditions of market expansion and obsolete competition that marked the 1960s and 1970s no longer obtain, however. In the 1980s, more women have come into the work force, but the rate of *growth* in female employment has slowed significantly and will continue to do so. Working

---

[7]The numbers used here for 1960 and 1985 are from different sources and hence subject to possible variation in definition. In fact, what was counted as "fast food" in 1960 and in 1980 probably included significantly different kinds of establishments. Precision, of course, is not absolutely essential when the change is so dramatic. Nevertheless, interested students are entitled to know the sources so as to make their own judgments. The 1960 estimate is from Urban B. Ozanne and Shelby D. Hunt, *Economic Effects of Franchising* (Washington, D.C.: U.S. Government Printing Office, 1971); and the 1985 figure is from *Restaurants & Institutions*, January 8, 1986.

women have become a stabilizing, rather than a dynamic, force in food service demand.

The early eighties were a time of recession. Although the economy was expanding, the mid-1980s was a time of retrenchment for consumers.[8] Even though the "yuppies" are the focus of much attention, these high-income, young urban professionals constitute only about 5 percent of the population. Much of the move toward two-income families seems to have been aimed at maintaining family incomes in the face of an inflation that has moved faster than have most incomes.[9] That is, the second incomes were needed.

Moreover, the competition is fierce for other uses of the dollar, including furnishing households for young marrieds and extending also to cars, boats, campers, VCRs, and other durable consumer goods. Growth forecasts are supported by population trends, but a slowing in growth of personal income together with competition with other uses for consumer dollars make it likely that restaurant growth will occur at a slower pace than previously. The days of revolution are probably over, but we can look forward to continuing evolution.

The competitive environment of the late 1980s and 1990s includes competition within the industry and competition for food service customers with businesses like convenience stores. Competition with other industries for consumers' dollar spent on goods and services used in the home is important as well. Before discussing this environment, though, we should note its likely effects on industry structure.

The competitive battle of the 1980s and 1990s is taking place among the giants. For instance, McDonald's sales in 1985 topped $11 billion. The pressures of competition on the independents and small chains are likely to be severe when companies of this size are engaged in a struggle. Tomorrow's giants will almost certainly start with a new idea and build to a success from a single, first unit, but only the most effectively managed operations will be able to survive, let alone grow, in the competitive 1980s and 1990s.

COMPETITION WITHIN THE FOOD SERVICE INDUSTRY

Competition within the food service industry has several parts: advertising and promotion, development of new products, expansion of day parts, expansion of service, price, and location. Each is discussed briefly.

Advertising and Promotion

In 1985, restaurants spent over a billion dollars for television advertising alone. Indeed, McDonald's, the second largest advertiser in the United

---

[8]Courtenay Slater, "Cautious Consumers," *American Demographics,* March 1985, p. 4.
[9]Frank Levy and Richard C. Michel, "Are Baby Boomers Selfish?" *American Demographics,* April 1985, pp. 38–41.

Franchise units follow a common advertising theme developed by the franchisor and bring a national campaign into local media. (Courtesy of Country Kitchen International, Inc.)

States (after Procter & Gamble), spent $686 million on marketing of all kinds.[10]

In competitive times, special promotions are of particular importance in the overall marketing program. Operations may offer coupons that reduce the price of items sold, offer premium merchandise (such as special glassware) at bargain prices, or offer consumers opportunities to compete in games. According to CREST's *Family Report,* in 1977 only 6.5 percent of visits to restaurants involved this kind of promotion, but by 1984 that proportion had risen to 11.3 percent.

Development of New Products

New products are used competitively in a number of ways. (New products are also discussed in Chapter 19.) First, they are used to expand a restaurant's customer base—to draw in more customers. Sometimes a company

[10]*Restaurants & Institutions,* July 23, 1986, p. 202.

introduces new products defensively or offensively because competitors have begun to gain market share. Wendy's efforts to attract more women to its restaurants are a good example of new products' being used to expand a customer base. In 1979, Wendy's new product was the salad bar, and Wendy's was the first among the major chains to introduce it. In 1983 Wendy's upgraded its salad bar, and also in 1983 it introduced its baked potato line. Both products, salads and baked potatoes, had the desired effect of expanding Wendy's market share among women.

Chicken nuggets are a good example of a defensive product introduction; that is, a number of chicken restaurant chains felt they had to jump on the nugget bandwagon because they were losing customers to McDonald's new McNuggets. Indeed, McDonald's was becoming one of the largest chicken chains in North America, and so the chicken restaurants needed to defend their market share.

Burger King launched a counteroffensive in 1985 against the growing appeal of gourmet burgers when it reformulated its Whopper. Burger King raised the Whopper's meat content by 17 percent, from 3.6 to 4.2 oz. and changed the bun size so as to alter the bun-to-meat ratio as well as the appearance of the product. McDonald's responded by introducing the McDLT. McDonald's was successful in maintaining its market share, and by early 1986, Burger King had begun to lose market share despite its reformulated Whopper.[11]

Expansion of Day Parts

Serving more *day parts,* or meal occasions, means, at the least, more productivity out of the operation's capital investment (land, building, equipment, and furnishings) by remaining open longer and thus raising sales volume. This tactic is reflected in the increased number of chains offering breakfast and/or moving toward 24-hour operations. Additional operating hours, however, also means an expanded payroll.

When volume can be improved during existing operating hours, not only can capital costs be spread over a larger volume, but in many cases current operating costs need not be increased by very much. The popularity of McDonald's McNuggets as a snack food brings in guests for a snack in off-meal hours, when the operation probably has idle staff. Similarly, most units are open for dinner, but many make only moderate sales. Thus, efforts to find entrees that will "reposition" the unit in the consumer's mind *as a dinner-occasion restaurant* will certainly continue.

Expansion of Service

The greater use of takeout and delivery is an important service expansion.

---

[11]*Nation's Restaurant News,* March 10, 1986, p. 143.

The significance of this competitive development can best be seen in George Rice's comment that in 1985 the number of meals and snacks eaten *inside* the restaurants did not rise, but that those eaten off the premises were what accounted for the industry's growth.[12] As we noted earlier, the lion's share of takeout and delivery goes to fast food, but this service expansion is also enjoying success in the finer restaurants and family restaurants.

Price

Michael Culp of Prudential Bache pointed out that restaurant prices used to increase in the range of 8 to 10 percent but are now rising from 3 to 4 percent.[13] The days of easily passing on higher costs to the consumer are past, and instead, careful management at the unit level is necessary.

Location

The best restaurant sites are often already occupied. Thus, to obtain new locations, firms have resorted to purchasing all or part of regional chains so as to secure their locations for conversion. Another strategy has been to expand into what had once not been considered viable fast-food locations. For example, we are now seeing franchised fast-food units on college campuses and military bases, at toll-road service plazas, in downtown office buildings, and even in museums. Wendy's is testing operations in K Marts and has begun to expand from a successful test in Days Inns economy motels. And McDonald's has gone to great pains to customize its downtown office building locations and overcome landlords' objections to fast food.

Downsizing is also a way of expanding, as is seen in McDonald's snack units, as well as mobile units—one more way of bringing the business to the customers so as to acquire and keep market share. Downsizing and mobile units are really a part of a location strategy.

The practice of colocating—locating two noncompetitive businesses on the same site—is spreading, too. For instance, Dairy Queen and Mr. Donut have agreed to exploit sites jointly. Similarly, Winchell's Donuts have developed a ministore to be located inside existing ARCO gas stations, and Dunkin Donuts also has taken a similar tack with gas stations.[14]

COMPETITION FROM RELATED BUSINESSES

Both convenience stores and full-line grocery stores have become serious competitors with fast-food restaurants.

[12]George D. Rice, "Foodservice Industry Review and Forecast," *Proceedings of the 13th Annual Chain Operators Exchange* (Chicago: International Foodservice Manufacturers Association, 1986).
[13]Michael Culp, "What's Hot in Fast Foods?" *Barron's*, April 23, 1985.
[14]*Nation's Restaurant News*, January 27, 1986, p. 72.

Limited food service in convenience stores eats into fast-food's market share. (Photo courtesy of 7-Eleven.)

Convenience Stores

In 1972, convenience stores—"C stores" for short—had 1.5 percent of fast-food sales but by 1985 accounted for 9.7 percent[15] and occupied 48,110 locations.[16] Although the traditional C store customer has been thought of as an 18- to 24-year-old male, a recent study by the National Association of Convenience Stores revealed that 44 percent of C store customers are female and two-thirds of them are white-collar workers or homemakers. Clearly, the stereotypes that suggested that C stores competed only in a small part of the fast-food market must be reexamined. Accordingly, the food service managers of Southland's 7-Eleven chain, the nation's largest C store operator has called fast food 7-Eleven's "greatest area of opportunity." Indeed,

[15]*NRA News,* March 1986, p. 21.
[16]*Restaurants & Institutions,* January 8, 1986, p. 179.

Grocery store deli departments are working hard to get a share of the food service market. (Photo courtesy of Piggly Wiggly.)

in 1984, 7-Eleven had fast-food sales of $900 million. In addition to fountain beverages, hot dogs, deli sandwiches, nachos, and microwave products, many C stores are now offering sandwiches that are made on the premises for greater eye appeal and freshness.[17] In fact, *Restaurant & Institutions* reported that in 1986 food service in C stores increased 50 percent over that in 1984.

Supermarkets

Supermarkets have been adding salad bars, delicatessens, and bakeries which are competing directly with food service.[18] In addition, 25 percent of supermarkets with salad bars offer eating areas.[19]

Grocery stores are also offering ready-to-eat take-out foods which are sold by the pound at prices well below what a restaurant must charge. In Denver, one grocery chain has replaced meat cutters with chefs, and a New Jersey chain has hired a leading restaurant consultant to redesign its stores

[17]*Nation's Restaurant News,* October 12, 1985, p. 1.
[18]*Restaurant Business,* August 10, 1985, p. 209.
[19]*Nation's Restaurant News,* May 13, 1985, p. 56.

and assist in training its staff. Stores offer items such as oven-ready stuffed pork chops, stuffed flank steak, and stuffed poultry. One dimension of the challenge is suggested by *Nation's Restaurant News:* "As frozen, store bought pizza becomes a stronger competitor to the pizza chains with improvements in quality and the trend toward convenience, pricing could become the critical factor in the future struggles for shares between the chains and the super markets."[20]

The Home As a Competitor

A study conducted by Purdue University's Department of Restaurant, Hotel and Institutional Management concluded that it is actually less expensive to eat fast food than it is to eat at home if meal preparation and cleanup time is given a realistic value.[21] The danger is, however, that the consumer may not choose to eat out even if it is a bargain. The growth of in-home "entertainment centers," particularly in the affluent households whose occupants make such ideal potential restaurant customers, raises the question of whether more people may choose to stay home to enjoy themselves. Thirty percent of homes have VCR players, and that number could rise to 40 percent, at current rate of VCR sales.[22] Forty percent already have cable television.

Nearly half of all American homes have microwave ovens, and this makes the grocery freezer a dangerous competitor. Accordingly, food manufacturers have developed special luxury products, and many, such as Lean Cuisine and Le Menu, appeal to consumers' diet consciousness. Indeed, given the speed with which consumers can prepare frozen foods in a microwave and the time saved in eating quickly at home and moving to the next room for entertainment, eating at home may come to be seen as the most serious competitor of all of food service.

Figure 4.2 shows that the prices of food prepared and eaten away from home have been growing since 1980 at a somewhat more rapid rate than have the prices of food prepared away from but eaten at home. Thus, restaurants may have to compete not only with one another but also with food consumed at home, if these trends continue. This could be an especially difficult problem in any economic downturn. When consumers were asked how they stretched their budgets, over half (51 percent) said they ate out less often, and 54 percent said they entertained more at home. Not eating out—in an era of convenient eating in—is one of the easiest ways to cut back on spending. And the already-growing number of restaurants offering takeout and home delivery suggests that the industry is already seeking to meet the renewed competitive threat of eating at home.

Other consumer "lifestyle" competitors are skipped meals and the

[20]*Nation's Restaurant News,* August 12, 1985, p. F24.
[21]*Nation's Restaurant News,* August 19, 1985, p. 21.
[22]*Nation's Restaurant News,* February 17, 1986, p. 106.

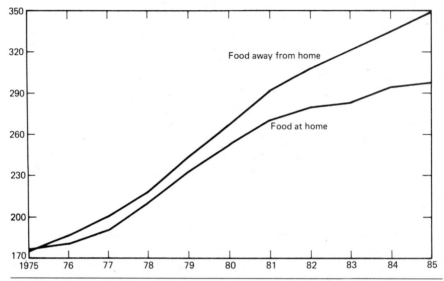

FIGURE 4.2 Relative price levels, 1975–1985 (1967 = 100), of food at home and food away from home. (Adapted from USDA/Prudential Bache.)

brown bag. The brown bag—a lunch brought from home—is probably prin-cipally an economy measure, and it might not be profitable to meet that particular price competition. On the other hand, consumers skip an average of two meals per week. No breakfast accounts for 65 percent of skipped meals, joined by no lunch, for 30 percent.[23]

Nutritionists tell us that skipping breakfast is actually not good for us. It can result in a weight gain because of insulin fluctuation and because of a tendency to have a high-calorie snack later or to overeat at lunch. Skipping breakfast also impairs performance, both physical and mental. And having just coffee and no breakfast has an even worse effect. The practice of skipped meals, then, might be thought of as a *marketing opportunity*. For example, individual restaurants or an industry group could use a public-ser-vice format to urge people to have a nutritious meal so as to improve their chances of losing weight and to feel better and work better.

EMPLOYMENT TRENDS

The changing age of America's population fits the good news—bad news pattern. The good news is the market opportunity arising from the higher

[23]John J. Rohs, *The Restaurant Industry* (New York: Wertheim & Co., 1985), p. 9.

TABLE 4.1   Population Changes for
Young Workers, 1975–2000 (in millions)

Year	14–17	18–24
1975	17,128	28,005
1980	16,140	30,357
1985	14,731	28,739
1990	12,950	25,794
2000	15,382	24,601

Source: U.S. Bureau of the Census.

average income as the baby boomers move into their peak earning years. The "baby bust," however, means shortages of restaurant labor, which are already being experienced in some areas and are likely to get worse for the next few years. There are roughly 3.5 million people working in fast-food operations, and nearly three-fourths of them are between 16 and 20 years of age.[24] Table 4.1 shows the dramatic change in the number of young workers between 1975 and 2000. The number of young people under 17 will be lowest in 1990, whereas the number of those between 18 and 24 will not hit bottom until 2000.

A study by Arthur D. Little & Co. for the National Restaurant Association projected a labor shortfall of nearly 200,000 food service workers by 1990 and approximately 1 million by 2000, assuming normal industry growth. The report pointed out that other industries employing large numbers of young workers such as retailers, service stations, hospitals, and banks would also be experiencing a labor shortage. An NRA report based on the Little study advised aggressive recruiting, upgrading pay and working conditions, and seeking out new labor sources. Increased labor productivity could be obtained, the study suggested, by using new technology such as automated or high-speed equipment and by improving management practices by streamlining menus, improving scheduling efficiency, and cross-training employees. It seems likely, too, that the labor shortage will encourage self-service.[25]

MANAGEMENT OPPORTUNITIES

The restaurant industry probably offers more opportunities to aspiring young managers than do all but a few of the high-tech fields, because there is a shortage of qualified managers at most levels today. This means that not

[24]*Wall Street Journal,* May 28, 1985, p. 33.
[25]*Food Service and the Labor Shortage* (Washington, D.C.: National Restaurant Association, n.d.).

only will the first job be fairly easy to get, but advancement is also likely to be possible for the hardworking qualified junior manager even if industry growth is not at the explosive level of the 1960s and 1970s. In the face of the labor shortage, though, managers should develop their "people" skills, because managing people—always important to our business—is likely to become more important.

There can be no question of the importance of good managers to the industry. In one study of food service chain executives, 85 percent of those surveyed listed management recruitment and development as among their firm's greatest problems. The well-equipped graduate, then, is likely to find real opportunity for growth in food service management.[26]

ENTREPRENEURIAL OPPORTUNITIES

The demographics that lead to a labor shortage are only one reason for the greater number of opportunities. The aging baby boomers are already raising the demand for variety and innovation in restaurants. Many existing fine dining establishments are finding it necessary to adapt to today's more casual tastes, and many new restaurants are being started by young entrepreneurs, particularly those with culinary training or experience.[27]

The most successful new chef owners generally have several years of experience, but many younger people with less formal culinary training are also finding success. The main criteria appear to be a good marketing sense, that is, knowing how to create a restaurant to satisfy an identified group of consumers, and a solid grasp of operating fundamentals.

SUMMARY

In this chapter we identified and discussed the major factors that will shape the food service industry. We began with equipment. New equipment like POS systems offer the opportunity for tighter controls. Other equipment improves the speed and availability of service and thus increases guest convenience. Although energy costs were a major force for change in the recent past, they are less likely to be so in the future, barring a political crisis.

Next we turned our attention to competition. Within the industry, this is increasingly a battle of the giants with advertising and promotion, new product development, service expansion, and convenience of location, all tools used by operators and chains. Competition comes from retailers normally considered outsiders—C stores and grocery stores. The consumer's

---

[26]W. E. Sasser and I. P. Morgan, *Growth of Second Tier Food Chains* (Philadelphia, Laventhol and Horwath, 1977).

[27]*Nation's Restaurant News*, May 20, 1985, p. 231.

home, itself, has become a major competitor. And the consumer's interest in spending money on other luxuries like a new VCR or some other high-priced item.

Finally, the shortage of labor spells both problems and opportunities. People with managing skills will clearly be at a premium.

KEY WORDS AND CONCEPTS

To help you review this chapter, keep in mind the following:

Complex delivery systems
Feasibility of automation
Computers
Scaled-down units
Mobile units
Energy costs
Restaurant expansion

New product development
Day parts
Co-locating
In-home entertainment centers
Baby-bust
Employment and Entreprenurial
    Opportunities

REVIEW QUESTIONS

1. Will any of the elements of the restaurant industry change in the next 10 years? If so, in what way?

2. What is the principal "revolutionary" invention in the food service industry?

3. Why are "chilled" foods popular?

4. What are the main areas of competition within the food service industry?

5. What are the main related businesses that compete with the food service industry?

6. How has the aging of the baby boomers affected the restaurant business?

C H A P T E R

Courtesy of Warner-Lambert.

INSTITUTIONAL FOOD SERVICE

THE PURPOSE OF THIS CHAPTER

One of the major reasons for the rapid growth in food service is that people have changed their eating habits along with their ways of life. Much of the growth in the food service market can be attributed to the increase in food consumption in institutional settings instead of at home. People eat in office or plant cafeterias; children and young people eat at their schools or colleges. The enormous growth in health care has led to a growing need for patient and employee food services in hospitals and in other health-care facilities.

This chapter provides you with information and a perspective on these growing markets. You will find this information useful even if you plan to work in the hotel business or in commercial food service. As we emphasized in Chapter 1, the hospitality industry requires a great deal of mobility and flexibility. You may find opportunities beckoning from the institutional area later in your career, because many commercial companies have begun to operate in the institutional food service area.

Moreover, there are differences in operating style and compensation between those who work for companies contracting in institutions and those who work for the institution itself. This chapter should help initiate and clarify your thinking about those issues, too.

THIS CHAPTER SHOULD HELP YOU

1. Explain the principal differences between institutional and commercial food service.

2. Identify the four major segments of institutional food service and list several characteristics of each.

3. Understand the way in which the school food service system can be seen as a model for other public sector food service programs.

4. See the growing congregate meals program for the aging in relation to the rapid growth of that population segment.

5. Identify and discuss the three major preparation systems.

6. Explain the merits of—and consumer resistance to—vended food service.

7. Discuss the relative advantages and disadvantages of contract food service companies as opposed to institutions operating their own food services.

8. Evaluate the differences in compensation between managers employed by commercial firms and those employed directly by the institution.

9. Express a considered opinion of the possible attractiveness of opportunities for you in the important growth area of institutional food service.

COMPARING INSTITUTIONAL AND COMMERCIAL FOOD SERVICES

Dividing food service into commercial and institutional segments is somewhat artificial and misleading, as some of the same firms that profit from providing institutions with food services also operate in other areas of the hospitality industry. ARA Services, for instance, operates hotels in national parks, and Marriott, one of the largest contract food service companies, is also a major hotel and fast-food company.

There is, however, a difference between restaurant and institutional food service. Institutional food service was once a "captive market," in contrast with restaurants, where guests have a choice of facilities and menus. This distinction still exists, but its force has been greatly reduced. Companies such as ARA and Marriott have found that a marketing approach that begins with guest preferences and the assumption that patients, inmates, soldiers, and students are, in fact, *guests* wins more friends than the old "eat it and like it" institutional attitude. The institutional guest *does* have a choice in the long run. College students who don't like the food withdraw from board plans; patients who have a choice of hospitals often choose the

A marketing orientation that offers the guests the services *they* want is important to today's institutional market. (Photo courtesy of Saga Corp.)

institution with superior food service; and even inmates find ways to assert their food preferences. In an age of consumerism, moreover, even guests who can't "vote with their feet" and go someplace else, don't hesitate to complain. Therefore, competition among the various food service contractors is often decided on the basis of marketing techniques and management skills.

Even though many companies provide both restaurant and institutional food services and use similar marketing and managerial techniques in both areas, the major difference between the two markets is that the food service in institutions is a small part of a large operation with a larger purpose of overriding importance—health care, education, or manufacturing, for instance. In the restaurant, the challenge is to please the guest. In the institution it is necessary to meet the needs of both the guests and the client (that is, the institution itself).

The distinction between client and guest is important. The client is the institution and its managers and policymakers. These are the people who award the contract or, when the institution operates its own food service, hire and fire the food service manager. Pleasing the guest (that is, the individual diner, patient, student, resident, or inmate) is important, but the client must be pleased as well.

A commercial restaurant makes a profit by pleasing its guests. There may be a substantial difference in an institutional setting between the needs and wants of the guest and those of the client. In school food service, for instance, the client's (that is, the school's) goals are providing not only adequate nutrition but also nutrition education by showing the students what a nutritionally balanced meal is like.

If the institution's food service is operated by a contract company, that company must arrange its contract with the client so as to provide a profit, usually in the form of a subsidy to the operation. In an institutionally operated food service program, a profit is often *not* sought, but some stated budget target *will* need to be met.

These examples show how institutional feeding can differ from a restaurant operated for profit. They should also suggest that it is no easier to operate an institutional food service at a profit. Even though that profit may derive from a subsidy from the client, the operating company must still reach a budgetary target. In fact, "making your costs"—that is, achieving a target cost ratio—can be more difficult in an institution with a low budget than turning a profit in a commercial restaurant is.

The two segments also have different operating problems. For example, the number of meals and portion sizes are much easier to predict in institutional operations. Because of this greater predictability, institutional food service operations often operate in a less hurried atmosphere than that in restaurants, in which customer volume and menu popularity often fluctuate. And whereas management people tend to work long hours in commercial food service, the working hours in institutional food service are usually shorter, or at least more predictable.

On the other hand, although a guest may visit a restaurant frequently, few of them eat as regularly in their favorite restaurant as do the guests in institutional operations. Thus, varying the menu for a guest who must eat in the same place for weeks, months, or even years at a time can be a demanding task.

CONTRACT COMPANIES AND INSTITUTIONAL OPERATIONS

An important division within institutional food service is that between contract food service companies (hereafter, contract companies) and institutional organizations that operate their own food service (hereafter, institutional operations). The huge institutional market is still dominated by institutional operators, but the contract companies' share has been increasing. Table 5.1 shows that contract companies now provide nearly one-third of institutional food services. Health care is the area in which contract companies have the smallest market penetration, but it has been increasing, from only 8 percent of the health-care market in 1981, compared with 11 percent

TABLE 5.1   The Institutional Food Service Market, 1986

	Size of Total Market (millions of dollars)	Degree of Penetration by Contract Companies
Business and industry	$ 5,908	64%
Colleges and universities	5,036	34
Hospitals and nursing homes	11,794	11
Primary and secondary schools	3,671	24
Total	$26,409	29%

Source: NRA News, December 1985.

in 1986. Contract companies have had even more success with public schools. The two areas in which the contract companies have expanded the least are colleges and universities and business and industry, but note that the contract companies are already well established there. Contract companies manage just over one-third of college and university food services and two-thirds of business and industry.

INSTITUTIONAL FOOD SERVICE OPERATIONS

There are four major divisions in institutional food service: business and industry, college and university, health care, and school and community. Two different ways of viewing the relative size of these divisions are summarized in Table 5.2. In the first column are the actual dollar sales as estimated by the National Restaurant Association (NRA). Because institutional sales are often subsidized, however, *Restaurant & Institutions* magazine believes that they can best be compared if their sales are estimated at their commercial value. The magazine therefore, used purchases as a base to reach an estimate that is comparable to commercial restaurant sales, and these figures are the second set presented in Table 5.2. According to the NRA method, institutions account for about 14 percent of food consumed away from home, but according to the magazine's method, the institutions' commercial equivalent volume makes up nearly a quarter (23.9 percent) of the total food service market.

BUSINESS AND INDUSTRY FOOD SERVICE

Business and industry food service provides food for the convenience of both the guest (the worker) and the client (the employer). The client wants inexpensive food with enough variety and quality to satisfy the workers, as the client knows that food can directly affect the employees' morale. Quick

TABLE 5.2 Institutional Sales: Actual and Commercial Value, 1986

	Institutional Sales	Percentage of Institutional Market	Commercial Value of Institutional Sales	Percentage of Institutional Market
Business and industry	$ 5,908	22.3%	$10,489	25.5%
Colleges and universities	5,034	19.1	6,164	15.0
Hospitals and nursing homes	11,794	44.7	11,438	27.8
Primary and secondary schools	3,671	13.9	13,043	31.7
	$26,409	100.0%	$41,134	100.0%

Source: NRA News; Restaurants & Institutions.

service is also important, because the time for coffee breaks and lunch is limited.

The underlying forces that drive the B and I market (as the business and industry segment is called) are the size of the work force and the level of employment. The size of the work force affects the long-term outlook. When it was growing, the work force was a strong positive force, during the years when the baby boomers were leaving school and entering employment. Now that that surge is over, however, the Bureau of Labor Statistics estimates that the work force will increase at a modest 1.9 percent per year until 1995, and this slower growth will clearly affect B and I sales.

Within the work force, the trend toward more office and other white-collar employment is determining where the B and I volume will be. For example, some of the largest factory accounts will be reduced in size or even closed. On the other hand, the volume of food service in commercial and office buildings is growing at a significantly faster pace than it is in manufacturing plants. In periods of low unemployment, B and I volume may rise, but on the other hand, B and I is especially sensitive to downturns in employment.

Aside from prisons, mental hospitals, and other custodial institutions, no part of the institutional food service market is insulated from the rest of the food service business, and this is certainly true for the business and industry segment. As Joe Fassler, president of Greyhound Management, put it, "Ten years ago your competitor was the other contract feeder. Today, other contract feeders are not our primary competitors. It is the commercial market."[1] One way that contract companies can meet the competition from commercial operations outside the institution is by developing their own version of popular restaurant strategies. Greyhound for instance, developed a fast-food operation, called "Eatins' Easy," for its accounts. The new units generally include a range of products: burgers, fried chicken, fish, and hand-carved meat.

The advantages of this new format are startlingly similar to the advantage that fast food has in the commercial restaurant business:

> The operation has an identity that helps secure patronage from an increasingly brand-conscious food service customer.
>
> The facility is simpler to build than is a full-menu concept, and the investment required is only about half as much.
>
> Operating costs are lower, too, because of the simpler menu and because customers are accustomed to self-busing in fast food.[2]
>
> Fast food is fast—in-plant feeding at General Motors plants takes only 3 minutes, compared with 12 minutes under earlier formats.

The merchandising of food service is receiving more attention, too. ARA, for instance, developed promotional programs for a number of menu selections that it has served for some time, but up until now without marketing planning and promotional support. These promotional programs include "Fresh Starts," a breakfast program with daily specials from around North America; "Kettle Classics," a variety of soups; and "Salad Garden."[3]

The purpose of employee food service operations changes with different employee levels. Many companies maintain executive dining rooms boasting fancy menus and elegant service. Such dining rooms are often used to entertain important business guests—customers, prospective employees, the press, and politicians. Executive dining room privileges can also be an important status symbol among managerial employees.

COLLEGE AND UNIVERSITY FOOD SERVICE

To understand college food service, one must understand the "board plan"; that is, students eating in residence halls may be required to contract for a minimum number of meals over a term or semester. The food service operation benefits from this arrangement in two ways. First, the absentee factor ensures that some students will miss some meals they contracted for, which permits the food service operation to price the total package below what all the meals would cost if every student ate every meal there. This makes the

[1]*Restaurant Business*, December 10, 1985, p. 189.
[2]*Nation's Restaurant News*, August 12, 1985, p. F56.
[3]*Restaurant Business*, November 1, 1985, p. 166.

package price attractive, and because most college food service operations permit unlimited seconds, students can "load up" at those meals they do attend.

Second, and more important, the board plan provides a predictable volume of sales over a fairly long period—a term, a semester, or a year. At the start of that period, the operator can closely estimate what the sales volume will be. Because attendance ratios and the popularity of various menu items are fairly predictable, the operator can also estimate how much food to prepare for each meal.

Although some colleges offer only a full board plan (three meals a day, seven days a week while school is in session), flexible board plans have become more and more popular on many campuses, particularly those on which contract companies operate the food service. For example, some plans exclude breakfast, whereas others drop the weekend meals. There is now a wide variety of plans. Indeed, one food service company offers 91 different board plans on college campuses around the country.

With a flexible plan that invites students to contract for only the meals they expect to eat, the absentee rate goes down and the average price charged per meal goes up, because of the lower absentee rates. Nevertheless, in plans that drop a significant number of meals, the total price of the meal contract also drops. In any case, both the full board plan and partial plans generally charge students on the basis of the average number of meals they consume.

Another approach that is gaining ground is for students to contract for some minimum dollar value of food service and to receive what is, in effect, a credit card with the amount they have paid credited to the card. As they use the card, the amount of each meal is electronically or manually deducted from the balance. Students receive the food purchased through their card at some discount from what competitive commercial operations charge, and so it is still a bargain. The contracts, on the other hand, give the operator a basis for projecting the demand for the school year for scheduling, purchasing, and general budgeting, and it also guarantees some minimum level of sales volume.

Flexible board plans represent one part of a marketing approach to college food service, an approach that adapts the services available to the guests' needs and preferences. In addition, with the arrival of fast-food firms on a few large campuses, college food service operations have begun to develop their own branded formats to meet the demand for this kind of service, in much the same way as have the operators in B and I described earlier. ARA, for instance, developed "Itza Pizza," a pizza delivery concept; "El Pollo Grande," featuring Mexican foods; and "Bagel Wagon," a mobile business that sells freshly baked products.[4] The food services might also

---

[4]*Restaurant Business,* November 1, 1985, pp. 166–168.

In college food services, several different board plans may be available. Often, different styles of service—from fast food to formal dining—are offered to give a sense of variety. (Photo courtesy of Saga Corp.)

feature Hawaiian luaus or outdoor steak fries, just to give their customers a sense of variety and change of pace. A contract company has to sell the client (the institution) so as to obtain or keep an account. But it must also sell the guests (the students) every day with quality and variety. Otherwise, the students will unsell the client and demand a change in food service.

One contract food service executive, C.J. Labante of ARA, summed up the goals of a college food service organization as follows:

The business manager wants to maximize the dollars returned to the university (the difference between the charge to the student and the actual cost of operations). Food service on most campuses is income producing.[5] The student, on the other hand, wants to pay the minimum for food service. But he wants to receive a high quality program, food he enjoys.

Students want to be served in a nice atmosphere. There is nothing worse than going into a stultified, aseptic atmosphere every day of the school year.

[5] The "income" produced for the institution by college food service is generally not a true net profit but, rather, a contribution to the interest cost and depreciation of the dormitory facility in which it is housed. Even in state schools, dormitories are usually constructed with money raised from sale of bonds, and the bondholders must be repaid in both principal and interest.

Service management, I believe, is the art of trying to optimize the objectives of our clients and customers and, at the same time, to make sure we earn a reasonable bottom line profit.

College food service contracting companies stress the need for a strong communications program between the food service staff and the students. Many operators consult regularly with a student advisory group. All agree that, in addition to good food and tight cost controls, a successful college food service operation must have "people skills"; that is, it must be able to deal effectively with the guests.

College students are generally pleasant to deal with, but they can be very demanding. They need to be consulted in planning, and patient attention to complaints is important, too. An unhappy *group* of college students— with a natural bent for boisterousness—can be a difficult group to deal with. Open lines of communication are essential to avoid the "us" versus "them" polarization that leads to trouble.

College enrollments should continue the decline that began in the early 1980s and is expected to last until the mid-1990s. Both contract companies and institutional operators will be affected by this trend, but the contract companies may be able to use it to their advantage through more vigorous marketing of their services to prospective client institutions. That is, as college enrollments drop and food service volumes drop right along with them, institutional budget targets will become harder to meet. The contractors will then have a competitive edge in seeking new accounts as the colleges seek the economies of scale that these companies offer.

HEALTH-CARE FOOD SERVICE

Health-care food service can be divided into three general categories: large hospitals (over 300 beds), small to medium hospitals, and nursing homes. In all three of these settings, health-care professionals—dietitians, along with such paraprofessionals as dietetic managers and dietetic technicians—play important roles.

The Dietetic Professional

"The dietitian," according to an authoritative study of the profession, "is a 'translator' of the science of nutrition into the skill of furnishing optimum nourishment. The word 'translator' is used in its familiar context of 'translating ideas into action.'"[6]

The largest group within the profession—between 60 and 75 percent— is made up of clinical dietitians concerned principally with the problems of special diets and with educating patients who have health problems that re-

[6]*The Profession of Dietetics: Report of the Study Commission on Dietetics* (Chicago: American Dietetic Association, 1972).

quire temporary or permanent diet changes. Another 15 to 25 percent of dietetic professionals are administrative dietitians concerned principally with the management of food service systems, for the most part in health care. (Dietitians also work in education and in non-health-care food services, and their commitment to community nutrition is growing rapidly as well.)

Dietitians who complete a bachelor's degree program and professional training (either in an internship program or in a coordinated undergraduate program that includes both academic classwork and professional experience) and who pass a registration examination are registered in the professional organization, the American Dietetic Association. Registered dietitians (R.D.s) are required by hospital accreditation standards and government regulations to supervise health-care food services either on a full-time basis or as consultants.

The dietary department in a large hospital is headed by either an administrative dietitian or a hospital food service manager. A nondietitian who is employed as the hospital food service manager is supported by a chief of nutrition services, who is a registered dietitian. Large hospitals generally employ a number of clinical dietitians who spend considerable time with patients and prepare special diets. Once a special diet has been written, the clinical dietitian translates it into production orders for the cooks and tray assemblers and then makes certain that these orders are followed. An important part of the dietitian's work is interpreting the diet to patients, helping them understand the need for the diet, and preparing them to undertake their own specialized diet planning.

In a smaller hospital, the food service manager is somewhat less likely to be a registered dietitian. In such cases, however, a consulting registered dietitian will provide professional guidance.

The Dietetic Technician

A somewhat newer role in health care is that of the dietetic technician, who has completed an appropriate associate degree program. Technicians occupy key roles in medium and large hospitals, working under the direction of registered dietitians. Dietetic technicians screen and interview patients to determine their dietary needs or problems and, in large hospitals, often have supervisory responsibilities. In smaller hospitals, technicians may run dietary departments under the periodic supervision of consulting registered dietitians. One of the most important areas of opportunity for dietetic technicians is in extended-care facilities, such as nursing homes, where technicians serve as food service managers under the supervision of a consulting registered dietitian.

Technicians must take a registration exam, and fully qualified technicians are registered by the American Dietetic Association. To save money, many hospitals now employ fewer registered dietitians, and so are delegating more and more work to dietetic technicians.

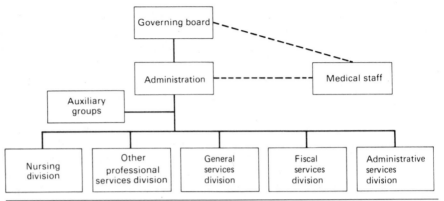

FIGURE 5.1 Functional organization of medium-sized hospital. (American Hospital Association.)

The Dietary Manager

The dietary manager also has an important role in health-care food service. Dietary managers must have had a considerable amount of on-the-job experience and must also have completed a 90-hour course of instruction covering subjects such as food service management, supervision, and basic nutrition. A separate organization, the Dietary Managers Association, provides for the education and certification of dietary managers who are not members of the ADA.[7] Dietary managers are used principally in nursing homes. Some dietary managers have completed the dietetic technician's more extensive two-year course of instruction and may use either title.

Dietary Department Organization

The organization of the dietary department should be considered in the context of the overall health-care facility organization. Figure 5.1 depicts the organization of a medium-sized hospital. The work of the nursing division is, in general, self-explanatory. Other professional services include laboratories, X-ray services, and pharmacies. The dietary department is found in the general services division along with other support services, such as plant engineering and housekeeping. The fiscal services division includes functions such as accounting, receiving, and storage. Thus, in some hospitals, receiving and storage may be carried out for food service by another support unit. Administrative services include the personnel and purchasing func-

[7]Ayres G. D. Carter and Ann L. Schrech, *The Role of the Dietary Manager: An Overview of the HIEFSS Role Delineation Study* (Hillside, Ill.: Hospital, Institution, and Educational Food Service Society, 1983).

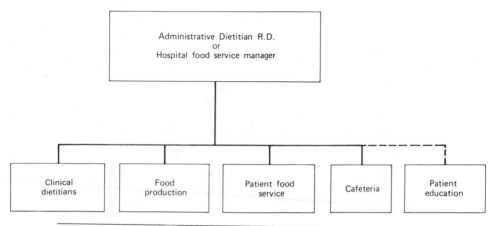

FIGURE 5.2 Functional organization of the dietary department.

tions. Here again, note that another division may assume these functions for the dietary department. This already-complex organization is further complicated by the medical and surgical staffs—the professionals on whose services the entire institution is centered.

Work in hospital food service is fast-paced, and many employees find the medical atmosphere exciting. The organizational complexity and need for *nutrition care* (the provision of special therapeutic diets) as a separate concern makes a career in health-care food service one of the most complex and demanding of the food service careers.

The organization of the dietary department will vary in its assignment and reporting relationships according to the size and function of the hospital. The main functions appear in Figure 5.2.

The same kitchen usually prepares the food for all the employees, house diet patients, and visitors. Some hospitals maintain a separate diet kitchen; others allow the same crew to prepare the special diets following appropriate recipes. Patient food service personnel deliver the food to the floors and return dishes and other equipment to the kitchen after the meals. The cafeteria serves the staff, visitors, and in some cases, ambulatory patients. Some large hospitals offer internships and other educational programs for dietetic professionals, just as they do for nursing and medical school graduates.

Nursing homes, extended-care facilities, and smaller hospitals perform these similar functions on a smaller scale. Thus, such an institution may employ only a consulting dietitian and may combine food production and patient food service. Or the cafeterias in some nursing homes may be expanded to serve all ambulatory patients, often in traditional dining rooms.

Trends in Health-Care Food Service

In the past, health care was a "recession-proof" food service market with a strong growth potential. Although health care is still less sensitive to economic conditions than are many other food service segments, the government's standardization of fees under "Diagnosis Related Groups" (DRGs) brought its growth to a halt.[8] This is because the government previously paid Medicaid and Medicare bills on a cost-plus basis. But this led to a runaway inflation in medical costs, with the annual increase peaking in 1980 at 15.3 percent.[9] Once the government introduced standardized reimbursement, private health insurance plans began to follow in order to cap their own costs. In addition, the nursing home equivalent of the DRG, called the RUG (Resource Utilization Grouping), was introduced in 1986.[10]

A major effect of DRGs, and RUGs has been to limit the number of days in hospitals or nursing homes for which Medicare or Medicaid will pay. This has reduced the length of the average health-care stay, the occupancy levels, and, thereby, the hospitals' revenue. In addition, DRGs and RUGs limit the other costs that will be reimbursed, further lowering revenue. Health care has consequently had to learn to live with less, which has had a dramatic impact on dietary departments: Because there are fewer patient meals to be served, the number of staff has often been reduced.

But on the other hand, the lower hospital occupancy levels have led to greater competition for patients, and the dietary department often plays a key role in this competition, offering optional room service, upscale restaurant facilities on the premises, restaurant-style menus for patients, and even dessert carts. In addition, many hospital dietary departments now offer to cater functions outside the hospital and encourage outsiders to come to eat in the hospital—all measures aimed at increasing the dietary department's contribution to the hospital's revenues.

Some hospitals are moving to centralized cook–chill systems because they offer substantial savings. And because these systems are expensive to build, hospitals are selling cook–chill meals to other, nearby institutions. The additional sales volume helps pay for the equipment and reduces the preparation facility's operating and capital costs.[11]

Entrepreneurial Opportunities. Because of the increasing number of elderly people in our population, more and more people require assistance living at home. Indeed, this number has probably been increased by the institution of DRG/RUG measures, which force health-care institutions to move out people as quickly as possible.

[8]*Restaurant & Institutions*, January 18, 1984, pp. 112–120.
[9]*Restaurants & Institutions*, January 23, 1985, pp. 140–144.
[10]*Restaurants & Institutions*, January 8, 1986, pp. 148–153.
[11]*Nation's Restaurant News*, February 11, 1986, p. F3–4.

To meet the needs of these people living at home who cannot care for themselves, a number of home-care services have sprung up. Some offer simply housekeeping services but others provide "sitter" service and limited nursing care. In addition, nutritional support companies offer nutritional care such as special diets. These home-assistance companies offer people with adequate training an interesting opportunity to go into business for themselves with a minimum of investment.

SCHOOL AND COMMUNITY FOOD SERVICE

Perhaps nowhere on the dynamic American scene has recent change been as rapid as in the roles and aspirations of women. These changes have, in fact, altered the structure and function of the family in the United States. Over the past 35 years, accelerating adjustments in our views of women and the family function have had an enormous impact on food service in general. We suspect that these changes have not yet had their heaviest impact on government-supported food service programs.

The best objective measure of the change in the role of women appears in the proportion of women employed outside the home or seeking such employment. This proportion is referred to as the *female labor-force participation rate*.

In 1900, about 20 out of every 100 women in the United States entered the work force, that is, were employed outside the home or were seeking employment. In 1920, after World War I, this number was only about 23 in 100 (actually, 22.7 percent), an overall change of less than 14 percent in the participation rate. From 1920 to 1940, the rate rose to just under 26 in 100, again, a change of just under 14 percent.

With World War II, the rate of change increased radically. The basis for estimating the 1940 rate and the 1947 rate changed slightly, as 1947 was the first year in which the rate was computed by current methods. Allowing for this difference, however, the rate rose from just over one-quarter (25.8 percent) of the women working in 1940 to nearly one-third in 1947 (31.8 percent), a rate of increase in that 7-year period of approximately 23 percent, compared with less than 14 percent for each of the two preceding 20-year periods.

In the 20 years between 1954 and 1974, the female participation rate jumped even higher, increasing from 34.6 percent to 45.6 percent. This was a change of 32 percent, or more than twice the rate of change experienced during the first two 20-year periods in this century. From 1970 to 1983, as Table 5.3 demonstrates, work-force participation increased dramatically for women in the age groups normally associated with raising children (ages 20 to 54), with the growth in the number of working women between the ages of 25 and 34 being particularly pronounced. Some combination of the grow-

TABLE 5.3 Projected and Actual Growth in Female Labor-Force Participation Rates, 1947–1995

Age Group	Participation Percentage						Rate of Change	
	1947[a]	1970	1980	1983	1995[a]		1947–1983	1980–1995
16–17	29.4%	34.9%	43.6%	39.9%	48.0%		35.7%	20.3%
18–19	52.2	53.5	61.9	60.7	68.9		16.3	13.5
20–24	44.8	57.7	68.9	69.9	82.0		56.0	17.3
25–34	31.9	45.0	65.5	69.0	81.7		116.3	18.4
35–44	36.3	51.1	65.5	68.7	82.8		89.2	20.5
45–54	32.7	54.4	59.9	61.9	69.5		89.3	12.3
55–64	24.3	43.0	41.3	41.5	42.5		70.8	2.4
65 and over	8.1	9.7	8.1	7.8	7.0		–13.16	–10.3
Total	31.8	43.3	51.5	52.9	60.3		89.6	14.0

Source: Bureau of Labor Statistics; *Statistical Abstract of the United States, 1986* (Washington, D.C.: U.S. Government Printing Office, 1986).
[a]Bureau of Labor Statistics, 1986 estimate.

ing social acceptance of working mothers and the effect of inflation and recession in reducing the rate of increase in family income probably accounts for these most recent developments.

We will consider these female labor-force participation rates in detail because of their enormous impact on the demand for food service. In 1900, only one in five women expected to work outside the home. Today, some two-thirds of women between the ages of 18 and 54 work or are seeking employment. And by 1995, that proportion will have increased to roughly 8 out of 10. The result, of course, is that many more women are midday food service customers. Moreover, the increase in family income provided by a second job allows more families to dine out in the evening. And a working wife, tired after a day's work, is quite likely to want to spend money for this purpose.

To see the impact of working mothers even more clearly, we should examine more closely the recent female labor-force trends. Table 5.3 shows that the change in women's labor-force participation has not been the same for all age groups, and these differences directly affect government-supported food service programs.

Labor-force participation by women under the age of 20 was not unusual in 1947. In fact, more than one-half the women 18 and 19 years old worked in the labor force in that year. At that time, as women married and bore children, they typically withdrew from the labor force. Recent years, however, have seen a shift from working women to working mothers.

As Table 5.3 shows, the increase in the participation rate for women in the child-bearing years was much greater than the increase in the rate for all women. As more and more mothers went to work, they increased the demand for different ways to provide meals away from home for their children.

Although the dramatic change in the number of women working outside the home has affected nearly every institution in our society, in the area of institutional food service, its greatest impact has been on school food service and care for the elderly.

The National School Lunch Program (NSLP)

Early History.   Historians have traced the earliest concern for feeding children outside the home to "private societies and associations interested in child welfare and education."[12] The first program of this kind seems to have started in 1790 in Germany. However, a national government first entered the field in Holland in 1900, with Switzerland following six years later.

---

[12]For an authoritative, extended treatment of the history of the NSLP, see Gordon W. Gunderson, *The National School Lunch Program: Background and Development* (Washington, D.C.: Food and Nutrition Service, U.S. Department of Agriculture, n.d.). Much of the following history of school lunches before 1970 is taken from Gunderson's excellent study.

In the United States, concern about hunger and nutritional deficiency deepened during the Depression of the 1930s. Ironically, the Depression was a time of agricultural surpluses. The earliest support for major, continuing federal involvement in school feeding arose, then, as part of the effort to use these surpluses constructively.

Concern for the nutrition of poor children, concern for the national interest, the need to stimulate demand for agricultural produce, and the need to accommodate young people too far from home to return there for lunch all helped build support for the school lunch program before World War II. A new, important factor during and after that war was the changing role of women, discussed previously.

We have already noted that the women at work were, more and more, mothers. They thus had to make some provision to feed their children a midday meal, as they could not do it themselves. Thus, what was once a function of the family increasingly became an obligation undertaken by that familiar community organization, the school. Under these circumstances, it is not surprising that political support for the National School Lunch Program (NSLP) grew, and so did the size of the NSLP's financial appropriation.

With the change of administrations in 1981, the U.S. government reassessed many social programs, including food service programs.

Current Support. One reason for the rapid growth of the school lunch program in the 1960s and 1970s was the enormous growth in the school population that resulted from the baby boom. That factor is now past, and moreover, funding support for school food service from the federal government has been drastically curtailed and refocused. For instance, in 1985, only 9 percent of the federal contribution went to middle-class children, compared with three to four times that proportion in the late 1970s. Most of the cash assistance—$2.43 billion—is provided for free or reduced-price meals served to low-income children.[13] Even though this diminished federal support has changed the management of the school lunch program, it has served well the changing life-styles of the American family. Indeed, the question is how school food service will be paid for, not whether the country will have such a program.

Federal support in total (including donated commodities) has remained at a level of approximately $3.2 billion since the Reagan administration took office. In the light of inflation, this means a reduction in real funding. The number of schools participating in the school lunch program has declined from nearly 94,000 in 1981 to just over 85,000 in 1985. Although some of the decline can be attributed to schools' withdrawing from lunch programs, some of the decline can also be attributed to schools closings because of the

---

[13]*Nation's Restaurant News*, December 9, 1985, p. F5.

Most experts agree that providing an attractive setting for school lunch programs has a favorable impact on participation rates. (Photo courtesy of American School Food Service Association.)

declining school-age population. Currently, the program reaches about 24 million children. The proportion of free and reduced price lunches, in keeping with a policy of targeting disadvantaged children for assistance, has risen from 45 percent in 1980 to 52 percent in 1985.

The School Food Service Model

Even though the school lunch program has substantially changed in recent years, it remains an interesting model for transferring family functions to a segment of the hospitality industry. The question of public hospitality agencies' performing what were once family functions remains a lively one. Many are opposed to what they view as an unnatural, even antifamily, trend in our society. On the other hand, with the high and growing number of women in the work force, it is generally agreed that somebody must provide the services no longer available in the home. Although America's reaction to the changes in the family's role is still changing, we can learn a great deal from the model of service that has developed in the school lunch program.

The first element in the model suggested by the school food service is that the program meet several clearly defined social needs. Although using up surplus commodities was an important early factor, the program appears to address more general social problems today. The program provides nutritious meals to needy children who might otherwise go hungry, and it helps make well-balanced meals available to all students.

USDA regulations require that school lunches conform to a basic pattern and provide one-third to one-half of a student's minimum daily nutritional requirements. The following four elements must be present in prescribed quantities.

1. Body-building foods, such as meat, fish, eggs, and cheese, that provide protein and iron. (Bread and butter are served with these foods to supply carbohydrates and fat.)
2. Vegetables or fruits high in vitamin A.
3. Vegetables or fruits high in vitamin C.
4. Milk, to provide calcium as well as protein.

The approved lunch pattern offers more than a nutritionally sound meal. It has become part of the educational program itself, teaching students what foods are necessary to health and growth.

As we noted earlier, many mothers have left the home to work. Thus, receiving an adequate noonday meal has become important not just to the needy students but to the affluent as well. In sum, then, the NSLP serves socially useful function by providing basic nutrition, offering a significant nutrition education program, and rendering important assistance to families with working mothers.

The second element in the NSLP model is that it pools subsidies. The federal subsidy usually requires matching state or local funds. Because the subsidies from the various levels of government are pooled, the result constitutes a "bargain." The student's lunch, even if he or she paid the full price, is less expensive than it would be if purchased anywhere else—even if it were brought from home.

The attractiveness of this bargain encourages participation, and participation ensures the third element of the model, a high volume. This high volume makes the meal program more efficient, and it results in further economies. In short, it improves the bargain.

The pattern of administration is the fourth and final element. There is general monitoring of the fairly broad guidelines at the national and state levels, but most operational decisions are made entirely at a local level. Technical advice is, of course, always available. Thus, the model encourages adaptation to local tastes and conditions.

The "bargain" that school lunches offer to its young consumers and

Because working mothers can rarely take summers off, a special summer food service program has become an important service to families with working mothers. (Photo courtesy of U.S. Department of Agriculture, Food and Nutrition Services.)

their families never has been completely dependent on the federal subsidies. Both state and local governments (and in some communities, charitable organizations) have contributed to the cost of school lunches in direct subsidies of varying amounts.

The Response To Funding Changes.   If there were any realistic danger to the school food service program as a result of funding level changes, the remarkable response of the school food service community to what was initially seen as a threat should certainly put anyone's fears to rest. That reaction, which is a tribute to the dedication, inventiveness, and resilience of school food service management, has had two related aspects: marketing and cost control. A consciousness of the "sovereign consumer," already present in many school lunch operations, has spread to a much broader audience among school lunch managers. With increasing costs passed on to the paying child, efforts to market the school food service competitively have been intensified. For example, to increase participation, youth advisory councils have been set up in some schools to provide customer feedback in much the same way as it is in colleges.[14] As a result, school lunchrooms have been remodeled to make them more attractive.

Successful promotions along the lines found in commercial operations are increasingly common.[15] Self-service bars have been introduced to provide a service that looks, and is, competitive with commercial food service. Moreover, nutrition is a central appeal that is a part of the nutrition education mission of school food service, and a promotional approach that is quite successful in reaching increasingly nutrition-conscious young people.[16]

An article on merchandising in the *School Food Service Journal* gives the kind of advice that might be heard from the home office of a company in the commercial sector, calling for some kind of promotional event at least once every two weeks, to compete with fast-food operations. Moreover, school lunch personnel must begin to function as sales people: "In the school food *service* industry, you're inviting paying customers into your lunch room to eat your good products. . . . Nonprofit does not mean no profit or no business sense. You're a business."[17]

Even though the salaries of commercial operators and many other institutional employees are generally higher, the life-style advantages of employment in school food service shouldn't be overlooked in assessing career opportunities in this field. Some programs run year round, but most offer reasonable hours, time off at Christmas and spring break, and the summers free for family or other pursuits.

FOOD SERVICE PROGRAMS FOR THE AGING

In our discussion of the school lunch program, we examined such basic causes as the national concern for adequate nutrition and an increase in the number of working mothers. A similar set of forces is at work in the creation of a food service program to serve aging Americans.

The first force is demographic—population trends related to births, deaths, and average ages in the country. Few people realize how radical the demographic changes have been in recent years. As recently as 100 years ago, only a small proportion of the population survived past the age of 50; "old age" began in a person's thirties[18] But by the beginning of this century, improved health care, better nutrition, better control of communicable diseases, and many other factors led to a radical increase in life expectancy. The strong influence of retirees in our society began, as Peter Drucker pointed out, when the babies born in the 1890s did not die in the 1940s, as

[14]*School Food Service Journal*, September 1984, pp. 22–23.

[15]*School Food Service Journal*, March 1985, pp. 124–127.

[16]*School Food Service Journal*, May 1985, pp. 26 and 109–112.

[17]*School Food Service Journal*, June–July–August 1985, p. 26.

[18]For an extended discussion of this issue and its more general social consequences, see Peter Drucker, *The Unseen Revolution* (New York: Harper & Row, 1976).

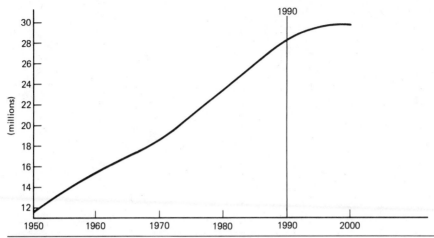

FIGURE 5.3   People 65 to 84 years old, 1950–2000. [Adapted from Peter K. Franchese, "Consumer Perspectives," *Proceedings: Chain Operators Exchange, 1985* (Chicago: International Foodservice Manufacturers Association, 1985).]

they would have a generation earlier. We are, in fact, the first society in history in which a large proportion of our population has survived not just past 50 but well into their sixties, seventies, and eighties.

As Figure 5.3 illustrates, America's elderly population already is large, and the number of people over 65 will grow until the end of the century. (After the turn of the century, this population group will grow even faster—but that is beyond the scope of our discussion here.) The population group with the highest growth rate today, as illustrated in Figure 5.4, is the group of very senior citizens over 85 years of age.

In the commercial market, the greater number of retired people means a new leisure class. Those between age 65 and 75 are likely to be healthy, active, and—with improved pension and social security programs—relatively affluent. This group already has affected travel markets as well as other leisure services such as dining out.

In this chapter, however, we will focus on the relatively less prosperous elderly for whom institutional programs have been designed. People over 75 are more likely to fall in this category, as they are more likely to be financially needy and to require assistance to survive. The rapid growth of this group is one reason for the increasing demand for institutional services for the elderly.

A second force at work is the change in the family. At the turn of the century, few women and even fewer married women went to work. And at that time, the few persons who did survive into old age lived with their grown children or other relatives. Today, however, working women and men

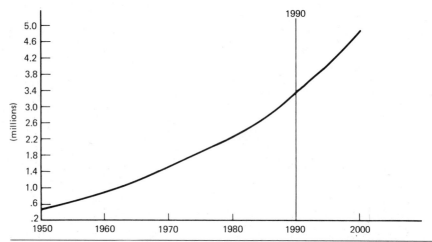

FIGURE 5.4 People 85+ years old, 1950–2000. [Adapted from Peter K. Franchese, "Consumer Perspectives," *Proceedings: Chain Operators Exchange, 1985* (Chicago: International Foodservice Manufacturers Association, 1985).]

have little energy left over to care for their aging parents and relatives. Therefore, different social arrangements are emerging to accommodate the increasing numbers of elderly people.

Some senior citizens can afford to enter retirement communities or other retirement centers that provide a host of services. But many elderly persons cannot afford these expensive arrangements. Although social security benefits give them some cash income to cover the costs of housing and clothing, an alarming proportion of our senior citizens of modest means receive inadequate nutrition. In fact, over 15 percent of elderly Americans live below the poverty line.

One solution to the problem of caring for the elderly (a solution that our society seems ready to accept because of the NSLP precedent) is an inexpensive food service administered under a program generally referred to as *congregate meals*. According to the Administration on Aging (AoA),

> The national nutrition program for the elderly is designed to provide older Americans, particularly those with low income, with low cost, nutritionally sound meals. Emphasis is given to providing these meals in group settings. The nutritional projects provide at least one hot meal a day (meeting one third of the daily nutritional requirements) five days a week to older citizens (60+) and their spouses of any age.

Although participants would be given an opportunity to pay for their meals, "no means test will be made and no one will be turned away on the basis of their inability to pay for a meal."

The congregate meals program offers older Americans not only sound nutrition but also a chance to continue their participation in community activities and to combine food and friendship. (Photo courtesy of U.S. Department of Health and Human Services, Administration on Aging.)

This legislation responds not only to the problems of low income among the elderly but to their other problems as well. To quote the AoA again:

> Regulations promulgated by the Secretary of HEW provide that individuals eligible to receive meals are those persons age 60 or over who (1) cannot afford to eat adequately, (2) lack the skills and knowledge to select and prepare nourishing and well-balanced meals, (3) have limited mobility which may impair their capacity to shop and cook for themselves, or (4) have feelings of rejection and loneliness which obliterate the incentive necessary to prepare and eat a meal alone.

In facing the problems of the elderly, this food service program sets goals for itself that go beyond the obvious nutritional goals:

> In addition to promoting better health among the older segment of the population through improved nutrition, the program can help reduce the

isolation of the aged, offering older Americans an opportunity to continue to participate in community activities and to combine food and friendship.

Social services for the elderly have also begun to emphasize deinstitution-alization. Early experiences in caring for our ballooning elderly population have taught us that it is both less expensive and more humane to help the elderly live in their own homes or apartments rather than in an institutional environment such as the county home for the aged. Food services provided by community or neighborhood organizations, which often administer other services as well, help maintain the elderly in their homes.

In fiscal year 1984, over 144 million congregate meals were served to nearly 3 million elderly, 56 percent of whom were in economic need. The cost to all parties (that is, government, participants, and other funding agencies) was over $574 million, and nearly 8000 sites were used for this service, most of them operating on a five-day week.[19]

PREPARATION AND DELIVERY SYSTEMS

Most institutions use one of three preparation systems: conventional systems, ready food systems, and convenience food systems. *Conventional food service systems*, still the most common, prepare food "from scratch" in their own kitchens for every meal. Many institutions prefer these operations, because management has acquired the impression that "from scratch" food tastes better and is more readily accepted by consumers. In markets in which labor is plentiful, and especially in larger institutions in which the number of people served is large enough to justify the use of a full kitchen crew, this traditional form of food service is still economically feasible.

In a *ready foods operation*, the institution's preparation employees work five days a week, eight hours a day, to prepare, plate, and then freeze or chill the food. A different crew reconstitutes and serves the food. This system is most frequently found today in large hospitals, but the use of central commissaries is also becoming common in school food service. The use of food chilled to 33 to 35° F (1 to 2° C) instead of to the frozen state is becoming increasingly common in both hospitals and school food service.

Convenience foods systems depend on foods provided by frozen food manufacturers. The institutions that adopt this system are usually small. The portion cost of the food is relatively expensive, but its use permits a food service when adequate kitchen facilities are not otherwise available. More-

[19]*Fiscal Year 1984 National Summary of Program Performance* (Washington, D.C.: Administration on Aging, n.d.).

On a hospital's tray line, regular and special diets are assembled for transportation to the patient's room. (Photo courtesy of Saga Corp.)

over, the higher unit cost may be offset by the smaller food service payroll, because fewer and less-skilled employees are required for this system.

The most common institutional delivery system (the means of delivering prepared food to the guest) is the cafeteria. But some executive dining rooms offer waitress service, and patient food service has too many different equipment configurations and modifications to discuss here. In school food service, however, in which basically the same meal is served at many sites in a

Centralization of food preparation is increasingly common in school food service.
(Photo courtesy of U.S. Department of Agriculture, Food and Nutrition Service.)

school district on any given day, more and more districts are moving to centralize food production in commissaries. The savings available from this strategy are impressive.

In Portland, Oregon, for instance, the annual savings from centralizing production for its 75 separate school lunch facilities was $600,000. Of this, $100,000 per year resulted from smaller food inventories, and an additional $500,000 came from lower labor costs. Not surprisingly, one factor in reducing the payroll was simplifying management in the school system. Through attrition, 68 kitchen managers at the school level were eliminated, replaced by a "lead assistant" in each satellite kitchen. The Portland school system also uses a quick chill system, and since it centralized its lunch preparation, the participation rate has risen, apparently as a result of the improved and standardized quality of its products.[20]

[20]*School Food Service Journal*, June–July–August 1984, pp. 152–154.

Once food preparation is centralized, transportation becomes essential, and so many school systems now operate their own transportation systems. (Photo courtesy of U.S. Department of Agriculture, Food and Nutrition Service.)

VENDING

Between 1975 and 1985, the dollar sales in vending nearly doubled, from $9.3 billion to $17.6 billion. Over three-quarters (76.4 percent), or $14 billion, of that represented either food or beverages (including candy and soft drinks). Table 5.4 shows the dollar sales of items sold through vending machines. After studying the table, you may wonder whether vending is really food service. Although three-quarters of vending volume directly competes with food service, roughly 65 percent of that volume comprises just hot and cold drinks. Still, the remaining balance is $5 billion. Moreover, many people seem to be replacing one or more meals with several snacks, and so vending does compete, especially with fast food, in the snack market.

Table 5.5 compares vending sales in 1975 and in 1985. Although the dollar total for all vending is given at the bottom of the table, remember that dollar comparisons are distorted by inflation. For this reason, the detailed

TABLE 5.4 1984 Vended-Product Volume

Product	Percentage of Total	Dollar Volume (millions)
Hot drinks	7.5%	1,240
Cold drinks	40.8	6,730
Packaged confections and snacks	16.3	2,680
Bulk vending (ball gum, nuts, etc.)	1.3	188
Milk	2.1	351
Ice cream	0.5	80
Pastries	1.9	320
Hot canned foods	0.9	149
Vended food service (sandwiches, salads, etc.)	5.3	880
Cigarettes	20.4	3,370
Cigars	0.2	21
All others	2.8	458
	100.0%	$16,477

Source: *Vending Times,* "Census of the Industry," 1985.

comparisons between product groups are in *units*. Even though some product categories have dropped somewhat, the heavy sellers, cold drinks and snacks, have risen substantially, as has vended food service in general. Because of these increases and the large drop in vended cigarettes, foods and beverages continue to be the major market for vending. Notice that vended food service (sandwiches, salads, and the like) has risen by 28 percent, and the following two brief case studies suggest the competitive impact of vending within the food service field:

An office building housing some 2500 employees was built in the heart of a large city. The designers refused to incorporate a restaurant, because kitchen facilities and storerooms would take up space destined for other uses. Dishrooms and the necessary plumbing and air ducts required for a kitchen would also have added to the cost of the building.

In addition, the building's management did not feel qualified to operate its own food service and had heard that leased restaurants often took up much of the building managers' time. Finally, management felt that a restaurant would also create traffic problems at the loading dock, with the numerous deliveries and garbage and trash removal.

Although capital expense and operating complications argued against a restaurant, the designers wanted a food service available in the building as a convenience to the occupants. Consequently, they designed vending res-

TABLE 5.5   Number of Units Sold through Vending, 1975 and 1985

Item	1975	1985
Hot drinks	4,563,000,000 units	4,820,000,000 units
Cold drinks	2,920,000,000	7,310,000,000
Packaged confections and snacks	6,760,000,000	7,600,000,000
Milk	1,105,000,000	89,000,000
Ice cream	304,000,000	230,000,000
Pastries	844,000,000	725,000,000
Hot canned food	265,000,000	233,000,000
Vending food service (sandwiches, salads, etc.)	790,000,000	1,015,000,000
Cigarette packs	4,510,000,000	2,530,000,000
Total dollar sales	$9,332,000,000	$17,548,800,000

Source: Vending Times, "Census of the Industry," 1986.

taurants that would provide an ample menu selection, including not only sandwiches but also scrambled eggs, sausage, and pancakes for breakfast, and fried chicken, french fried potatoes, salisbury steak, and other traditional entrees for lunch and dinner. Although entrees such as these currently account for only 5 percent of food service vending sales, their presence constitutes an important service for the guest and, perhaps, a harbinger of future food service trends.

The food (including sandwiches, which make up some three-quarters of the vended food service sales) is prepared at the vendor's commissary. The food is delivered before the building's regular operating hours, to avoid congestion.

In another city, a professional building accommodating about 500 people opened a small table-service restaurant just off the lobby. The occupants of the building were unhappy with the quality of the operation, however, and the operator finally went out of business. Its eight employees were replaced by a vending restaurant that offered a variety of specialty sandwiches prepared in the vendor's commissary and heated for service in a microwave oven. The operation required one attendant on duty from 8:00 A.M. to 4:30 P.M. on weekdays.

Guests are rarely enthusiastic about vending restaurants, but their impersonality can be reduced by "attended vending," which provides a specially trained hostess who makes change, gives refunds, and handles complaints. Still, vending remains primarily a mechanical, self-service process.

On the positive side, vending restaurants are convenient, can solve economic and operational problems for building and plant managers, and can increase food service variety. Most food service vending operations are found in public buildings, plants, factories, and offices, in which the clientele is too small to justify a full-fledged food service operation and too far from other restaurant facilities for the employees to reach them easily on their lunch hours.

The variety of products that vendors sell is growing and improving. Nearly one-half of the companies offering vended food services have their own commissaries, and their vending outlets usually are equipped with microwave ovens. In 1984, nearly 86 percent of vending food service companies operated microwave ovens in their accounts, and 305,000 of these units were in operation in conjunction with food service vending.

Most vending sales are in the B and I segment: over half (57 percent) in factories, 18 percent in office locations, and 8 percent in government, military, and other public locations. Colleges and universities accounted for 10 percent of sales, and grade and high schools accounted for 2 percent. Health care provided only 4 percent of vending sales.[21]

Vending has clearly become part of the "eating" market, as defined in Chapter 2, rather than the dining market. Vending companies have found that if they offer *manual vending* (that is, a cafeteria staffed by "real, live" people) during some of their hours of service, all of their products are more likely to be accepted. One vendor speculated that this is true because the personal touch allows the guests to associate the vended food with the people who provide food services in the more traditional cafeterias.

Vending offers the hospitality industry a means of extending food service hours to meet the convenience of guests, and to provide acceptable service where it would be economically impossible to provide full manual food service. Sanitation in vending is important and can be troublesome. And the rejection of vending is likely to continue. Nevertheless, this component of food service, now serving $5 billion worth of food in direct competition with restaurant meals and more than $7 billion more in snacks and drinks, should not be ignored by either the food service student or the operator.

WHO OPERATES AN INSTITUTION'S FOOD SERVICE?

Now that we have discussed the clientele served by institutional food services, we can examine the arguments for and against the use of contract companies or institutional in-house food services. The principal arguments involve (1) economies of scale, (2) control of operations, and (3) management expertise.

[21]"Census of the Industry," *Vending Times,* July 1986, p. 50.

RESPONSIBILITY FOR INSTITUTIONAL OPERATIONS

Many institutions see no need to pay the overhead and profits of a contract company. Operating on the assumption that their own employees can manage as efficiently as a contract company can, these institutions choose to keep the overhead and profit they otherwise would have to pay to an outside company. These institutions can control their operations, and to some extent they can limit the staff turnover traditionally associated with contract companies, who frequently promote or transfer their employees. "If we like a person," said one university official, "we might lose him to a contract company. In our own operation, if we treat him right we have a good chance of keeping him—of maintaining staff stability."

Institutional Operators

The magazine *Restaurant & Institutions* publishes a study of large organizations in food service called the "400," which reports on the 400 largest hospitality operators in the United States. Each year, the 400 lists roughly 50 institutional operators in this group of largest organizations, including several health-care institutions, state universities or university systems, and numerous public agencies.

Contract Companies

Each year, 25 to 30 of the 400 largest U.S. food service organizations are contract companies, according to the annual *Restaurant & Institutions* "400." A contract company provides an institution with two kinds of managers: the unit manager and the regional and district managers who train, evaluate, and supervise the unit manager's work and ensure management continuity.

Another important service that contract companies offer is centralized purchasing. ARA Food Service listed some typical savings that it achieved:

- A purveyor change made in central Texas that saved the company and its clients $104,000 a year.
- Negotiations with dairy suppliers in the same central Texas market that resulted in annual savings of $90,000.
- An audit of a supplier's books (impractical and too expensive for a smaller operation) that resulted in determining and recovering overbillings of $13,500.
- Consolidation of the purchases of several different accounts into one account that saved $30,000.

Because ARA negotiates on a national scale, for example, for its coffee purchases and because the consolidated purchases for the firm annually run to 18 or 20 million pounds, ARA can ensure price stability for three to six months as well as minimum costs consistent with market conditions.

Contract companies also offer to their clients, at cost, extensive facilities planning services. These services include operational design (equipment), interior design, procurement, supervision of construction, and equipment installation. Specialized accounting and market planning services may also be offered to clients.

Many companies have developed specialized marketing techniques adapted to the needs of individual institutions. Thus, for instance, Ogden Food Services has developed a fast-food variation of their Nedick's hot dog, sandwich, and orange-drink operation to meet college student's preference for economy and speed.

CONTRAST IN CONTRACT COMPANY AND INSTITUTIONAL BENEFITS TO EXECUTIVES

A survey by *Institutions/Volume Feeding* magazine revealed market differences in the operating style of contract companies and institutional operators. That survey found that institutional management people felt a higher degree of job security and less of the "intense and unrelenting pressure to achieve continuously higher performance levels" evident among commercial chain executives. On the other hand, institutional executives reported frustration at being just one department in a large organization in which organizational politics play an important role in determining policy and in which decisions affecting the food service operation may be made at a higher organizational level.

Table 5.6 summarizes the different aspects of compensation emphasized in the commercial and noncommercial sectors. Although pay was somewhat lower in the noncommercial operation (38 percent of noncommercial managers earned more than $20,000, compared with 59 percent of commercial

TABLE 5.6 Fringe Benefits among Food Service Operations

Fringe Benefit	Percentage of Those Offering Benefit	
	Commercial	Noncommercial
Pension plan	25%	75%
Medical insurance	65	80
Other insurance	44	46
Living accommodations	5	15
Cash bonus	25	5
Profit sharing	28	9
Stock option	12	4
Company car	38	4

Source: Institutions/Volume Feeding, Cahners Publishing.

operators), the fringe benefits were better in the noncommercial sector. Those emphasizing monetary reward for performance were, as expected, better for many of the commercial executives.

OTHER INSTITUTIONAL FOOD SERVICE SEGMENTS

Two other food service segments, military food service and in-flight and transportation food service, deserve mention here to round out your picture of the institutional market. Both offer career opportunities and often a chance to travel.

MILITARY FOOD SERVICE

Fourteen of the *Restaurant & Institutions* "400" are military food service groups. As listed in Table 5.7, these groups fall into four categories: military food service; post and base exchange food service organizations; military officers', noncommissioned officers', and enlisted soldiers' clubs; and military health-care units. All four groups employ both civilians and military commissioned and noncommissioned personnel. For information on careers in this area, of course, you need go no farther than your local armed forces recruiter.

IN-FLIGHT FOOD SERVICE

Perhaps we should have called this section "Transportation Food Service" because Table 5.8 does include one railroad company, Amtrak, but the real center of gravity in this segment is the airlines. Seven airlines plus Amtrak are among 400 largest hospitality firms. A number of companies also have in-flight food service divisions, operating as contract caterers. The companies listed in the table, however, are much like institutional operators.

The airline food service business is fast paced and requires people who work well under pressure. The uncertain number of passengers on an outbound flight, sudden cancellations or additions to the airlines' schedule of flights, and the various equipment configurations used in different aircraft make in-flight food service a challenging field. And some carriers offer free or reduced-price travel as a fringe benefit.

THE FUTURE OF INSTITUTIONAL FOOD SERVICE

The forces working in the restaurant business discussed in Chapter 4 will affect institutional food service as well. Trends in the restaurant sector can be expected to influence institutions, as fast food already has. Contract companies will continue to offer the greatest benefits to the smaller institutions,

TABLE 5.7 U.S. Military Food Service

R&I "400" Rank	Agency	Dollar Volume[a] (millions)	Number of Units
23	U.S. Navy	$852.4	666
28	U.S. Army	676.6	1,089
37	U.S. Army Clubs and Recreation	518.9	1,116
46	Army and Air Force Exchange Service	428.2	2,773
49	U.S. Air Force Open Mess System	412.5	502
55	U.S. Air Force	323.7	639
79	U.S. Navy Officer and Enlisted Mess System	218.5	267
80	U.S. Marine Corps.	214.9	199
120	Navy Resale System	136.4	537
222	U.S. Coast Guard	59.6	388
247	U.S. Marine Corps. Club System	51.0	163
285	U.S. Army Medical Dept.	45.0	51
369	U.S. Air Force Medical Service	32.6	82
387	U.S. Navy Medical Command	30.3	27

Source: Restaurants & Institutions, July 9, 1986.
[a]Estimated equivalent to commercial sales volume established by *Restaurants & Institutions.*

TABLE 5.8 In-flight and Other Transportation Food Services

R&I "400" Rank	Company	Sales[a] (millions of dollars)
65	Pan American World Airways	$258.2
66	Eastern Airlines, Inc.	253.1
72	Delta Air Lines	230.0
98	Trans World Airlines	173.2
130	Northwest Orient Airlines	119.0
244	Republic	51.0
337	Amtrak	35.0

Source: Restaurants & Institutions.
[a]Commercial equivalent estimated by *Restaurant & Institutions.*

but most of the larger institutions likely will continue to feel that they can achieve adequate economies without outside help. Moreover, institutions of all sizes will continue to believe that institutional control of the food service operation can be facilitated by direct control.

The force of consumerism will be felt in those institutions in which food service systems account not for an occasional meal but for 25 percent or more of a guest's nutritional intake.

SUMMARY

First in this chapter we compared institutional and commercial food services. Even though institutional food service is considered a "captive market," it is good business to please both the client (the institution) and the guests.

We then differentiated contract companies and institutional operations and examined each. Institutional food service has four major divisions: business and industry, college and university, health care, and school and community. In regard to business and industry, we discussed the introduction of fast-food and contract companies in factories and companies. We talked about the various ways that colleges and universities feed their students: the different kinds of board plans and the ways of attracting students to and keeping them in the plans. In health-care food service, we described the dietetic professionals: clinical dietitians, dietetic technicians, and dietetic managers. We then reviewed the dietetic department organization and the trends in the health-care food service—how dietetic departments are trying to help hospitals stay solvent. We next discussed school and community food service. First, we related the reasons for the establishment of a national school lunch program, including the increasing participation of women in the labor force and the concern for poor children. We described the school food service itself and the outlook for its future. Turning to food service programs for the aging, we found that the main reasons for their popularity are the greater number of elderly people in our society and the many living below the poverty level.

In our discussion of preparation systems, we described three: conventional food service systems, the most common, which prepares food from scratch; ready food operations, in which one crew prepares the food and another reconstitutes and serves it; and convenience food systems, which uses foods provided by food manufacturers.

We then examined vending systems: what they vend, how they are received, and how they will fare in the future.

Our next topic was the operation of institutional food services.

We also considered the arguments for and against contract companies and institutional in-house operations.

In closing, we outlined the other institutional food services: military food service and in-flight and transportation food service. We ended with a brief look at the future of institutional food services.

KEY WORDS AND CONCEPTS

To help you review this chapter, keep in mind the following:

Contract companies

Institutional operations

Dietitians

Dietetic technicians

Dietetic managers

Congregate meals

Conventional food service system

Ready food service system

Convenience food service system

Vending

REVIEW QUESTIONS

1. What are some of the differences between commercial restaurants and institutional food services?

2. What is the difference between contract companies and institutional food services?

3. What are the four divisions of institutional food services?

4. What are the different kinds of dietetic professionals, and what do they do?

5. How have dieticians' roles changed?

6. How has the greater participation of women in the labor force changed the school food service and care for the elderly?

7. Outline the congregate meals program for the elderly.

8. Is vended food service popular with its customers? Why or why not?

9. What are the other institutional food services?

P A R T 3

LODGING

Hotels and motels are big business—and a career field that is attractive to many students. The next four chapters will describe the lodging business from several points of view.

In Chapter 6 we will look briefly at the history of lodging and then shift our attention to the ways that hotels and motels meet various needs of guests and those of the community. Several types of location are discussed. The chapter ends with a look at the importance of franchising in lodging.

Chapter 7 describes the major departments of a hotel and discusses how they function, focuses briefly on financial measures used to assess hotel operations, and, finally, considers career possibilities in several areas of lodging.

Chapter 8 recognizes that the revolution technology is working in lodging. We will examine the vital role the computer is playing in the front office, security, and energy management. We will also look briefly at an exciting new service many hotels are offering: videoconferencing. The chapter concludes with a look at the "smart guest room."

In Chapter 9 our concern is the forces that are changing lodging. These include the economics of the hotel business and the factors that shape the hotel investment decision, and the management companies that serve hotel properties. The chapter—and this section of the text—concludes with a brief look at the outlook for the lodging industry.

THE HOTEL AND MOTEL BUSINESS

THE PURPOSE OF THIS CHAPTER

The best way to understand the major kinds of lodging firms is to see them in the light of changing travel patterns and consumer needs. This chapter stresses the uses to which lodging is put by travelers and the surrounding community. This emphasis provides you with a view of the functions performed by this component of the hospitality industry. Franchise systems also provide important services to the consumer. Accordingly, this chapter discusses franchise operations in some detail.

THIS CHAPTER SHOULD HELP YOU

1. Relate changing patterns in the hotel-motel business to changing transportation patterns and changing needs of customers.

2. Discuss the economic forces and cost patterns that helped the motels challenge the hotels and then helped the motor hotel challenge the motel.

3. Categorize the hotel-motel market by location, service mix, and function or use for the traveler.

4. Understand the economic and social functions of lodging in a community.

5. Become acquainted with the role of franchise systems in lodging today.

Arthur Hailey's novel *Hotel,* written in the early 1960s, described a kind of hotel that even then was passing from the scene—a "grand old lady," an independently owned hotel staffed by old-timers who all seemed to have some personal bond with the aristocratic owner, Warren Trent. The wheeler dealer who finally displaced Trent was a none-too-thinly disguised portrait of an actual hotel tycoon who, in those days, made a practice of acquiring old properties and modernizing both their physical plants and their operating organizations. But if Hailey's novel addressed change in the hotel business, it covered only a small part of that change. Modernization now means much more than the mere sprucing up that Mr. O'Keefe, the hotel tycoon, planned for Hailey's St. Gregory Hotel.

Professional lodging has always followed the patterns of transportation of its time: caravansaries, inns along the Roman roads, post houses, and so forth. It has responded, too, to changes in destination patterns. Toward the end of the nineteenth century, North American hotels grew up to serve the rail traveler. Often, the hotel was physically connected to the railroad station. A few of these hotels still survive, and some, such as Toronto's Royal York, remain thriving centers. Of the hotels built during the first half of this century, those not physically connected to the railroad station were usually convenient to it and to the major destinations in the downtown sections of cities. Indeed, there may be a revival of this pattern if there is also a revival of rail travel, with the high-speed rail corridors proposed for the 1990s.

THE EVOLUTION OF LODGING

The two principal determinants of hotel location, transportation system and destination, changed in the great period of economic expansion that followed World War II. As a result, several waves of hotel and motel building have changed the face of American innkeeping.

THE MOTEL

Although a few "Mo Hotels," or motels, were to be found in the Southwest even in the late 1920s, and "tourist courts" began to appear in the 1930s, the big wave of motel building followed World War II.

The end of the war released a pent-up demand for automobiles. During the 1930s, depressed economic conditions prevented many people from buying a car; then during the war, automotive production concentrated on military needs. The explosive growth in auto travel that followed the end of the war brought people into the travel market, as both buyers and sellers.

The first motels were small, simple affairs, with commonly under 20 units (or guest rooms). These properties lacked the complex facilities of a hotel and were generally managed by resident owners with a few paid employees.

They were built at the edge of town, where land costs were substantially lower than those downtown. The single-story construction that typified motels until the late 1950s (and even the two-story pattern of later motor hotels) offered significant construction economies, compared with the downtown high-rise properties built on prime real estate. Capital costs represent the largest single cost in many lodging establishments, and so the lower land and building costs and the lower capital costs that resulted gave motels significant advantages. These savings could be, and generally were, passed on to the guests in the form of lower rates.

Probably more important, motels offered a location convenient to the highway. Because the typical guest traveled by car, he or she could drive downtown, returning to the accommodations in the evening. Meanwhile, inexperienced travelers, who had always been put off by the formality of hotels, with their dressy room clerks, bellhops who had to be tipped, and ornate lobbies, preferred the informal atmosphere of the motel, a "come as you are" atmosphere in terms of both dress and social preferences. In the motel they might be greeted by the owner working the front desk. Motel operators were proud of their informality. The personal touch they offered guests and the motel's convenience and lower prices were their stock in trade. Few motel operators had formal training, and many would gladly tell one and all that their lack of professional training was the very secret of their success.

THE MOTOR HOTEL

For a few years, it appeared that hotels (in general, the relatively large downtown properties) and motels (usually the small properties located at the edge of town) would battle for the new mobile tourist market. Unhappily for both the hotel and the mom-and-pop motel, the situation was not that simple.

In 1952, Kemmons Wilson, a Memphis home building and real estate developer, took his family on a vacation trip. He was depressed by the dearth of accommodations to meet his family's and the business traveler's needs. He returned to Memphis with a vision of a new kind of motel property that combined the advantage of a hotel's broad range of services with a motel's convenience to the auto traveler. That insight revolutionized the lodging industry.

Motels became larger and began to offer a wider range of services. Dining rooms or coffee shops, cocktail lounges, and meeting rooms appealed to the business traveler. Swimming pools became essential to the touring family. Room telephones, usually present in hotels but generally absent in motels, became the rule in motor hotels, thus requiring a switchboard and someone to operate it. Whereas hotels and motels once had offered coin-operated radios and television sets, free television and then free color television became the rule.

In 1953, the first Holiday Inn, with 100 rooms, opened. Today, 1624 inns and many innovations later, Holiday Inn operates approximately 317,506 rooms in over 50 countries and territories, and its format has been adopted by many other successful motor-hotel chains and franchise groups.

Although there were experiments with smaller inns having 50 to 75 rooms, most lodging companies determined that generally a 100-unit facility was the smallest that made economic sense. That size permitted full utilization of the minimum operating staff and provided a sufficient sales size to amortize the investment in such supportive services as pools and restaurants.

THE AIRPORT MOTOR HOTEL

In the 1950s and 1960s, as air travel became more and more common, a new kind of property appeared, designed especially to accommodate air travelers. Even though these travelers arrive by air, they rent cars often enough to justify a lodging design similar to that of the motor hotel. Thus, the principal distinction of the airport property is its location. Airport motor hotels tend to emphasize their small- to medium-sized meeting-room capacities, because of the preponderance of business meetings at these properties.

THE DOWNTOWN HOTEL

Although the older downtown hotels faced new competition on the edge of town, new properties in the downtown market areas were fairly scarce because of changes in the transportation system and traveler destinations.

At about the same time that U.S. cities began their urban renewal, the interstate highway system began to penetrate the downtown areas. The downtown renewal area, with its new office and shopping complexes, often revived interest in hotel construction designed to serve these new destinations. Urban renewal, coupled with the limited-access interstate highways, opened up the city to the nation's highway travelers.

Downtown properties have many advantages. They are near the large office complexes and retail stores: by day they are near business destinations, and by night they are close to many of the large city's entertainment centers. Although the downtown property generally depends less on "off-the-road" travelers than do the motor hotels, their guests arrive often enough by automobile (and use rented cars often enough) to justify ample facilities for automobiles. These facilities commonly include a motor entrance, a waiting area often called the motor lobby, and on-premises parking accessible to a guest without any assistance from (and tips for) the hotel staff. In fact, many older downtown properties have been remodeled to include most of these facilities. Though on-premises parking has not always

Hotels such as Western International's Bonaventure in Los Angeles mark the resurgence of the downtown hotel in the 1970s and 1980s. (Photo by Alexandre Georges.)

been feasible, reasonably convenient off-premises parking, with valet service to pick up and drive the car, is common. Thus, although not all downtown properties include the words title motor hotel in their name, nearly all first-class downtown properties offer the services associated with them.

There are, of course, many other ways to classify hotels and motor hotels, by location for instance:

Downtown.   Central business district in a city of 50,000 or more.

Midtown.   Central city shopping or office area other than central business district in a city of 50,000 or more.

Suburban.   In a suburban or on the fringe of a city of 50,000 or more.

Airport.   On or contiguous to a commercial airport property.

Small Town.   Anywhere in a town under 50,000.

Roadside.   On a federal, state, or local highway but not in any of the above locations.

The Hotel Bonaventure's architect, John Portman, has become famous for developing fascinating interior play spaces in the centers of cities. (Photo by Alexandre Georges.)

Resort.   Virtually all motor hotels today have recreational, entertainment, or leisure attractions, but a "resort" is defined as one that is also a destination for travelers as opposed to an enroute overnight location.[1]

Temple also offered us three functional definitions:

Basic.   A motor hotel mainly dependent on room business. It would have a smaller than average commercial area with only one dining room (fewer than 100 seats) and one lounge.

[1]J. B. Temple, "Marketing for Motor Hotels," *Lodging,* June 1976, p. 26.

Standard.   A motor hotel dependent on a mix of rooms business, meetings, and food and beverage operations. It would have an average size commercial area, dining accommodations with more than 100 seats and meeting facilities for at least 100 people.

Complex.   A motor hotel with a large commercial area, multiple dining rooms, and accommodations for large meetings.[2]

Categories of hotels and motels are not just academic abstractions. These categories tell us something about the properties' economic and social function—what the guest uses them for. This is vital information to any manager who realizes that it is the customer with needs and interests who ultimately determines value and, therefore, operating format and procedure. Before we leave this subject, then, let us look at hotels and motels not by type of location but in terms of use.

THE USES OF LODGINGS

All lodgings have some functions in common: shelter for the night and food and drink either on the premises or nearby. Different travel purposes, however, create different guest needs.

THE BUSINESS TRAVELER AND THE TRANSIENT PROPERTY

The backbone of most hotels' business is the business traveler. Each hotel's proportion of business travelers varies, of course, and also varies seasonally; for example, hotels usually have more tourists in the summer. This proportion also changes in the national market from year to year and according to a number of factors, including the business cycle. For example, in good times, there is more business travel, and during recessions, travel budgets are cut.

In a witty article in the *Cornell Hotel and Restaurant Administration Quarterly* entitled "How Architects Design Rooms Differently," a hotel architect, Morris Lapidus, emphasized practicality and comfort: "a no-nonsense room [has] some touch of luxury so that [a guest] feels that even though he's deprived of the pleasures of home, hearth, and fire he still has adequate working area where he can make his notes and get himself collected." Lapidus recommended giving the business guest convenience so that he can relax, and "enough psychological compensations to make up for his isolation."[3]

[2]Temple, "Marketing for Motor Hotels," p. 26.
[3]Morris Lapidus, "How Architects Design Rooms Differently," *Cornell Hotel and Restaurant Administration Quarterly,* May 1974, p. 69.

Grand hotels, such as Loew's Anatole Hotel in Dallas pictured here, provide a ceremonial setting that helps symbolize the importance of convention events. (Photo courtesy of Loew's Hotels.)

THE CONVENTION TRAVELER AND THE CONVENTION HOTEL

Most convention hotels attract ordinary business travelers as well, and so these two markets are often linked in travel statistics. Lapidus provided an interesting and colorful description of the convention hotel and its function:

> The convention hotel is a new form of American hybrid. All of us are familiar with the great American convention, where an organization or corporation

Large function rooms, like this one, are necessary to serve the general sessions of large organizations. The Grand Ballroom at the Mayflower Hotel in Washington, D.C., offers a sumptuous setting for organizations to honor their top brass and impress their members. (Photo courtesy of the Mayflower Hotel.)

gathers as many members as it can in one particular place and fills up a horrendous agenda with lectures, meetings, group discussions, film shows, workshops and lots of drinking. The main reason for all this endeavor is to conduct a forum for ideas, to keep members apprised of what the parent organization has been doing, and to get everybody's idea of where they are going and how they should get there. It is also a nifty tax write-off.

The convention hotel should be a ceremonial hotel, so far as meeting areas are concerned. This is the place where the "tribe" honors the chiefs, hands out the awards to diligent warriors, and welcomes the initiates. The organization's brass must look and sound good on the platform at meetings and banquets. The warriors—and the warriors' wives when present—should

The convention hotel must have supersuites "for the chiefs," as Lapidus put it, such as the one shown here, from New York's Waldork Astoria. (Photo courtesy of Hilton Hotels.)

be equally seated and treated. And the novitiates, for whom it is an honor just to be there, must have an opportunity to feel part of the inner circle.

The convention hotel must also have supersuites for the chiefs and many comfortable but similar rooms for the warriors. The novitiates may be housed more economically although this is seldom the case. They may share rooms and not be permitted to bring along their wives until they're full-fledged warriors.[4]

Lapidus also observed that the guest rooms at conventions are often social centers where friends or business associates come for a drink or an informal meeting. These rooms thus should be spacious and should separate the dressing area from the living quarters. The best arrangement, Lapidus declared, is to provide one double bed and a couch that can become a second double bed in larger rooms. Of course, there is a need for more modest single rooms for "warriors and novitiates," to use his analogy.

[4]Lapidus, "How Architects Design Rooms Differently," p. 69.

Las Vegas's MGM Grand offers a wide variety of entertainments, including gambling, extensive sports facilities, a movie theater, and several restaurants. (Photo courtesy of MGM Grand.)

THE TOURIST MARKET

Many motor hotels, particularly those serving highway locations, accommodate traveling families in the tourist season. During this period, rooms can be rented to three or six people or more, at higher rates (and higher food and beverage sales). To serve this market, a room with two double beds and room for a rollaway is essential. (The same room can be rented as a single, and often at a lower rate, to business travelers during the rest of the year.) Because the traveling family is more price sensitive than is the business traveler, luxury in the room itself is distinctly secondary and luxury in the overall plant (size of swimming pool, luxury food service facilities) is not usually emphasized in these properties.

MIX OF USES

Obviously, no *convention hotel* refuses individual guests or families. Nor would a *transient property* turn down a *destination visitor*. As a practical

The MGM Grand offers opulent suites to "high rollers"—and to any others who are disposed to pay for luxury. (Photo courtesy of MGM Grand.)

matter, none of these categories is perfect; they just suit our need to describe some of the principal functions of hotels. Most properties draw their guests from all segments of the market during the year.

RESORT HOTELS

A transient property is where a guest arrives tired in the evening and leaves the next morning. A destination property, on the other hand, invites a guest to spend as much as a week or more and provides the extensive leisure facilities a vacationer expects. Accordingly, most resort guests are willing to pay higher rates for these services.

Some destination resorts offer a mix of activities suited to the sports enthusiast. The Homestead in Hot Springs, Virginia, for instance, offers in its advertising

horseback riding, woodland walking, trout fishing, mineral spa, swimming, three 18-hole championship golf courses, tennis, buckboard and surrey driving, skeet and trap shooting, ten pin and lawn bowling, loafing, and skiing.

Budget hotels generally have smaller commercial buildings. A Days Inn, pictured here, offers cut-rate gasoline as an "extra" economy service. (Photo courtesy of Days Inns.)

And the Greenbrier in White Sulphur Springs, West Virginia, describes itself as "a 6,500-acre estate secluded in the beautiful Alleghenies." In addition to sports, the Greenbrier, like most such "adult resorts," offers extensive meeting and convention facilities.

> The new conference center includes ballrooms, auditoriums, theatre, exhibit hall and 25 meeting rooms fully equipped with the latest audio-visual equipment. Capable of serving groups of 10 to 1,100.

A quite different kind of "adult destination" (where, as in the Homestead and the Greenbrier, children are always welcome) is found in Las Vegas, the number-one hotel city in terms of hotel sales. Las Vegas is famous for its gambling, but its resort hotels offer much more (including, sometimes, features for the children). For example, the Las Vegas Hilton advertises itself as the place

> where the real superstars play in Las Vegas. Now the largest, most complete resort in the world. Incredible dining in eight unsurpassed restaurants, including the spectacular Japanese Fantasyland, Benihana Village! Plus an 8½ acre outdoor recreation deck and even a unique "youth hotel" for the youngsters alone.

These adult-centered resort hotels do, of course, welcome children, but other complexes are designed primarily with the family, and especially children, in mind. The most famous of these is Walt Disney World (WDW). Although the resorts we described include many other activities, we can properly say that at WDW, several hotels are integrated within a larger entertainment center. That center includes not only the theme park for which WDW is best known but also all varieties of water sports on a large lake, a sophisticated campground sporting its own entertainment centers, three golf courses, and the customary amenities and luxuries available at each hotel. In contrast with WDW, the increasingly common regional theme parks do not create as much demand for hotel accommodations because they serve guests who come from within a reasonable driving distance of their homes.

LODGING AS A COMMUNITY INSTITUTION

You may have seen the following slogan behind the counter in some business:

This is a nonprofit business. We didn't plan it that way; it just happened!

To a greater degree than in many other industries, that not-so-funny joke applies to hotels and motor hotels, except that the meager profits may not be all that unexpected. To see why, we need to shift our attention from the purposes of the individual guest to those of the community.

In many small towns, the hotel or motel is more or less a public institution. It is a gathering place for local leaders and provides hospitality for visitors to the city's principal businesses. Because of these community benefits, some small-town hotels have been built more or less as nonprofit operations, with both ownership and even capital lent without any real expectations of overwhelming profit. The benefits to the community—and to its principal institutions—are seen as sufficient to offset a lack of profit. Such resignation as this may not be the rule, but it is far from uncommon.

In practice, however, most hotel operators discover that an unprofitable hotel is also an unsuccessful hotel. Over the long haul, the need for operating subsidies, or the simple absence of sufficient financial return, makes the property lose its luster and then become downright unattractive. Eventually the owners grow reluctant to pay adequate executive salaries and to spend the funds necessary to maintain the physical plant. Gradually the plant decays, the organization loses its enthusiasm, and the hotel closes its doors.

The community need for hotel services, however, often leads real estate developers to promote hotels as a part of real estate developments in large cities. A developer acquires the rights to a large tract of land and plans a complex of office buildings, department stores, and other retail establishments. The development may be situated downtown; it may work with urban redevelopment; or it may settle at the edge of the city as part of an office

park or an industrial park consisting of offices, light manufacturing, or ware-
housing and distribution centers. Although the development's overt purpose
is suggested by its title (urban redevelopment, office park, industrial park),
one of the first buildings to go up will probably be a hotel or motor hotel.
The developers hope, of course, that it will earn a profit, but they build it
mainly because of its importance to the overall development.

The developer may not be particularly interested in entering the hotel
field, but the development surely needs the hotel.[5] Visitors with business in
the area need a place to stay. Headquarters units need space for sales meetings and other technical conferences. Those with offices or who are otherwise working in the area need a place to eat lunch, get a snack, meet for a
drink, and perhaps entertain out-of-town guests at dinner at the end of the
day.

Most development projects are preceded by a feasibility study of the
project's economics. Two extracts from such feasibility studies, conducted
in a medium-sized city (Middleton) in a basically rural area and a large metropolitan center (Bigton), suggest some of the developer's underlying motives. (Because these are confidential documents, the identity of the cities
has been disguised.)

> [This is] one of a series of studies dealing with the proposed Middleton
> Square developments in the Washington Street Urban Renewal Project area in
> Middleton.
>
> The urban renewal area covers six city blocks between the existing downtown
> area and the shore of Lake Washington. The proposed Middleton Square
> development contemplates a comprehensive, integrated development of new
> office structures (one of which is already under construction), adequate
> automobile parking, a full range of retail facilities including a major full-line
> department store, and the 300-room hotel which is the subject of this analysis.
> All of these facilities are expected to upgrade and modernize Downtown
> Middleton.

In a study conducted in a Bigton hotel development under consideration, the
following information came under the heading of "Impact and Location":

> A new, large, and spectacularly designed hotel in Downtown Bigton would
> have a significant impact on Bigton. Properly promoted, the proposed hotel
> would not only focus more attention on Bigton as one of the nation's great

---

[5]To this point, we have been concerned with various types of lodging establishments—hotels, motels, motor hotels, budget motels, and others. Accordingly, we have used the fullest,
most specific designation we could. From this point on and in the next chapter, however,
we will be concerned with transient lodging in general. To be brief, we will use the word
hotel to describe the lodging establishment in general, although occasionally, we will revert
to the fuller description for emphasis.

metropolitan centers, but the hotel would also substantially improve the inventory of transient lodging accommodations in the downtown area, and thereby strengthen that area's competitive position in the lodging market. If the hotel is as successful as predicted in this analysis, it will attract comparable competition to the downtown area—further reinforcing that area's position in the local lodging market.

The function of a hotel property, then, sometimes involves what economists call *externalities*—benefits external to the hotel itself, such as community development, the enhancement of property values in the area in general, and service to people who need food and lodging and would not visit the area without them. It's hardly surprising, then, that many new hotel properties have financial difficulties. This is particularly true for properties built during waves of real estate speculation such as those that occurred in the late 1920s, the early 1970s, and the mid-1980s. For sophisticated hotel operators, however, this kind of situation creates real opportunities.

FRANCHISE SYSTEMS

The word *franchise* comes from the language of political science and refers to a right bestowed by some authority. For example, when Kemmons Wilson created a successful operating format for a motor hotel, he began to *enfranchise* others with the right to use Holiday Inn's name. To do this, he adopted a practice similar to the *referral groups* already in existence and operated mainly by Quality Courts and Best Western Motels,[6] (now Quality Inns and Best Western). At that time, as now, the franchiser provided the use of a name and some managerial and technical know-how. In the motor-hotel field, however, the role of the franchising company was crucial.

A NATIONAL IDENTITY AND BRAND NAME

In a market of national travelers, the identity of the individual property has little meaning except to the local townspeople and its frequent visitors. On the other hand, "Hilton Inn," "Sheraton Inn," or "Holiday Inn" convey meaning to travelers from any part of the nation. To these travelers, the mere mention of these names suggests the kind, degree, and probable cost of the services available.

National franchising companies spend portions of their own budgets on advertising in appropriate regional markets and in the national market. Most

---

[6]There is an important technical difference between a *franchise system* (in which the franchising company grants a right) and a *referral system* (in which a property and its ownership become members). There is not a great deal of difference, however, in how they operate, though the referral group is sometimes characterized by greater owner autonomy. For our purpose, the word *system* will denote either kind of operation.

One of the major benefits that a franchise company offers is a nationally advertised brand name. (Photos courtesy of Sheraton Hotels and Days Inns.)

franchise systems also levy an advertising fee on each franchisee and pool these funds. Thus, the collective advertising fund makes it possible to purchase ads too expensive for an individual property. These include such media efforts as commercials on national radio and television and layouts in national magazines.

Franchise hotel–motel companies also print national directories showing the location of each of the system's properties. Perhaps the most important services that franchisers offer the guest—and therefore, the operator—are referral systems and quality assurance programs.

REFERRAL SYSTEMS

When a guest wants to make a reservation, he or she can call a single number and either have a reservation at a distant point confirmed immediately or obtain help in locating alternative accommodations. Once the guest begins a trip, accommodations for subsequent nights' stops are only as far away as the room telephone. Thus, once a hotel system has a guest's patronage for a single night, it is in a position to sell the guest all subsequent accommodations. Moreover, most referral or reservations systems are either computer based or use a WATS (Wide Area Telephone System) line. WATS systems permit leasing of telephone lines, which drastically reduces the cost per call for high-volume use.

The first successful computerized reservations system was Holiday Inn's Holidex. Each inn has a terminal connected to a central computer by telephone wires. For each day of the year the local innkeeper "deposits" a certain number of rooms of each type available. The computer acts as a kind of "bank" or clearinghouse for all Holiday Inns. The computer sells all rooms "on deposit" for the day in question without consulting the inn in which the reservation is made. As each room is sold, the inn is notified of the guest's name, the type of room wanted, and other information (arrival time and so on). This information is then used to make up a reservation card for the arriving guest.

If the local innkeeper must increase or decrease the number of rooms available for a given day, or stop taking reservations entirely for that day, he or she sends a simple message through the inn's terminal to the central computer, which alters, as instructed, the number of rooms available. At the end of each month, the innkeeper receives a report of sales refused and can use this as a basis for planning sales strategies and front-desk procedures or for constructing additional rooms, if the demand is present.

Some chains rely solely on a WATS reservation system. Callers call an 800 number (at no charge to them) that reaches a central reservation office. Using leased WATS lines to reach the receiving property, that office then calls the property and secures a reservation, if possible, and confirms it for the guest. (Some WATS systems also use computers and "deposit" rooms in a way similar to the Holidex system, except that terminals are not present in all properties.) With either a WATS line or a computer-based system, an effort is made to accommodate the guest in a nearby property in the system if the guest's first preference is not available.

Many large systems use both a computer reservation system and WATS lines, and the largest systems supplement these with regional sales offices. Some smaller systems use teletype or telephones when the reservation volume does not warrant the high fixed cost of a computer or a WATS line.

INSPECTION SYSTEMS: QUALITY ASSURANCE

Almost all franchise and referral groups specify a minimum level of physical plant and service requirements before admitting a new operation to the system. These requirements generally include a restaurant, a swimming pool, certain types of furniture and fixtures, and such operating services as room service and a 24-hour front desk.

In addition to specifying operating standards, a system usually enforces

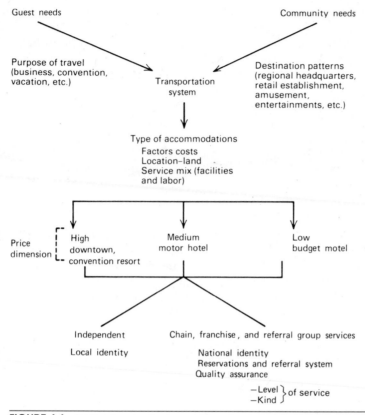

FIGURE 6.1   Determinants of value and function in hotels, motor hotels, and motels.

the maintenance of these standards through regular inspections made by either the systems inspection department or an established member of the system. The detail and care devoted to quality assurance by the modern motor hotel system is based on chain or referral group inspection systems.

DETERMINING HOTELS' VALUE AND FUNCTION

In this chapter, we described the evolution of the accommodations industry since the end of World War II, emphasizing the guest's needs and wishes and the community's needs as causes for this evolution. We must now organize these needs and this evolution into a clear pattern.

Figure 6.1 coordinates the demand for accommodations (at the top of the figure) with the guest's needs. These needs include the purpose of travel and the needs of the community, based on the community's destination patterns. The interaction between the accommodation needs of the individual and those of the community is shaped by the transportation system available in the community. Destinations become significant only if they can be reached.

Thus defined, purpose dictates accommodation type, and these types are further affected by the costs of making services available. These costs are determined principally by location and land value as well as by the *service mix*. The service mix refers to the relative elaborateness or simplicity of the facilities and the labor they require to render their services.

Because capital and operating costs, and hence rates, increase more rapidly than does the price level in general, new marketing strategies emphasize upgrading amenities.

Whether their rates are high, medium, or low, accommodations commonly participate in franchise and referral groups adhering to a common identity and providing the traveler with the convenience of a reservation system and the assurances of a certain level and kind of service. In many markets, however, independents with a strong local identity remain important.

Although the model of Figure 6.1 is neither precise nor predictive, it does help trace cause and effect as they interact to determine the functions and resulting service profiles of hotels, motor hotels, and motels.

SUMMARY

We began this chapter by relating the history of lodging, leading up to the introduction of motels and then motor hotels and airport motor hotels. We also discussed downtown hotels.

We then outlined the uses of lodging by transient business travelers, convention travelers, and tourists and described the differences in the hotels targeted to them. We also looked at resort hotels and how they differ from other kinds of hotels.

Lodging as a community institution was our next topic. This included a discussion of why a community needs hotels and why they may be built, even though they may not make any money and, indeed, may even lose money.

We also again considered franchise systems and the advantages of having a national identity and a brand name. In our description of making reservations in a franchise system, we explained referral systems. We briefly discussed inspection systems as well.

Lastly, we summed up the chapter with a figure that showed how value and function are determined in the different kinds of hotels.

KEY WORDS AND CONCEPTS

To help you review this chapter, please keep in mind the following:

Motor hotels
Airport motor hotels
Downtown hotels
Business travelers
Convention hotels

Resort hotels
Externalities
Franchise systems
Referral systems
Quality assurance/inspection
   systems

REVIEW QUESTIONS

1. What are the main reasons for the motel's popularity?

2. How do motor hotels differ from motels and hotels?

3. How do the needs of business travelers and convention travelers differ?

4. What different kinds of travelers do transient properties and destination properties serve?

5. What are the externalities of a hotel property?

6. What are some of the advantages of a franchise hotel?

Courtesy of Holiday Inns, Inc.

HOTEL AND MOTEL OPERATIONS

THE PURPOSE OF THIS CHAPTER

It is impossible to teach someone how to "run a hotel"[1] from a book. Only practical experience can teach a subject so complex. Nevertheless, this chapter describes (1) the major operating and staff departments, (2) the support departments, and (3) the patterns of income and cost that affect hotel operators. This decision should help you organize your own observations and start you on the way to learning "how to" by providing a frame of analysis for your field experiences and your subsequent professional life. Finally, this chapter outlines the major hospitality career entry points and the paths available for advancement.

THIS CHAPTER SHOULD HELP YOU

1. Name the major functional departments in a hotel and explain how they relate to one another.

2. Trace the general flow of work accomplished in the major departments and their key subunits.

3. Explain why the food and beverage department, though not the principal source of profit, is so important to a hotel's success.

4. Relate the principal sources of income and expense to the appropriate department according to the Uniform System of Accounts for Hotels.

---

[1]Hereafter, in the interests of simplicity and economy, we generally will use the word *hotel* as a generic term to describe all kinds of transient lodging—hotels, motels, and motor hotels.

5. Explain how accounting statements can be used to measure the performance of key executives and department heads in the hotel.

6. Define and use the key operating ratios and terms that describe an operation.

7. Explain the relationship of the financial structure of a hotel to its cost of operations.

Hotel properties range from tiny to huge in size. Although large properties such as the Chicago Hilton or Bally's Grand in Las Vegas catch the public's imagination, the majority of properties built in recent years offer between 100 and 200 units. Because most students will encounter these kinds of properties in their work, the examples in this chapter will assume a motor hotel in the 100- to 125-unit range.

Surprisingly enough, most properties perform basically the same functions, but the way in which they do them varies with the property size. When there are significant variations in routine practices in larger properties, we will note them. Our emphasis, however, will be on the similarity found throughout the hotel business rather than on the variations.

MAJOR FUNCTIONAL DEPARTMENTS

Figure 7.1 shows the basic functional areas of any hotel or motor hotel. This figure includes elements not found in some motels, however, as some motels lack food and beverage departments, and many do not have a gift shop or garage. Our purpose, however, is not to draw a chart that represents all properties inclusively; that would be impossible. Rather, we have outlined the major activities usually present in most properties.

A large property may employ a general manager under whom an executive assistant manager assumes responsibility for day-to-day operations. There is often a resident manager who supervises several departments on his or her side of the house, as Figure 7.2 shows, and a food and beverage manager who reports to the "exec."

On the other hand, in the 100-unit inn diagrammed in Figure 7.3, the general manager may be responsible—with an executive housekeeper and perhaps a front-office manager or chief clerk—for running the rooms and for supervising an assistant manager responsible for food and beverage. Thus, the executive staff may vary from two or three persons supported by a few department heads and key employees in a small property, to a large bureaucratic organization made of the many layers of authority necessary to operate a large complex property.

It is important to note that a smaller property may have functional areas

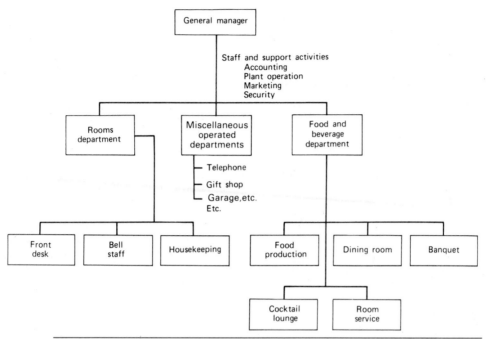

FIGURE 7.1 Major functional areas found in hotels and motor hotels.

(food production, bar, dining room, dish, pot, receiving, and cleanup, for instance, in the food and beverage area) but no true department heads. The restaurant in a small inn may be run by a restaurant manager who directly supervises all the employees with help from *lead employees* in each functional area on each shift. For instance, the hostesses for the day and evening shifts may provide leadership to the dining room during their shifts; a head cook on each shift does the same for the kitchen. The manager may be responsible for hiring and discipline on both shifts, usually along with someone designated as an assistant when the manager is off duty. This arrangement is economical and convenient in small properties as long as the restaurant manager delegates enough responsibility to avoid becoming overcommitted.

THE ROOMS SIDE OF THE HOUSE

Room rental is a hotel's main business and its major source of profit. The day-to-day operations of the typical rooms department yield a *departmental income* (the revenue remaining after the direct operating costs of the department are taken out) of about 70 percent, compared with 15 to 20 percent for the food and beverage department. Thus, the people on the rooms side of the house are crucial to the operation's overall success.

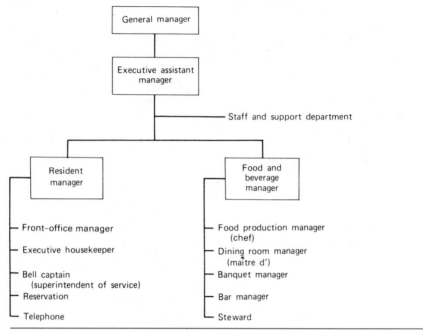

FIGURE 7.2 Simplified organizational chart for large hotel.

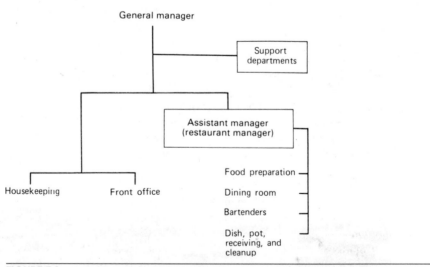

FIGURE 7.3 Functional organizational chart for small motor hotel.

The territory of the front desk. The major elements found in most front offices are present here: (1) reservation files for future dates, (2) telephone switchboard, (3) telephone information rack, (4) house (tray) ledger, (5) front-office accounting machine, (6) room rack, and (7) reservations for today. Although the front desk looks different when it is computerized, its functions are essentially the same.

The Front Office

More than any other group, the desk clerks represent the hotel to its guests. They greet the guests on their arrival and make them welcome (or not, depending on their manners). If something goes wrong, most guests will complain first to the front desk. And when the guests leave, the desk clerk checks them out. If anything has gone wrong, this will be a good time to catch it. ("I hope you enjoyed your stay, sir"—and then *listen* to the answer.) Although the duties of the desk overlap, they will differ with the work shift.

In the following discussion, a small inn serves as a model. The functions in a larger property may be broken down into specialties (reception desk, cashier, mail, and key clerk) performed by different persons. Our purpose is to describe the work and the functions. Your own observations will illustrate for you the variety of ways in which the work is organized. When a computerized front-office property management system (PMS) is used, fewer charges will be posted by hand if other charging departments are "on

If a guest voices any complaints at checkout, the morning clerk should deal with them tactfully so that the guest will return.

line" to the PMS, that is, interconnected so that charges automatically are picked up by the front-office computer.

The *morning clerk* works from 6:45 A.M. to 3:15 P.M. With a half-hour meal break, this is an eight-hour day. Because the evening crew comes in at 2:45 P.M. and the night auditor goes off duty at 7:15 A.M., all shifts overlap so as to ensure a smooth transition from one shift to the next. Some properties maintain a logbook in which information or events with which later shifts should be familiar are noted. The new shift's first task on coming on duty is to check the logbook to make sure they're fully briefed.

The morning shift's work is concentrated in the early hours (from around 7:30 A.M. until midmorning) on checking out guests. At the same time, of course, the employees on this shift answer the guests' questions and perform other routine tasks. But their main responsibility is checking out guests.

When a guest is ready to leave, the clerk verifies the final amount of the bill, posts any recent charges, and assists the guest in settling with cash, check, or credit card, according to the house credit policy. This credit policy, which lays down guidelines for accepting checks and specifies the acceptable credit cards, is an important part of any clerk's training.

Although the technical aspects of the clerk's work are important, the

This room rack indicates that most of the rooms are vacant. Some of them are not yet ready to rent, and so the rack card shows them as "on change."

courtesy a clerk accords a guest is at least as important. A departing guest must have an opportunity to register complaints if he or she has had problems. The morning clerk's work thus includes a special responsibility for ensuring that guests leave with the intention of returning to the hotel on their next visit to town.

As guests check out and their rooms become vacant, the clerk notifies housekeeping, or if the housekeeping department is on line to the PMS, it will automatically be notified. This permits housekeeping to make up the rooms promptly so that they will be ready when new guests check in later that day. As the rooms are made up, housekeeping notifies the desk so that early arrivals an be accommodated in rooms that are ready to rent. Alternatively, the room status can be changed to *ready to rent* at housekeeping's computer terminal later, when the room is made up.

Reservations[2] for the coming evening have accumulated in previous days, and many guests will come in during the morning. If a manual reservation system is being used, sometime before noon the planning for the evening begins with the *blocking* of vacant rooms on the room status board, often called the *room rack*. There are many different front office systems.

---

[2]In large hotels, and particularly in convention and resort properties, the reservations office is a specialized area within the front office.

ON CHANGE

_____

_____

_____

_____

_____

_____

_____

_____

_____

HOLIDAY PRESS FORM 3-115   PRINTED IN U.S.A.

ROOM   1 Person $_____

2 Persons $_____

3 Persons $_____

4 Persons $_____

TYPE _____

CONNECTS WITH _____

The room status card gives the rate for the room and other important information. When inverted in the rack, it indicates that the room is "on change," that is, not yet ready to rent. (Courtesy of Holiday Press.)

The simplest has a _rack card_ for each room. (The color of the card denotes the room type—yellow for singles, blue for doubles, orange for suites, or some similar combination.) When guests are checked in, a portion of the form that the guest fills out, usually called the _registration card,_ is inserted in the room rack, which shows that the room is occupied. When the guest checks out, the registration card is removed, and the rack card is inverted to indicate the room is _on change,_ which means that it is being made up for the next guest. When housekeeping indicates that a room is ready, the card is turned again to indicate ready to rent.

Toward the middle of the morning, the clerk blocks the evening's reserved arrivals by placing a card in the room rack. On very busy days, reservations may be closed (which means that no reservations for that night will be accepted) before the beginning of the business day. On most days, however, the transient hotel gradually fills with reservations that come in during the day.

When a PMS is used, this procedure is much simpler. Although special-request rooms are individually blocked, most rooms are assigned automatically by the computer, taking account of whether rooms are on charge or ready to rent, according to information supplied continuously by checkouts and the housekeeping department. As you can see, the PMS makes front-office work much easier. In fact, a room rack is no longer necessary and is replaced by summary information made available in various reports that can be called up instantly on the computer's screen.

It is important that reservations be accepted only if a room will be available; therefore, a close watch must be maintained on checkouts, reservations, and early arrivals so as to avoid *overbooking*. Overbooking means accepting reservations for more rooms than the hotel has available. In the past, hotels deliberately overbooked to a certain extent, for several reasons. The most important was that many reservations turned out to be "no-shows"—the guest did not arrive as expected. Guests generally would not pay for a reservation even when they had "guaranteed" it (that is, guaranteed payment even if they didn't arrive). A study by the American Hotel–Motel Association on the attitudes of actual no-shows indicated that these people (1) considered not showing up for a guaranteed reservation unfair but (2) claimed they had never done so!

With this kind of attitude, collecting from no-shows was not promising. Obviously, a hotel cannot afford to hold rooms empty, and so many operators carefully computed a "no-show percentage" and oversold their rooms by that amount. Regular reservations usually were held until 6:00 P.M. The percentage of no-shows at that time was generally quite high. Guaranteed reservations were to be held all night. Because some of these would not show anyway, a policy of conservative overselling was quite common. When a guest arrived with a guaranteed reservation that could not be honored, most hotels arranged other accommodations at their expense and paid the guest's transportation expenses to the other hotel.

The overbooking problem occasionally was worsened by some unforeseen event—for instance, a sudden change in weather that resulted in a cancellation of all flights out of town. Thus, guests who had expected to leave stayed over, and they generally could not be forced to leave. As a result, arriving guests found the reservations they had planned on were not available. Situations like this occurred infrequently, but they led to hard feelings and even some successful lawsuits. For this reason, in the late 1970s the practice of guaranteeing a reservation with a credit card became common. This practice, in effect, means that the room is paid for in advance. The guest will be charged for the room by the credit card company, which will pay the hotel whether or not the guest appears. When a guest cancels a guaranteed reservation (before 6:00 P.M. on the night of the reservation), most reservation systems provide a *cancellation number,* which is given to the guest as proof that he or she actually did cancel. Some hotels that do not use cancellation numbers ask the clerk to give his or her first name.

The *afternoon clerk's* work is shaped by the fact that the heaviest arrival time begins, in most transient houses, a little after 4:00 P.M. The afternoon clerk, therefore, takes over the reservation planning begun by the morning clerk and greets the guests as they arrive.

First impressions are crucial, and the desk clerk's warm welcome often sets the tone for the guest's entire stay. By remembering the names of repeat visitors, meeting special demands when possible (such as for a ground-floor room), and bearing in mind that the guest has probably had a hard, tiring day of work and travel, the desk clerk can convey the feeling that the guest is among friends at last. The clerk checks in the guest, and that process establishes the accounting and other records necessary for the stay. (At many hotels, an important part of checking in a guest is learning his or her expected date of departure. This information facilitates the reservation planning process just discussed.)

The *night auditor* is a desk clerk with special accounting responsibilities. When things quiet down (usually by 1:00 A.M.), the auditor posts those charges not posted by the earlier shifts, including (most especially) the room charge. He or she then audits the day's guest transactions and verifies the balance due the hotel from guests as of the close of the day's operations. The auditing process can be quite complicated, but simply stated, the auditor compares the balance owed to the hotel at the end of yesterday with today's balance. He or she verifies that the balance is the correct result of deducting all payments from yesterday's balance and adding all of today's charges. This process, summarized graphically in Figure 7.4, not only verifies today's closing balance of guest accounts owed to the hotel but also systematically reviews all transactions when an error in the balance is found. For this reason, the night auditor's job is important, requiring intelligence, training, and integrity.

Telephone

Because the system of accounting for hotels recognizes the telephone activity as a separate department for revenue purposes, one often hears about the *telephone department.* But only in the largest hotels is there a really separate organizational unit to match this designation, and in such hotels, it is headed by a chief operator. The telephone service in many properties is

The room status board or room rack gives the clerk who is assigning a room to an arriving guest the information necessary to avoid putting the guest in a room that is already occupied or that hasn't yet been made up.

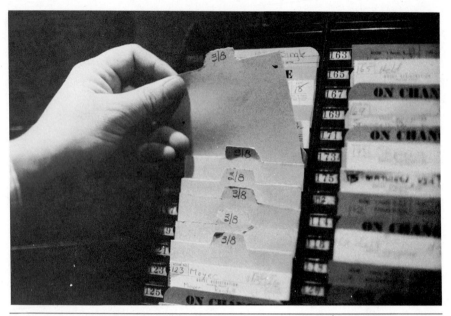

The morning clerk "blocks" rooms for tonight's reservations.

handled by a person who also serves as a second desk clerk. Many properties, particularly those of approximately 100 units with automatic phone systems, require the desk clerks to operate the switchboard as part of their regular duties.

Housekeeping

Housekeeping, that less-than-glamorous but essential department, is as much a production department of a hotel as the front desk and bell staff are service departments. It is clear that without clean rooms to rent, a hotel would have to close. For this reason, the management should always pay close attention to morale factors such as pay and worker recognition in the housekeeping department.

The housekeeping department is usually headed by an executive housekeeper. In a smaller property, a linen room assistant may double as an assistant housekeeper and inspector. In larger properties, the executive housekeeper will have at least one assistant and several supervisors, generally known as inspectors, who supervise maids in a designated area.

In some hotels, housemen take responsibility for cleaning the halls and heavy work such as moving furniture. These employees often form a separate subdepartment. Hotels with their own laundries often assign the supervision of that area to the housekeeping departments. Generally a working

"Yesterday's" Closing Balance of	
Accounts Owed the Hotel by Guests	

<u>MINUS</u>   all payments received today

<u>PLUS</u>   all charges guests made today

<u>EQUALS</u>
"Today's" closing balance

FIGURE 7.4   The night audit: a schematic view.

laundry supervisor or lead worker handles routine supervision under the executive housekeeper's general direction.

The Bell Staff

Many motor hotels do without a bell staff, because most of their guests prefer to "room" themselves. On the other hand, the bell staff plays an important role in the larger and more luxurious hotels. The process of rooming a guest includes more than just carrying luggage and showing a guest to a room. Rather, it begins when the clerk assigns a room. At this point the bellman takes charge, welcoming the guest in both word and manner and, on entering the room, demonstrating its operations and features. He or she shows the guest how to operate the air conditioning and turn on room and bath lights. The bellman will usually turn on the television and run through the channels and networks available. He may also indicate when the food service is open and provide other information the guest may need.

In luxury hotels, the *concierge* offers the guests important services. He or she is expert in giving directions to local attractions, securing tickets to shows, and recommending tours and other entertainment. The concierge knows about local transportation, tour schedules, and nearly any other information a tourist might want. The concierge concept is unique to luxury hotels, or to luxury floors in larger hotels catering to a range of pocketbooks. In most hotels, the front desk and bell staff generally share the work that the concierge does in the luxury property, although the decreasing size of most bell staffs today restricts this service. Nevertheless, it is important to see that the guest (who is, after all, usually an outsider to the community) has some place in the hotel to turn for information. He or she is likely to need up-to-date information about airport limousine schedules; the hours of religious services and the locations of churches; and such entertainment possibilities as sporting events, movies, and the theater. Some hotels give employees special training in how to give directions and provide lists of local attractions.

The use of the concierge has expanded substantially in luxury hotels and in large hotels in which some floors have been set aside for upscale service. For instance, CN Hotels offer three levels of service: premier, silver, and gold. Guests staying in the silver category follow a separate, simplified check-in procedure at the concierge's desk in the lobby, and those staying on the gold floors check in with a special concierge on their floor and are roomed by the concierge rather than a bellman. Training as a concierge today is an excellent part of an aspiring hotel manager's background in the increasingly luxury-conscious segment of the industry.

FOOD AND BEVERAGE DEPARTMENT[3]

There's an old saying among hotel people that "if you can run the food, the hotel will run itself." Like most folklore, this exaggeration carries more than just a grain of truth. Perhaps a personal recollection will illustrate this point:

> My first job as an innkeeper was in a hotel with a leased food and beverage department. That is, the owners had leased the food and beverage department to a food service management company to "keep the food problems out of our hair," as they put it. This is sometimes a disastrous "solution," and it certainly was in my case.
>
> A banquet held in the hotel was fouled up, and I, as the innkeeper, was apologizing to a prominent automobile dealer for the problems he and others had had. I concluded my explanation by commenting that unfortunately, because the restaurant was leased, there was not much I could do about it. His reply has always stayed with me.
>
> "Tom," he said, "suppose you came down and bought a car from me and a few weeks later had mechanical trouble. Suppose my service department couldn't fix the trouble, and you came to me to complain and I told you, 'It's beyond my control. My service department is leased.' Would you ever buy another car from me? Your food and beverage department is *your* service department."
>
> I was genuinely hard put to give any adequate answer to his question— because there wasn't any.

Of course, the car dealer was right. Service in any part of the hotel is important. But nothing seems to enrage guests quite so much as slow breakfast service, cold soup, or tough steak.

Many hotels in recent years have emphasized the food and beverage department's role as a profit center, that is, a specifically identified, profitable part of the hotel's operation. The typical hotel food service department creates about half as much in dollar sales as does the rooms department but generally provides between 10 and 15 percent as much profit as that generated by the rooms department.

---

[3]The student may wish to review the section of Chapter 2 regarding restaurant operating ratios, as they are also used in the industry in discussing hotel food and beverage operations.

Many old-time hotel keepers still regard the food and beverage department as a key marketing activity whose main purpose is to secure guest patronage for the hotel and only secondarily to generate profits. These operators don't throw money away. But they may price food and drink very reasonably and offer large portions or exceptionally good quality to attract patronage from the community. The reasoning is that this approach will attract guests to stay in their rooms.

On the other hand, more and more economy properties—and even some that like to think of themselves as luxury hotels—are severely limiting their food and beverage operations. Typically, these hotels, often in the so-called all-suite category, offer a free continental breakfast, and some even offer a free cooked-to-order breakfast. In addition, rather than a cocktail lounge, some all-suite hotels offer a free cocktail hour. Some chains are also returning to leased food and beverage operations, usually with a separate franchised operation on the premises.

Restaurants

Many motor hotels offer coffee-shop service, a more or less formal dining room, and a cocktail lounge. The hotel restaurant's hours of operation are related to the guests' needs rather than just to food and beverage profits. For example, many hotels open at least one food room at 6:00 A.M. to serve those who are early risers because they have come from another time zone, have an early plane to catch, or want to beat the morning traffic. The few guests who turn up before 7:30 in the morning hardly ever warrant the added payroll hours for cooks, waitresses, and the cashier. But if their schedules are accommodated, they are likely to return to the hotel and spend those rooms-department dollars that provide a 70 percent profit margin.

Similarly, the dining room's sales volume falls off dramatically in most properties between 8:30 and 9:00 P.M., but many hotel dining rooms stay open to accommodate the few late-arriving guests. The bar, too, may serve only a few guests in the mid-afternoon or after 9:00 P.M., but again, the full service a guest expects must be available.

Although management personnel need not always be present at opening or closing time, some lead employee, such as the cashier or first cook, must accept responsibility for unlocking and locking food storage areas, turning lights and equipment on at opening and off at closing, setting up the cash register or closing it out, and so forth. Because of the large number of operating hours, one hostess is generally responsible for the day shift (from 7:00 A.M. to 3:00 P.M.), and a second is in charge of the evening shift (from 3:00 P.M. until closing). In smaller properties, one of these supervisors may be designated to act for management when the restaurant manager is not on duty.

Hotel menus, too, take on a special character related to the guests' needs. Breakfast and the evening meals are the most important to the tran-

The services available at most hotels include a cocktail lounge whose hours of operation are designed as much to accommodate the rooms guests as they are to make a profit on the bar itself. (Photo courtesy of Sheraton Hotels.)

Food and beverage are, quite literally, the service department in a hotel or motel. (Photo courtesy of the New York Sheraton Hotel.)

sient hotel guest, who may not have arrived in time for lunch or may be away from the hotel for that meal. (Clearly, this statement does not apply to destination properties such as resorts). Once again, personal experience furnishes a good illustration of this point:

> At breakfast, I always provided orange juice freshly squeezed in the dining room where the guests could see that it really was fresh. This was foolishly expensive from the restaurant's standpoint, but I received enough guest comment slips saying "I stay at this hotel because of the fresh orange juice" to convince me that we weren't really being extravagant.

> At the evening meal we offered, as a "Traveling Man's Special," one complete meal at a rock-bottom price featuring a low-cost appetizer, a wholesome but inexpensive entree, salad, and dessert. In a freestanding restaurant, this would make no sense because it would reduce the check average, taking sales away from more expensive items on the menu. But many travelers are cost conscious because they are paying their own expenses or, as with government employees (and professors!) they receive only limited reimbursement for their travel costs. A "bargain meal" thus attracts such customers to a hotel. Some guests told us they ate the inexpensive meal—but had a couple of cocktails before the meal and charged the whole amount on their expense accounts. The total cost was still within their company's travel allowance.

Banquets

Some large properties offer a catering department (or banquet department) headed by a catering manager who books and sells banquets. Smaller properties include this activity among the restaurant manager's duties. Larger properties have special full- and part-time banquet service staffs. Smaller properties draw banquet service personnel from their regular crew and often supplement them with part-time employees.

Banquets are often profitable, but once again, in many properties the banquet menus and banquet rooms are meant principally to serve the rooms department. Thus, a meeting may occupy one conference room all day. Perhaps the hotel supplies a coffee break and a luncheon in another room. It probably charges the business people little, if anything, over what those meals and snacks would cost in the dining room. Moreover, it may not charge extra for the meeting facilities. If such a meeting accounts for 20 or 30 guest-room rentals—or even only 10 or 15—the logic we have mentioned before clearly applies. The 70 percent profit on room sales makes desirable this use of banquet space.

Food Production

In most properties, the person in charge of food production is called the *chef.* A chef is a person who has completed, either formally or informally, the training that qualifies him or her to be a master cook. The chef should

Modern hotels usually offer at least one informal dining room or coffee shop in which guests in informal attire will be comfortable. (Photo courtesy of Sheraton Hotels.)

also be a manager who can purchase food; hire, train, and discipline employees; and plan appetizing meals priced to yield a profit. All too often, however, the title of chef is bestowed on somebody who is, at best, a head cook. The cost of a *true* chef is, you see, beyond the means of most operations.

An increasingly common title in American food service is *food production manager.* Although these managers are almost invariably accomplished cooks, they emphasize kitchen management and rely on strict adherence to written recipes, rather than on their craft skills, to ensure quality. The type of management chosen by a property generally reflects the dollar volume of food sales. More sales may permit the expense of a chef or food production manager. Smaller properties may have to content themselves with a chief cook. In this case the restaurant manager generally supervises the kitchen quite closely.

With the greater availability of quality frozen prepared foods as well as the growing acceptance of limited menus, an approach to food service that requires limited culinary skills is becoming more and more common in hotels that don't try to reach the luxury standard.

Large convention properties may support a separate subdepartment, often made up of part-time workers who just prepare banquet food. Some properties even use a separate banquet kitchen.

Because of the hours of operation, a manager should clearly designate early and late supervision hours. This supervision may require a lead cook—or perhaps the restaurant manager or an assistant—to work as a supervisor.

The Exceptional Case.   As a student of food service, you should be aware that in a few hotels—usually older and smaller ones—the food department actually generates more profit than the rooms department does. In these cases, the innkeeper or owner is an unusually talented foods person and devotes the greatest portion of time to the food department. In these properties, as in all the others, however, the success of the foods department invariably increases room sales.

Sanitation and Utility

Sanitation is so important that many food service programs offer entire courses on the subject. Our purpose here, then, is not to cover every aspect of sanitation but to note the work of restaurant employees in the area of cleanup and sanitation. The fact that many students preparing for management take one or more courses in sanitation tells us how important this unglamorous work really is.

The category of employees we will discuss here include *dish, pot, receiving,* and *cleanup* workers. Receiving—checking incoming goods against the quality and quantity specified—is a responsible and skilled job in large hotels. The receiver reports directly to the hotel's accounting office. In smaller properties, however, receiving is combined with the work of some other station; the employees' skill levels in this area are minimal, and duties are limited to *counting* and *weighing* goods as they are received and *storing* them in the appropriate places. In these instances the receiver's job may be combined with that of the morning pot washer, for example. Breakfast often produces fewer pots to be washed than other meals do, and most food supplies are delivered between 7:00 and 11:00 A.M. In these cases, management inspects the incoming products. In larger properties, however, checking the quality of goods received is one of the receiver's most important jobs.

Dishwashers are important in at least three ways. First, a restaurant that runs out of clean dishes in the middle of a meal period would be a joke if the problem were not so serious. Second, the failure to wash dishes properly exposes the guest to food poisoning and the hotel to a serious loss of public confidence. Finally, dishwashing is closely involved in controlling a group of costs that, in most restaurants, loom as the largest expenses after food and labor: the breakage of china and glass, the disappearance of silver, and the cost of cleaning supplies.

Although breakage does occur in other areas (the waitresses and waiters account for the second largest breakage total, followed by the cooks), the dishroom is where the most dishes are handled and where breakage is the greatest. A careful dishroom crew can do a great deal to control and even reduce this large expense.

Although many other areas use cleaning supplies, probably the largest soap user is the dishwasher. Too little soap results in poor sanitation. (In fact, mechanical soap-control devices generally control soap dispensing, but sloppy work and misuse of the automatic equipment can result in problems.) Too much soap or improper handling can result in significant and costly waste. Similarly, the improper use and cleaning of the dishwasher can lead to costly repairs. For example, draining the machine at the close of business without remembering to turn off the heat can burn out a portion of the dish-washer. Expensive repairs—and the problems of operating a restaurant with-out a dishwasher while those repairs are being made—can be the result.

Breakage is not generally a problem in pot washing, but the restaurant's work depends as heavily on clean pots and pans as it does on clean dishes. Like dishwashers, pot washers also use significant amounts of costly soap. Pot washing, physically, may be the hardest job in the restaurant. It involves bending over a hot sink, breathing in the soap fumes, and strenuously scrub-bing pots to get the "burned on" food loose. In some large operations "pot machines," like dish machines, help with this work. But few smaller prop-erties can afford this investment in equipment and space, and so pots are generally washed by hand.

The night cleanup crew is often composed of the closing dishwashers and pot washer, though a separate cleanup crew may be hired by larger prop-erties. Cleanup is probably the most "unsung" work in the restaurant; and yet inadequate sanitation, at the very least, eventually results in a poor pub-lic image for the restaurant. Worse, a single outbreak of food poisoning can damage a property's reputation for years—to say nothing of the discomfort the guests suffer!

Many students find that the only summer jobs they can land are in the "sanitation and utility" areas. Unfortunately, students often view these jobs as a waste of time. In fact, many industry leaders brag that they "started in the dishroom." This boast is neither an accident nor a public-relations artif-ice. One of the keys to success in our field is encouraging unskilled workers to perform well in jobs that offer little intrinsic satisfaction. This encourage-ment starts with respect for the people who take these positions, a respect that often comes from having done the work yourself. (A little recognition and humane treatment can be awfully important to a job that others consider the "bottom rung.")

In some hotels, the supervisor of these functions is the steward, who may also be responsible for purchasing. In the typical property, however, the restaurant manager or, most often, his or her assistant is the supervisor in this area. This is another reason for mastering these jobs while a student. The assistant restaurant manager job in most hospitality operations—restaurants, hotels, and institutions—is most commonly assigned to people just out of management training programs. Success in this job often launches a successful career, and a good working relationship with subordinates is helpful in this entry-level job. Few things will help you toward that goal more than the ability to roll up your sleeves and help out when one of your crew gets "stuck." (But always be careful not to turn yourself permanently into a manager-dishwasher just to win popularity contests.) Of course, you need not plan to spend your life in the dishroom, but never be afraid to say you started there!

STAFF AND SUPPORT DEPARTMENTS

Some departments or activities in the hotel offer no direct guest services. Instead, they maintain systems for the property as a whole, such as sales, marketing, and engineering. Some of these activities do, however, service the departments that deal directly with the guests: accounting and personnel immediately come to mind.

Sales and Marketing

Marketing means designing a hotel to suit the needs and tastes of potential guests—or shaping the operations of an existing property to its most likely guests. A second marketing function is encouraging the guests to choose your property by emphasizing all of those service activities that make the property pleasant and convenient. Finally, marketing is promoting the activity among various potential guests and groups of guests. (This duty is often thought to be all there is to marketing, but it actually comes after the first two.)

Marketing is a general management function that involves all levels of the operation. One important day-to-day activity in this area is sales promotion. In large properties, a sales manager and one or more sales persons are responsible for finding sales leads and following up on them with personal sales calls and booking functions. Some properties define the sales department's work as the national convention market. Others identify local firms as the principal place to concentrate their efforts. Determination of just which market to approach is a crucial top management decision usually made by the general manager, the sales manager, and even the ownership. In chains, corporate policy may dictate these decisions, but most often the precise market for a particular property must be specifically designated by the local management. (Some properties—in particular, resort hotels—hire outside sales firms called *hotel representatives* to represent them in key markets.)

In smaller hotels, the innkeeper is responsible for managing sales. He or she will commonly make the sales calls personally and entertain people from potential sales accounts in the hotel. In some properties, the innkeeper is assisted in this work by a full- or part-time sales representative.

Because the work of the marketing department is essential, a major trade association, the Hotel Sales Marketing Association (HSMA), has developed to conduct educational and informational programs for both sales personnel and general management. This organization, which publishes excellent materials on sales techniques of all kinds, has a student membership available, and many hospitality management programs have student HSMA chapters.

Engineering

The engineering function is so important that many programs have one or more courses devoted to the disciplines that support it. Once again, we will simply describe briefly the work of this area. Large- and medium-sized hotels usually employ a chief engineer who supervises an engineering staff. Together, they are responsible for operating the hotel's heating and air conditioning; for maintaining its refrigeration, lighting, and transportation (elevator) systems; and for overseeing all of the hotel's mechanical equipment. Breakdowns in these areas seriously inconvenience guests. And of course, utility costs have always been significant and in recent years have been increasing at an alarming rate.

In small properties, the engineer is often little more than a handyman who carries out routine maintenance and minor repairs. Outside service people supply the more specialized maintenance skills. In these properties, the innkeeper often supervises the engineering (or maintenance) function.

In any property, large or small, general management should at least

1. Determine what periodic maintenance of equipment is required (oiling, filter changing, making minor adjustments, and the like).
2. Establish a schedule for accomplishing that work.
3. Develop a reporting system and physical inspection system that assures management that this work is carried out properly and on time.

Accounting

Sometimes referred to as the *back office* (in contrast with the front office or front desk), accounting is charged with two quite different duties, accounts receivable and financial reporting and control. In large hotels, the accounting department may be headed by a comptroller and consist of several skilled clerical workers. Chains generally develop sophisticated corporate accounting departments that supervise work at the individual property. In a small property, on the other hand, the work is usually done by some combination of the innkeeper's secretary, a chief clerk, and an outside accountant.

When guests check out, they may pay their bills with cash, but they often charge this expense instead. The accounts receivable (bills owed by guests) in a hotel are divided into two parts. First, a *house ledger* (or tray ledger), kept at the front desk, is made up of bills owed by guests in the house. Charges by guests posted after they have left and charges by other persons, such as restaurant patrons not in the hotel, are kept in what is often called the *city ledger*. The name is derived from an earlier time when charging hotel bills was not common. Instead, guests paid cash when they checked out, and any charge not in the house ledger was a charge from some local customer, someone "in the city" rather than "in the house" who had a charge account at the hotel. Incidentally, the word *ledger* originally referred to a book on whose pages these records were kept. Today, records of charges are maintained on separate forms called *guest folios*. Increasingly, they are maintained "in memory" on a computer. The function, however, and even the terminology are the same.

The other, less routine, accounting function preparing operating statements, conducting special cost studies, and overseeing the hotel's cost control systems. In small properties, much of this work is done by an outside accountant, whereas the larger properties often have their own full-time accounting staff headed by a comptroller or chief auditor.

INCOME AND EXPENSE PATTERNS AND CONTROL

As with so many subjects discussed in this chapter, whole courses are often devoted to the topic of this section, and another chapter of this book is devoted to control as a management function (Chapter 15). Our purposes here, therefore, are preliminary: we intend to provide you with an understanding of the control structure of a hotel and a limited introduction to the vocabulary of control in hotels and restaurants.

THE UNIFORM SYSTEM OF ACCOUNTS

Hotel accounting is generally guided by the Uniform System of Accounts for Hotels, which identifies important profit centers in hotels as *revenue departments*. The uniform system first arranges the reporting of income and expense so that the relative efficiency of each major department can be measured by the *departmental income* (which was once called *department profit*). Table 7.1 shows a typical rooms-department schedule of income and expenses for a 120-room motor hotel, and Table 7.2 shows a food and beverage department schedule for such a property. The rooms-departmental income and the food and beverage departmental income figures help the innkeeper evaluate the performance of key department heads working in those areas.

To determine the property's overall efficiency, a manager deducts four

TABLE 7.1 Rooms-Department Schedule of Income and Expenses

	In Dollars	In Percent
Room sales	$2,555,110	100.0%
Departmental expenses		
Salaries and wages	355,160	13.9
Employee meals	10,220	0.4
Payroll taxes and employee benefits	76,653	3.0
Laundry and dry cleaning	38,327	1.5
China, glass, silver, and linen	25,551	1.0
Commission	38,316	1.5
Reservation expenses	17,886	0.7
Contract cleaning	7,665	0.3
Other expenses	76,647	3.0
Total rooms expenses	$ 646,425	25.3%
Rooms departmental income	$1,908,685	74.7%

categories of *undistributed operating expenses* from the total of the various departmental incomes. These costs—administrative and general expense, marketing and guest entertainment, property operation, and maintenance and energy costs—are judged to be costs that pertain to all departments in a way that cannot be perfectly assigned to any one department.

The amount remaining after deducting these four categories of expense from the total of departmental income is called *total income before fixed charges*. (Until recently this amount was called, somewhat more colorfully, *house profit*.) This figure is probably the best measure of the success not only of the total property but of the general manager or innkeeper as well.

For this reason, many managers receive bonuses based on their performance as measured by this figure. It is fair to evaluate the manager without regard to the remaining costs, which can best be described as capital costs. Almost all of these costs—rent, property taxes, insurance, interest, and depreciation—are a direct function of the cost of the building and its furnishings and fixtures. The responsibility for these costs lies with the owners who made the decisions when the property was first built and furnished. These costs, therefore, lie beyond the control of the manager. Table 7.3, a typical statement of income and expense for a 120-room property, shows how all of these figures relate to net profit.

TABLE 7.2 Food and Beverage Department Schedule of Income and Expenses

	In Dollars	In Percent
Food sales	$1,031,382	72.9%
Beverage sales	381,993	27.1
Total food and beverage sales	$1,413,375	100.0%
Cost of sales		
Food cost (after credit for employee meals)	$ 347,544	33.6%[a]
Beverage cost	81,046	21.4%[a]
Total food and beverage cost	428,590	30.3%
Gross margin	984,785	69.7%
Public room rentals	25,440	1.8%
Other income	18,374	1.3
Gross margin and other income	$1,028,599	72.8%
Departmental expenses		
Salaries and wages	159,347	32.5%
Employee meals	21,201	1.5
Payroll taxes and employee benefits	101,763	7.2
Music and entertainment	40,988	2.9
Laundry and dry cleaning	12,720	0.9
Kitchen fuel	4,240	0.3
China, glass, silver, and linen	26,854	1.9
Contract cleaning	5,654	0.4
Licenses	2,826	0.2
All other expenses	70,669	5.0
Total food and beverage expenses	$ 746,262	52.8%
Food and beverage departmental income	$ 282,337	20.0%

[a]These two cost percentages apply respectively to food sales and beverage sales, whereas all other ratios are total sales.

TABLE 7.3 Highway Motor Hotel Statement of Income and Expense for Year Ending December 31, 19XX

	In Dollars	In Percent
Revenues:		
Rooms	$2,555,110	60.2%
Food—including other income	1,031,382	24.3
Beverages	381,993	9.0
Telephone	101,865	2.4
Other operated departments	80,643	1.9
Rentals and other income	93,376	2.2
Total revenues	$4,244,369	100.0%
Departmental costs and expenses:		
Rooms	$ 646,425	15.2%
Food and beverages	1,131,038	26.6
Telephone	131,575	3.1
Other operated departments	55,177	1.3
Total costs and expenses	$1,964,215	46.2%
Total operated departments' income	$2,280,154	53.8%
Undistributed operating expenses:		
Administrative general	$ 415,948	9.8%
Marketing	195,241	4.6
Property operation and maintenance	241,929	5.7
Energy costs	199,485	4.7
Total undistributed expenses	$1,052,603	24.8%
Income before fixed charges	$1,227,551	29.0%
Property taxes and insurance:		
Property taxes and other municipal charges	$ 110,353	2.6%
Insurance on building and contents	21,222	0.5
Total property taxes and insurance	$ 131,575	3.1%
Income before other fixed charges	$1,095,976	25.9%

	In Dollars	In Percent
		TABLE 7.3 *continued*

	In Dollars	In Percent
Capital costs:		
Depreciation and amortization	$ 331,060	7.8%
Interest	428,681	10.1
Total capital costs	$ 759,741	17.9%
Net income before income taxes	$ 336,235	6.4%

KEY OPERATING RATIOS AND TERMS

In Chapter 2 we introduced some key ratios and food service terms, which are used in hotel food service as well. In addition, the hotel industry has other indicators of an operation's results:

Occupancy is generally indicated as a percentage.

$$\text{Occupancy percentage} = \frac{\text{Rooms sold}}{\text{Total rooms available}}$$

Average rate is an indication of the front desk's success in selling both the least expensive and the higher-priced rooms.

$$\text{Average rate} = \frac{\text{Dollar sales}}{\text{Number of rooms sold}}$$

The average rate is also a mix of the double-occupancy rooms sold (rooms with two or more guests). This is reflected by the ratio

$$\frac{\text{Number of guests per}}{\text{occupied room}} = \frac{\text{Number of guests}}{\text{Number of occupied rooms}}$$

Because housekeeping is the largest and most controllable labor cost in the rooms department, many hotels compute the average number of rooms cleaned in the following ratio:

$$\frac{\text{Average rooms cleaned}}{\text{per maid day}} = \frac{\text{Number of rooms occupied}}{\text{Number of 8-hour maid shifts}}$$

All of these ratios are usually computed for the day, the month to date, and the year at year's end. Comparisons of these indicators with earlier operating results and with the budget provide important clues to an operation's problems or success.

CAPITAL STRUCTURE

We will discuss some of the financial dimensions of the hotel business further in Chapter 9. At this point, however, we need to describe briefly the capital costs found on the hotel's income statement because they are a significant part of a hotel's cost structure. *Capital costs* include rent, depreciation, and interest. A related cost, property taxes, can be included here because these taxes are dependent on the value of the land and the building.

Depreciation is a bookkeeping entry that reflects the assumption that the original cost of the hotel building, furniture, and fixtures should be gradually written off over their useful life. Interest, of course, is the charge paid to the lenders for the use of their funds.

The hotel industry is *capital intensive*. That is, it uses a large part of its revenue to pay for capital costs, including real estate taxes. Close to 20 cents of every sales dollar go to cover costs related to the hotel's capital structure.

Hotel development is attractive to some investors because it is highly *leveraged*. Leverage, as a financial term, refers to the fact that a small amount of an investor's capital can often call forth much larger amounts of money lent by banks or insurance companies on a mortgage. A fixed amount of interest is paid for this capital, and so if the hotel is profitable, the investor's earning power will be greatly magnified. But the investor's modest initial investment need not be increased. Earnings go up, but interest does not. Nor does investment—hence the word *leverage*.

Leverage, as developers have discovered repeatedly, can be a two-way device. Operating profits boom in good times and cover fixed interest payments many times over. When times turn bad or the effects of overbuilding begin to be felt, revenues fall, but interest rates (and required repayments on the principal of the loan) do not. The result is a wave of bankruptcies.

ENTRY PORTS AND CAREERS

An old adage says that there are three routes to advancement in the hotel industry: sales and marketing, accounting, and food and beverage. According to this adage, sales and marketing is the best route to the top in good times, but accounting, with its mastery of cost control, is the surest route in bad times. These three routes do seem to lead to advancement, but they are by no means the only places to start.

FRONT OFFICE

Many people begin their careers in the lodging industry in the front office, the nerve center of the hotel and the place where its most important sales take place. Obviously, the front office is an important area, and front-office techniques can be mastered fairly quickly. Moreover, this mastery still leaves a good many of the hotel's important operating functions outside the front office yet to be learned. Although some executives have risen to general manager from the front office, most of them are found in small properties. If your ambitions include advancement to general manager, you will want to think carefully about building on a successful front-office experience by adding experience in another area.

Many people find front-office work, with its constant change and frequent contact with guests, the most rewarding of careers. Moreover, improved pay scales in this area in recent years have upgraded the long-term attractiveness of this work, as has the increasingly sophisticated use of the computer in the front office. Another advantage of working in this area is a more-or-less fixed work schedule, though the afternoon shift's hours (from 3:00 P.M. to 11:00 P.M.) and those of the night auditor (from 11:00 P.M. to 7:00 A.M.) are viewed by many as drawbacks to those specific jobs.

ACCOUNTING

It is certainly true that during the Depression of the 1930s, many of the successful managers were accountants. Today, however, accounting has become a specialized field, and successful training in this area can be so time-consuming that one can hardly expect to master the other areas of the operation. Although accounting may not offer as easy a route to the general manager's slot as it once did, it does offer interesting and prestigious work for those who like to work with numbers. Moreover, the hours in this area tend to be reasonably regular, and the pay is usually good.

Although accounting per se is not as common a route to general manager as it once was, a new offshoot of accounting, operations analysis, is quite a different story. Operations analysts conduct special cost studies either under the direction of the auditor or as a special assistant to the general manager. Some operation analysts work in corporate headquarters. The operations analyst's job is such a good training ground for young managers that a regular practice of rotation through this job for promising young managers has become, in some companies, a feature of management development.

SALES AND MARKETING

The key to the success of any property is sales. Thus, it is not surprising that many successful hotel operators have a sales background. On the other hand, salespeople often find that a grounding in front-office procedure and in food and beverage operations (with special emphasis, respectively, on reservations procedure and banquet operations) leads to success in sales. Successful sales personnel are much in demand, and a career in sales offers interesting and financially rewarding work.

The importance of sales and marketing tends to increase when there is an oversupply of rooms in a market. Increasingly, the marketing manager for a hotel is asked to conduct market research or to analyze market research done by others. Indeed, a common requirement for senior positions in marketing is the ability to prepare a *marketing plan*. Such a plan evaluates the local environment and the competition, sets goals for the plan period (usually one to three years), and presents the strategy and tactics to fulfill the plan. A solid educational background is a great help to the modern hotel marketing manager.

FOOD AND BEVERAGE

Food and beverage is one of the most demanding areas of the hotel operation, and it is an area in which Murphy's law most often applies: "If anything can go wrong, it will!" Success calls for the ability to deal effectively with two separate groups of skilled employees—cooks and serving personnel. Along with mastering both product cost-control techniques (for both food and alcoholic beverages) and employee-scheduling techniques, the food and beverage manager must also work in sanitation and housekeeping and master the skills of menu writing. He or she must complete all these duties against at least three unyielding deadlines a day: breakfast, lunch, and dinner.

Many general managers brag that "I'm basically a foods person." Their success probably can be traced to the factors we discussed earlier in the chapter: the food and beverage department is the service department of the hotel, and in any competitive market, a successful food and beverage operation helps fill the hotel. Food and beverage managers may, however, find themselves stereotyped by firms as "foods people" and their advancement hindered because owners prefer to keep them in their specialty, in which qualified managers are so scarce. In cases in which advancement to general manager is blocked, qualified managers have not usually had trouble finding another job.

We should note that there are a number of hotels, particularly in the economy market, that are deemphasizing food service. This is true even for some upscale, all-suite properties. This trend, however, is found in only a minority of properties, and we will argue in the next chapter that food service is still the key to a hotel's competitive strategy. Although there are many management opportunities for those without a food service background, people competing for the top positions will still be ahead with a strong food and beverage background.

An advantage of careers in food and beverage is career-progression flexibility. Accomplished management and supervisory people in the food and beverage field almost always enjoy the option of moving to work outside the hotel in restaurants, clubs, or institutions. Although food and beverage probably requires longer hours than does any other area in the business, it is typically a well-paid position and offers not only career flexibility but unusually solid job security as well. Finally, it forms a sound basis for advancement into general management.

OWNING YOUR OWN HOTEL

Many students are attracted to the hospitality management field because they would like some day to own their own businesses. Whereas new hotels require large investments, existing operations can sometimes, under special circumstances of two different kinds, be purchased with little or no investment. First, after a wave of overbuilding and during economic recessions (and particularly when these two occur simultaneously), bankruptcies become common. And when banks must take over a hotel, they need someone to handle operations. They are often willing to give to a person with the know-how to take the property off their hands an opportunity for an ownership interest.

Some older hotels in smaller cities offer another kind of opportunity. They may have lost their competitiveness as hotels, while still occupying prime downtown real estate in a good food and beverage location. Because of this fact, together with an older hotel's extensive banquet facility and liquor license, the property may be revitalized by a well-run and imaginatively promoted food operation. The profits of that food operation may then be plowed back into improving the hotel facilities. The improved facilities *and* the property's improved reputation, earned by its newly successful food and beverage operation, often result in a greatly improved rooms business. Examples of such operations can be found in many parts of the country. Where they are found, they always share these three characteristics: excellence in the food operation; unusually effective promotion, generally enhanced by the manager's community involvement; and very, *very* hard work by that manager, who seems to live and breathe the hotel and restaurant business.

The hotel business offers many rewarding careers in front office, accounting, marketing and sales, and food and beverage. For those whose ambition and temperament makes them want to extend themselves, the top job is within reach and ownership is in sight. Arthur Hailey captured an important fact about hotels: they are romantic, intriguing, exciting places in which to work.

SUMMARY

The first topic we discussed in this chapter was the major functional areas of a hotel and who runs them. Although big hotels have true departments and department managers, smaller hotels would designate these as areas, supervised by lead employees.

We next examined the rooms side of the hotel. The front office is particularly important, as it is the guests' first real contact with the hotel. The front office generally has a morning clerk, an afternoon clerk, and a night auditor, all with both different and overlapping duties. All help in making reservations, either through a computerized reservation system or by hand. Other rooms-side departments are the telephone department, the housekeeping department, and the bell staff.

The food and beverage department is very important to the hotel, as it may determine whether guests return to the hotel (or come in the first place). We described the kinds of restaurants that various kinds of hotels offer, banquet facilities (if any), food production, and sanitation and utility.

We next looked at hotels' staff and support departments: sales and marketing, engineering, and accounting. The accounting department is sometimes referred to as the back office. We explained the hotel departmental income and expenses, operating ratios and terms, and, finally, capital costs.

We finished the chapter with a look at the best routes to advancement in the hotel industry—front office, sales and marketing, accounting, and food and beverage—and the advantages and disadvantages of each. We also discussed the possibility of owning your own hotel.

KEY WORDS AND CONCEPTS

To help you review this chapter, keep in mind the following:

Rooms department
Food and beverage department
Miscellaneous operated
  departments
Rooms-department income
Food and beverage department
  income
Front office: welcoming and
  complaints

Back office
House ledger (tray ledger)
City ledger
Total income before fixed charges
  (house profit)
Undistributed operating expenses
Occupancy
Average rate

Night audit
Overbooking
Telephone department
Housekeeping
Bell staff
Rooming the guest
Staff and support departments
HSMA

Number of guests per occupied
   room
Average number of rooms
   cleaned per maid day
Capital costs
Capital intensive
Leverage
Career paths

REVIEW QUESTIONS

1. How do functional areas differ from functional departments? By whom are functional areas run?

2. Describe some of the duties of the morning clerk, the afternoon clerk, and the night auditor.

3. Outline the process by which room reservations are made.

4. What are some of the duties of the telephone, housekeeping, and bell staffs?

5. What does the saying "If you can run the food, the hotel will run itself" mean?

6. Describe the different kinds of restaurants that a large hotel might have.

7. Why is the sanitation and utility area a good place for a summer job?

8. What are hotels' support departments that do not offer any guest services?

9. What are capital costs?

C H A P T E R

Courtesy of NCR.

AUTOMATING OPERATIONS AND SERVICES IN HOTELS

THE PURPOSE OF THIS CHAPTER

Technology is having a major impact on the effort to offer guests more value for their lodging dollar. First of all, it helps operators contain and control costs. Secondly, it enhances services we offer the guest. At the heart of these developments are the computer and the microchip. Understanding how computers are making hotels easier to operate in some ways but, at the same time, require more training of managers will underline the importance of adequate education for those who seek responsible positions as managers and supervisors in the hotel business of today and tomorrow.

THIS CHAPTER SHOULD HELP YOU

1. Understand the fundamental elements of a computer system.

2. Appreciate the spreading automation of hotel accounting and operations that results from key interconnections of departments with a property management system.

3. Become familiar with the function of major applications of technology in hotels in controlling costs or improving guest services.

4. Identify the principle benefits of property management systems.

5. Know how a "menu driven" front-desk system simplifies training and operations.

6. Describe the improvements in guest security that technology has brought to the "smart hotel room."

7. Understand how videoconferencing adds value to a hotel for some groups of guests.

COMPUTERS: THE HEART OF LODGING TECHNOLOGY

The key to most automation in hotel operations and services is the computer. Computers come in various sizes and have various names but they all, from microprocessors to mainframes work in essentially the same way. For those who have had a computer course, this section will be a review. But for those who are not as familiar with computers, we have italicized important technical terms the first time they appear. These terms appear in a glossary at the end of the chapter.

One word that we will often use in regard to computers is *systems*, as referring to the interactive whole.[1] A computer, for instance, is just a box or chip unless something is input to it. Furthermore, nobody will know what the "box" is doing unless it has output devices. Thus, we can speak of a *computer system* as containing *input devices*, a *central processing unit (CPU)*, and *output devices*. A computer system is shown diagramatically in Table 8.1. At a hotel's front desk, the keyboard is generally the input device used. The central processing unit (CPU) is the heart of the computer. Most hotels use *cathode ray tube (CRT) screens* and printers as output devices.

The CPU[2] has three elements, the *control unit*, the *arithmetic/logic unit*, and *memory*. The control unit interprets instructions from computer programs, directs the CPU's other parts, and also controls the input and output devices. Some find it useful to think of the control unit as the computer's brain.

The *arithmetic/logic unit* performs calculations (that is, adding, subtracting, multiplying, and dividing) and logical operations such as comparing one set of numbers with another.

The computer's *memory* holds instructions in the form of computer programs and data that have been input, such as charges and payments to a guest's bill. In addition, while the computer is working, its memory holds the results of work in progress, and when a calculation is completed, it holds the information that has been processed and the answer. In some cases, data may be stored outside the computer in what are called *external memory*

---

[1] For a further discussion of applications of the systems concept to hospitality management, see Thomas F. Powers, "A Systems Perspective for Hospitality Management," *Cornell Hotel and Restaurant Administration Quarterly,* May 1978, pp. 70–76.

[2] The description of the CPU is adapted from Jerome S. Burstein, *Computers and Information Systems* (New York: Holt, Rinehart and Winston, 1986), chap. 5, esp. pp. 131–135.

TABLE 8.1   Fundamentals of a Computer System

The elements found in any computer are fundamentally the same. They are the means for (1) supplying data to the computer, (2) processing the data, and then (3) making the results available in a usable form. The main units are described below.

Input	Processing	Output

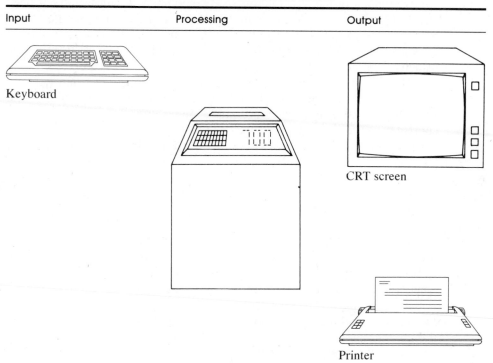

Keyboard

CRT screen

Printer

Input	Processing	Output
The most common input device is the keyboard, where both instructions and data are typed into the computer	The CPU is made up of three units: • The *control unit* runs programs and oversees the computer's functioning. • The *arithmetic/logic unit* performs all calculations. • The computer's *memory* stores programs and data	*Printers* make copies of reports or guests' bills when a permanent record is requested. *CRT* screens are used by clerks and other computer operators to check the status of records and reports while the computer is operating and to monitor input data as they are entering it.

devices. An example is the special programs used to perform the night audit, which are often held on a night auditor's *disk* except when in use.

The computer operates by converting all information to *binary numbers,* which are quite different from the number system we are used to. The binary number system is based on just two numbers, 0 and 1, and has been compared to an on–off switch or a true–false test. Each character (letters or numbers) is stored electronically as some combination of eight zeros or ones. A single binary number is called a *bit,* and a *byte* is a string of bits (usually eight bits per byte) that the computer processes as a unit.

The size of a computer is often expressed in terms of the information it can hold in memory, usually stated in thousands (abbreviated K) of bytes. Thus, a 256K computer's memory holds 256,000 bytes of information. The computer converts programs as well as the data input into binary numbers, stores and manipulates them as necessary, and then transforms the resulting information into "human-readable," as opposed to "machine-readable," form.

INTERFACES

Many hotels' accounting and operating systems are *interfaced* (electronically interconnected) to the computer (see Table 8.2). In this way, for example, housekeeping can be informed instantaneously, via its terminal screen (or printer), of guest checkouts. Or if the telephone system is interfaced to the computer, when rooms are made up, the maid (or inspector) can dial an appropriate code on any phone, thus informing the front desk that a room is ready to rent. When the hotel's call-accounting system is interfaced, long distance calls are automatically posted on the guest's folio. (Remember that in this system, the guest folio is not a piece of paper but a set of electronic impulses stored at an appropriate address in the computer's memory and printed out as hard copy only when needed.) Another common interface is with the food and beverage point-of-sale (POS) terminals. If a guest charges a check to his or her room, it will be entered at the POS end, and the charge will be instantaneously posted to the guest's ledger in the computer.

Payroll interfacing allows the computer to register the start and stop times for each worker. Using these data, the computer prepares the payroll checks, labor-use reports, labor-use analyses, and labor forecasts.

Terminals are said to be *smart* or *dumb*. For instance, there may be two or more terminals at the front office, one of which (a "smart" terminal) contains the computer itself. The other terminal is connected to the computer, uses the computer to make all calculations, and has no computational power of its own—it is a "dumb" terminal. On the other hand, the dining room may contain a "smart" terminal with enough computational power to total guests' bills, keep track of cash received, and produce a number of

TABLE 8.2 Common Interfaces in Hotel Computer Systems'

Chain Headquarters

Telephone System
- Housekeeping inputs room status by phone.
- Phone control (on/off) is at checkout and check in.
- Guest's name is displayed for operator when guest dials from room phone. Guest's name can also be displayed in outlets.

Point-of-Sale (POS) Terminal
- Posts food and beverage charges directly to guest's folio.
- Posts group charges to master folio.
- Posts other charges (gift shop, in-house movies). Verifies credit.

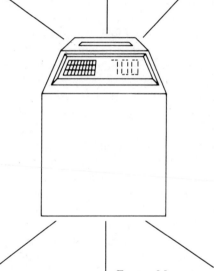

Call Accounting
- Posts long distance call charges directly from phone company to guest's folio.

Energy Management Systems
- Controls air conditioning.
- Shuts off lights at checkout.
- Regulates peak usage levels.

Payroll
- Time clock registers start and stop of work hours.
- Computer prepares actual payroll and checks.
- Computer "modeling" of labor utilization includes
  Labor-use reports
  Labor-use analyses
  Labor forecasts

food and beverage reports. At the heart of this "smart" POS as well as of call-accounting systems, energy control units, and other "smart" terminals is a *microprocessor,* a tiny, single-purpose computer in the form of a single silicon chip, smaller than your fingertip.

The hotel's computer may also be interconnected with the company's main computer in a remote head office. This interconnection may be permanent and continuous, in which case the property's computer is said to be *on line* to the head office. Very often, however, the head office uses periodic (usually daily) *polling* to monitor the unit's activity. In polling, the head office's computer in effect "calls up" the property's computer using long distance lines and, in computerese, asks for the appropriate reports and data. These are transmitted almost instantaneously in *machine-readable* form via the phone line to the head office's computer. Polling is usually done late at night when phone rates are at their lowest.

In some cases, the *data* generated by the property will be further analyzed at the head office. The resulting report can then be *downloaded,* that is, transferred in machine-readable form from the central unit to the property, in what is essentially the reverse of polling. With polling, usually unprocessed or partially processed data are carried to the central office. With downloading, finished reports or other communications are sent to the individual properties.

Computers come in several sizes. Most hotel computers are *microcomputers,* the type of computer most commonly known as a personal computer (PC). *Minicomputers* are faster and have more memory than a microcomputer does. A larger or more complex hotel might use a minicomputer, or the head office's computer in a small hotel chain might be a minicomputer. The largest computers are known as *mainframes.* In the hotel business, mainframes are used in the head office to compile operational reports and manage functions like companywide accounting, payroll, and accounts payable. National reservations systems also rely on mainframe computers.

HARDWARE AND SOFTWARE

Most of what we have been discussing relates to *hardware,* the actual physical equipment in a computer system. Equally important is the *software* or computer programs. Many computer programs used in hotels are *canned programs,* that is, standard software packages that have been designed for special purposes such as front-office accounting. Some units develop their own software which is more expensive but may give greater flexibility to meet special needs.

COMMON USES OF TECHNOLOGY IN HOTELS

Most of the uses of technology we will be examining are computer or microprocessor based. Some of them improve the efficiency and cost effective-

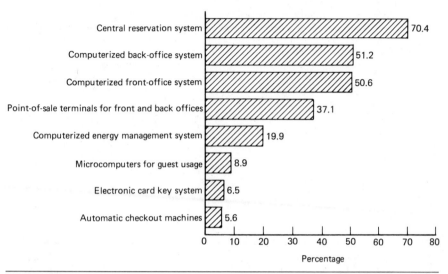

FIGURE 8.1   Technological characteristics of property automation (U.S. Lodging Industry 1986. Laventhol & Horwath.)

ness of operations by doing jobs better, faster, and with fewer errors. Some, such as *videoconferencing,* offer what amount to new services. Others directly affect guests by giving them a greater sense of luxury, personal security, or convenience. The frequency of use of some major applications of technology is shown in Figure 8.1.

TECHNOLOGY AND OPERATIONS

The major improvement in operations attributable to technology is the computerized property management system. Other technological innovations in hotel operations include call accounting, security, and word processing.

Property Management Systems (PMS)

The Property Management System (PMS) has been defined by Prof. Alan J. Parker of Florida International University's School of Hospitality Management as consisting of a number of individual programs that, together, manage the front- and back-office systems.[3] (The functions of the PMS are highlighted in Table 8.3.) The PMS may also include both the hardware and the software needed to automate the front and back office. In an article in *Lodging* magazine, Douglas Engel and Joseph Marko offered several reasons that so many hotels have adopted the PMS:

1.   To improve operational efficiency by eliminating repetitive tasks and by having information current and readily available.

[3]*Lodging,* October 1984, p. 63.

TABLE 8.3 Property Management Systems

Front-Office Functions

Core Features	Optional Features
Guest Accounting and Service • Check in and checkout • Folio accounting • Telephone information	Guest history Travel agent accounting Budgeting statistics Word processing
Operations • Guest reservations • Night audit • Group registration and folio accounting • Housekeeping: Room status	

Back-Office Functions

Core Features	Optional Features
Accounts payable Payroll General ledger	Inventory Purchasing Budgeting Forecasting Purchasing

---

Other Service Functions

Sales and marketing analysis
Package and meal plans
Function-room scheduling
Banquet and catering sales
Word processing
Promotional mailings
Maintenance scheduling
Forecasting
Graphics: Menus

Source: Adapted from Douglas Engel and Joseph Marko, "Property Management Systems," *Lodging,* February 1986, pp. 17–20.

2. To improve guest service through accurate, faster dissemination of information and new opportunities to keep track of guests' likes and dislikes.

3. To improve internal operational controls by adding a level of standardization that is difficult to establish and maintain in a manual system.

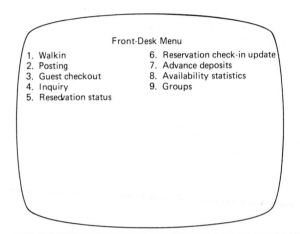

Front-Desk Menu

1. Walkin   6. Reservation check-in update
2. Posting   7. Advance deposits
3. Guest checkout   8. Availability statistics
4. Inquiry   9. Groups
5. Reservation status

FIGURE 8.2   A sample PMS menu.

4. To save money by improving efficiency, reducing payroll, and eliminating outside service bureau costs.

However, the actual operating savings in properties of fewer than 300 rooms will probably be eaten up by additional computer-related expenses such as specialized maintenance and supplies.[4] But greater convenience for guests is increasingly a competitive necessity when over half the competition offers that convenience. While it is hard to put a dollar value on operational efficiency and control, these two are, increasingly, needed to operate at competitive costs in an increasingly automated industry. The adoption of the PMS seeks to improve the relationship between room rate and value to the guest: it enhances services and helps hold down costs.

A PMS is *menu driven*. In many systems, the *menu,* or list of possible courses of action, is shown on the CRT screen, as in Figure 8.2. In other systems, the menu or list of operations doesn't come on the screen. The options are there, but the clerk is expected to know what they are and how to deploy them. The display of the menu, however, prompts the operator and has the advantage of making training and operations easier.

The starting point for a clerk is probably a menu of options such as that shown in Figure 8.2. For a walk-in guest (one without a reservation) the clerk presses "1." The screen will then change to the "guest walk-in menu" (technically, the "guest walk-in routine"), such as that shown in Figure 8.3. Note that this menu is displayed at the bottom of the screen. This is because from this point on, the clerk will be working with a guest record that will be

[4]*Lodging,* February 1986, p. 17.

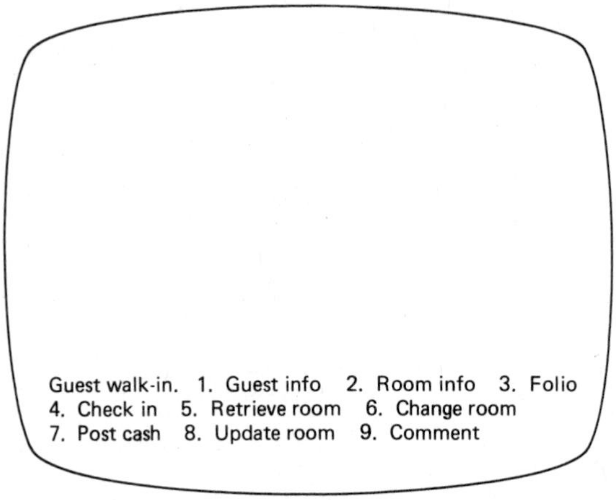

Guest walk-in. 1. Guest info   2. Room info   3. Folio
4. Check in   5. Retrieve room   6. Change room
7. Post cash   8. Update room   9. Comment

FIGURE 8.3   Guest walk-in menu.

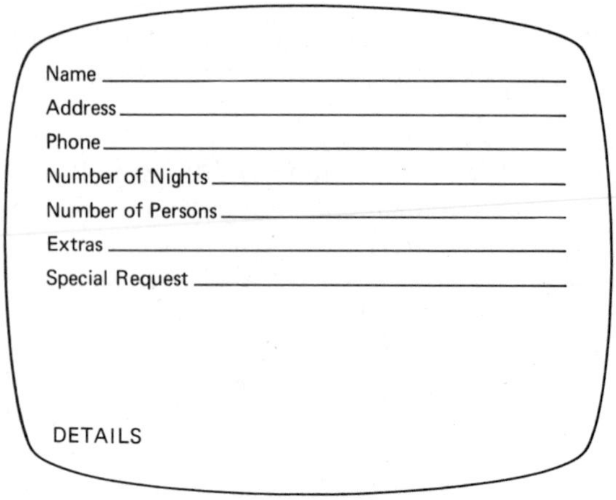

Name _____

Address _____

Phone _____

Number of Nights _____

Number of Persons _____

Extras _____

Special Request _____

DETAILS

FIGURE 8.4   Guest information format.

displayed in the space above the menu. The clerk continues the process of registering a walk-in guest by pressing "1" for "Guest information" plus "Enter." At this point the screen presents the guest-information form for registration, as shown in Figure 8.4. Note that a *submenu* (subroutine) *prompt* tells the clerk that he or she is now in the process of filling in the details. The process moves along, prompted by the options at the bottom of the screen. The computer displays for the clerk the different types of rooms and rates available, assigns a room number when given a room type, and creates a folio for the guest, all on instructions from the clerk. A similar set of operational routines is available to check in a guest with a reservation, to post charges, to check out a guest, to update a guest's records, and so forth.

The system also provides reports that give an overview of the operation's status at any particular time. For instance, the computer may report on the reservation status for today or any future day, on reservations not yet arrived, on the number of rooms occupied, on change or ready to rent, and so forth.

This is not the place to try to display an entire system, and the above examples are intended merely to give you a feel for what a menu-driven system is and how, by displaying prompts which give the clerk action options, it can speed the process of managing the business of the front desk and improve guest service. We can also see how the menus and submenus could facilitate and speed training by displaying information.

Call Accounting

For many years, hotels relied on charges called back by the long distance operators after a guest completed a long distance call. Now in most hotels, the voice callback has been replaced by at least a teleprinter. As the call charges are printed out, the teleprinter paper is torn off and used as a voucher to post long distance calls. If the callback system is interfaced with the PMS, the calls will automatically be posted to the guest folio almost as soon as the call is completed. This saves the clerks' time and ensures that all charges will be posted and will be posted before the guest departs.

Security

Most hotels still use conventional metal keys but a small but growing number are using a variety of electronic "one-time" key systems that offer added security. The problem with conventional keys is so common that Hailey's novel *Hotel* uses it as the basis for one episode. Guests often lose their keys, and thieves find it easy to obtain keys by stealing or buying them. In the *Hotel* episode, a thief who earns his living from hotel room theft based on filched keys disturbs a guest—and you can imagine that it *would* be disturbing to wake up and find someone rummaging around in your room!

Electronic key systems replace the mechanical lock and key with a plastic device. The plastic key is encoded with a unique number for each guest registered in the hotel. A microcomputer at the front desk encodes the key and has literally millions of combinations available for each guest room.[5] The computer system provides a printout of all the keys issued and indicates who issued each key. In the event of a theft, this makes it possible to determine who might have had access to a room. Maids' keys, pass keys, maintenance keys, and so on also are encoded by the microcomputer.

Each guest room's lock is controlled by a microchip. Some of the chips

[5]*Lodging,* October 1984, pp. 41–42.

are physically connected to a main power source and interfaced with the front office's microcomputer that issues the keys. Others operate on long-life batteries, and when a new key is issued, the room's microchip is reset to the new combination. Both systems enable the room's microchip to record the most recent entries—up to 14 in one system—by type of key (guest, maid, passkey, and the like). In most systems the individual keys can be used again after they are reprogrammed but present no threat if lost or discarded after the guest has checked out.

Word Processing

Jon Williams, the AH&MA's manager of computer services, points out that word processing ties together two technologies, the typewriter and the computer.[6] Material is typed into a microcomputer (in some cases, word processing uses the memory of a larger, propertywide computer), and the operator can read what is typed on the screen. If changes need to be made, the appropriate material is recalled to the screen, and any insertions or deletions are made. Most word processors provide automatic page numbering, page formatting, and a spelling check. Word processing is useful for all correspondence but is especially helpful for direct mail. A form letter appears as individually typed, and in fact, certain words, sentences, or paragraphs can be inserted. Using a feature called a *mail merge*, the word processor can prepare personalized, individually typed letters for each name on a mailing list that has been separately input to it. Word processing not only improves the quality and quantity of output but also reduces labor requirements.

VIDEOCONFERENCING

Videoconferencing is another space age technology that uses computers and microprocessors. Videoconferencing allows companies and other groups to bring people together—after a fashion—by providing them with sight and sound if not physical presence. As it has developed thus far, groups find that the necessary preparation and entertainment format somewhat restrict its uses. It is hardly suitable for an informal chat. Rather, it is used for such events as new product introductions, large sales meetings, and other motivational meetings that lend themselves to the prepared format required by electronic media. Thus far, the impact of videoconferencing has not been highly competitive with the hotel business. That is, a video conference generally hasn't canceled out conventions that might have gone to a hotel. It is probably being used today in place of—or, commonly, in addition to—printed media and direct mail.

The main elements of the videoconferencing system are an *originating site*, an *earth station*, or *communications satellite*, and a special receiving

---

[6]*Lodging*, March 1985, p. 77.

GLOSSARY OF COMPUTERS IN LODGING

Arithmetic/logic unit.   The part of the computer that performs calculations (adding, subtracting, multiplying, and dividing) and logical operations such as comparing one number with another.

Binary numbers.   The number system used in computers. In the binary number system there are only two digits, zero and one, which in the computer represent the presence or absence of an electrical impulse. They have been compared to an on–off switch.

Bit.   A single binary number, a zero or a one.

Byte.   Eight bits, the unit generally used by the computer.

Canned programs.   Prepared software, standardized programs.

Cathode ray tube (CRT).   A video monitor used as an output device in computer systems.

Central processing unit (CPU).   The computer's processing component, is made up of the control unit, the arithmetic logic unit, and the computer's memory. The CPU can be thought of as the "guts" of the computer.

Computer system.   The interactive whole that makes up the computer: the input device or devices, central processing unit, and output devices.

Control unit.   The part of the CPU that controls input, processing, and output. It can be thought of as the computer's brain.

CPU.   See *Central processing unit.*

CRT.   See *Cathode ray tube.*

Data.   Raw or unprocessed facts, like a record of sales transactions.

Disk storage.   An external storage unit.

Downloading.   The dissemination of processed information by a central computer. Some hotel chains "download" to their units instructions or management reports processed in the central office.

Dumb terminal.   A terminal that displays transactions but that has no computing or storage capacity.

External memory device.   An auxillary storage that supplements the computer's memory capacity.

Hard copy.   Computer records printed out on paper (as opposed to being displayed in the CRT).

Hardware.   The physical components of a computer system, as opposed to its *software* or program elements.

Information.   Data that have been processed so that they are useful and have meaning, as in a cashier's shift report, a daily operations report, or other management report.

Input devices.   Generally, any data-entry device. The most common input devices in hotels are keyboards. POS terminals may also be thought of as input devices.

Interface.   The point at which two components in a system interact, or the act of interaction between components. Commonly used to denote the interaction of two elements in a computer system.

Machine readable.   Data or information in a form that can be read (only) by the computer, such as information coded in binary numbers.

Mainframe.   A large computer such as is used in central reservations systems.

Memory.   The computer's capacity to store data and information as electronic impulses.

Menu, menu driven.   Computer software that is often composed as a series of subroutines that can be used by the operator. The operator chooses a subroutine from a "menu" of options. The system then displays the appropriate form for action, along with a prompt indicating a further menu of choices for action.

Microcomputer.   A small computer such as a personal computer.

Microprocessor (microchip).   A single silicon chip that contains the computer's control and arithmetic/logic unit.

Minicomputer.   An intermediate-sized computer, between a microcomputer and a mainframe.

On line.   Directly connected to or interacting with the computer.

Output devices.   Devices that translate machine-readable information into a form that people can read. In hotels, the CRT and printer are the most common devices.

Personal computer (PC).   A microcomputer designed to be used by individuals in the home or in business. Many front-desk systems use PCs.

PC.   See *Personal computer*.

PMS.   See *Property management system*.

POS.   Point of sale (cash register).

Polling.   The process by which one computer interrogates another, according to a predetermined pattern, to transfer data and information to the polling computer.

Property management systems (PMS).   A combination of programs that automate the front and back offices. PMS may also indicate front- and back-office hardware.

Smart terminals.   Terminals that can be programmed and have computational capacity.

Software.   Computer programs.

Subroutine prompt.   Display of a menu presenting subroutine options within any given routine.

System.   A set of interrelated elements, an interactive whole.

Word processor.   Computer systems that can be used to input, edit, and print text material such as letters and reports.

---

disk at the *receiving site*. The program is transmitted from the originating site or sites to a *satellite-transmitting antenna* called an *uplink*. The satellite transmits the signal to one or more receiving sites.[7]

Many hotel companies have equipped their properties for videoconferencing because it generates food and beverage and conference-room revenues and even some guest-room sales. HI-NET Communications linked 1500 U.S. properties in 1986, offering the ability to show a video conference both in the meeting rooms and in every guest room in the property. (HI-NET also offers closed-circuit television programs, including pay-per-view movies.[8])

Installation of a system of this kind obviously improves the services available to corporate and other group customers, thereby adding to the value of a property for a particular market.

At least one expert observer of the hotel business, Daniel R. Lee, feels that various forms of electronic conferencing will, in the long run, compete with lodging, particularly in the small-meeting market. Lee estimated that roughly half of the demand for lodging is based on the need for communication between people at distant points and that half of that, or 25 percent of lodging demand, does not require intimacy, such as one-on-one meetings. It is this "nonintimate" communication function that Lee sees as competing with the market for lodging. Lee also noted that communication devices such as electronic chalkboards and microprocessor receivers and transceivers improve videocommunications as a meeting medium. The simplest video-supported communication is slow-scan television. Pictures or images are digitalized and transmitted through a normal telephone line. No satellite

[7]*Lodging,* October 1984, p. 37–38.
[8]*Hotel and Motel Management,* June 1986, pp. 36–37.

GLOSSARY OF VIDEOCONFERENCING TECHNOLOGY

Downlink.   The electronic equipment in an earth station that receives satellite signals.

Earth station.   Sending and receiving communication equipment that interacts with a satellite and with locations that are transmitting or receiving video signals.

Originating site.   Place at which the television signal is produced for transmission to a satellite.

Receiving site.   Place at which signals are viewed on television, such as hotel meeting rooms.

Satellite.   An electronic device in space that sends and receives signals.

Satellite-Transmitting Antenna.   The earth station's sending device, sometimes called an *uplink*.

Slow-scan television.   A telecommunication system using ordinary telephone lines to transmit images. Two-way voice transmission generally accompanies slow-scan TV on a separate phone line.

Uplink.   The satellite-transmitting antenna of an earth station.

Videoconferencing.   An electronic system that transmits television images, generally via satellite, from one or more originating sites to one or more receiving sites.

---

hookup is required for this kind of communication. "The process," Lee stated, "is much like a slide show with a new still image shown to the audience every 5 to 20 seconds. Two way voice communication is accomplished through a separate telephone line."[9]

Slow-scan TV is limited both in the quality of the video image and the number of sites which it can link. The more sophisticated video conference that we discussed earlier is more costly, but, Lee notes, many companies (he cites IBM, Aetna, Sears, and ARCO) are developing their own teleconferencing systems with the specific goals of improving corporate communications and decreasing executive travel costs.

The vigorous response of lodging companies to this competitive challenge suggests that they will play a major role in videoconferencing as it emerges. As Lee pointed out, however, the revenue sources—food and bev-

---

[9]Daniel R. Lee, *Lodging* (New York: Drexel Burnham Lambert, 1984), p. 107.

erage and conference-room rental—that videoconferencing will tap are much less profitable than is the guest-room revenue related to small meetings, and so even if the room revenue lost is largely replaced by videoconferencing revenue, the impact on profits will still be negative.

Lee noted that research indicates that people do prefer person-to-person meetings to the more impersonal videoconference but that these reports do not take costs into account. "In fact," he asserted, "much of the shift toward teleconferencing will not be voluntary. Once it is widely available and the cost savings become known, businesses and other major travel users may mandate its use by their employees."[10]

Any negative impact from videoconferencing and the related communications technology is likely to be felt only gradually. It may slow down the increase in demand for lodging, but by Lee's estimate, its effect is likely to "amount to only some 10 to 15 percent of today's total lodging demand," with that effect spread over the next 10 to 20 years.[11]

ENERGY MANAGEMENT[12]

As much as 10 percent of the hospitality industry's costs are either directly or indirectly for energy for such things as lighting, air conditioning, and heating. Because energy costs are escalating, there has been much attention in recent years on developing equipment to control them. As with so much other technology in the hospitality industry, the computer and microprocessor are central to this effort. To understand hotels' energy management control systems, we must begin with how a hotel's energy charges are computed by the power company. There are two elements in such a bill, demand and usage.

Demand

Demand charges are based on the peak load—that is, the maximum demand for power—that the property requires during the billing period. In some operations, equipment may be turned on when an employee comes to work. Let's suppose that the morning cook comes in at 5:30 A.M. to open the restaurant at 6:00 A.M. This is a convenient time to turn on the air conditioning for the day. So the first thing the cook does is to flip the switches turning on the air conditioning and then to turn on the kitchen exhaust fans and the stoves and ovens. All that equipment at once creates a very heavy demand, and so a very simple way to minimize this would be to give the cook a timed schedule for turning on the equipment. Of course, automated equipment can also be used to turn on the equipment.

[10]Lee, *Lodging,* p. 10.
[11]Lee, *Lodging,* p. 10.
[12]For a fuller discussion of this topic, see Frank D. Borsenik, *The Management of Maintenance Systems and Energy in the Hospitality Industry,* 2nd ed. (New York: Wiley, 1987).

Peak-load control systems can be set to turn off equipment such as the air conditioning during the day when the hotel's total electricity use approaches the upper demand level set by management. Usually, equipment is turned off according to a predetermined set of priorities and then only for periods of 15 to 20 minutes.[13]

Usage

The electric bill is based not only on the peak demand but also on the total electric use. Programmable thermometers can be used in some parts of the hotel to avoid wasting power. For instance, if a meeting room is to be used for a luncheon at noon, the thermostat may be set to turn the air conditioning on at 10:30 A.M. and off at 1:45 P.M.

The temperature inside a building is the result, in large part, of outside temperature. Thus, thermostats may be set to turn up the air conditioning at 9:00 A.M. as it warms up outside and then to turn it down at 5:00 P.M. as the temperature drops. With "optimized start" and "optimized stop" equipment, however, instead of relying on a regular time-of-day setting, thermometers sense the actual outside temperature. For example, if it warms up later than 9:00 A.M. on a summer day because it is cloudy, the increase in air conditioning can be delayed to meet the actual conditions of that day.

Control Systems

Computers and microprocessors record and analyze energy use and actually control the equipment requiring energy. An energy management program is based on the hotel's actual use of energy. A remote sensing system can be linked to a PC programmed to summarize energy use and operating patterns and to provide detailed reports. The equipment may be controlled by a central computer to which all of it is connected. Alternatively, equipment may be wired to individual microprocessors that provide sensing and logic in order to control the units under different operating conditions. When separate microprocessors are used to control equipment settings, they can be tied together for monitoring purposes.[14]

THE SMART GUEST ROOM

To this point, we have been looking at a number of ways in which technology can improve a hotel's operating systems in the whole property. We can briefly highlight some of the ways in which the individual guest's experience is or will be enhanced. The technology we will be describing already exists and is in use in some applications. So far, however, some devices have not come down enough in price to be usable in guest rooms.

[13]Robert E. Aulbach, *Energy Management* (East Lansing, Mich.: American Hotel and Motel Association Educational Institute, 1984), p. 143.

[14]Aulbach, *Energy Management*, p. 144.

We have, for instance, discussed electronic locks and keys. There also are systems available that dispense altogether with keys, using thumbprints or a scan of the retinas of the guest's eyes. It is also possible to have the lights turn on as the guest enters the room (and to monitor rooms that are supposed to be empty), by using ultra high frequency or infrared monitors. In addition, individual guest room safes, using an individually reprogrammable chip that is set to a number designated by the guest, are in use in some hotels. There also is a device that permits the guest to view a person knocking at the guest-room door through the room's closed-circuit television screen.

A service that is increasingly popular is a well-stocked refrigerator in a guest's room offering cocktails, beer, wine, and snacks. When the guest removes an item, the appropriate charge is automatically registered at the front desk. If the system is interfaced with the PMS, as the guest removes the item from the refrigerator, the charge is automatically posted to the guest's room.

A fairly new service but one likely to spread very rapidly is the video guest checkout. There are few things as annoying to guests as having to stand in a long line to pay their bill on departure, especially if they have a plane to catch. But an in-room video checkout permits guests, by using a touch pad on the room TV, to call up their bill for inspection. If all of the charges are accepted, the guests can then direct that the bill be charged to whatever credit card they used to check in. The video checkout will be available systemwide by the end of 1988 in one chain (Marriott), and it seems clear that the competition will have little choice but to follow suit as quickly as possible.

Greater personal convenience, greater personal security, and a feeling of being in effortless control of one's immediate environment all add up to both greater convenience and the "fantasy factor" of the guest's experience, which we will discuss in the next chapter.

SUMMARY

We first gave a brief sketch of computers: the various kinds and their principal parts and functions. Then we focused on how computers are interfaced to hotels' accounting and operating systems.

The chapter next began a discussion of the new technologies that are used in hotels, including property management systems (PMS) and how they are used in making reservations and registering guests' long distance calls. Electronic key systems are another new technology that help ensure guests' security. Word processing facilitates the hotel's correspondence. Finally, videoconferencing enables people to "meet," via computer, and although it could reduce the use of hotels, it has not done so yet, and many hotels themselves are offering videoconferencing facilities.

We also examined energy management: demand, usage, and control systems. Ending the chapter was a description of a "smart" computerized guest room, some of whose features are now in use.

Hotels on the upside of the market are offering—through technology as well as improved facilities and enhanced services—improved value to the guest. Most hotels are also seeking to use technology and careful total system design to hold down rates. In a competitive industry, that is a race that will continue.

KEY WORDS AND CONCEPTS

To help you review this chapter, keep in mind the following and refer to the two glossaries for additional key words:

Computers	Output
Systems	Interfaces
Input	Word processing
Processing	Videoconferencing

REVIEW QUESTIONS

1. What are the principal parts of a computer?

2. What are some of the uses of computers in hotels?

3. How does a hotel use a PMS?

4. How do hotels use computers in regard to telephone calls and security?

5. Describe videoconferencing and how hotels have responded to it.

6. How are computers used to manage energy consumption?

7. Describe a "smart" guest room.

Credit: Courtesy of John Portman and Associates. Photo by Jaime Ardiles-Arce.

FORCES SHAPING THE HOTEL BUSINESS

Fundamental to an understanding of the hotel business is an understanding of the complex economics of lodging. This helps us to comprehend the development of new hotel formats, which have burgeoned in the past few years. Competition within the hotel industry involves location and product but, in recent years especially, also operating decisions about facilities, service levels, and amenities. With these fundamental considerations in hand, you are in a better condition to assess and perhaps chart your career prospects in an industry in a state of rapid change.

THIS CHAPTER SHOULD HELP YOU TO

1. Understand the economics of the hotel business.
2. Become aware of the forces that create hotel building cycles.
3. Discuss the dimensions of the hotel investment decision and its impact on operations.
4. Assess the advantages of management companies for owners—and for yourself as a prospective employer.
5. Identify individual entrepreneurial opportunities that may accompany reverses in the hotel business generally.
6. Identify the major segments of the lodging industry and relate them to customer segments.

7. Assess the competitive value of services and amenities offered, or not offered, by various lodging segments and companies.

THE ECONOMICS OF THE HOTEL BUSINESS

To understand the hotel business we will begin with its economic dimensions. Hotel developers and operators make long-term decisions, but in the face of shorter-term cycles. A hotel's lifetime is usually thirty or forty years and often a hundred years or more, but the cycle of hotel building is more like ten years or fewer in length.

In fact, the hotel business is cyclical, capital intensive, and highly competitive. Even though many competitors have expanded lodging capacity, it is a business whose real (inflation-adjusted) growth prospects need to be questioned. Finally, because of the hotel company's large capital investment, we should recognize that it has two kinds of customers: guests who want to rent a room and developers who want to build hotels.

A CYCLICAL BUSINESS

The hotel business is cyclical. First, the demand for hotel rooms rises and falls with the business cycle. Generally, the demand for hotel rooms changes direction three to six months after the economy does, as reflected in the gross national product.[1] This is not surprising, as both business and pleasure travel are easy expenditures to cut out in a declining economy and to restore when it improves. In any local market, the hotel business is likely to have its own cycle, related to the supply of hotel rooms, rather than the demand for them. But the cycle generally starts with the demand for rooms, potential or actual. Perhaps the easiest way to see this cycle is to work through an imaginary, but quite realistic, example.

An Example of the Hotel Business Cycle

"Oldtown," a quiet city of 100,000, has been a stable community with a balanced economy for many years. Not long ago, during a period of general economic expansion, a large national company built a large factory complex in Oldtown. The ripple effect from this spread to the suppliers for the factory complex as well as a number of other companies who, when they heard about the factory complex, learned what an attractive site Oldtown was. Employment soared: some people were transferred to Oldtown, and others moved there seeking jobs.

Our story now shifts to Major Hotels' corporate offices where in a meeting with the vice-presidents of operations and real estate, the vice-president for development suggests that Major ought to look into building a hotel in

[1]John J. Rohs, *CFA Lodging Industry Update* (New York: Wertheim & Co., 1986), p. 13.

Oldtown. There is immediate agreement to do a preliminary study. Three months later the preliminary study shows encouraging results, and so several lines of activity are set in motion. A consulting firm is hired to do a formal feasibility study; an architect is hired to do preliminary design work; and informal conversations with Major's bankers begin. Six more months pass. The results of the consultant's feasibility study confirm Major's preliminary study: The preliminary design is a beauty, and everybody agrees this could be a great hotel; and the bankers, having looked at the studies and the design, decide to process quickly Major's loan application. (They have had a surge in deposits and need to get that money into interest-earning loans. They need to lend, just as Major needs to borrow.) Best of all, the ideal location has been found, and negotiations to acquire a site are going well.

At a meeting of Major's executive committee, a formal proposal to go ahead is presented. The discussion touches briefly on the competition, but everyone quickly agrees that Oldtown's existing hotels are tired and will be no match for the proposed property. When somebody asks, "Is anybody else going in there?" the answer is, "A few people have been nosing around, but there's nothing firm as far as we can tell." Everyone agrees that it is time to purchase the site and sign a design contract with the architect. Because this is a meeting, everybody's commitment is a public matter.

The same series of events is taking place at Magnificent Hotels, LowCost Lodges, Supersuites, and a couple of other companies. But because each company keeps things fairly quiet until everything is settled, there are only vague rumors that others are also interested in Oldtown.

Finally, 18 months after the first vice-presidential meeting at Major, the company announces that a 300-room hotel will be built in Oldtown, and the ground breaking is set two weeks hence. The story is front-page news. Over the next six months, similar announcements from Magnificent, Low Cost, and Supersuites make the front page, too.

At Major, these other companies' announcements make quite a stir. At a meeting of the executive committee, they all shake their heads and agree that those other companies are crazy; they have no sense at all in overbuilding like this. One very junior vice-president who is sitting in raises the possibility that Major should abandon the project, but he is quickly shouted down. Thousands of dollars have already been spent on feasibility studies and architectural work; a site has been purchased; and contracts have been signed for construction. "Besides," says the financial vice-president, "what would our banks say if we pulled out now? Do you think we'd get another loan commitment as easily next time?" Because *everybody* has agreed to the project publicly, for any to admit that he or she was wrong would also be publicly embarrassing.

Eighteen months later, Major's beautiful new property opens, and the general manager hands the following situation report to the vice-president of operations:

> Within four blocks of my office, there are a thousand rooms under construction. Every place my sales staff goes, they trip over our competitors' people. Magnificent is slashing its convention rates for next year; LowCost has announced a salespersons' discount when its hotel opens next month; and Supersuites is offering free cocktail parties every evening.
>
> I think we will do all right after the first couple of years because our operation is going to be stronger and of better quality, but don't expect much for our first two or three years until we are established.

There are no further announcements of lodging construction in Oldtown.

We have spent quite a bit of time looking at this cycle of events to illustrate the significance of factors such as the complexity of the decision to build a hotel, the lead time required, the preliminary expenditures, and the public corporate and individual commitment to the decision. This cycle shows that an increase in demand can set off a series of events that usually cannot be stopped even when it becomes clear that the market is or will be overbuilt.

In some markets, the demand keeps increasing, and in three to five years another round of building starts, this time fueled by all the old faces plus—for those who didn't get in the first time—a need to be represented in the growth market. In other markets, it takes years for the demand to catch up with the overbuilding.

Our example was of a local market, but this is usually part of a larger, national market. Different local events related to a general national period of prosperity set off building booms in many local markets because demand for hotel rooms is closely related to general economic conditions. When the national economy turns down, so does the hotel business. Figure 9.1 illustrates hotel construction's cyclic behavior from 1968 to 1986.

Hotel building tends to come in waves or cycles which end, much to everybody's surprise, in a temporary or more or less permanent overbuilding. Figure 9.1 shows the cycle of hotel construction between 1968 and 1986. This cyclical pattern is fundamental to our understanding of the lodging business.

A CAPITAL-INTENSIVE BUSINESS

For the restaurant business, the biggest costs by far are food and payroll, followed by other direct operating expenses. Thus when sales fall precipitously, so do expenses. Hotels also have some large variable costs, most being in the food and beverage department. Lodging itself, however, is capital intensive; that is, it requires large investments of capital in fixed plant and equipment. And capital costs such as depreciation, interest, insurance, and property taxes are fixed costs. Thus, even if there are many vacancies at Major's new hotel, its the capital costs that will continue regardless of business and must be met, or the mortgage lender will (generally) foreclose.

FIGURE 9.1   Hotel construction starts were high in 1985. [Randall C. Zisler and Robert A. Feldman, *The Real Estate Report* (New York: Goldman Sachs, April 1986).]

What may happen in this situation is complicated. The mortgage holder—let's say an insurance company—may foreclose, and then it will own a hotel that it doesn't know how to operate. If it acquires a lot of hotels in this way, which sometimes happens, it may hire a management company or even establish its own hotel-operating division. (In fact, in 1986 the Prudential Realty Group owned and operated 102 hotels with 35,000 rooms.) Most mortgage holders, however, just want to find another company to take over the mortgage. They are in the business of lending money at interest, and they want a "performing loan" (one that is making payments on time) on their books rather than a hotel full of guests looking for an owner to complain to if their eggs aren't cooked right.

The original developers probably were able to borrow 60 to 70 percent of the total cost of the property and arranged to meet the rest of the investment through their own resources or by attracting other equity investors (owners rather than lenders). If the property's mortgage is foreclosed, the equity holders' stake (30 to 40 percent of the investment in this example) will be lost.

The property may be sold by the mortgage holder at a "distressed price," at, let's say, 65 percent of its original cost. The new owners will receive a significant operating advantage because their capital costs will be lower, reflecting the lower purchase price. This advantage can and frequently does mean a lower rate structure for the recapitalized property. Other properties find it difficult to meet this new lower rate if they have not been "through the wringer" (that is, bankrupted and sold at a discount to reflect the owners' equity being "washed out.") Indeed, a recapitalized property with lower fixed costs can destabilize the market and, in bad times, set off a wave of financial crises in that market through rate reductions that can't be matched by the existing capital costs at other properties.

We will argue later that this is a problem but also presents major windows of opportunity for qualified management people in the hotel business.

A COMPETITIVE BUSINESS

This is not the place for an extended theoretical discussion of monopoly, oligopoly, monopolistic competition and so forth. We do need to note, though, that some businesses like automobile and aluminium manufacturers are dominated by a few sellers. In these industries, competition may be fierce but prices tend to remain stable; some economists speak of administered prices—prices set by company decisions rather than market forces.

Room rates in lodging *tend* to be fairly stable because most properties do have a high fixed-cost structure. (Hotel payrolls, by the way, have a large fixed rather than variable element related to the minimum crew needed to stay open. This combines with capital costs to make for a high overall fixed cost.) The lodging business is much more competitive than is auto manufacturing or other oligopolies. There are "many buyers, many sellers," and everybody can easily find out what rates are being charged. (In the language of economists, these conditions describe good, if not perfect, competition.) In these competitive conditions, every tactic tends to be met by a counterattack, and lower rates in one property put immediate price pressure on other properties in the same market segment and often, indirectly, on properties in other sectors as well.

The highly competitive structure of the industry makes local or regional oversupply of rooms a very serious business. Competition means that at the bottom end of the cycle, some companies can get bruised. Older and outmoded properties may be "withdrawn from the market," that is, torn down or converted to another use, often sooner than expected.

A GROWTH BUSINESS?

In its 1985 report on trends in the hotel business, Pannel Kerr Forster estimated that there were 2.7 million rooms in the United States, with 400,000 more scheduled to be built by 1992.[2] That is about a 15 percent increase in the number of rooms, around 2 percent per year. A 2 percent growth rate certainly doesn't qualify lodging as a growth industry (10 or 20 percent might), and the number of rooms is really not the best measure of growth.

---

[2]*Trends in the Hotel Industry, USA Edition 1985* (Houston: Pannel Kerr Forster, 1985).

Rooms sold is a much better indicator and has been growing at roughly 1 percent a year since the end of World War II. The truth is that lodging is not a growth industry.[3]

We should note that this is neither a good nor a bad thing, simply a fact of life. The hotel business does suffer from a shortage of qualified managers, and there are certainly many opportunities at all levels for people who are interested in the business. Moreover, although there may not be growth in the national market, many regional markets offer growth opportunities, as do market segments such as economy and all-suite properties. From an economic perspective, however, the lack of a strong growth trend in total demand should be understood, particularly in the light of our discussion of product segmentation later in this chapter.

Many factors appear to be slowing the growth of lodging demand. First, travel patterns and consumer preferences have changed. With faster travel, executives can fly into a city, do their business, and fly home on the same day. Shorter trips have become the rule. In addition, long distance telephoning is substituting more and more for face-to-face meetings, and videoconferencing could have a similar, though smaller, impact. In pleasure travel, campers and trailers, or even second homes, are often used instead of transient lodging. People who spend their vacation in their summer cottage are obviously not hotel customers at that moment.

The lodging industry's pricing practices have almost certainly contributed to these trends. Throughout the early 1970s, hotel prices increased at about the same rate as did other prices. From 1972 until quite recently, however, room rates increased substantially faster than did the costs of other goods and services, as illustrated in Figure 9.2. In 1984, room rates increased roughly five percentage points more than other prices did, and, in 1985, about three and a half points more.[4] As early as 1984, the president of Quality Courts charged that hotels were frightening guests away because of their "excessive product pricing and a decrease in the perceived price value relationship."[5]

[3]When I first made such a statement in 1974, in an article in *The Institute Journal* published by the American Hotel Motel Association Educational Institute, it caused considerable irritation in some quarters in the hotel business, presumably because "growth" was good, and so nongrowth must be bad. I am happy therefore, to note that I now have plenty of company among the experts. For instance, Daniel Lee, security analyst at Drexel Burnham Lambert, stated, "Although cyclical, the lodging business is not a 'growth' industry" (Daniel R. Lee, "A Forecast of Lodging Supply and Demand," *Cornell Hotel and Restaurant Administration Quarterly*, August 1984, p. 37); and Glenn Withian, managing editor of the *Cornell Quarterly*, stated, on the basis of Laventhol & Horwath data, "The number of hotel rooms occupied per day has remained relatively flat for more than three decades." (Glenn Withian, "Hotel Companies Aim for Multiple Markets," *Cornell Hotel and Restaurant Administration Quarterly*, November 1985, p. 51.)
[4]Rohs, *Lodging Industry Update*, p. 9.
[5]*Nation's Restaurant News*, December 17, 1984, p. 93.

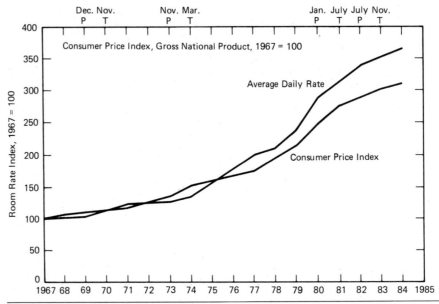

FIGURE 9.2 Consumer price index versus average daily rate. (Pannell Kerr Forster & Co., *Trend of Business—1986.*)

Price increases have not been limited to room rates. According to Laventhol & Horwath analyst Bjorn Hansen, "Hotels have been very aggressive in raising their (food) prices—and customers are starting to show resistance." Saul Leonard, of the same firm, observed, "If you're an egg eater, you've got to spend at least $15 to eat breakfast in a hotel. You can get breakfast at a nearby coffee shop for $1.29."[6] When the cost of both food and room are added together, the cost of hotel-based travel has soared even more than the escalation in just room rates suggests.

DIMENSIONS OF THE HOTEL INVESTMENT DECISION

Despite price resistance, overbuilding in some markets, and the cyclical nature of the business, new hotels continue to come on the market. This is because developers need hotels to open up new or redeveloped areas and because lenders are interested in granting mortgages to hotel builders and developers. There are at least three dimensions of a hotel investment: financial, real estate, and operation.

[6]*Nation's Restaurant News,* November 4, 1985, p. F3.

FINANCIAL

The decision to build a hotel may be motivated by purely financial considerations related to interest rates, tax-law changes, or the desire to hedge against inflation. For instance, as James McGraw, executive vice-president of the Sheraton Corporation, pointed out in regard to the early and mid-1980s "People built hotels with cheap money [money "rented" at low interest rates] and made money on the loan if not the hotel."[7]

The 1981 tax law encouraged hotel development by allowing shorter tax lives for properties, thus enabling higher depreciation deductions. This was a great advantage to people and corporations with large incomes in the highest tax brackets because the depreciation acted as a tax shield. The 1986 tax reform act, however, reversed these advantages, resulting in a significant decline in new hotel construction.

Investors are also attracted to hotels because they are an inflation hedge. As one real estate investment and operating company explained in a brochure addressed to potential investors, "Hotels have the ability to respond almost instantly to changes and fluctuations in the economy and market. For instance, while office and retail properties are usually locked in to long-term leases—some lasting as long as 20 years—hotel rates can be changed virtually overnight."[8]

REAL ESTATE

Hotels also may be built because a community or area development needs the property; that is, the hotel may be necessary to a larger project. The underlying value of the real estate and its appreciation may be a more important consideration to some investors than is the profitability of the hotel. For example, a number of foreign investors in North America have apparently been willing to invest money in hotel properties for their longer-term appreciation and as a safe haven for their funds.

AN OPERATING BUSINESS

The hotel's operation is often the first investment dimension that most students of hotel management automatically think of. We have already discussed hotel operations in Chapter 8, but it is worth noting here that operations may be a secondary consideration to some investors.

Risks and Rewards

Our discussion of the cyclical nature of the hotel business suggested that it can be risky for investors. On the other hand, "On an operating basis, hotels have historically outperformed all other types of property. Figures given in

---

[7]James D. McGraw, "Suite Hotels Panel Discussion," Eighth Annual Hospitality Investment Conference, New York, June 9, 1986.

[8]"VMS Hotel Investments: A Unique Destination for the Individual Investor," n.d., p. 3.

a recent report state that hotel properties showed a compound annual return of nearly 22 percent—higher than any other form of income producing property."[9] Thus, although there are risks, clearly there are also substantial rewards to investors to compensate for that risk.

MANAGEMENT COMPANIES

Hotels are often built by people who have neither the skill nor the interest to operate them, and so to answer their needs, management companies have come into existence.

The first management company may have been the Cesar Ritz Group. Before the turn of the century, Ritz, with his famous chef, Escoffier, was "paid a retainer to appoint and oversee the managers of separately owned hotels. That arrangement allowed the hotel to advertise itself as a Ritz hotel."[10] The first U.S. "hotel management company" was the Treadway Hotel Company, which began operating small college inns in the 1920s.[11] During the 1930s, the American Hotel Corporation managed bankrupt hotels, but as late as 1970 there were only three or four management companies in operation in the United States. The period since then has been characterized by rapid hotel property development and several periods of "shakeout." Many hotel owners (and their mortgage holders) found themselves in financial difficulty. Under these circumstances the number of management companies grew rapidly, and in 1985, the president of one of the larger companies, Robert M. James, estimated that there were about 125 management companies, although only a few of them were national organizations. The arrangement between the management company and the hotel owner is called a *management contract* and was spelled out by Professor James Eyster of the Cornell Hotel School:

> A management contract is a written agreement between a hotel–motor inn owner and operator in which the owner employs the operator as an agent (employee) to assume full operational responsibility for the property and to manage the property in a professional manner. As an agent, the operator pays in the name of the owner, all property operating expenses from the cash flow generated from the operation; it retains its management fees, and remits the remaining cash flow, if any, to the owner. The owner provides the hotel—motor inn property to include land, building, furniture and fixtures, equipment,

---

[9]"VMS Hotel Investments," p. 1.

[10]Daniel R. Lee, *Lodging* (New York: Drexel Burham Lambert, 1984), p. 23.

[11]Information in this section is taken from Robert M. James, "Management Companies," *Lodging*, June 1985, pp. 105, 128.

and working capital and assumes full legal and financial responsibility for the project.[12]

There are two kinds of management companies. First, most chain organizations such as Hilton, Holiday Inns, or Sheraton serve as management companies for hotels under their franchises. Independent management companies, on the other hand, operate properties under several franchises. According to James, the independent companies offer the owners more control over daily operations and more flexibility in terms and in brand affiliation than do the chain companies.

The independent management company offers several advantages to those starting a career in the hotel business. The company with a successful track record will have experienced and knowledgeable people in its senior ranks. Working with and under such well-qualified and broadly experienced managers can be an education in itself. Moreover, a larger company will probably have properties of varying sizes and franchise affiliations and thus offer both opportunities for career progression from smaller to larger properties and a broad variety of experiences. Naturally, as with any company you are considering working with, it is a good idea to inquire about the company's reputation before signing on in a responsible position. And, again, as with any company, a good way to get to know a prospective long-term employer is through employment in the summer or part time during the school year.

Entrepreneurial Opportunities

We discussed the outlook for careers in the hotel business at the conclusion of the Chapter 7. We should pause here to note the significance of the management company's function for those who want to have ownership interest in a hotel. Management companies serve a need for mortgage holders and developers that can also be filled by individuals. These individuals, who, through education and experience, prepare themselves to manage a hotel, can regard a time of economic reverses for the industry as a time of opportunity for themselves. Particularly with locally financed (that is, mortgaged) properties that get into trouble, there is a real opportunity from time to time to get into an ownership position in return for assuming an existing mortgage. This kind of opportunity is more likely to come up with older properties, and so the importance of a good food background—in order to merchandise the property—is clear.

---

[12]James J. Eyster, *The Negotiation and Administration of Hotel Management Contracts,* quoted in Robert M. James, "Management Companies," *Lodging,* June 1985, p. 105.

LODGING TRENDS: SEGMENTATION OR FRAGMENTATION?

Until quite recently, the North American lodging industry was product oriented and relatively standardized.[13] In effect, the hotel business defined its customers' needs for them by offering a standardized product. The market a few years ago could be represented by three major types. First were first-class properties—Hilton, Westin, and Marriott, for instance. A second major group was made up of companies serving business and tourist travelers with a very good standardized product such as Holiday Inns, Quality, and Ramada. The third group was lower-cost properties made up of older independent motels and, especially from 1975 onward, a growing group of properties built specifically for the rate-sensitive market, such as Days Inns. By the mid-1980s, however, the lodging market had changed dramatically, and products designed to suit the needs of specific travelers' market segments had emerged.

The emergence of properties aimed at specific market segments led some to speak of the fragmentation of the market. Part of this change was the reduction of services at one end of the market and the expansion of personal services at the other end. Luxury accommodations are the specialty of some hotel companies such as the Four Seasons. Other companies provide differentiated, upscale, service-intensive "executive floors" in mid-scale properties. Another interesting development is the introduction of the all-suite hotels, hotels that are less service intensive but that feature a higher-quality guest room.

We turn our attention now to a brief discussion of the major segments of the market. We will conclude this section with a review of the significance of hotel developers in the emergence of "new" segments.

ECONOMY LODGING

In the early 1980s, Days Inns, Econolodge, and other established economy chains found themselves competing with Quality's Comfort Inns. And by the mid-1980s, the lower-priced, budget-oriented properties had become a major force in the market. Especially the entry of Holiday Corporation into the economy market, with Hampton Inns, meant that the large corporations with "deep pockets" (that is, with ready access to the funds to finance expansion) had arrived. The size of the economy segment in 1986 was suggested by a survey of economy chains which showed that the largest 50 chains of economy lodging were operating about 325,000 guest rooms, or nearly 15 percent of the market in approximately 3300 locations.[14]

Economy properties offer "standard-sized, fully furnished, modern

<hr>

[13]I am indebted to Mr. Ray Yelle, president of Commonwealth Holiday Inns of Canada, for his observations regarding the transition that is taking place in lodging competition.
[14]*Hotel Motel Management,* May 19, 1986, pp. 22–26.

Some budget properties offer no food or pool, just a high-quality room and excellent housekeeping. These properties have targeted business travelers as their principal market. (Photo courtesy of Red Roof Inns.)

rooms at rates 20 to 50 per cent below area average rates."[15] In conventional motor inns and hotels, the commercial building or its equivalent—lobby, restaurants, cocktail lounge, and meeting and banquet rooms—is a major part of the initial investment. But in the economy format, some or all of these facilities are eliminated.

Hampton Inns, Holiday Corporation's economy chain, generally contain 110 to 130 units and offer a lobby and breakfast area and a hospitality suite.[16] Some economy properties offer a limited food service or have a franchised restaurant on the premises, such as Wendy's or Arby's at Days Inns. Many economy chains rely on a location near local restaurants, whereas others, such as La Quinta Motor Inns, provide a freestanding restaurant on the same site as the motel.

The plans for expansion in the economy market announced by corporations such as Holiday and Quality, as well as the already-established chains like Days Inns and Motel 6, have at least two limitations. The first is the cyclic nature of the business. Many industry observers feel the hotel business is already overbuilt in most markets, even in the economy segment. The second factor is the refranchising cycle.

[15]*Hotel Motel Management,* May 19, 1986, pp. 22–26.
[16]*Hotel Motel Management,* June 30, 1986, p. 38.

Most budget properties offer a simpler variety of the same basic services that other motor hotels provide. (Photo courtesy of Days Inns.)

Refranchise or Convert?

Franchises are usually granted for several years, commonly 25 or 30. At the end of the original franchise agreement, new terms will be negotiated if the franchise is to be renewed. By the early 1980s, a number of older mid-priced hotels were due for refranchising. Generally the refranchising has meant huge investments for upgrading the hotel. Not only must the rooms be redecorated, but often the air-conditioning plant must be replaced. The lobby and food service units must also be refurbished, and other major capital improvements such as an indoor swimming pool may be required. Although such an investment may make sense in some locations and may be financially possible for some owners, others find that the upgrading required is not economically justified or feasible.

Obviously, the properties that do not upgrade and refranchise do not just "go away." Some simply become independents, many of which then compete in the economy market. An increasing number choose to "convert" to another company. For instance, Quality's economy chain, Comfort Inns, includes a number of reconversions from its own mid-scale Quality Inns and

Budget motel rooms are basically similar to rooms in more expensive properties. (Photo courtesy of Days Inns.)

from other franchise groups. The existing inventory of older mid-scale properties is a competitive threat to the economy segment because it may make sense for more and more mid-scale properties to minimize their investments by refranchising to the standard of the economy market.

MID-SCALE PROPERTIES

Existing mid-scale properties are generally upgrading their facilities as new properties are built and older ones are refranchised. New players are also arriving in this market.

The Courtyard Concept

Probably the best-known and perhaps the most-copied new concept is "Courtyard by Marriott." This product was developed after extensive consumer research and testing in the Atlanta area. Based on successful prototypes, Marriott proposed spending $3 billion to develop, by 1990, 300 courtyards with over 50,000 rooms. The courtyard concept in many ways resembles the economy market, in that the commercial building is scaled down dramatically to include a very small lobby and minimal food and beverage facilities. In turn, the scaled-down food and beverage operations require much lower payrolls. The restaurant menus are highly simplified and rely on convenience and preprepared foods. Finally, only limited meeting space is provided, generally just one or two small conference rooms.

Instead of capital investment in public space for food and beverage facilities—and expenditures for their operation—the courtyard property invests in unusually well-appointed and large guest rooms and offers them at highly competitive rates. Most of the rooms contain king-sized beds, separate working and dressing areas, a sofa bed, in-room coffee service, a phone with a long cord, and remote-control television with cable and free movies. Rates range from $40 to $60. The property features a central landscaped courtyard with a swimming pool and a "socializing area." Northern locations have indoor swimming pools. Operating costs are minimized by clustering the courtyards in areas that can support more than one property, so as to achieve economies in management and marketing expenses.[17]

The courtyard concept is clearly popular with other companies. Whether companies have deliberately copied Marriott or simply reached the same conclusions is not clear. Nevertheless, the announcements of new products that are similar to Marriott's courtyards have become so frequent that some in the trade describe them as "courtyard clones."

Older Properties

Some older mid-scale properties move to the economy category. Others, however, seek to position themselves in the mid-scale market, but without the extensive upgrading required in the typical refranchising. One new chain, Park Inns, was established with the avowed intent of serving mid-scale franchisees that are not happy with their refranchising. Company officials forecast that by the end of the decade more than 700 U.S. hotels will have changed their corporate affiliation.[18]

With their full complement of food, beverage, and meeting facilities, these older properties will continue to offer physical plants that are competitive with those of the new and refranchised properties. And because many of these properties are 20 to 30 years old, they may have lower capital costs, reflecting their depreciated values. This could result in a considerable reduction in their break-even point, which means that they can offer significantly lower rates for roughly comparable facilities. The mid-priced category, which in 1985 represented roughly 70 percent of the market, is highly competitive. It is pressed from below by economy properties and from within by new entrants and older properties that may offer lower rates.

UPSCALE PROPERTIES

The upper end of the lodging market has been split into three types, *upscale*, *all-suite*, and *luxury*. Some companies, such as Hilton, Westin, and Shera-

[17]Company sources.
[18]*Hotel Motel Management*, February 3, 1986, page 31.

Guest rooms at Courtyard by Marriott are designed with distinct functional areas for relaxing, working, sleeping, and dressing. King-sized beds are a feature in 70 percent of the rooms. (Photo courtesy of Marriott Corp.)

ton, compete principally in the upscale market. (Note, however, that Hilton Inns and Sheraton Inns are often judged to compete in the mid-scale market. The *inn* designation often denotes a franchised property operating in a smaller or suburban market.) The competition in this segment is with mid-scale chains moving into the market and with all-suite properties.

Mid-scale companies have invaded the upscale market: Holiday with the Crown Plaza Holiday Inn, Ramada with the Ramada Renaissance, and Quality with the Quality Royale. Another competitive tactic of mid-scale operators aimed at gaining a share of the upscale market is that of "executive floors." An increasingly common approach—sometimes referred to as "a hotel within a hotel"—is having rooms in midscale properties offer luxury features, more amenities, and expanded services such as free newspapers, overnight shoeshine service, and a complementary breakfast. But perhaps the greatest competition in the upscale market is from the all-suite properties.

All-Suite Properties

Market research suggests that two-thirds of all business travelers are potentially all-suite customers; that is, they can afford all-suite rates. One-third of these people have tried an all-suite hotel, and two-thirds intend to try one.[19] Since their inception, all-suite hotels have outperformed the market in terms of occupancy, room rates, and profit. In fact, 35 to 40 percent of their gross revenue has been available to cover fixed charges, compared with only 25 percent from standard hotels.[20]

A conventional hotel room has 300 to 400 square feet, whereas an all-suite unit ranges from 500 to 800 square feet. This generally includes a separate dining room—which may be used as a work or lounging area—a bedroom, and a kitchenette. The suite appeals especially to business travelers who want a more spacious, homelike atmosphere as well as a space for work and relaxation. On the weekends, the roominess is a special advantage for traveling families with children because both parents and children can have rooms of their own without additional cost.

The rates at all-suite hotels are generally competitive with those of comparable conventional properties. This is possible because their food and beverage service is quite limited. As with economy properties, the elimination or severe curtailment of investment in food and beverage facilities (capital costs) and food and beverage operations (operating costs) makes the provision of larger and more luxurious guest rooms economically viable. Most all-suite units offer a complementary breakfast, and many offer cocktails at no charge in the late afternoon and early evening. This permits the property to schedule employees for only the hours required for this limited service and to offer the service in a predictable, economical format.

All-suite properties are less dependent on the off-the-road, drop-in traveler and consequently can afford a less expensive location away from the expressway interchange favored by many hotel companies. In fact, the all-suite hotel company is commonly located near its corporate clients.

In some respects, the all-suite hotel label is misleading because there are suite properties at every level of the market, from Quality's Comfort Inns' all-suite properties to L'Ermitage at the very top of the luxury scale. Although some authorities suggest that all-suite units could take up 10 percent or more of the market by the early 1990s,[21] all-suite properties may eventually become the rule outside those areas with exceptionally high land costs and outside the strictly budget category.

The Long-Stay Market

One particular all-suite segment deserves specific mention, and that is the property designed for long-stay guests. The market leader in this area has been Residence Inns.

---

[19]Michael M. Dickens, president, Guest Quarters Inc., Address to the 8th Annual National Hospitality Industry Investment Conference, New York, June 9, 1986.
[20]Felig Jarvis, "All Suite Hotels," *Lodging*, June 1985, pp. 103, 121, 122.
[21]Rohs, *CFA Lodging Industry Update*, p. 16.

Residence Inns estimates that the extended-stay segment is 5 percent of the lodging market. Residence Inns' data also show that almost half (40 percent) of its guests are extended-stay guests, that is, those who stay 5 to 29 days. The next biggest group (30 percent) is long-stay guests, remaining 30 or more days, whereas only 30 percent stay a more conventional four or fewer days.[22] According to Residence Inns, a typical guest is between 25 and 44 years old and earns $35,000 or more per year. Three-quarters of its guests have professional, managerial, or administrative jobs, and the rest are in technical occupations (15 percent) or sales (13 percent). Eighty-five percent of Residence Inns' business comes from the 500 largest companies in the United States, and roughly half of its guests earn over $50,000 per year. Thus, Residence Inns has chosen a highly profitable specialized market with clearly defined needs.

LUXURY HOTELS

Another property type that has grown from being relatively rare to becoming quite common is the luxury hotel, as typified by the Four Seasons or Mandarin properties. These hotels—a tier above those labeled as upscale—are characterized by very comfortable, even opulent guest rooms, excellent food service, and highly skilled personal service. As Isador Sharpe told an industry group, "Success in the luxury market requires excellence—with extraordinary consistency."[23]

The executive floors mentioned earlier in connection with the mid-scale market have their parallel in the luxury and superluxury markets in the "Towers" concept. Originally begun at the Waldorf Astoria Hotel in New York City, the Waldorf Towers were aimed at wealthy travelers, heads of corporations, and visiting diplomats and heads of state. Hilton found this segmentation strategy one worth developing further and did so, first in the Palmer House Towers in Chicago and then in several other properties. The idea has been adopted by other upscale hotels to maintain not only the profit but also the glamour and reputation that accrue to those who host the wealthy, famous, and successful.

OTHER SPECIALIZED SEGMENTS

Conference Centers

More money—$40 to $60 million—is spent each year on corporate education than in colleges and universities. This therefore is a very attractive market and one for which many hotels compete. Specialized conference centers

---

[22]Jack P. DeBoer, chairman and chief executive officer, Residence Inns, Address to 8th Annual National Hospitality Industry Investment Conference, New York, June 9, 1986.
[23]Isador Sharpe, Address to the Eighth Annual National Hospitality Industry Investment Conference, New York, June 9, 1986.

Residence Inns, a leader in the long-stay market, offers an all-suite property especially designed to meet the needs of guests who will be staying for more than a few days. The exterior courtyard view shown here resembles a low-rise condominium development. The guest facilities are designed for business entertaining. (Photos courtesy of Residence Inns.)

Luxury hotels offer not just comfort but also elegance in every appointment. Pictured (opposite) are a guest room and a mirrored bathroom from the Park Hyatt on Water Tower Square in Chicago. (Photo courtesy of Hyatt Hotels.)

have grown up to meet the particular needs of this market. Some of the centers are operated by large companies such as General Motors, IBM, or AT&T. Others, however, are built as separate businesses to compete for the conference business. Some meeting coordinators prefer these kinds of properties because of their special design and their ability to focus their whole attention on the conference. Several conference centers are operated by hotel companies. Marriott, for instance, operated 22 such properties in 1986 and was actively seeking more management contracts in this area.[24] The facilities provided at such centers usually include tennis, swimming, golf, and game rooms. Some centers also offer gyms, saunas, bowling, horseback riding, and libraries.[25]

Condominiums

Condominiums, or "condos" as they are often called, generally offer the features of an apartment building—multiroom apartments with full kitchens—sometimes combined with those of a hotel, such as on-premise food and beverage service. The units, however, are usually sold to individual owners, but the overall property is operated by a management company. Condos that compete with hotels are often located in a resort area.

Two kinds of condo ownership are available. Some condos are sold outright, and their owners have the right to year-round occupancy. Another, increasingly common practice is to sell "time-shares," the right to occupy the condo permanently and as an owner for a limited and specific time, with others having that right for other time periods. The price of a time-share usually depends on the desirability of the particular time period, with less attractive time periods costing substantially less than peak periods do. On the other hand, some time-sharing arrangements require the owners to buy shares in high, middle, and off seasons. Thus, for instance, a time-share package might be offered for one week each in the months of July, October, January, and April. Time-share–swapping networks enable the owners to swap with one another a week they own in Miami for, say, the same week or even a different week in Aspen.

Condos are competitive with hotels in two ways. First, they represent a form of interindustry competition in the same way that a second home or a camper does. That is, the owner of a condo in a resort location is much less likely to be a hotel customer because his or her funds are already invested in a vacation property.

Besides being an alternative to a hotel for their owner, condos—both those sold outright and those marketed as time-shares—are often rented out by the management company when the owner does not want to use the prop-

---

[24]*Hotel Motel Management,* June 9, 1986, pp. 19–21.
[25]David E. Arnold and Joan K. Spence, *The Executive Conference Center—A Statistical and Financial Profile.* (Philadelphia: Laventhol & Horwath, 1982).

erty. This makes them very real competitors on a day-to-day basis, with the hotels in their market. Some condo properties, particularly those offering many services, are operated by hotel companies and are marketed as resorts. Indeed, some companies have sold significant portions of a resort as condos or have built a condo component into their plan for the development and financing of a new resort. In effect, the sale of condominiums has become an important source of financing for the owners of the resort.

SEGMENTATION: FOR GUESTS OR DEVELOPERS?

Much of the development of new product segments—economy, all-suite, executive floors, superluxury—can be related to specific market segments. For example, economy segments are aimed at rate-conscious consumer groups such as retirees. (Days Inns reported that 11 percent of its rooms are occupied by seniors.) Residence Inns has a clearly targeted segment in mind, and its range of products, from executive floors to superluxury, is for the expense-account market. On the other hand, the appeal of the all-suites—"two-thirds of the market," upscale executives and families with children—sounds like targeting nearly everyone who isn't overly concerned about price. Indeed, one market analyst characterized segmentation as "an 'unique' strategy which seems to have been universally adopted."[26]

Glenn Withian, Managing Editor of the *Cornell Hotel and Restaurant Administration Quarterly*, suggests that the consumer market is not the sole driving force behind segmentation, however; segmentation also meets the business needs of the hotel companies, their potential franchisees, and the developers. Segmentation first offers a strategy to hotel companies to maintain growth in a mature market. If, for instance, there are already a number of established Holiday Inns in a market, that city may still be ripe for a Hampton Inn or an Embassy Suite. This pleases both the potential franchisee looking for an investment opportunity and the franchisor.

> Most hotel companies are largely service companies that sell a product—a specific kind of hotel—to developers. . . . Today, hotel companies are offering developers a range of hotels so the company can match the hotel product to the site. Having multiple brands or chains allows hotel companies to provide a product to meet developer needs.[27]

[26]Randall C. Zisler and Robert A. Feldman, "The Real Estate Report" (New York: Goldman Sachs, April 1986), p. 15.

[27]Glenn Withian, "Hotel Companies Aim for Multiple Markets," *Cornell Hotel and Restaurant Administration Quarterly*, November 1985, pp. 39–51. In the argument cited here, Withian is quoting industry analyst Daniel Lee.

From an ethical point of view, there is nothing even faintly questionable about these tactics. The franchisor is in the business of selling franchises; the franchisee wants to invest in a property; and a developer needs a property to round out a project. Each pursues his or her own interest in an informed way. The resulting increase in competition is a business risk that should surprise no one.

Nevertheless, the interests of hotel companies, franchisees, and developers heighten the possibility that markets will be overbuilt, that the cycle we discussed at the beginning of this chapter will be more pronounced then if the players limit their attention to just consumer demand.

SOLUTIONS TO OVERSUPPLY

One solution to an oversupply of rooms in a market is, as we said earlier, time and a continuing growth in demand. The other solution is to withdraw from the market or to convert the property to other uses. For instance, 13 hotels with about 5700 rooms were taken off the market in New York City between 1980 and 1985, either through conversion to another use such as apartments or because they were closed. It is estimated that 1.1 percent of hotel rooms are withdrawn each year.[28] Although the closing of a hotel is usually a sad day, especially for its owners, staff, and frequent guests, most properties do eventually reach a point that the continued investment to maintain and refurbish a property is not warranted. Indeed, inherent in the notion of depreciation is the fact that properties wear out.

In periods of oversupply, properties are more readily judged substandard because the newer and better properties are more likely to be filled first. And a number of industry observers have suggested that during the last half of the 1980s we might expect such activity to be more common than in other periods.[29]

COMPETITIVE TACTICS: SERVICES AND AMENITIES

In the competitive hotel marketplace, one of the means of differentiation is designing a hotel property to suit the needs of a particular market segment. In many cases such strategies involve changes in the mix of services and facilities from what was once the industry standard (see Figure 9.3). For example, some properties have curtailed their services, and others have ex-

---

[28]Lee, *Lodging*, p. 73.

[29]See, for instance, Rohs, *Lodging Industry Update*, p. 8, or the remarks of several speakers at the 8th Annual National Hospitality Industry Conference. Hervey Feldman, president of Embassy Suites, referred to the mid-1980s as the worst crisis our industry has ever faced. Carl Mottek, president of Hilton Hotels, referred to the mid-1980s as the universal buyer's market, and James Pickett, president of Pickett Companies, called it a time of obsolescence, disruption, demolition, and conversion.

panded them, in what one analyst sees as a response to the "polarization" of consumers.[30]

In this discussion, remember, we will be looking at all kinds of changes, both increases and reductions. Whenever we speak of *reductions* in facilities or service levels, you should remember that such reductions permit greater investment in guest rooms or lower room rates, and often both. That is, the reduction is generally matched by an improved consumer benefit.

The industry is trying to find appropriate price–value relationships for particular consumer segments. Indeed, segmentation—in facilities, services, and rates—marks a major shift in the lodging industry from an operational focus to a marketing focus.[31] The incidence of nonfood and beverage guest services is summarized in Figure 9.3.

HOTEL FOOD SERVICE

One characteristic of many of the newer lodging formats is the reduction in food services.

Bed and Breakfast—Plus

The practice of giving away a continental breakfast is certainly not new but has been common in small motels for some years. But the advertised, stand-

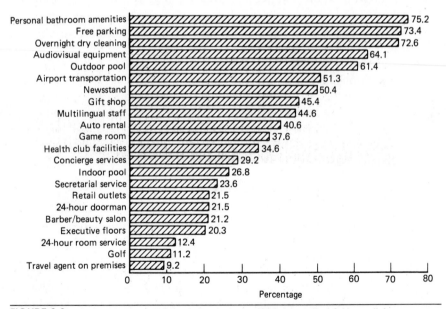

FIGURE 9.3   Guest services. (U.S. Lodging Industry 1986. Laventhol & Horwath.)

[30]Rohs, *CFA Lodging Industry Update*, p. 15.
[31]*1986 US Lodging Special Analysis* (New York: Laventhol & Horwath, 1986), p. 2.

ardized availability of a "free breakfast," that is, one covered by the price of the room, has a special appeal. In the economy market, for instance, a continental breakfast of juice, pastry, and coffee is generally all that is provided. In some all-suite properties, as well, a continental breakfast is the standard, but a number offer a full, cooked-to-order breakfast. All-suite properties also commonly provide a free cocktail party, typically from 5 to 7 P.M. Residence Inns have a grocery-shopping service available without cost to their guests, and some of their properties also have arranged for food service delivery from local restaurants.[32]

Many all-suite properties also provide a scaled-down, on-premise restaurant. But very few, if any, however, offer substantial meeting and banquet facilities. Some all-suite operators, such as the Hotel Luxeford operations, go to a great deal of trouble to arange for their food service to be operated by a well-known, local restaurateur.[33] In the all-suite market, then, there is not the uniformity in curtailment of food service that is found among most budget properties. In general, however, elimination or at least simplification is the rule.

Quick-Service Delis and Leased Food Service

Fast-food operations such as Arby's and Wendy's are replacing "Daybreak" operations at Days Inns. In Toronto, Pat & Marios, a roadhouse chain, operates the restaurant in the high-rise airport Venture Inn, one of a chain of Canadian budget hotels. Delicatessens are also proving successful in some Radisson, Hyatt, and Ramada properties.[34]

Most Embassy Suites lease their food service units to other operators. All of these lease arrangements with fast-food and roadhouse chains have the advantage of giving the food service headaches to another specialist company. And some customers favoring a particular fast-food service may actually be drawn to the property for that reason, and virtually all customers will know what to expect. The disadvantage is that the lodging operation loses a large measure of control over its "service department."

On-Site Franchised Restaurants

Probably the best-known practitioner of the on-site franchised restaurant is La Quinta Motor Inns. This economy motel chain offers a build-to-suit leased restaurant on the motel site. It has used this arrangement with several restaurant companies, including Denny's, Cracker Barrel, Bob Evans Farms, Waffle House, and Shoney's. According to *Nation's Restaurant News*, La Quinta is now also interested in fast-food chains such as McDonald's and Wendy's because they are serving breakfast—and because of

---

[32]*Nation's Restaurant News*, April 1, 1985, p. 33.
[33]*Nation's Restaurant News*, March 10, 1986, p. 44.
[34]*Nation's Restaurant News*, April 22, 1985, p. 3.

the speed of their breakfast service. Generally, such a lease specifies the minimum number of hours of operation and allows the guests to charge their food to their room.

Conventional Hotel Restaurants

A single direction for hotels' food services is by no means clear. Some hotel operators are finding that they can't compete successfully with local top-quality food service restaurants in attracting local trade and so are building smaller restaurants and reducing the number of the food service outlets in the hotel from two or three to one.[35] Even some luxury hotels, according to Laventhol & Horwath's Bjorn Hansen, are opting for more casual outlets rather than formal dining rooms.[36]

On the other hand, Marriott chose to send several of its chefs to study in the south of France, and a number of other hotels have contracted with leading French and American chefs for consulting services.[37] Thus, these companies are, if anything, increasing their emphasis on fine food. Indeed, the president of Doubletree Inns stated, "Strong, community oriented restaurants and lounges add 7 to 8 points to our occupancy rates." In a similar vein, the president of Royce Hotels explained, "If you call secretaries in West Palm Beach and ask them where to stay, they probably say Royce because they eat in the restaurant and visit the lounge. Eighty percent of our business is generated through local referrals."[38]

Restaurants As a Competitive Strategy

Hotel restaurants do not generally make money after all of the charges are considered. Bjorn Hansen of Laventhol and Howarth has estimated that after allocation of all overhead, a hotel restaurant actually loses about 5 percent on sales.[39] The reasons for this difficulty were discussed in Chapter 7, where we saw that food service was the hotel's "service department." The argument for devoting all the time and effort to food service, however, is made fairly well by the Doubletree and Royce presidents in the previous paragraph. Food service in many markets adds points to occupancy, secures local referrals, and the resulting higher occupancies more than offset the limited profits of food service.

Whereas newer formats minimize food service at the present time, these properties currently have the advantage of being brand new. When they have several look-alike competitors, all offering the same advantages, the competitive situation may prove more complex.

[35]*Nation's Restaurant News*, November 4, 1985, p. F5.

[36]*Nation's Restaurant News*, August 12, 1985, p. F58.

[37]*Nation's Restaurant News*, January 20, 1986, p. F3.

[38]*Nation's Restaurant News*, March 10, 1986, p. F29.

[39]Bjorn Hansen, "Hotel Food Service: Where's the Profit?" *Cornell Hotel and Restaurant Administration Quarterly*, August 1984, p. 96.

At the point when the lodging market becomes highly competitive, the chances are that the importance of a good-quality food and beverage operation will be "rediscovered" by more and more operations. On the other hand, it is quite clear that there is and, for the foreseeable future will be, an important segment of the lodging industry that does not offer any significant food service.

OTHER SERVICES AND AMENITIES

A wide range of services, distinctive physical plant features, and products outside the food and beverage department are used by hotels to differentiate a property from its competitors.

The Concierge and Superfloors

The basic function of the concierge is to provide guest service and information. The cross keys, symbol of the concierge, is intended to convey a degree of expertise and knowledge significantly above that of the bell staff. The concierge knows the right restaurants, the best shows, and can probably get reservations or tickets if they are required. In many ways, the concierge acts as a friend to the stranger out of town, giving service and rendering that "extra" in service that makes a stay a distinctive experience in hospitality.

Many hotels are adding a concierge to the lobby staff, and a number of companies associate the concierge closely or exclusively with their super-floors, that is, special areas such as executive floors and tower suites. On these floors special lounges and other services are commonly provided. Although there are many variations, perhaps the easiest way to examine the practice is to look at one hotel company.

At CN Hotels' new Toronto property, L'Hotel, three classes of *service* are available: premiere, silver, and gold. The word *service* is emphasized because the basic product, the rooms and its furnishings, is virtually the same in all three classes. The silver and gold floors are a part of a strategy of meeting the particular service tastes and needs of upscale, frequent travelers.

Guests entering the hotel intending to go to the premiere—or "regular"—floors (about 65 percent of the hotel) register at the front desk and are shown to their room by a bellman. The concierge in the lobby provides them with standard services such as information, reservations, and tickets.

Guests entering the hotel intending to go to the silver floors register at the lobby concierge's desk using a special express registration procedure. Upon arriving at their floor, they are met by a host or hostess and shown to their room. (Their bags are sent up by the doorman.) The silver floor has a small but very comfortable lounge that offers the guests a complimentary continental breakfast, an honor bar (that is, guests may pour their own drinks and sign a chit for them) from 4 to 10 P.M. daily, and complimentary canapés served from 5 to 7 P.M. Other services include complimentary local phone calls, complimentary cable television with remote control, complimentary tea or coffee with their wake-up call, evening turn-down service, and an overnight shoeshine. Special personal amenities include hair dryers, plush bathrobes, extra plush towels, fresh fruit, and freshly cut flowers. Rooms on the silver floor cost about 25 percent more than those on the premiere floors do.

Guests on the gold floors are generally recognized by the doorman because they are repeat guests. They are sent directly to their floor, where they are met by the gold floor concierge and shown to their room after the very brief registration formalities are concluded in the gold lounge. In the center of the gold lounge, consisting of several rooms furnished in the style of a private club, is the office of the concierge and his or her staff. Prompt, personal service is emphasized in the lounge. The continental breakfast on the gold floor is deluxe, and all the amenities offered on the silver floor are provided here as well. In addition, each room is supplied with a small box of fine chocolates. The gold lounge offers an honor bar, secretarial services, and a "board room" for small meetings. The full dining-room menu is available from room service. Guests on both the silver and gold floors are offered complementary limousine service to the center of downtown. Rates on the gold floor are about 45 percent higher than are those on the premiere floors.

Service-differentiated floors are not an automatic success, and CN has had to conduct a heavy advertising campaign to promote them. The demand for the upscale floors had increased, however, by 30 percent a year and a half after they opened, and this increase gave promise of continuing.

Before concluding this discussion, we should comment again on the wide variety of practice. Luxury hotels, such as the Four Seasons or Dallas's Turtle Creek, offer substantially the same services as those available on the gold floor, but to *all* their guests. On the other hand, many motor hotels and virtually all economy properties have completely eliminated the bell staff, on the theory that today most people prefer not to be bothered with a bellman. Perhaps the notion of the polarization of the industry applies with special force to services such as those we have just discussed.

Fitness Facilities

According to the *Washington Post,* 2000 hotels—10 times as many as three years earlier—list some kind of health and fitness facility in their advertising.[40] Health-club memberships have been growing at a 20 percent rate; company fitness programs are becoming common; and more than half of all U.S. firms expected to start programs within the next decade. Thus, all these people who have committed themselves to a fitness program quite naturally don't want to break their routine when they travel, and so it is not surprising that hotels and motels are adding fitness programs. Resort and convention

[40]*Lodging,* January 1985, p. 60.

hotels invest in more elaborate facilities, whereas economy and mid-scale properties tend toward more modest arrangements. The basic equipment required are exercise bikes, treadmills, rowing machines, weight-training equipment, and floor mats.[41]

The notable fact about fitness centers is the speed with which they are—and can be—added to a property. This kind of service can be expensive to add, but it is also a fairly easy service to add—and easy for competitors to copy as well.

Amenities

Susan Chandler, a marketing and amenities consultant, suggested that once the basics the guest requires (which she defined as shampoo, soap, and a shower cap) have been provided, an important purpose of amenities is to exploit what she calls the *fantasy factor,* "responding to the person within the guest—whom he or she would wish to be . . . and bolstering their most cherished image of themselves." She emphasized that this fantasy factor can be activated by thoughtful service such as remembering the guest's name or providing VIP recognition somewhat in the manner of the gold and silver floors. Chandler also noted, however, that basic amenities can cost as little as 30 cents per room per day up to $3.50 or more.[42]

According to a joint study by Procter & Gamble and the AHMA, the five most popular personal amenities that guests use are shampoo, larger bars of soap, toothpaste, hand and body lotion, and mouthwash.[43] Table 9.1 lists other items, and Table 9.2 gives a more comprehensive view of services and product usage.

TABLE 9.1 Popular Guest Room Amenities in Order of Frequency of Guest Usage

1 Shampoo	8 Shoeshine cloth
2 Larger bars of soap	9 Stationery
3 Toothpaste	10 Cologne or perfume
4 Hand and body lotion	11 Shower cap
5 Mouthwash	12 Sewing kit
6 Bath gel	13 Suntan lotion
7 Hair conditioner	

Source: Lodging Magazine.

[41]*Hotel and Motel Management,* June 1985, pp. 79–83.
[42]*Lodging,* January, 1986, pp. 25–28.
[43]*Lodging,* July–August, 1986, pp. 26–29.

TABLE 9.2   Services and Products Used by Guests

Service or Product	Percent Using
Television	91%
Personal care items	76
Restaurant/coffee shop	70
More than two towels	69
Wake-up call	59
In-room coffee maker	54
Cocktail lounge	29
Swimming pool	29
Pay TV	20
Exercise facilities	15
Check cashing	10
Room service	10

Source: Lodging Magazine.

ASSESSING SERVICES AND AMENITIES

As a competitive tactic, what stands out is the ease with which many of the services and amenities we have been discussing can be copied. The first hotel or motel in a city that put in a television set undoubtedly had an advantage—but not for long. And shampoo—once rarely seen in a hotel room—has now become commonplace. Indeed, in regard to personal-care amenities, it is becoming necessary to have them just to avoid damaging the property's reputation, but it is difficult to see them as offering any lasting competitive advantage. Similarly, exercise facilities are an easily duplicated service. But finding or training a good concierge is almost as difficult as providing memorable food service. Again, food service is very difficult to do well, and its very complexity ensures that it will not be easy to copy. Although some property types may be able to dispense with food service and rely on restaurants in their neighborhood, it seems likely that they will have greater difficulty in differentiating themselves from their competitors. Soap, shampoo, or a weight room probably won't help either. As the ultimate differentiating service, food service's role seems secure.

THE OUTLOOK FOR THE LODGING BUSINESS

Perhaps the easiest way to introduce our discussion of the outlook for the lodging business is with a personal recollection:

The first job I had in the hotel business was in my father's hotel, the Fargon, in the year I graduated from high school, 1949. The hotel advertised that every room had access to a bath—which was true, as there were two of them on each floor. Our least expensive room was a "plain court room," which rented for $1.40 per night. These were tiny rooms that looked out on a small air shaft. The plain outside room was not much larger, but it did have an outside window. It rented for $1.65. Both rooms had access to a bath,—down the hall.

Of course we had rooms with "connecting bath," too. As I recall, a single-with-bath rented for the princely sum of $2.50, and a double was somewhere above $3.00. The rooms were clean but small and had no radio and, of course, no TV.

Lest anyone think poorly of my father's hotel, let me tell you that this was an AAA-approved hotel and that in his day, my father had a reputation as a leader in the industry. In fact, this book is dedicated to him out of respect for his achievements.

UPGRADING

The fine little hotel in which I worked in high school couldn't even compete in today's market. The story of the hotel industry since that time is one of continuous upgrading: radios, televisions, swimming pools, larger rooms, bigger beds, plushier rooms. And that story line seems unlikely to change. The industry is highly competitive, and so improvements are quickly matched. Hotel guests have consistently opted for the improved property with the higher rates. This has created a place at the lower end of the market for economy properties. It is interesting that the first Holiday Inns in the early 1950s were, in many ways, the economy chain of *their* day, and that gradually the upgrading process has moved them to what is called mid-scale today.

Today's economy properties resemble closely the Holiday Inn rooms of a few years ago, and we are now seeing economy chains announce *their* move into the mid-scale market.[44]

CYCLES

Rather than a growth industry, the hotel business is a cyclical one in a fairly static market. This makes competition even fiercer, and the most successful competitive tactic in the long run has been to improve the product even if the rate increases. Hotel rates are likely to be driven up by the increased costs associated with upgrading, though very severe competition in the face of periodic overcapacity may delay rate increases from time to time.

Although overbuilding at one end of each cycle seems to be a chronic problem, that is not necessarily bad news for aspiring hotel management

---

[44]*Hotel and Motel Management*, June 1985, p. 5.

people. The opportunities that failing properties have provided in the past have been the basis for some of the most successful hotel careers. Conrad Hilton, as Hilton Hotels President Carl Mottek recently pointed out, bought the Waldorf Astoria for 4.5 cents on the dollar and made it successful because he and his organization knew how to run it. Not everyone can buy on that scale, but there are many other entrepreneurs whose history is the same on a smaller scale. A cyclical business presents opportunities to those who know the business.

The intensity of the cycle that ends in overbuilding appears, if anything, to be heightened by the increasingly prominent role played by developers. The real estate developer's need for a hotel to complete a project and give it appeal has encouraged the development of oversupply in some markets, but as we've argued, that has meant opportunities for many. In 1970, there were only 3 or 4 management companies; in 1985, there were over 125, large and small. These management companies came into being because a hotel belonging to somebody else was an opportunity for them.

Food Service

The new hotel formats increasingly emphasize the guest room and rely on outside restaurants—or leased, on-premise restaurants—to provide an essential service. In doing so, they may have given up a key competitive tool, but there doesn't seem to be any question but that food service will play, at best, a secondary or, at worst, a nonexistent role in the economy sector of the lodging business. The consumer has accepted that and come to expect it in return for holding down room rates. Still, we will probably see a resurgence in food and beverage above the strictly economy properties, and so anyone entering the field would still do well to seek a solid grounding in restaurant operations.

The demand for improved service—and all the difficulties of attracting and keeping good service employees we discussed earlier—apply to hotels as well. "People" skills to deal with demanding guests and scarce employees will be at a premium.

Growing Markets

Certainly, the demographics we have discussed suggest a growing leisure travel market. Middle-aged people have the highest propensity to travel, and the rate at which older people travel was projected by one expert to increase by 20 percent over a ten-year period.[45] The exploding leisure class of retirees beckons the industry nearly as strongly as does the arrival in middle age of the baby boomers. The future looks bright but competitive.

---

[45]Lee, "Lodging," p. 31.

SUMMARY

The hotel business is highly competitive, characterized by periodic increases in the number of rooms available. Accordingly, we say it is cyclical. Because it requires such a large investment in fixed assets, it is capital intensive. Often hotels are built to meet not only the guests' needs but also the investors' needs. The growth in the number of management companies running hotels under contract is, in large part, the result of real estate developers' building new properties to meet *their* own needs. Segmentation, too, has contributed to the growth in rooms supply as each company seeks to be represented with each of its products in all major markets.

Hotel companies are competing through market segmentation, by developing specialized products for particular markets and by curtailing investment and services in some areas, principally food service, so as to permit competitive rates even with upgraded guest rooms. Other competitive tactics include offering (or not offering) various special services and amenities. Even though food service is being eliminated or deemphasized in some segments, superior food service remains an important competitive point of difference for many properties. The greatest problem in the hotel business is developing new ways of balancing room rates and lodging value to meet consumers' current needs and preferences.

KEY WORDS AND CONCEPTS

To help you review this chapter, keep in mind the following:

Management companies
Economy lodging
Mid-scale properties
Upscale properties
All-suite hotels
Luxury hotels
Refranchising

Courtyard concept
Long-stay market
Conference centers
Condominiums
Concierges
Superfloors

REVIEW QUESTIONS

1. How does the hotel business react to the business cycle and to the local market?

2. What are capital costs? Why is the hotel business a capital-intensive business?

3. How have travel patterns and consumer preferences changed in regard to the demand for lodging?

4. What are the main elements of a hotel investment decision?

5. Why did management companies come into being?

6. How do independent and chain management companies differ?

7. Into what kinds of properties has the hotel business now been segmented? Briefly describe each.

8. What does the decision to refranchise entail? To convert?

9. What is the courtyard concept?

10. What is an all-suite hotel?

11. Briefly outline the arguments both for and against segmentation.

12. In what areas are hotels best differentiated from one another? What area is least likely to be copied? Why?

13. In what way have hotels changed the most?

TRAVEL, TOURISM, AND THE HOSPITALITY INDUSTRY

For some sectors of hospitality such as hotels, tourism and travel, for business as well as pleasure, are an absolutely essential portion of the market. For food service, too, travelers are a vital market segment. In the next three chapters, we will examine this fundamentally important area of economic activity.

Chapter 10 begins with a look at the forces that are behind the strong growth projected for travel and tourism. We also examine travel trends, develop an understanding of the economic and noneconomic significance of tourism and consider the impacts of international travel.

In Chapter 11 the important question why people travel, and where they travel to, is our subject. We will be interested in centers of attraction for mass-market tourism, such as theme parks and casino gambling, and, on a different note, parks and the natural environment. We look, too, at smaller centers of travel, which are often the focus of shorter trips. Finally, we concern ourselves with "temporary attractions," such as fairs and festivals.

Chapter 12 focuses our attention on what are really allied industries from the hospitality industry's point of view, such as passenger transportation and travel agents. We will also consider the camping business as a competitor and alternate to conventional lodging.

C H A P T E R 10

Courtesy of the Greater New Orleans Tourist and Convention Commission.

TOURISM: FRONT AND CENTER

THE PURPOSE OF THIS CHAPTER

Travel and tourism at the local, state, and even national levels and vital to the health of our economy, as well as to the hospitality industry. Indeed, tourism is big business and growing rapidly in North America and worldwide. Because the economic and social impacts of tourism are so significant, no hospitality manager can afford to overlook the subject. This chapter discusses the economic dimensions of tourism as well as the social and cultural impacts.

THIS CHAPTER SHOULD HELP YOU

1. See the importance of tourism in the economy as a whole.
2. Understand the factors that are supporting the growth of travel and tourism.
3. Become familiar with current travel trends.
4. Know the significance of the travel multiplier in assessing the economic significance of tourism.
5. Recognize the importance of tourism in providing employment.
6. Recognize the significance of tourism as a part of international trade and as a source of concern in America's balance of payments.
7. Understand why tourism is not an industry.
8. Assess the noneconomic positive and negative impacts of tourism.

Tourism's importance to the hospitality industry is obvious. Some parts of the industry, such as hotels, derive almost all of their sales from travelers. Even food service attributes roughly 25 percent of its sales to travelers. And many leisure-oriented businesses with a major food service and hospitality component, such as theme parks, are also dependent on travelers.

In the economy as a whole, the importance of tourism and the hospitality industry is increasing each year. Indeed, as employment in "smokestack" industries—that is, manufacturing—falls, the service industries, especially those businesses serving travelers, must take up the slack, by providing new jobs. Tourism, then, is central not only to the health of the hospitality industry but also to the economy as a whole.

Tourism is the collection of productive businesses and governmental organizations that serve the traveler away from home. According to the U.S. Travel Data Center, these organizations include restaurants, hotels, motels, and resorts; all facets of transportation, including rental cars, travel agents, and gasoline service stations; national and state parks or recreation areas; and various private attractions. The industry also includes those organizations that support these firms' retail activities, including advertising companies, publications, transportation equipment manufacturers, and travel research and development agencies.

TRAVEL AND TOURISM

Travel and tourism are as American as baseball, hot dogs, apple pie, and the interstate highway system. In fact, Americans take over a billion trips each year.[1] In 1985, over 41 million Americans took one or more trips.[2] Moreover, tourism is growing rapidly, fueled by more leisure time, rising family incomes, and the more favorable demographic trends we have discussed in earlier chapters. We can look briefly at each of these factors.

GROWING LEISURE

There are several reasons for the increase in leisure time. People at work now have more time off. Most companies' vacation policies have become more liberal. And the number of legal, paid holidays has increased, and significantly for tourism, more of these are timed so as to provide three-day weekends.

[1]*Economic Review of Travel in America* (Washington, D.C.: U.S. Travel Data Center, 1985), p. 6.

[2]*National Travel Survey—1985 Full Year Report* (Washington, D.C.: U.S. Travel Data Center, 1986), p. A–1.

Although the typical workweek has stayed at 40 hours for many years, flex time and other flexible scheduling arrangements are giving more people more leisure time. In Europe, some manufacturing industries have even broken with the 40-hour workweek norm, and in Sweden, the average workweek is now 28.8 hours.[3] In the United States as well, we may soon see pressure for shortening the workweek.

INCOME TRENDS

The two-income family has become a major factor in travel. Within the two-income family, however, there are two, somewhat different groups. In some cases, the wife has chosen to work because she wishes to follow her professional or occupational interests. This is an upscale group commonly associated with "yuppies," though it is by no means limited to professional people, despite what the term *yuppy* (young *u*rban *p*rofessionals) implies. An alternative reason for wives to work, however, is to maintain the family's income, especially in adverse circumstances. In many households, the husband's income has not kept pace with inflation and the cost of maintaining a satisfactory standard of living. In others, layoffs have meant that the husbands are unemployed for a period, forcing the wives to go to work to maintain the family's income.

The latter group of two-income families shows the other side of the replacement of blue-collar jobs with service industry jobs: When workers find that they must replace a $15-an-hour manufacturing job with a $5-an-hour service job, the chances are good that their spouses will have to return to work to help maintain the family's income.

What is emerging is a group of prosperous, free-spending, two-income families, plus another group that must be more careful about spending its money. The latter, however, has chosen to sacrifice the convenience to the family of having the wife at home. Nonetheless, many of these families are able to maintain their income at or near the prosperous level they aspire to, meaning that they remain significant prospects for the travel and tourism business.

Almost all two-income families have time pressures. When both parents work, the household chores still need to be done and children must be cared for. This means that many people may have to sacrifice leisure time for household and family maintenance chores. Therefore, when they do get away, time is at a premium, and they seek "quality time." Though sensitive to price/value comparisons, these travelers generally seek good value for their money rather than low-cost recreational experiences.

[3]Kenneth E. Hornback, "Social Trends and Leisure Behavior," paper delivered at the 1985 National Outdoor Recreation Trends Symposium, Myrtle Beach, S.C., February 24–27, 1985.

DEMOGRAPHICS

Our earlier discussion of the "middle-aging of America" suggested the impact of demographic changes on tourism. Middle age generally means higher income and a greater propensity to travel. Only 18 percent of Americans fall into the latter half of middle age, from 50 to 64, but the people in this age group dominate the luxury travel market.[4] These travelers are typically "empty nesters," whose children have left home. At the same time, they are at or near their peak earnings.

Another significant demographic development for tourism is the increasing number of senior citizens. Indeed, authoritative estimates indicate that 27 percent of households headed by a person aged 65 or older have enough discretionary income to do some leisure traveling. Although this group, made up largely of retirees, is generally not as prosperous as is the group we just discussed, they have much more leisure time. Accordingly,

Camping serves the needs of American travelers of all ages, including the growing number of retired Americans for whom leisure is a full-time way of life. (Photo courtesy of the National Park Service.)

[4]Jeffrey P. Rosenfeld, "Demographics on Vacation," *American Demographics*, January 1986, p. 40.

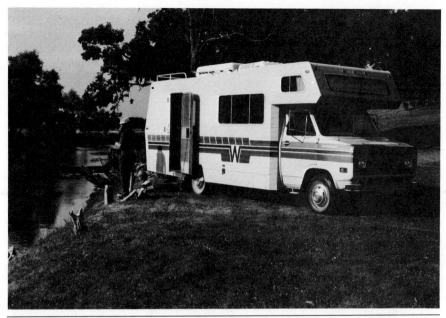

In the United States outdoor recreation is the fourth most popular reason for travel. (Photo courtesy of the Recreational Vehicle Industry Association.)

elderly travelers often choose group travel at off-peak times and seasons and tend to be more price conscious. The travel industry has responded with numerous special price arrangements aimed at senior travelers.[5]

TRAVEL TRENDS

The main reason in 1985 for traveling was to visit friends and relatives. Other pleasure travel ranked just behind that, and business and convention travel was in third place. Roughly two-thirds of all trips were vacation trips.[6] Table 10.1 summarizes the purposes of traveling.

A trip is defined as travel of 100 miles or more away from home. Another statistic in Table 10.1 is the person trip—simply the number of trips times the number of people taking them. For instance, two persons taking a trip together account for one trip but two "person trips." The discrepancy in Table 10.1 between the percentages of trips and of person trips probably

[5]Rosenfeld, "Demographics on Vacation."
[6]*National Travel Survey*, p. A5.

TABLE 10.1 The Purpose of Travel

Purpose of Trip	Percentage of Trips	Percentage of Person Trips
Visit friends or relatives	37%	40%
Other pleasure	32	35
Business or convention	24	17
Other	7	8
	100.0%	100.0%

Source: National Travel Survey—1985 Full Year Report (Washington, D.C.: U.S. Travel Data Center, 1986).

arises from the fact that more people travel together on vacation and pleasure travel jaunts, whereas more people travel alone on business trips.

MODE OF TRAVEL

After automobiles, airlines are the second most common means of travel, and airline travel has increased in recent years. In 1985, for instance, air travel accounted for 20 percent of all travel, up from 17 percent in 1984. Bus travel accounted for only 2 percent, and train and "other" travel, an additional 1 percent each.[7]

PRICE SENSITIVITY

The trends in auto and air travel support the notion that travel is price sensitive. That is, as gas costs have risen, travel by car has fallen significantly. Moreover, according to studies by the Hertz Corporation, consumers are now buying smaller cars, keeping them longer, and driving them shorter distances.[8] This is hardly surprising. After the purchase of a house, the auto is usually a family's largest consumer expenditure. And as the cost of autos has risen in recent years along with operating costs, particularly gas, consumers have traded down. As recently as 1976, an intermediate-sized car was the average on the road, but that fell to a mid-sized car between 1977 and 1982. Then in 1982, the average moved down a notch further to a compact. Moreover, in 1972, the average age of cars on the road was 5.7 years, according to the Hertz study but had risen to 7.6 years by 1984. We are seeing consumer sensitivity to costs, then, in the drop in auto use and the fact that people are replacing cars less often. Though cars remain far and away the most common form of transport, as they become more expensive

[7]*National Travel Survey,* p. A3.
[8]Hornback, "Social Trends and Leisure Behavior."

to own and operate, consumers change their behavior to moderate the impact of rising costs.

Conversely, the deregulation of airlines has led to greater price competition and lower fares. And as the cost of air transport has fallen, the frequency of air travel has increased dramatically.

TRAVEL AND LODGING

According to the National Travel Data Center, roughly 40 percent of travel (in 1985, 40.9 percent of person trips, 42.8 percent of all trips) included overnight stays in hotels or motels. And the majority of hotel and motel users are pleasure-oriented travelers. In fact, 47 percent were traveling for pleasure such as sightseeing, entertainment, or outdoor recreation. Twenty percent of hotel and motel guests were visiting friends and relatives. The balance—or one-third of lodging guests—were attending conventions or on business. But because pleasure travel tends to be concentrated in the summer months, it is still reasonable to say that the year-round backbone of most hotels' business is the one-third of travelers who are on business.

The business travel market is an upscale market, made up of more-affluent, better-educated persons likely to be employed in white-collar jobs. Over half of business travelers, for instance, have completed college, compared with 22 percent of the adult population. Over two-thirds have white-collar jobs—double the national rate—and 42 percent have household incomes of $40,000 or more, three times the national average. Roughly one in five business travelers (22 percent) are frequent travelers, but these people account for 70 percent of all business trips taken in the United States.[9]

WOMEN AND TRAVEL

Women's role in business and the professions has been expanding rapidly, and consequently women business travelers have increased in importance to hotel operators. To explain this, in 1973, women accounted for only 18 percent of all managers, but by 1984, one in three managers were women. In the same period, the percentage of female lawyers rose from 6 to 16 percent. The growth in the number of female physicians was healthy but less dramatic, from 12 to 16 percent. And the number of women who decided to become their own bosses has shown the greatest growth rate, jumping 10 percent from 1980 to 1982, ten times the growth rate for men.[10] Clearly, the hospitality and tourism businesses' new emphasis on women travelers is a response to market trends.

[9]*National Travel Survey.*

[10]Suzanne D. Cook, "The Business of Travel," *American Demographics*, July 1985, The travel statistics, however, are updated from the *National Travel Survey*, p. 26.

THE ECONOMIC SIGNIFICANCE OF TOURISM

In total business receipts, tourism has consistently ranked second or third among all businesses. Only grocery stores—and in some years, automobile dealers—have greater sales. Measuring the industry in terms of employment, tourism provides more jobs than does any other industry except the health services.[11]

Although tourism currently generates over $250 billion in receipts, that is only a superficial, first-order measurement of travel importance. You may recall the term *multiplier* from your economics courses. A multiplier measures the effect of initial spending together with the chain of expenditures that result. (For example, when a traveler spends a dollar in a hotel, some portion of it goes to employees, suppliers, and owners, who in turn respend it—and so it goes.) Although the precise computation of the *travel multiplier* need not concern us, some experts estimate that the final impact of tourism is three to three and one-half times greater than is that of the initial expenditures of the tourists themselves. Figure 10.1 illustrates how the multiplier works in practice.

TRAVEL INDUSTRY RECEIPTS

Travel industry receipts are growing faster than is the economy in general. In good years, tourism generally grows about as fast as does the economy as a whole, and sometimes faster. In recession years, however, tourism actually holds up better than does the rest of the economy. Hence, tourism is an important source of both growth and stability in the local, state, and national economies.

As figure 10.2 illustrates, since 1974, travel industry sales have outpaced the general level of economic activity as measured by the gross national product (GNP). In fact, travel industry sales, adjusted for inflation, have increased at a compound rate of 3.4 percent, compared with GNP growth of 2.8 percent.[12]

TOURISM AND EMPLOYMENT

Approximately one in every twenty civilian employees is employed in an activity supported by travel expenditures. That is roughly 5 million persons. The impact of tourism on employment in areas closely related to tourism is depicted in Figure 10.3. Although only about one-quarter of food service employment can be traced to tourism, a much larger proportion of hotel and motel employment serves travelers away from home.

The U.S. Travel Data Center explained the significance of tourism to employment:

[11]Cook, "The Business of Travel."
[12]*Economic Review of Travel in America*, p. 8–9.

The travel industry continually outperforms the overall economy in creating new jobs. Since 1958, the earliest year for which appropriate data are available, payroll jobs in travel-related businesses have increased 221 percent, more than two and one-half times as fast as the overall economy.

The travel industry has contributed to job growth far in excess of its size. Just in the last decade travel industry employment has increased by nearly sixty percent, three times the growth rate for all U.S. industries. The 2.9 million new jobs provided by the industry since 1974 comprise eighteen percent of the national increase in employment.[13]

Tourist Spending for	Tourist Industry Expenses	Secondary Business Beneficiaries
Hotels	Wage, salaries, and tips	Employees
Restaurants	Payroll taxes	Government agencies
Entertainment and recreation	Food, beverages, and housekeeping supplies	Food industry
Clothing		Beverage industry
Personal care	Construction and maintenance	Custodial industry
Retail	Advertising	Architectural firms
Gifts and crafts	Utilities	Construction firms
Transportation	Insurance	Repair firms
Tours	Interest and principal	Advertising firms
Museums and historical	Legal and accounting	News media
	Transportation	Water, gas, and electric
	Taxes and licenses	Telephone companies
	Equipment and furniture	Insurance industry
		Bank and investors
		Legal and accounting firms
		Air, bus, auto, and gas
		Taxi companies
		Government companies
		Wholesale suppliers
		Health care

FIGURE 10.1 The tourist dollar multiplier effect: tourist dollar flow into the economy. Source: Michael Evans, *Tourism: Always a People Business* (Knoxville: University of Tennessee, 1984).]

[13]*Economic Review of Travel in America*, p. 29.

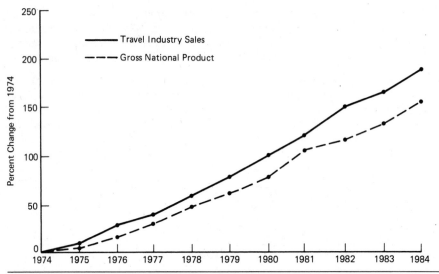

FIGURE 10.2   Travel sales and GNP, 1974–1984 (U.S. Travel Data Center.)

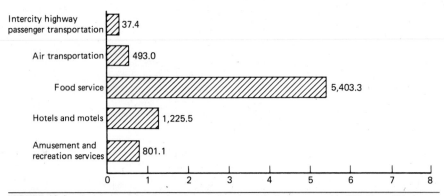

FIGURE 10.3   Employment in industries serving tourists (in thousands). (U.S. Travel Data Center.)

The growth of tourism employment relative to total employment is summarized in Figure 10.4.

PUBLICITY AS AN ECONOMIC BENEFIT

Communities often spend large sums of money to advertise their virtues to visitors and investors. They establish economic development bureaus to bring employers to town and even offer tax rebates and low-cost financing. Tourism also offers a chance to achieve many of these same benefits. That

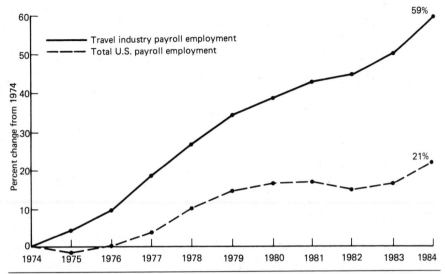

FIGURE 10.4   Growth in travel industry employment and total U.S. employment. (U.S. Travel Data Center.)

is, a tourist attraction brings visitors to a city or area, and they can then judge for themselves the community's suitability as a place in which to live and work. The impact of a major tourist event is suggested by the experience of Vancouver, British Columbia, with Expo '86. The number of visitors to British Columbia in 1986 rose a whopping 80 percent over that of the previous year! Because British Columbia abounds in natural beauty and splendor, probably many visitors considered relocating there, and many more may have decided to make at least a return visit.

THE UNITED STATES AS AN INTERNATIONAL TOURIST ATTRACTION

There are two measures that reflect the overall popularity of the United States as a travel destination. Table 10.2 shows the first of these, the total of all receipts from tourists. But because currency values are fluctuating, this total should be compared with a measure of physical volume such as tourist arrivals, which are shown in Table 10.3. Both tables show the receipts and arrivals for the entire world and for the Americas.

The rapid growth in tourist spending that characterized the late 1970s subsided in the first half of the 1980s. The United States' share of the world market has fluctuated between rather narrow limits: from 11 to 13 percent in terms of dollar receipts and between 6.5 and 8.3 percent in arrivals. The

TABLE 10.2   U.S. Share of World and Americas Region International Tourism Receipts, 1970–1985 (billions of dollars)

Year	World International Tourism Receipts	U.S. Share	Americas Region Tourism Receipts	U.S. Share	U.S. Tourism Receipts
1970	$ 17.9	12.8%	$ 4.8	47.8%	$ 2.3
1975	38.6	11.9	9.7	47.4	4.7
1980	95.3	10.5	20.9	50.7	10.6
1981	97.7	12.4	25.2	51.2	12.9
1982	94.6	13.1	22.9	54.1	12.4
1983	97.5	11.7	24.6	46.4	11.4
1984	100.8	11.3	25.7	44.3	11.3
1985	105.0	11.4	26.6	45.1	11.6

Source: U.S. Travel and Tourism Administration.

United States' market share in terms of both receipts and arrivals fell substantially between the late 1970s and the first half of the 1980s.

A comparison of Tables 10.2 and 10.3 shows that the United States' share of arrivals (6.5 percent in 1985) worldwide was significantly lower than its share of dollar receipts (11.4 percent in 1985), which suggests that international travel to the United States is more expensive for many travelers than is travel to other countries.

In both numbers and expenditures, the number of American visitors abroad has long exceeded the number of foreign arrivals and receipts in this country. In the 1950s and 1960s, the American economy was much stronger than that of most European countries. Thus, the dollar's purchasing power remained strong abroad, and foreign travel constituted a real bargain for Americans. Then the serious inflation in the United States during the late 1960s and the 1970s and the growing strength of the European economy reduced the dollar's purchasing power abroad and boosted the purchasing power of many foreign currencies in the United States.

In 1982, after 20 years of increases, the number of overseas visitors to the United States and the level of visitor expenditures began to decline. This trend continued in 1983 and 1984 and was only moderately reversed in 1985 when the number of visitors rose by a half million and spending rose by $600 million. In the same period, U.S. travelers' expenditures abroad increased by 8 percent to nearly 15 percent.

Underlying these developments were the rising value of the U.S. dollar and unfavorable economic developments outside the United States. As the value of the U.S. dollar rose, travel to the United States once again became

TABLE 10.3 U.S. Share of World and Americas Region International Tourist Arrivals, 1970–1985 (millions)

Year	World International Tourist Arrivals	U.S. Share (percent)	Americas Region International Arrivals	U.S. Share (percent)	U.S. International Tourist Arrivals
1970	158.7	7.8%	35.7	34.7%	12.4
1975	206.9	7.6	41.6	37.7	15.7
1980	279.0	8.0	56.1	40.1	22.5
1981	287.8	8.3	53.9	44.1	23.8
1982	287.5	7.6	51.4	42.7	21.9
1983	292.3	7.4	51.2	42.4	21.7
1984	312.3	6.7	52.4	39.7	20.8
1985	325.0	6.5	53.5	39.8	21.3

Source: U.S. Travel and Tourism Administration.

more expensive for visitors. Conversely, travel outside the United States once again became a bargain that Americans sought.

In 1985, 21.3 million foreign visitors spent $12 billion in the United States. In the same period, however, 28.9 million Americans spent $17.3 billion overseas. An additional amount—the difference between what Americans spent on foreign airlines and what visitors from overseas spent on American carriers—accounted for another $5 billion of unfavorable balance. The proportions of the continuing travel deficit are shown in Table 10.4 and Figure 10.5.

International travel has had the same effect on the United States' bal-

TABLE 10.4 United States Travel Deficit, 1970–1985 (millions of current dollars)

1970	$ 2,487
1975	3,216
1980	1,354
1981	478
1982	2,081
1983	5,549
1984	8,597
1985	10,280

Source: U.S. Travel and Tourism Administration.

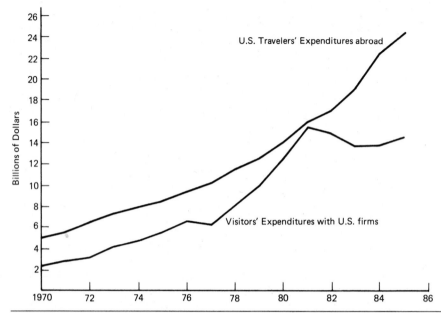

FIGURE 10.5   The travel gap reopens. (U.S. Travel and Tourism Administration.)

ance of payments (the difference between American spending abroad and American receipts from overseas) as exports (sales overseas) and imports (purchases from overseas) have. Because our balance of payments influences the strength of the U.S. dollar in world markets and in the domestic economy, both governmental and private agencies actively promote travel to the United States in a number of ways. For example, a federal agency, the United States Travel and Tourism Administration, was established specifically to attract travelers to this country. Tourism is now a major export industry in the United States.

As Figure 10.6 shows, more than one-half of our receipts from foreign visitors come from our Canadian and Mexican neighbors. Visitors from Japan, England, West Germany, and France make up another 14 percent of the market.

Whatever the economic and political ramifications of the travel gap may be, the fact is that overseas visitors—over 21 million of them in 1985 spending $12 billion—make up a huge market. It is clearly one that those serving travelers in the United States cannot afford to ignore.

In the hotel industry, some properties in large cities with large numbers of foreign tourists attribute one-third or more of their occupancy to visitors from outside the country. And many hotels, responding to the needs of foreign visitors, are anxious to hire multilingual managers, clerks, and service

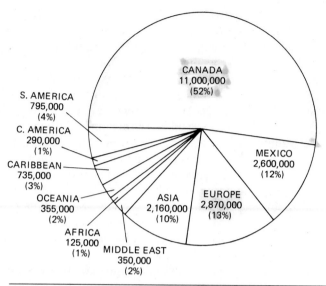

FIGURE 10.6   1985 International tourist arrivals to the United States. Total arrivals: 21,280,000. (U.S. Travel and Tourism Administration 1986 Annual Report.)

personnel. Some hotels have also begun actively to promote foreign business through representation at travel trade fairs abroad and through solicitation of foreign tour business from travel agents.

IS TOURISM AN INDUSTRY?

Let us pause here for a moment to review the concept of the hospitality industry we developed in Chapter 1. We concluded that such an industry could be characterized by a common heritage, by the similarity of operating problems shared by the various components, and by the high mobility that managers and workers enjoy. For instance, a supervising manager might well move from a restaurant into hotel management and then to some form of institutional work such as club management or college housing and food service.

Although we constantly use the term *hospitality industry,* there is no such thing as a corresponding tourism industry. This is because tourism is a highly varied, though often interrelated, bundle of economic activities. Although these economic activities often court the same customer, the services rendered, and the operational problems encountered, are different enough to limit the mobility of a trained employee or manager from one activity to another. This is the principal difference between the hospitality industry and tourism.

It is true, of course, that some positions in one component of the hospitality industry cannot be transferred within the industry. A desk clerk, for instance, has skills peculiar to the hotel business, and a greenskeeper's knowledge is useful mainly in the club business. The heart of the hospitality industry, however, is food service, in which there is a great deal of intra-industry mobility for workers in food service; any manager qualified in food service operations can probably move with comparative ease to other parts of the industry. But the field of tourism lacks this kind of common thread.

A few more examples will illustrate our point. An airline, a car rental agency, and a hotel may share the same customer, but the services they provide differ strikingly. The airline provides its transportation strictly from point to point on some predetermined schedule. The car rental agency also provides transportation and related support services, but it dictates neither a schedule nor a destination. Moreover, its customers travel alone or with companions of their own choosing. Hotels, in its turn, provide a stationary shelter for some period specified by its guests.

Some operational problems of tourism and hospitality are superficially similar. For instance, the reservation systems used by hotels and motels and car rental companies are based on a model originally developed for the airlines. In actuality, though, operational problems within tourism vary widely. For instance, aircraft maintenance, automobile maintenance, and hotel maintenance obviously require different facilities, skills, and planning. It is unlikely that the same person could, for instance, service an airline radar system, an automobile generator and voltage regulator, and a hotel's plumbing and air conditioning.

Differences also appear in the structure of the firms. The airline and car rental fields are dominated by a few very large companies, but the hotel industry is a highly competitive field on which not even the successful motel chains can claim a corner.

Most importantly, as we said earlier, there is little ease of movement among the tourism segments. Tourism is not one career field but many. Thus, the car rental agent seeking work at an airline ticket counter would have to be retrained. A skilled waitress works in tourism and might have learned a great deal that would be useful as a stewardess, but we don't hear much about waitress experience as a qualification for employment as a stewardess.

The important point to see here is that although tourism may be a related set of economic activities, it is not an industry for which overall educational career preparation is possible.

Some hotel companies such as Westin and airline companies such as United now have the same owners. The president of Westin Hotels some years ago became president of the holding company that owns Westin and United Airlines, and so it is true that there is some interindustry mobility, but it is principally at very senior levels.

Hospitality managers should, of course, acquire a general understand-

One feature that ties together the hospitality industry is the importance of food service to every segment. This is just as true of theme parks, as Great Adventure's Yum Yum Palace, shown above, suggests. (Photo courtesy of Great Adventure.)

ing of tourism, as the two fields share many professional interests. Tourism also constitutes an important market for many hospitality firms. For example, the success of the airlines in selling to travelers will directly affect the occupancy rates of the hotel industry, and the hotel guest may well want the service of a rental car.

State, regional, and local travel promotion also is important to hospitality firms, and so such promotion deserves their support. In general, however, the relationships among the industries that serve the tourist, though complementary and interdependent, do not extend into the interindustry career ladders.

NONECONOMIC EFFECTS OF TOURISM

So far we have stressed the economic impact of tourism, for instance, its effect on the gross national product and employment. But tourism also has other impacts, both unfavorable and favorable.

CROWDING

A successful tourist attraction may, in effect, self-destruct from its own success. One of the major potential problems of tourism is crowding: so many people want to see the attraction that its own success destroys the attraction's charm.

At successful theme parks, this problem is addressed by designing places where guests will be waiting in line as "staging areas" with interesting views and even live or mechanized entertainment to distract the visitors. Another theme park tactic is to have lots of cleanup help, so that paper, cigarettes, and other trash never accumulates, thus reducing or eliminating some of the evidence of crowding.

Another example is that in areas of scenic beauty such as popular national parks, trails often become more and more difficult as they progress. Indeed, most people turn around and return to the parking lot once the pavement ends. And even fewer continue once the unpaved trail actually becomes difficult to follow. In effect, reducing the amenities is a subtle form of unstated rationing of which the ultimate example is the wilderness area, where entrance is only on foot or by horse. Difficulty of access can thus reduce crowding.

Along with crowding, tourism can result in noise, odors, and pollution. A special form of crowding is the traffic jam. Not surprisingly, people who live in a tourist attraction area may have mixed or hostile feelings about further development because of their concern for privacy, the environment, or just their ability to get safely to and from home on crowded highways.

Another possible impact of crowding is "crowding out." For example, a beach or other scenic area formerly used by local people may be bought and its use restricted to paying visitors. This has happened on several Caribbean islands and in some cases resulted in the local populace's becoming unfriendly or even hostile as they found their beaches becoming inaccessible to "natives." This led to sharp clashes between the local people and the visitors, an unfriendly environment, and then a drop in the number of visitors.

These potentially unfavorable developments related to tourism give rise to the notion of "carrying capacity," that is, that an area can accept only a certain number of visitors without being hampered as a desirable destination.

FAVORABLE NONECONOMIC EFFECTS

But not all noneconomic effects are necessarily unfavorable. Tourist success can often fuel local pride: Some tourist "events" such as festivals and fairs may be staged to celebrate some aspect of the local culture. Agricultural fairs, for instance, which draw thousands—and sometimes hundreds of thousands—of visitors, celebrate a region's agricultural heritage and its favored crops as well as provide for important educational activities such as 4H meetings and contests.

In other cases, a local tradition may be observed. In a Portuguese community, it may be a blessing of the fishing fleet; in an area where many of

Hersheypark offers an eighteenth-century German village commemorating the early settlers in the area surrounding Hershey, Pennsylvania. (Photo courtesy of Hersheypark.)

German descent live, it could be "Oktoberfest." In these cases, adults are reminded of their background, and the young see their heritage dramatized as visitors come to admire it. Indeed, much early travel was for the purpose of pilgrimage, and religion still plays an important part in travel in some areas.

Because of its important impact on the hospitality industry tourism is significant to students of hotel, restaurant, and institutional management. But even if this weren't your field of study, it would be important for you to know about it. This is because whatever problems tourism raises, its positive impacts not only economically but also culturally and socially make it an important phenomenon of contemporary mass society.

SUMMARY

This chapter opened with a definition of tourism and the reasons that it is important to the hospitality industry. We then explained why people are traveling more: more leisure time, rising family incomes, and more middle-aged people who have the time and money to travel.

The main reason for traveling is pleasure, and then business. Although more people travel by car than by any other means, as cars have become more expensive to buy and to operate, people have been turning more and more to air travel, the second most popular mode of travel. In addition, most hotel and motel users are people traveling for pleasure, followed by those traveling on business. More women now are traveling, as well.

The economic significance of tourism is clear: Tourism ranks second or third in total business receipts. Moreover, about one in twenty people is employed in an activity supported by travel expenditures. Indeed, communities seeking potential employers may profitably use tourism as an attraction.

The United States is also an international tourist attraction, its popularity often based on the value of the U.S. dollar versus that of other currencies. Foreign visitors to this country are an important means of alleviating the U.S. balance-of-payments deficit.

We then discussed whether tourism is really an industry in the way that the hospitality business is. And finally, we closed the chapter by touching on the noneconomic effects of tourism, both unfavorable (such as crowding) and favorable (such as festivals, fairs, and the celebration of local traditions).

KEY WORDS AND CONCEPTS

To help you review this chapter, keep in mind the following:

Tourism	Travel industry receipts
Pleasure travel	Tourist attraction
Business and convention travel	Noneconomic effect
Travel multiplier	Crowding

REVIEW QUESTIONS

1. What is tourism, and what organizations does it include?

2. What factors have caused the increase in tourism?

3. What are the main reasons that people travel?

4. Which age groups travel most, and what kinds of trips does each group take?

5. What are the recent trends in automobile and airline travel, and what are their causes?

6. Is tourism important economically to the United States? Explain.

7. At the present time, are many foreigners visiting the United States? Has this always been the case? Explain.

8. What is the U.S. hospitality industry doing to attract foreign visitors?

9. Describe some of the noneconomic favorable and unfavorable effects of tourism.

C H A P T E R

Courtesy of American Airlines.

DESTINATIONS: TOURISM GENERATORS

THE PURPOSE OF THIS CHAPTER

Travelers are going places! Destinations and attractions are magnets that set the whole process of tourism in motion. In this chapter we look at the motivations of travelers as well as the nature of mass-market travel destinations. Many of these are, to all intents and purposes, a part of the hospitality industry and offer attractive career prospects. Even if this were not the case, you would want to be familiar with the economic and operating characteristics of destinations to round out your understanding of tourism.

THIS CHAPTER SHOULD HELP YOU TO

1. See the relationships between travelers' motives and the attractions at destinations.

2. Distinguish between primary and secondary attractions.

3. Identify the characteristics that make the destinations of mass-market tourism different from those of the more aristocratic travel patterns of just a few years ago.

4. Know more about the kinds of activities theme parks offer to entice travelers.

5. Take advantage of the increasing significance of regional theme parks in planning your work experience.

6. Appreciate why the economics of casino gambling makes some communities consider legalizing them in new markets.

7. Become familiar with the significance of large- *and* small-scale urban play centers as a part of the tourism plant of any community.

8. Evaluate the importance of "temporary" attractions, such as fairs and festivals.

9. Assess the importance of natural attractions to tourism.

MOTIVES AND DESTINATIONS

If people had no place they wanted to go, tourism would be in trouble. In fact, people travel for many reasons, for instance, work and recreation. In this chapter we will be concerned almost exclusively with recreation, but even for this, the motives are varied because recreation is more than "just play." Webster tells us that recreation also means reviving, giving new vigor, refreshing, and reanimating as well as amusing, diverting, or gratifying.

Recreation has a function, then, in life. It is, in some ways, not just the opposite of work; it is its counterweight. Recreation relates to relaxation but also to stimulation, to gaining renewed energy, as well as to playing. As a necessary and vital part of life, not surprisingly the things that attract different people are highly varied. For instance, perhaps the earliest motive for travel was religion and the sense of renewal of commitment that was—and is—experienced by the pilgrim. Today's pilgrimage attractions include Lourdes in France and Fatima in Portugal and, in the New World, Guadeloupe in Mexico and Ste. Anne de Beaupre in Quebec.

Health interests have also long been a major travel motive. In ancient times, the Romans were drawn to springs thought to have health-giving properties, which became fashionable again in the eighteenth century. Hot springs in the United States, such as Hot Springs, Arkansas, and French Lick Springs, Indiana, are less popular today than they were a few generations ago. In regard to another kind of health interest, the Mayo Clinic attracts so many people that its home in Rochester, Minnesota, probably has more hotel rooms per resident than does any other city in the United States.

Scenic beauty, especially the mountains and the seashore, have long been a major attraction. Scenic beauty is often coupled with *health-building activities*—hiking, skiing, and swimming, for instance—so that both body and mind are refreshed by vistas and activities. Today's state and national park systems are the most extensive response to these touring motives in history.

Sporting events, from the first Olympics in 776 B.C. to the Kentucky Derby and the Superbowl, have attracted thousands of serious sports enthusiasts as well as untutored onlookers. Indeed, sports arenas have become such big business that some institutional food service companies have created special divisions just to manage sports food service.

Culture, including history and art appreciation, are judged by some as not very interesting stuff—yet every year the battlefields of yesterday throng with thousands of visitors on guided tours, the Louvre is one of France's major cultural treasures, and the Art Institute of Chicago is one of that city's significant draws. Perhaps because work is so important to Americans, another major attraction in Chicago is its Museum of Science and Industry which celebrates the American heartland's industrial prominence. Music and theater festivals all across Europe and North America are used more or less consciously by many cities to enhance the cultural life of the area—and to attract visitors' spending to strengthen the local economy.

Theater and spectacle—whether Broadway's White Way or Walt Disney's theme parks—are currently among the most significant tourist attractions. And we should note that there are literally hundreds and thousands of less well known theaters and amusement parks that stimulate the local culture and local economy by catering to the interests of people close to home.

Mill and Morrison distinguish between what they call *primary or touring destinations* and *secondary or stopover destinations.*[1] Primary destinations have a wide market and draw travelers from a great distance. These kinds of destinations, such as Walt Disney World, attract visitors from the entire North American continent and all over the world. Because such a high proportion of their visitors are away from home, these primary agents create a heavy lodging demand. Orlando, Florida, for instance, is like Rochester, Minnesota, a city with a disproportionately high number of hotel rooms per capita.

Secondary destinations draw people from nearby areas or induce people to stop "on their way by." Some secondary destinations may in fact have a higher number of visitors than primary destinations do. The Grand Canyon, for instance, attracts fewer than 3 million visitors a year, though they come from all over the world. In contrast, many regional theme parks draw that many visitors, and Atlantic City, which is mainly a regional casino gambling center, attracts well over 10 times that many. In general, we can say that a primary attraction requires more services per visitor, but this does not detract from the importance of successful secondary attractions. Indeed, even smaller secondary attractions make important contributions to their locale.

The balance of this chapter will be an examination of those destinations and attractions to which hospitality services are important enough that the attraction can usefully be thought of as part of the hospitality industry. We will consider destinations such as theme parks and casinos as well as significant secondary destinations in urban centers such as sports centers, zoos, museums, and universities. We will also look briefly at attractions in the natural environment such as national parks, seashores, monuments and the

[1]Robert Christie Mill and Alastair M. Morrison, *The Tourism System* (Englewood Cliffs, N.J.: Prentice-Hall, 1985), chap. 8.

like. Finally, we will consider "temporary" destinations such as festivals and fairs. Our main interest will be in the impact of these kinds of destinations on opportunities in the hospitality industry, their significance for hospitality managers, and possible careers in such complexes.

MASS-MARKET TOURISM

Until quite recently, travel was the privileged pastime of the wealthy. The poor might migrate—to move their homes from one place to another in order to live better or just to survive—but only the affluent could afford travel for sightseeing, amusement, and business. That condition has not really changed; some affluence is still required for business and recreational travel.

The demand for alternatives to traditional lodgings has grown rapidly in recent years. Campgrounds are now more flexible in terms of operations and financing. (Photo courtesy of the National Park Service.)

At Walt Disney World and other theme parks, employees are "performers, not reformers." A relaxed, come-as-you-are atmosphere is intended to support the guests' fun, and dress codes, such as those in the more traditional resorts, are the exception in the newer-style operations. (Photo courtesy of Walt Disney World.)

What has changed is the degree of affluence in our society. We have become what economists call the "affluent society."

When travel was reserved for the higher social classes, its model was the aristocracy. In hotels, for example, dress rules required a coat and tie in the dining room. But as travel came within the reach of the majority of Americans, the facilities serving travelers adapted and loosened their emphasis on class. Many of the new establishments have, in fact, become "mass" institutions.

In a conversation with the author, a Walt Disney World training official summed up this change. Speaking of the attitude of some college-educated employees (when first hired) toward the guests that the employees considered "hicks," he said, "We point out to them that we, at Disney World, are *performers, not reformers*. We're here to help people have a good time, not to improve their manners or to change them in any other way." Thus, Disney World has virtually no dress code for guests. People come as they are. All comers are served and enjoy themselves as they see fit within the limits of reasonable decorum.

In Las Vegas casinos, mink-coated matrons play blackjack next to dungaree-clad cowboys. These are not "social clubs" that inquire who your father was or which side of the tracks you live on. The color of your money is the only concern. Likewise, anybody with the money can buy a reserved seat in any of the country's new superdome sports centers. What we see developing are new "play environments"—places, institutions, and even cities designed almost exclusively for play.

These essentially democratic institutions supply a comfortable place for travelers from all kinds of social backgrounds. Accordingly, as the popularity of these facilities increases, we see a new, more egalitarian kind of lodging institution beginning to flourish.

PLANNED PLAY ENVIRONMENTS

Recreation is as old as society. But a society that can afford to play on the scale that Americans do now is new. Some anthropologists and sociologists argue that "who you are" was once determined by your work, what you did for a living, but that these questions of personal identity are now answered by *how we entertain ourselves*. In his book *Future Shock*, Alvin Toffler speaks of the emerging importance of "sub cults" whose life-styles are built around nonwork activities. For these people, work exists as a secondary matter, as only a means to an end.

Play environments, of course, are not newer than play itself. Fairs at which work (or trade) and play were mixed date back to the mid-1800s in the United States and to medieval times, or even earlier, in Europe. The first amusement park was Vauxhall Gardens in England, built in the 1600s, and the first U.S. amusement park, Coney Island, dates from 1895. What is new, however, is the sophistication that a television-educated public demands in its amusement centers today, and the scale on which these demands have been met since the first modern theme park opened at Disneyland some 25 years ago. Disneyland, in effect, showed the commercial world that there was a way to entice a television generation out of the house and into a clean carnival offering live fantasy and entertainment.

MAN-MADE ENVIRONMENTS

THEME PARKS

According to the *Wall Street Journal,* a number of traditional amusement parks have closed their doors because they "offered little more than thrill rides and cotton candy and these days Americans want much more than that."[2]

According to industry sources, the United States has about 35 major themed attractions and 550 other, more traditional amusement parks.[3] Theme parks, which account for only 6 percent of all amusement parks, receive over a quarter of the park's receipts. These parks have clearly become an important part of both the national tourist market and the local entertainment market. The number of their visitors in 1985 was estimated at 230 million, the equivalent of roughly one visit for every person in the United States. In practice, though, about half the guests visit at least twice a year.

The *New York Times* described this new breed of park as follows:

Most new amusement parks are variations on the basic Disney conglomeration of colorful animal characters, reproductions of historical buildings, ingenious thrill rides, and quality stage shows, all in a lavishly landscaped, spotlessly clean outdoor setting suitable for a day long family excursion.

Gone are the rickety ferris wheel, the sawdust midways, the bingo barkers and the girly reviews that gave so many parks questionable reputations in the pre-Disney days.[4]

Themes

Just as restaurants are expected more and more to offer atmosphere as well as food, today's television-oriented traveler expects a park environment that stimulates and entertains in addition to offering rides and other amusements. One way to meet this demand is to build the park around one or more themes.

Canada's Wonderland follows themes such as "International Festival," "Medieval Faire," "Happyland of Hanna-Barbera," and the "Grande World Exposition of 1890." Walt Disney World in Florida offers "Main Street, U.S.A.," "Adventureland," "Frontierland," "Fantasyland," and "Tomorrowland."

Some parks are built around one general theme. For instance, Busch

[2]*Wall Street Journal,* August 2, 1972, p. 1.
[3]Personal communication with Ms. Pat Durickna, director of public relations, International Association of Amusement Parks and Attractions.
[4]*New York Times,* May 30, 1976, p. 20.

Audio-Animetronics are featured in the hippolike robots that are a part of the Adventureland cruise at Walt Disney World. (Photo courtesy of Walt Disney World.)

Entertainment's "Old Country," located near historic Williamsburg, Virginia, uses a seventeenth-century European theme for the park as a whole and within that general theme offers eight areas themed to specific countries or regions: Banbury Cross and Hastings (England); Aquitaine (France); Rhinefeld and Oktoberfest (Germany); Heatherdowns (Scotland); New France (early North America); and San Marco (Italy).

Whatever the theme, parks offer rides, one of the most popular being water rides. In fact, Busch has developed a separate theme park, adjacent to its Busch Gardens in Tampa, built around water and water rides. Adventure Island, as it is called, offers 13 acres of tropically themed lagoons and beaches featuring water slides and diving platforms, water games, a wave pool, a cable drop, and a rope gym.

Although some parks cater to nostalgia, (a romantic longing for the past), others recreate the past in a more realistic way. The "Towne of Smithville," in New Jersey, for instance has restored a mid-1800s crossroads community. It offers a Civil War museum and a theater as well.

Some parks take their themes from animal life. Busch Gardens in Flor-

Morning on the Veldt. With the towers of Timbuktu an impressive backdrop, giraffes and zebras gather for an early feeding on Busch Gardens' 60-acre Serengeti Plain, where more than 400 exotic mammals roam freely. (Photo courtesy of Busch Gardens.)

ida offers "The Dark Continent," a 300-acre African themed park which includes the Serengeti Plain, home of one of the largest collections of African big game. It also serves as a breeding and survival center for many rare species. The animals roam freely on a veldtlike plain where visitors can see them by taking a monorail, steam locomotive, or skyride safari.

Busch has also developed a park, Sesame Place in Langhorne, Pennsylvania, near Philadelphia, that blends physical and play activities with science experiments and computer games. In one experiment, called star lightning, the visitor can make gases, enclosed in a glass ball, interact with electromagnetic fields to create lightning and rainbow colors. Another experiment uses a laser and turning mirrors controlled by the guest to create a hands-on experience of the effects of reflection. Sesame Place also offers one-week computer camps, school field trips, and college-accredited computer courses for teachers.

Like virtually all modern theme parks, Sesame features full-sized cartoon characters, including Ernie and Bert from Sesame Street. And Big Bird and Oscar are featured in a video show in which the audience participates. Like other parks, too, Sesame Place offers rides and theater-style entertainment.

Busch does not limit its visitors to viewing animals. In other themed areas, it offers a wide variety of rides and shows. For instance, Timbuktu, a recreation of an ancient desert trading center, features the Phoenix boat-swing ride, a Dolphin theater, 1,200-seat Festhaus dining and entertainment complex, the Scorpion coaster ride, a carousel, the Sandstorm thrill ride, a games arcade, and African crafts. Marrakesh, a simulation of a walled Moroccan village, offers Moroccan craft demonstrations, an "All That Music" song and dance revue, shopping bazaars, belly dancers, snake charmers, and the Mystic Sheiks of Morocco, a brass-and-percussion marching band.

The sea offers other enticing themes. Marineland, in California, besides shows related to its ocean theme, offers to anyone who can swim a swim-through aquarium known as Baja Reef. For those who are certified scuba divers, there is available a trip in a special stainless steel cage into a 560,000-gallon tank filled with over 60 sharks.

Sea World, with successful parks in Florida, Ohio, and Southern California, features shows in a 3000-seat stadium for viewing "Shamu, the three-ton Killer Whale." In a 5-million-gallon lagoon nearby, dolphins perform

At Marineland, the Shark Dive Adventure offers visitors who are certified scuba divers a chance to submerge only inches away from sharks and other denizens of the deep. (Photo courtesy of Marineland.)

Some theme parks include specialized education program formats for students from kindergarten through university age. (Photo courtesy of Sea World.)

before a 2500-seat stadium. Like many theme parks, Sea World offers organized education tours featuring the work of Sea World's research organization. A liberal amount of education-as-fun is found in its regular, entertainment-oriented shows.

An official of the Disney organization summed up the theme parks' approach to education this way: "Before you can educate, you must entertain." Theme parks do, indeed, constitute a rich educational medium.

Scale

Theme parks are different from the traditional amusement parks not only because they are based on a theme or several themes but also because of their huge operating scale. As in nearly everything else, Disney leads the way in plant scale. The entire Walt Disney World (WDW) in Florida comprises 27,400 acres and has a 60,000 maximum one-time guest capacity. The food operation at WDW has 70 food locations that seat 10,000. The total system has a maximum capacity of 23,330 meals *per hour.* The career significance of WDW and similar enterprises is suggested by the fact that

The forces of evil, dragons, and dragonettes stir up the lagoon at Walt Disney's Epcot Center in Florida in an effort to disrupt the good guys whose mission is to paint the sky with rainbow colors. (Copyright © The Walt Disney Company, 1986.)

WDW has become the largest private employer in the state of Florida, with up to 17,000 permanent employees.

REGIONAL THEME PARKS

Theme parks catering to a regional rather than a national market have been growing at a rapid pace in recent years. This development seems to be based on the increasing cost of transportation and the pressure of inflation on many family incomes. Regional parks serve a smaller geographic area than, for instance, Disney World, and are often more targeted toward particular groups in their marketing.

For instance, Atlanta's Six Flags offers special parties for high school graduating classes and offers an annual Christian Music Festival featuring "top Christian talent" that might not be as popular in other regions of North America. In Pigeon Forge, Tennessee, near Knoxville, Dollywood recreates the Smoky Mountains of the late 1800s through crafts and country music as well as atmosphere, old-time "home cooked" food, and rides. Country music is a regular part of the "Parton Back Porch Theatre," and during the National Mountain Music Festival in July, it features Dolly Parton, for whom the park is named. A crafts theme is featured during a month-long National Crafts Festival in October. Regional parks such as Dollywood are clearly major sources of tourism: Dollywood attracted over 1 million visitors in its first year of operation.

Regional parks, though not as large as Walt Disney World, are not small. Six Flags over Georgia, for instance, is situated on 331 acres and offers over 100 rides, shows, and attractions. Rides in these parks are of impressive scale. Six Flags' Splashwater Falls, which rises five stories to fall into 250,000 gallons of water, has a carrying capacity of 1800 passengers per hour and cost nearly $2 million to build. Thunder River, a boat ride, cost $4 million to build, covers seven acres, and moves 167,000 gallons of water per minute. It, too, has a carrying capacity of 1800 per hour. Entertainment is on a large scale at Six Flags, too. The Southern Star Amphitheater has 4000 fixed seats and can be expanded to seat 20,000.

Not surprisingly, regional parks have a significant commitment to food service. Knott's Berry Farm, for instance, in Buena Park, California, the nation's oldest themed park, has 35 eating places on its 150 acres and additional food service in the adjacent Knott's Market Place. Not far away, Marineland features a Burger Galley, International Cafe, Pacific Pizza, an Ice Cream Shoppe, Seaside Sandwich Shop, and Corby's Corner. Marineland also has outdoor catering locations that can handle company picnics and special groups of from 150 to 5,000.

Employment and Training Opportunities

The regionalization of theme parks is a favorable development for hospitality students because of the opportunities they offer for employment and management experience. Theme parks often operate year round, but on a reduced scale from their summer peak. During the months when school is out and, too, when outside weather conditions favor park visitation, attendance soars. To meet these peaks, the crew expands each summer. To supervise this expanded crew, college-age people are chosen, usually from last year's crew, as supervisors, assistant managers, and unit managers. These positions are often quite well paid, but more significantly they offer a chance to assume responsible roles beyond those that most organizations offer to people of this age. Generally these opportunities are accompanied by training and management development programs.

The Butterfield stagecoach meets the iron horse in Knott's Berry Farm's Old West Ghost Town. Knott's stagecoaches are authentic antiques that date back as far as 1847. The locomotive, #41 out of the Baldwin works in Philadelphia, was made in 1881 and operated for many years pulling narrow-gauge passenger trains in the Rocky Mountains. Today's old-time adventurers can experience what travel was like on the American frontier a hundred years ago, with their journeys interrupted by "holdups" that are staged daily by masked outlaws from the staff of Knott's funfighters. (Photo courtesy of Knott's Berry Farm.)

As a personal note: I have graded more summer field-experience papers that I care to recall, and consistently the best opportunities and training experiences I have encountered have been in regional theme parks. A word of advice, then, is to take a close look at the regional theme parks in your area as a possible summer employer.

CASINOS AND GAMING

To move from the innocent amusement of theme parks to casinos and gaming may seem a giant step, but they do at least have a good deal in common as tourism attractions. We will look briefly at two quite different markets: Las Vegas and Atlantic City.

Some might think that Las Vegas and Atlantic City are the only two centers of gambling in North America, but a moment's reflection on the variety of legal gambling activities around us quickly leads us to discard that notion. Gambling is fairly widespread in the United States, including casinos, card rooms (legal in 9 states), horse racing (37 states), lotteries (25 states), and off-track betting (22 states). In fact, only 4 states (Hawaii, Indiana, Mississippi, and Utah) outlaw gambling altogether. An additional 8 states permit only bingo games (Georgia, Kansas, North Carolina, South

Carolina, Tennessee, Texas, Virginia, and Wisconsin). All 10 of Canada's provinces have legalized horse racing, and the provinces and 2 federal territories have lotteries and permit off-track betting.[5]

The question of gambling does raise serious moral and social issues, but it is clear that the practice, in one form or another, is quite widespread. Efforts to legalize casinos in several jurisdictions in both the United States and Canada have failed repeatedly. Though fairly widespread in the Caribbean islands, casino gambling is limited to only two states in the United States. Gambling's profit potential for companies and the favorable economic impact for communities is so great, however, that we are likely to see continuing pressure to allow it in other mainland jurisdictions. Areas that have seen significant efforts to gain legalization of casinos in one form or another include Miami, New Orleans, and Galveston, Texas. There has also been considerable interest in casinos in the Pocono Mountains in Pennsylvania, the Catskills in New York, and in Quebec. Given the importance of economic impact arguments, we should look at this aspect briefly at the same time that we examine the two existing continental North American casino centers.

Las Vegas

The first settlement in Las Vegas can be traced back to 1829, but the town's formation dates from 1905 when it was a small desert railroad town. Casino gambling was legalized in 1931. Following World War II, Las Vegas grew more rapidly as large hotels were built, and by the 1950s Las Vegas had become an established tourist destination combining casinos, superstar entertainment, and lavish hotel accommodations. Today, a city of 500,000, Las Vegas has over 54,000 hotels and motel rooms, nearly 1 for every 10 inhabitants. The city's annual occupancy rate ranges from the high seventies to the low eighties, as compared with a nationwide 67 percent. In 1986 there were 4,500 rooms under construction in Las Vegas and 4,000 more proposed, according to the Las Vegas Convention and Visitors Authority.

But Las Vegas has a good deal more to offer than casinos. The city is also known for its incredible stage shows featuring such extravaganzas as Bally's Grand "Jubilee." The show includes "Samson and Delilah" in which Samson tumbles the Philistine temple and its 35-foot idol. The sinking of the *Titanic* is recreated. Tribute is paid the doughboys of World War I in a reenactment of a dogfight between two 15-foot vintage aircraft—all this live and on stage!

Hotel room rates in Las Vegas are among the most affordable in the resort industry, and eating inexpensively is no problem. Many hotels sell breakfast for as little as 99 cents and offer a buffet-style dinner for less than

[5]*Marketing Bulletin*, Las Vegas Convention and Visitors Authority, December 15, 1985, p. 8.

The town that casinos built! The top picture shows Las Vegas as an insignificant desert railroad town just after the turn of the century. Pictured below is the famous Las Vegas "strip" today. (Photo courtesy of the Las Vegas Convention and Visitors Authority.)

$5.00. Las Vegas also sports 12 championship golf courses and 19 tennis and 7 racquetball facilities. Obviously, entertainment and sports facilities as well as lodging and food service bargains are used to attract visitors to play in the casinos.

But there also are national attractions around Las Vegas, which enhance the city as a destination. The famous Hoover Dam and Lake Mead, with its

500 miles of shoreline, are less than a half-hour away. Death Valley is a half-day's drive away, and the Grand Canyon is an easy day's drive from Las Vegas. Less well known attractions within an hour's drive include the Valley of Fire, Red Rock Canyon, and a clutch of ghost towns.

Las Vegas is thus a fully developed tourist mecca, served by 18 major airlines and 30 charter air companies. McCarron International Airport averages nearly 400 flights daily.

In addition to its recreational features, Las Vegas has a highly developed convention business, including a 1.1-million-square-foot convention center with another 1.3 million square feet available at major hotels in the area. A million conventioneers attend over 500 conventions held in the city annually, and another 13 to 14 million tourists pass through the city each year.

The fact is that there is not much else in Las Vegas other than tourism, the businesses that serve the tourist, and the businesses that serve those businesses and their employees. Las Vegas is the ultimate in destinations, the city that tourism built.

Plush casinos like this are the drawing card that attracts nearly 12 million visitors each year to Las Vegas, from highrollers to nickel slot players. (Photo courtesy of Las Vegas Convention and Visitors Authority.)

Of course, gambling is the mainstay of the Las Vegas economy; something over $2.5 billion is wagered each year in Las Vegas. Other traveler expenditures, however, are not inconsequential. Tourists spent an average of $88 per day in 1985; trade show delegates spent nearly $200 per day; and convention and meeting delegates spent $150 per day—all in addition to the sums expended in gaming.[6] That amounts to well over $2.5 billion in non-gambling expenditures per year.

In 1985, nearly 125,000 people were employed in the lodging, gaming, and recreation fields in Nevada. Of these, 77,000 were in Las Vegas, and another 32,000 worked in Reno, the other major gambling center in the state.[7] The spending of all these employers—along with the purchases of their employees—adds up to an enormous economic impact.

Atlantic City

Atlantic City has a lot to teach us about tourism, both good and bad. Atlantic City has always been a tourist city since its founding in the mid-1850s, and it was once the premier resort city on the East Coast of the United States, famous for its boardwalk and its resort hotels, catering principally to prosperous upper-middle-class Americans. But with the coming of automobiles, motels, lower-cost travel, and changing tastes in leisure, Atlantic City began to deteriorate. From 1960 to 1975, the city's population declined by 15,000, the number of visitors fell to 2,000,000, the number of hotel rooms decreased by 40 percent,[8] and Atlantic City became a case study in the difficulty of reviving a tourist center once it had gone downhill.

As one observer put it, Atlantic City was a tourist resort without any tourists.[9] From a peak tourist center for earlier generations, Atlantic City became virtually an abandoned hulk, rusting away at its moorings. Like many older, worn-out tourism centers, its plant was outmoded and in bad repair. Perhaps more serious, it no longer had any appeal in the market, and the revenue wasn't there to rebuild. Then in 1976, gambling was approved, and in 1978 the first casino hotel opened.

The city's turn around has been remarkable. From 1978 with the opening of the first casino through 1985, $2.7 billion was spent on new facilities, and over 50,000 casino and noncasino jobs were created. In 1986, over 30 million people visited Atlantic City, making it the number-one tourist destination in the United States.

The casinos are required to reinvest 1.25 percent of their gaming revenues in the community and state—an estimated $1.6 billion in the first 25

[6]*1985 Summary,* Las Vegas Convention and Visitors Authority.
[7]*Marketing Bulletin,* p. 7.
[8]*1985 Annual Report,* Atlantic City Casino Association, p. 6.
[9]Personal communication, David Gardner, executive vice-president, Atlantic City Casino Association. Mr. Gardner was employed as a city planner in Atlantic City during the 1960s.

years—through the state-run Casino Reinvestment Development Authority. Since casino gambling was approved, casino hotels have paid over $2.5 billion in taxes, regulatory fees, and required reinvestment.

Atlantic City is quite different from Las Vegas. Although there are two major cities within a day's drive of Las Vegas—Los Angeles and San Diego—Atlantic City has one quarter of the U.S. population within a 300-mile range. New York City, Philadelphia, and Washington D.C. all are within 150 miles. Over half of Atlantic City's visitors arrive by car, and another 45 percent arrive by bus. Because it lacks a modern, full-scale airport, less than 1 percent arrived by air in 1985.

Atlantic City's skyline is a study in contrasts. Its 11 new or renewed casino hotels are the latest word in casino glitter, but between them are open spaces where old buildings have been razed, and in many places hulks remain, boarded up. Outside the boardwalk's immediate vicinity, much of the city is still dilapidated slum housing, though that is rapidly being replaced with public housing for lower-income residents, private apartment developments aimed at the middle class, and, on the ocean front, expensive condominiums.

In contrast with Las Vegas's 54,000 hotel rooms, Atlantic City's 11 hotels now have only 11,000 rooms. In early 1987, there were, however, an additional 5000 rooms under construction and 3500 in the planning stages, including 3 new casino hotels. As you can see, by the early 1990s, the hotel inventory should be in the order of 20,000 rooms.

Atlantic City is in many ways still in the early stages of its turnaround, with a major takeoff likely to occur in the early 1990s. A rail line to Philadelphia to connect with the high-speed rail lines running from Washington to New York is expected to bring 2.2 million riders to Atlantic City annually. The process of developing Atlantic City's municipal airport, 10 miles away in Pomona, has begun with the refurbishing of its facilities.

In 1986, Atlantic City had 27 citywide conventions and trade shows which attracted 175,000 attendees, who spent over $115 million in the area. Although these are impressive figures by themselves, they are clearly smaller than Las Vegas's 1 million delegates. In fact, Atlantic City's present convention hall has less than half the exhibit space of Las Vegas's center, but a new convention center equal in size to the present one is planned for the early 1990s. A 1000-room, noncasino hotel will be incorporated into that center, which also is being built in conjunction with a new rail terminal.

As convention and exhibit space, as well as more hotel rooms, becomes available, along with greatly improved transportation facilities, the growth prospects for Atlantic City are bright indeed.

The economic impact of Atlantic City is also being felt outside this city of 40,000 people, in the 100,000-person Atlantic County, and in the wider South Jersey area. Atlantic City has led all other New Jersey labor markets in growth since 1980, according to the Governor's Economic Policy Council, and the New Jersey Department of Labor has identified Atlantic County as one of the fastest-growing areas in New Jersey.

Casino Markets and the Business of Casinos

The business of casinos, obviously, is gambling, at table games such as roulette, blackjack, and dice. In addition, a major and growing gambling pasttime is the slot machine. From the casino's point of view, what matters in evaluating a customer is his or her volume of play, because the odds in every game clearly favor the house. Big winners are good news for the casino because of the publicity they bring. But in the long run, the casino wins.

Casino markets can be divided into four general groups: tourists, high rollers at the tables, high rollers at the slot machines, and the bus trade. Tourists are those who visit the city to take in the sights, see a show, and try their hand at "the action"—but with the modest limits in mind as to how much they are prepared to wager and lose, usually up to $100 but often as much as $250 or $500.

The high roller, one casino executive told me, can be defined as a person who "plays with black chips," that is, hundred-dollar chips, and whose average wager is therefore $100.

The definition of a high roller varies. Casino officials in Atlantic City indicated a minimum gambling budget of $2500. In Las Vegas, James Kilby, Boyd Professor of Casino Management and Operations at the University of Nevada at Las Vegas's College of Hotel Administration, stated that "A $100 average bettor would be expected to have access to $10,000 during a typical 3-day visit to Las Vegas. Although some properties operate with a lesser-quality high roller, they are finding the cost equals or exceeds the revenue."[10]

For high rollers, gambling is the major attraction, but they thrive also on the personal attention given to them by the casino and hotel staff and the "comps"—complimentary or no-charge services and gifts—provided by the casino. Some high rollers wager more than the average and, a few, much more. In general, the level of "comps" is based on the volume of play—with some casinos prepared to provide free transportation, luxurious hotel suites, meals, and show tickets, for instance. For those who are heavy gamblers, the hotel may provide a limousine or even a helicopter to bring them from their home and return them—and keep on file such information as the hat, shoe, or suit size of the gambler's spouse; and the player's preference in food, wines, flowers, chocolate; and the like.

Some casinos rate high rollers in terms of the "buy in," that is, the amount of chips they buy, but an increasingly common measure is the player's theoretical loss. This is based on the estimated average wager and the average time spent at the table. What is of interest, here, is the dollar volume

---

[10]Personal communication from James Kilby, January 21, 1987.

of play, not whether the player wins or loses during any particular trip. But again, over the long run, the casino always wins. The theoretical loss is based on the dollar volume of play times the casino's average winning margin at the game. Some casinos are prepared to provide in comps as much as 35 to 50 percent of a player's theoretical loss.

More modest but still significant is the high roller slot player. In Atlantic City, a $500 gambling budget qualifies as a "slot high roller," but Kilby suggested $2,000 as the requirement—in cash on line of credit—for Las Vegas. Kilby also noted in connection with this higher amount that Las Vegas has a large number of $5 and $25 slot machines.

Comps and special recognition are extended to these players, too, according to their level of play. Some casinos have begun to issue cards with an electronic identification embedded in them. These cards are inserted into the machine to record the player's level of play, and comps based on the volume of play (not losses).

A final category could be called the "low roller," the bus trade. These are generally lower-income people, often retirees, and, surprisingly, often people on unemployment compensation. They, too, come for the gambling but usually have a budget of only between $35 and $70. They often are attracted by a bargain low price.

In Atlantic City, this bus trade provides the backbone of the year-round volume of business. In fact, on a typical day in Atlantic City, somewhere between 1000 and 1500 charter buses arrive laden with "day trippers," there for somewhere between 4 and 12 hours. These players, too, are attracted by relatively generous comps. A typical bus deal, costing $10 to $12 in early 1987, might have included round-trip bus transportation, a $5.00 meal discount coupon, and a $10 roll of quarters ("coin," as it's called in Atlantic City) to get them started.

Casino Staffing. The casino gaming staff is made up of dealers (and croupiers), a floor person (once called the floor man) who supervises several dealers, and a pit boss. (In craps, a boxman assists the dealer, handling the bank). In the pit—a group of similar games—the pit boss is assisted by a pit clerk who handles record keeping.

The pit boss is really a technician, expert from years of experience in the practice of the game. He or she generally supervises the play, approves "markers"—that is, approves the extension of credit (within house limits)—approves in-house food and beverage comps for known players, and generally provides personal attention to high rollers.

The floor person supervises between two and five dealers, depending on the game, and never more than four games. They are also responsible for closely watching repeat customers in order to estimate their average bet, a figure that is crucial to the casino's marketing intelligence.

Slot machine areas are staffed by change people working under a supervisor. Change people and supervisors, also offer recognition and personal contact for frequent visitors and slot high rollers.

Comps above a certain dollar level are generally approved by the casino's senior management. Comp services for a "junket" group are approved by the casino's marketing staff. Junkets are similar to tours that might be sold by a travel agent except that the "sights" are generally the casino and its hotel environment, and there may be no charge for any of the services because of the expectation of casino play by the visitor. Junkets are put together by the casino or, more commonly, by junket brokers in distant cities.

Working in casinos is very difficult. It requires a quick mind and an ability to work with people who are under considerable pressure. Players sometimes become abusive and unreasonable, and staff are expected to avoid, whenever possible, a difficult scene and permanently alienating a player and his or her friends. Not surprisingly, the higher the roller is, the greater will be the patience that may be expected of the staff.

Dealers need to be alert to players' attempts at cheating, and they themselves are constantly scrutinized by supervisors and security personnel because of the temptation of dishonesty where so much cash is changing hands.

The author would be uncomfortable if he did not close this section with a personal observation:

> Gambling does raise serious moral and social questions for many, including me. Often gamblers exceed the limit of what they can afford, damaging their ability to care for their families. My observation, moreover, is that gambling creates an environment that often degrades people and raises money and material things to a higher level than they deserve. A real and somewhat scary question, though, is whether this emphasis on money and things and the deemphasis on people are a result of gambling or whether gambling is a reflection of those traits at large in our society. Whatever my views on the moral and social aspects of casinos and gambling however, I don't feel that I can be a serious student of the hospitality industry and ignore such a large and growing part of our industry that appears to have so much appeal to our customers.

URBAN ENTERTAINMENT CENTERS

Urban entertainment centers vary widely. Some are designed on a smaller scale as a draw for local traffic and an enhancement to the local environment. Others are on a scale nearly as grand as those we considered in regard to theme parks, and there are many in between.

Sports stadiums have been with us since the time of Rome's Colosseum, but the latest variety of such centers is the covered "superdome," such as those in Houston and New Orleans. Describing the New Orleans superdome opening, the *New York Times* spoke of the 9.7-acre, 27-story facility as the "second in what promises to be a continental string of mammoth sports emporiums. Cities are now vying to build the largest, most expensive stadiums."[11] The *Economist* described the publicly owned domed stadium as essential to gaining the status of a big league city. "The tenant teams not only draw in the fans and help pay off the stadium bonds and overheads, they also create jobs and general business."[12]

These facilities host not only sports events but entertainers and rock concerts as well. They provide gathering places that entertain residents or visitors to a city. Typically, they reach out to an area around the city—and sometimes to the entire nation—drawing in the visitors and tourists.

A similar facility, the convention center, mixes business and pleasure. The visitors to a convention or trade show are on business. But many of these gatherings are more social than professional, and even the most business-oriented meetings are, in large part, devoted to having a good time.

Convention and trade show centers were once largely the preserve of great metropolitan centers such as New York with its Coliseum and Chicago with its McCormick Place. Increasingly, however, cities such as Seattle and New Orleans, large but of second rank in size, have developed urban entertainment centers as a means of challenging established travel patterns and increasing the travel business in their market.

In fact, the urban play (and business) centers now extend into cities of the third and fourth rank. Although medium-sized cities cannot bid in the national convention market for the large conventions, they often can attract smaller national meetings and regional conferences. For this reason, many cities successfully sell bond issues to build civic meeting centers that improve a community's ability to compete for its share of the travel market. That travel market, more and more city leaders are learning, means more sales for local businesses, increased employment, and more tax revenues.

Whether the results of these civic efforts always justify such an investment is open to question. In any case, though, somebody must operate these centers, and the skills involved (dealing with various traveling publics, providing food service, and managing housekeeping and building operations, to name only a few) clearly fall within the hospitality management graduate's domain. The significance of this new area of hospitality management may be measured by the fact that as we noted earlier, ARA Services has established a special division to manage such centers.

Increasingly, urban planners are including in their developments plazas designed to accommodate amusements, dining, and other leisure activities. The prototype of this kind of plaza is Rockefeller Center in the heart of New

[11]*New York Times,* August 4, 1977, p. 40.
[12]*Economist,* June 16, 1984, p. 25.

Superdomes host not only sports events but entertainers and rock concerts as well. The New Orleans stadium, shown here, covers nearly 10 acres. (Photo courtesy of Louisiana Superdome.)

York City, with its ice-skating rinks in winter, and horse shows, karate demonstrations, and model airplane contests in milder seasons.

Of the more recently constructed plazas, according to the *Wall Street Journal,* the First National Plaza in front of the First Chicago Building is a model for plazas to come. A computer controls the fountain, so that visitors won't get splashed on windy days. From May to October the plaza features free noontime entertainment, late afternoon concerts, an outdoor cafe, and a popcorn stand that nets $10,000 a summer! It also has, year-round, a restaurant, a bar, a legitimate theater, and retail shops.

City waterfront redevelopment projects, too, have become centers that attract visitors and enrich the lives of the local people. Often coupled with these are aquariums. Thirty American cities had aquariums under construction or in the planning stages in 1986, sparked by such successes as those in Baltimore and Monterey, California. Baltimore's National Aquarium, for instance, is credited with contributing some $90 million to the state's economy. At the Monterey Bay Aquarium, 2.4 million visitors helped restaurants at Fisherman's Wharf weather their winter sales slump. In addition, there have

In the center of downtown Chicago, The First National Plaza offers summer dining and entertainment. (Photo courtesy of the First National Bank.)

been so many visitors to the Monterey site that it set off a local hotel construction boom, according to the *Wall Street Journal*.[13] During the summer of 1986, the *New York Times* reported 20 major new aquariums either under construction or in the planning stages, a tribute to the drawing power of facilities already in place—and their ability to enrich the cultural life of the community.[14]

Museums were once thought of as stuffy, but the *Economist* recently characterized the best-equipped science museums as "grown up play pens. Interaction is the key word. Visitors can take a weather-reporting class, watch a fish spawning cycle, experiment with sounds and colors or bone up on elementary mathematics of chance. There are also plenty of satellites, laser guns and deep sea diving bells."[15]

Another kind of "living museum," a zoo, can be a major tourism generator. For instance, each year roughly 5 million visitors come to the San Diego Zoo. The zoo also operates an 1800-acre wildlife preserve 30 miles north of San Diego. The zoo and preserve, like so many other tourist desti-

[13]*Wall Street Journal*, November 22, 1985, p. 27.
[14]*New York Times*, August 10, 1986, p. 34.
[15]*Economist*, June 14, 1986, p. 82.

A shopping center with a difference. Canada's West Edmonton Mall is both a mall and a theme park. Among its attractions are four submarines, (above), plus a 5-acre swimming pool with a 6-foot surf shown on the next page. (Photo courtesy of Triple 5 Corp.)

nations, have a substantial educational mission. The preserve, for instance, is visited by 40,000 elementary and secondary schoolchildren each year. An important service provided to visitors, of course, is food service, and because the number of visitors to destinations such as aquariums and zoos—like so many other seasonal attractions—expands when school is out, these operations can offer summer experience opportunities to students, with a decent chance at getting into a supervisory position.

Shopping centers are usually thought of as catering principally to local

(Photo courtesy Triple 5 Corporation)

shoppers. But even so, such centers can be more than a little ambitious. The new St. Louis Centre suggests the scale of a large, locally centered mall and the often close relationship of such centers to the hospitality industry. The centre was begun as an urban renewal project in 1972 and was completed 13 years later, in 1985, at a total cost of $17.5 million. Comprising a two-block stretch of downtown St. Louis, the centre serves about 10 million people each year, of whom nearly a million are out-of-towners. The centre has 16 fast-food restaurants and 4 sit-down restaurants, whose combined annual food service volume is $12.5 million. An all-suite hotel is also planned for the centre in conjunction with the expansion of the city's convention center.[16]

Finally, we will look briefly at a mega–shopping center in Western Canada built on the grandest scale yet undertaken. In the case of the West Edmonton Mall, the aim from the very first was to attract tourists as well as

[16]Personal communication, Ms. Patsy Baldwin, assistant general manager, St. Louis Centre.

local residents to the center, as Edmonton, Alberta, a city of 560,000, could not support a mall of this scale by itself.

The scale quite literally boggles the mind. Consider its total indoor area of 5.2 million square feet, equivalent to 28 city blocks. The ceiling peaks at 16 stories with a mile-long, two-level main concourse, served by 15,000 employees. The interior plantings include $3 million worth of tropical plants—among which is a grove of 50-foot palm trees—and the 37 animal displays include Siberian tigers and a 300-pound grouper! The mall houses an amusement park and a water park with a 5-acre pool where you can surf on 6-foot waves, water-ski, ride the rapids, and get a suntan, even when the outside temperature is well below zero. The sights include an 80-foot-long Spanish galleon, an 18-hole miniature golf course, a 50,000-gallon aquarium, and four submarines (more than the Canadian navy has, in fact). The 33-foot-long computer-controlled subs will seat 24 people. Built by a family of Iranian immigrants, the Ghemezians, the mall is dedicated to the idea that shopping is more than just a utilitarian chore and can be an opportunity for fun. The mall has its own tourism promotion budget of $5 million (roughly equivalent to the budget of the province of Alberta)[17] and its own tour-packaging travel agency.

About 36 percent of the visitors to the mall are from Edmonton and its trading area. Another 18 percent are from Alberta outside the 60-mile trading area. The other 46 percent come from the rest of Canada and the United States. Half of these Canadian visitors and 75 percent of the Americans come specifically to visit the Edmonton Mall. U.S. visitors average a four-day stay. Visitors, interestingly enough, spend as much or more outside the mall as they do inside the mall.

On the average, 400,000 people visit the mall each week. Annually, the mall generates 6 million tourists (that is, people from outside Edmonton), of whom about a half-million come from the United States.[18] Naturally the mall has a major impact on hospitality industry firms in Edmonton and is itself a significant part of the local hospitality industry, with 10 restaurants, numerous fast-food operations, and a 360-room luxury hotel.

The Ghemezians have proposed even larger malls in Minnesota and outside either Buffalo, New York, or Toronto, Ontario. The *Minneapolis Star Tribune* estimated that if the proposed mall functions as projected, it will draw 6.5 million non-Minnesota visitors to the Minneapolis area and the mall, more than half a million more than Disney World's non-Florida draw. Some financial analysts have expressed skepticism about the long-term financial viability of malls this size, but if they do prove successful, we can expect to see more like them.

[17]*Wall Street Journal,* October 7, 1985, p. 1.

[18]Personal communication, Ms. Deane Eldredge, director of public affairs, Triple 5 Corporation.

TEMPORARY ATTRACTIONS: FAIRS AND FESTIVALS

Fairs date from the Middle Ages when they served as an important center for economic and cultural revival. Festivals also have their roots in early history and were originally religious events.

World's Fairs are year-long attractions, but even a local fair such as the agricultural fair in Duquoin, Illinois, which annually attracts a quarter of a million people to this town of 7000, can have a major impact on a city. Some fairs celebrate local industry, whereas others have cultural and historical roots, such as is the case with Mardi Gras in New Orleans. Tradition is not enough, however. A successful event must also have direction, purpose, and goals.[19] Indeed, a festival or fair is a quasi-business activity. Its success is measured by its ability to attract visitors, to cover its costs, and to maintain sufficient local support to keep it staffed, usually almost entirely with unpaid volunteers.

Events such as these affect the economy of the cities and regions that sponsor them. Local patrons spend from their family entertainment budget money that might have left the community. Visitors "spend in food, lodging, souvenirs, gasoline, public transportation and the like. In some cases the event itself makes purchases which add to the dollar stream of the community."[20]

The economic effects of fairs and festivals have a major impact on the community and especially on its hospitality industry. For this reason, hospitality industry managers are often prominent sponsors and backers of such events. We ought not lose sight of the fact, however, that, like so many other aspects of tourism, fairs and festivals also have important social and cultural benefits to their communities: They celebrate the local heritage and bring members from all parts of the community together to work as volunteers.

In some cases, a festival may even be used to help in the regeneration of a community. In New Haven, Connecticut, the Office of Housing and Neighborhood Development uses neighborhood festivals as a centerpiece in its Commercial Revitalization Program. The effect of a festival on a neighborhood's turnaround is described as follows:

> The signs of change are now visible to the community. The investment climate has improved substantially and outside interest has emerged. There may be a desire to "show off" improvement. Many new characters are involved and the character of the area is changing.[21]

[19]Marlene E. Boland, "The Dynamics of Community Festivals," Master's thesis, School of Rural Planning and Development, University of Guelph, 1985, p. 52.

[20]Laurence S. Davidson and William A. Schaffer, "A Discussion of Methods Employed in Analyzing the Impact of Short-Term Entertainment Events," *Journal of Travel Research*, Winter 1980, p. 12.

[21]*A Promotion Guide to Commercial Revitalization*, Office of Housing and Neighborhood Development, New Haven, Conn., no date, p. 9.

Large or small, then, these kinds of events can be a vital part of the life of a community, city, or region.

NATURAL ENVIRONMENTS

Not everything, by any means, that attracts tourism is manmade. In the public sector, national and state parks, forests, and waters should interest hospitality students just as much. These uniquely American recreation areas have been copied the world over. As far as hospitality innovation goes, they are, in fact, relatively new. The first park created by Congress, Yosemite, was established toward the end of the Civil War, in 1864.[22] The National Park Service itself was not established until 1916.

From 1950 to 1965, the number of visits to national parks increased by

The National Park System is an uniquely American innovation that has been copied the world over. (Photo courtesy of the National Park Service.)

[22]The first national park was Yellowstone, established in 1872. Yosemite was originally a California state park created by the U.S. Congress. It became a national park in 1890.

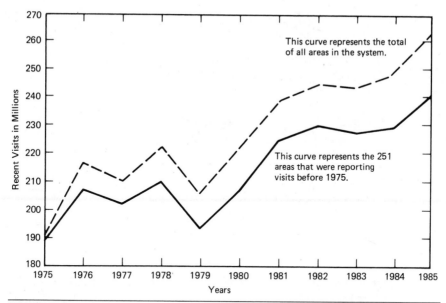

This curve represents the total of all areas in the system.

This curve represents the 251 areas that were reporting visits before 1975.

FIGURE 11.1   Visits to all areas versus pre-1975 areas, showing the effect of new areas and their initial high growth rate. (National Parks Statistical Abstract.)

nearly four times, from 33.3 to 121.3 million. In the next 15 years, this number more than doubled, rising to over 300 million in 1980.

Beginning in 1981, however, the number of visits to national parks flattened out, and there was actually a modest decline from 1982 to 1983. Figure 11.1 summarizes the 10-year visitation record and shows the impact of newly opened parks, which have accounted for much of the growth in the period.[23]

In 1985 there were 15,780,000 overnight stays in national parks. As Figure 11.2 indicates, only about 3.5 million of these were in hotels.[24] Camping is the major accommodation for park visitors and outdoor enthusiasts, a subject that we will discuss in the next chapter. In addition to nearly 16 million overnight stays in national parks, there were an estimated 30 million visitors who spent the night in state parks and perhaps another 12 million in national forests.

The National Parks Service Act of 1916 established the National Park System with the clear intention of providing recreation and, at the same time, preserving the parks intact for the enjoyment of future generations. The increased crowding of existing facilities has led those interested in preservation as well as recreation—including the National Park Service itself—to propose drastic limitations on use of private automobiles within parks.

[23]*National Park Abstract, 1985* (Washington, D.C.: National Park Service, 1985), p. 3.
[24]*National Park Abstract, 1985*, p. 32.

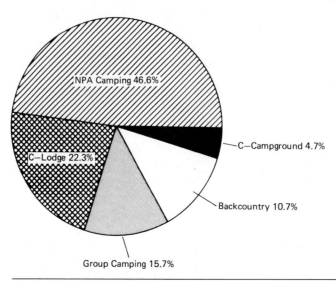

FIGURE 11.2   National Park Service overnight stays in parks: 15,780,166. (National Parks Statistical Abstract.)

The National Parks and Conservation Association (NPCA), a private group that supports a conservationist view of natural parks, has suggested that such accommodations as hotels, cabins, and campgrounds be restricted or even reduced within these parks. Similar proposals have been advanced for such high-intensity recreation activities as downhill skiing (with its requirements for ski lifts), snowmobiling, hunting (particularly in the eastern states), and seashore activities.

The NPCA does not argue that hospitality facilities and services should be unavailable. Instead, it proposes that *staging areas* with lodgings and other services be established in nearby communities and that these staging areas be connected with parks by low-cost transportation. Proposals like this would reduce private auto use and help preserve the natural beauty, a park's principal attraction and reason for being. It might also create major new commercial recreation areas and opportunities for hospitality firms and graduates of hospitality management programs. Moreover, given the leadership of the national parks in the field of recreation, this pattern might well extend to state parks and forests in future years if it is accepted by Congress and the people.

This huge tourism activity has created many opportunities for tourism enterprises serving the areas that surround natural recreation sites. Although park management is a specialized field addressed in professional education programs in parks and recreation management at colleges and universities, the management of the auxiliary services in and around parks—particularly food services, hotels, and motels—lies within the hospitality management career area.

SUMMARY

In this chapter we discussed recreation, its motives and its destinations. After explaining why people travel, we divided their destinations into primary or touring, and secondary or stopover. Then we talked about planned play environments, such as national and regional theme parks, casinos (as exemplified by Las Vegas and Atlantic City), urban entertainment centers such as sports stadiums and mega–shopping centers, and, lastly, the natural environment, especially national parks.

Along the way, we pointed out the possible employment opportunities for both temporary jobs and permanent careers. Destination attractions are often big hospitality businesses in themselves and act as magnets that keep the flow of tourism not only going but also growing.

KEY WORDS AND CONCEPTS

To help you review this chapter, keep in mind the following:

Recreation
Primary and secondary attractions
Planned play environments
Theme parks
Casinos
Casino markets

High rollers
Bus trade
Comps
Urban entertainment centers
Mega–shopping centers
Natural environments

REVIEW QUESTIONS

1. What are some of the reasons that people travel?

2. What is the difference between primary and secondary destinations?

3. Briefly describe a theme park that you have visited, and explain why you think it is popular.

4. How do national theme parks, such as Disney World, differ from regional theme parks, such as Six Flags?

5. Besides gambling, what advantages does Las Vegas offer?

6. What are "comps," and how do casinos decide to whom they will give them?

7. Do you think that mega–shopping centers will be successful? Why or why not?

8. What is a staging area, and why is it important?

BUSINESSES SERVING THE TRAVELER

THE PURPOSE OF THIS CHAPTER

In Chapter 10 we looked at the economic, social, and cultural significance of tourism. In Chapter 11 we focused on destinations and attractions, the generators of tourism. Now we turn our attention briefly to businesses that serve the tourists and are closely allied to the hospitality industry: passenger transportation, travel agents, and travel wholesalers. These businesses are a vital part of the tourism system of which the hospitality industry is also a part.

We will also look at a business some would say is a competitor of the hospitality industry. Camping is clearly competitive with hotels, but it is probably more useful to look at campgrounds as a part of our hospitality universe.

Finally, in this last chapter on tourism, we need to direct our attention to what lies ahead for tourism. We will find that real promise for growth is the key factor.

THIS CHAPTER SHOULD HELP YOU

1. Identify major trends in the travel business and possible future developments in this allied industry.
2. Understand the role of the travel agent as a retailer and wholesaler.
3. Relate the services of the travel agent to the hospitality industry, and particularly to hotels.

TABLE 12.1 U.S. Intercity Transportation by Common Carriers and Private Vehicles (billions of passenger miles)

	1975		1980		1985	
Vehicles	Miles	Percent	Miles	Percent	Miles	Percent
Common carriers	166.2	17.3%	236.5	21.1%	300.4	23.5%
Autos, trucks, and recreational vehicles	793.2	82.7	881.1	78.9	1002.6	76.5
Total	959.4	100.0%	1117.6	100.0%	1309.0	100.0%

Source: U.S. Travel Data Center.

4. Assess the campground industry's present situation and outlook.

5. Develop a picture of campground customers and their needs and of the economies of camping.

6. Appreciate the degree to which campgrounds and RVs are competitive with the hotel business.

PASSENGER TRANSPORTATION

In Chapter 10 we looked at travel trends as a part of tourism. Here, we'll briefly survey travel again, this time to gain a perspective on the travel business as an allied industry that works with hospitality firms in serving travelers. Tourist expenditures make up practically all of the sales of firms engaged in public intercity travel—*common carriers,* as they are called. Common carriers include the airlines, bus companies, and railroads.

In the past 10 years, the number of passenger miles of intercity travel has increased by just over 36 percent, as shown in Table 12.1, to over 1.3 trillion passenger miles. (One person traveling one mile equals one passenger mile, and four people traveling one mile equals four passenger miles.) Total travel by private vehicle has also increased, and travel by auto, truck, and RV (recreation vehicle) is still the dominant mode of travel. But private vehicles' *share* of travel has declined to just over three-quarters of passenger travel. Common carrier travel, however, has raised its share by 5.2 percentage points, a *share* increase of nearly a third.

The number of passenger miles traveled by air has doubled, accounting for nearly all of the increase in common-carrier volume, as shown in Table 12.2. The picture that emerges is of the airlines' overwhelming and growing dominance of the public transport market: In 10 years, the airlines have increased their share of the market from 14 to 21 percent.

TABLE 12.2 U.S. Intercity Transportation by Common Carriers (billions of passenger miles)

Sector	1975		1980		1985	
	Miles	Percent	Miles	Percent	Miles	Percent
Air	136.9	82.4%	204.4	86.4%	274.7	89.7%
Bus	25.4	15.3	27.4	11.6	27.1	8.8
Rail	3.9	2.3	4.7	2.0	4.6	1.5
Total common carriers	166.2	100.0%	236.5	100.0%	306.4	100.0%

Source: U.S. Travel Data Center.

CHANNELS OF DISTRIBUTION: TRAVEL AGENTS

Those who manufacture consumer goods talk about the several "layers of businesses" between the manufacturer and the final customer. Some of these intermediary businesses and agents are wholesalers, manufacturer's representatives, and brokers. Typically, these intermediaries move the product from the manufacturer to the retailer, who then sells to the final user, the retail customer. Although most hospitality firms provide goods and services directly to the customer without any intermediaries, the travel agent represents an important exception.

A travel agent may be either of two kinds of intermediaries who bring travel customers and tourist firms together. In 1986 there were roughly 28,000 firms specializing in arranging passenger transportation and accommodation. Of these, over 90 percent, some 25,500 firms, were travel retailers, that is, firms that sell directly to travelers and make individual travel arrangements for them. Another 9 percent were tour operators or wholesalers.

These firms schedule reservations with all of the firms that serve travelers—carriers, hotels, restaurants, and attractions such as those we discussed in the last chapter. Then they sell the services of these firms in return for a commission on those sales. Travel wholesalers often retail their own tours, but they also work with the retail travel agencies that sell the tour package to customers in their local markets.

Retail travel agencies book transportation for clients on all kinds of carriers. They also sell packaged tours and sometimes put together their own package tours, although this is not their primary business. Their commissions vary according to the services they provide.

Thirteen percent of all travelers consulted a travel agent in 1985, and 9 percent actually used an agent to make reservations.[1] Commissions on do-

[1]*National Travel Survey* (Washington, D.C.: U.S. Travel Data Center, 1986), p. 12.

Already an American institution, Walt Disney World's Cinderella Castle symbolizes North America's most famous theme park. (Photo courtesy of Walt Disney World.)

mestic air fares are about 10 percent, and those on international travel are roughly 11.5 percent. Hotel and cruise commissions range from 10 to 15 percent. In 1986, 67 percent of domestic and 80 percent of international air travel were booked through travel agents. Travel agents therefore play a major role in the hotel business, with 23 percent of domestic hotel reservations made through travel agents. The comparable statistic for foreign hotel accommodations is 79 percent, and a whopping 92 percent of cruise bookings are handled by travel agents.[2]

[2]Personal communication, American Society of Travel Agencies.

Hotels (especially resort hotels) often profit handsomely from associations with travel agencies. In return for the commissions they pay these agencies, the hotels have their properties represented in many local communities. The travel wholesaler, too, can be important to hotels, because a listing in a wholesale package guarantees a listing with all of the wholesaler's retail affiliates.

Some hotels, however, avoid travel agent representation and the accompanying commissions if it produces, on balance, relatively little income.

CAMPING

Much of the park visitation discussed in the last chapter constitutes what is called *day use:* the family piles into the car and visits the park for a day of hiking, picnicking, fishing, and so forth and returns home in the evening. Nevertheless, a significant portion of the use is overnight, and most of that use involves camping.

The growth in the number of overnight stays in parks was dramatic through the mid-1970s. Since that time, however, the number of overnight stays in national parks has shown a modest decline, although that in state parks has continued to expand. The explanation for these trends probably lies in travel costs. Many national parks are far from population centers and therefore reaching them requires considerable travel. There are more state parks, though they are generally smaller in area, and many are located near their state's population centers. It thus appears that many visitors have switched to parks nearer home as destinations, as has been the case with other destination categories. Another possible factor is the national parks' policy of discouraging the overuse of national parks by limiting in-park facilities.

Parks are campers' territory. As Table 12.3 shows, only a fifth of overnight stays in national parks were in concession hotels and motels. The state parks' proportion of overnighters who camped is even higher, probably about 90 percent. So even though there has been a switch in destinations, total park visitation *and* total camping continue to show healthy growth.

There are about 7000 campgrounds in the United States.[3] Although they range in size from very small to over 3000 sites, the average campground has about 150 sites and covers 50 to 60 acres. There is a trend toward longer operating seasons with somewhere between one-third and one-half of the campgrounds remaining open all year.

---

[3]Operating and facility data in this section are taken from Herbert E. Echelberger, "Nascent Trends in the Private Campground Industry," paper delivered to the 1983 National Outdoor Recreation Trends Symposium and *American Campground Industry 1984 Economic Analysis* (Burlington: U.S. Forest Service and the University of Vermont, n.d.).

Family camping is fast growing in popularity in North America. The A. C. Nielsen national research firm released data showing that more than 58 million adults camp out annually. This number is topped only by swimming, bicycling, and fishing as the most popular leisure activity. (Photo courtesy of KOA.)

TABLE 12.3 Overnight Stays in National Parks by Type of Accommodation (Millions)

Year	Concession Lodging	Campgrounds	Back Country, Groups, and Miscellaneous	Total
1950				4.5
1960				9.4
1970				16.2
1975				17.5
1980	3.2	9.1	3.6	15.9
1985	3.5	8.1	4.1	15.8

Source: National Parks Statistical Abstract.

Campgrounds are increasing in size and are expanding the services they offer. The more profitable ones are often part of a chain or franchise group. Like other forms of the competitive lodging industry, campgrounds feel pressure to match the improvements of their competitors and so continually are upgrading their amenities. For instance, cable TV hookups and baby-sitting have become more popular, and there also are available more food services, sports instruction, guide services, and entertainment at campgrounds. Many campgrounds also offer some kind of shelter as well as the raw campsite, with about a quarter of the campgrounds renting trailers to campers. Herbert Echelberger, a social scientist with the U.S. Forest Service and the University of Vermont, predicts that other amenities such as hiking trails, stocked fish ponds, beach frontage, and marinas are likely to become more common as the trend toward competitive upgrading continues.

PRIVATE CAMPGROUNDS

Private campgrounds participated in the growth in outdoor activity and park usage of the 1960s, and by 1972 there were more than 50 companies franchising or affiliating campgrounds. After the oil crises and recessions of the 1970s, only one major chain survived, Kampgrounds of America, or KOA. But even KOA declined in size from a peak 817 campgrounds in 1976 to approximately 675 in 1986.

In 1985, a small chain, Yogi Bear Jellystone Campgrounds owned by Leisure Systems Inc., began to expand, and by early 1987, Leisure Systems operated approximately 85 campgrounds in 33 states and 2 provinces. The company's plans were to double in size again in the next year. Interestingly, Leisure Systems campgrounds are intended as destination campgrounds. In fact, they refer to their operations as "camp resorts." Leisure Systems have an average size of 325 sites. Although there are a number of other small regional chain and franchise groups, there are no comprehensive data on them.

Larger campgrounds—and those that remain open year-round—have higher-than-average incomes and profits. The largest single source of income, accounting for roughly two-thirds of revenues, is campsite rental fees. Another quarter of income is derived from store sales and vending machines. The two largest items of expense in a campground, accounting for nearly half of its revenue, are salaries and wages and purchased goods and supplies. Utilities and capital costs are the next largest category of expenses, each accounting for about one-tenth of income. Other expenses include advertising, insurance, and property taxes.

CAMPERS

A series of studies conducted over several years by the Survey Research Center of the University of Michigan indicates the great popularity of camping among North Americans and sheds some light on consumer behavior in this area.[4] Most families are favorably disposed toward camping. Two-thirds of the heads of all households, in fact, agreed when asked if they thought camping was the best vacation a family could take. And when asked to choose between a vacation at a resort or a state or national park, more people (47 percent) chose a camping trip than a resort vacation (only 41 percent). The principal reasons given were a love for the outdoors and a preference for a peaceful vacation away from the hustle and bustle of everyday life.

The family most likely to go camping is young, lives in the West, and has three or more children. Its relatively large size may be why it prefers camping, because of the higher cost of hotel stays and restaurant meals. Over half the respondents in the survey said that a recreational vehicle (RV) gave as much or more value as did the other things on which people spend their money, a fact that will take on added significance in the next section of this chapter. Only a third of the respondents thought that an RV offered less-than-average value, and 25 percent thought that RVs actually offered better value.

Two-thirds of all families in the survey group had camped sometime in their lives, and a surprising 57 percent had taken at least one trip within the previous three years. Camping seems to be an activity that starts young. Eight-eight percent of the household heads who had gone camping did so before the age of 30, and 60 percent began before they were 15.

People who have camped indicate that they plan to camp more often in

---

[4]The studies cited here appeared in the April, May, and June 1982 issues of *RV Dealer*. The validity of the demographic data, however, was reconfirmed as of late 1983 by the center. The results are also generally consistent with earlier studies published in 1980, suggesting a continuity of behavior over a considerable period of time.

the future. When past camping and future intentions are combined, one-third of all respondents had camped recently *and* intended to do so in the future. As the director of the Survey Research Center remarked, "There are not too many other recreational activities, if any at all, that can boast of having the participation of one-third of the entire population."[5]

A survey of KOA campers in the province of Ontario during 1985 supports the Survey Research Center's conclusions. It reveals a loyal and prosperous customer group, that is, a market of frequent users. Ninety percent of those completing the survey planned to camp during 1986. Only 5 percent of the respondents had been campers for 1 year or less, and a surprising 64 percent had been camping for 11 years or more. Retirees, a large part of this market, made up 19 percent of the respondents. Twenty-two percent of the respondents had camped 40 or more days during the past year, 17 percent for 30 to 39 days and 27 percent for 20 to 29 days. Weekend use, as opposed to vacations, formed a significant part of the market. Ninety-one percent of the weekend campers intended to camp as much or more in the future as they had in the past; only 1 percent did not plan to camp again.

Measured by spending patterns, KOA campers apparently were prosperous. First, 78 percent used some kind of RV, and 93 percent of those users owned a recreational vehicle. Average spending of less than $500 on a camping vacation was the rule for 26 percent; from $500 to $1000 for 23 percent; and over $1000 for 42 percent. This spending, of course, came on top of an already-heavy investment in a "mobile motel room."

In general, private campgrounds tend to be located along the main routes of travel rather than in specifically scenic areas. Because they are operated for profit, private campgrounds must locate near main arteries of traffic where, like hotels and motels, they are most convenient to the traveler and hence more likely to enjoy a favorable occupancy rate.[6] Campgrounds operated by parks and other public agencies, however, are generally located in a scenic area, often removed from the main thoroughfares. Publicly operated campgrounds do not aim for a profit and these camps often experience lower occupancy rates in all but the peak season.

RECREATIONAL VEHICLES

To understand the significance of the growth of camping completely, we must trace the growth of the ubiquitous recreational vehicle (RV). Figure 12.1 shows RV sales statistics from 1971 to 1985. As the data illustrate, this type of accommodation is particularly susceptible to high gasoline prices and adverse economic conditions. Because over half of all new RVs (and over

---

[5]Richard T. Curtin, "American Families Esteem the Camping Experience," *RV Dealer,* April 1982, p. 30.

[6]Of course, many private campgrounds are in scenic locations. Rather, our point here is that the major determinant of location for successful commercial campgrounds is accessibility to a large volume of traffic.

Commercial campgrounds such as KOA are an important element in the growing recreation industry. (Photo courtesy of KOA.)

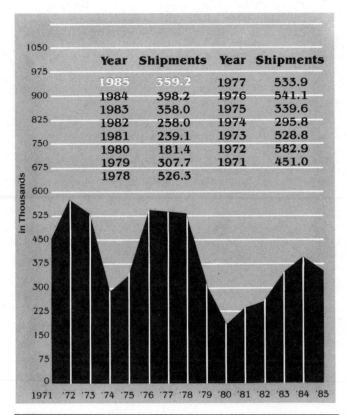

Year	Shipments	Year	Shipments
1985	359.2	1977	533.9
1984	398.2	1976	541.1
1983	358.0	1975	339.6
1982	258.0	1974	295.8
1981	239.1	1973	528.8
1980	181.4	1972	582.9
1979	307.7	1971	451.0
1978	526.3		

FIGURE 12.1   Recreational vehicle shipments, 1971–1985 (thousands of units). (Recreation Vehicle Industry Association.)

30 percent of used RVs) are sold on credit, the unusually high interest rates prevailing between 1979 and 1981 probably also hurt sales in that period. On the other hand, it is clear that many of these vehicles are sold even in difficult times. Moreover, after falling in poor periods, sales climbed back to exceed previous records in the mid-1970s and have shown considerable resilience in the 1980s. Clearly, the "wheeled motel room" is here to stay.

RV manufacturers have taken a number of steps to adapt their product to high gasoline costs. First of all, efforts to pare size and weight have commonly reduced overall weight by 10 percent, and in some cases by as much as 25 to 50 percent. Changing the shape of the RV to reduce wind resistance can account for as much as a 15 percent savings in fuel. In fact, Winnebago, one of the largest RV manufacturers, claims a gas mileage rating of 15 miles to the gallon for its latest models. Finally, with more small cars on the high-

A wide variety of recreational vehicles is available to fit various-sized families, budgets, and tastes. The camper pictured here sleeps seven. (Photo courtesy of Coleman Co., Inc.)

way, new-model towable vehicles have been designed that can be pulled by subcompacts.

In Chapter 7 we noted that the number of hotel rooms *sold* had increased at an annual rate of just above 1 percent since 1948. The information we have just examined suggests where those customers went. The Recreational Vehicle Institute of America estimated that RVs are used, on the average, for 23 days per year. Project, then, the total use of the 6 million RVs estimated by the RVIA to be in operation in 1981. At an average of 23 days of RV use per year, you can see that these vehicles generated the equivalent of 138 million room-nights in competition with motels and hotels. Now compare that figure with the approximately 553 million room-nights sold by all hotels in 1981. What this analysis suggests is that RVs and camping now have a significant share of the country's total transient-rooms business.

This RV will get 15 miles to the gallon, according to its manufacturer, because of its lighter weight and superior aerodynamics. (Photo courtesy of Winnebago Industries, Inc.)

A COMPARISON OF CAMPERS AND HOTEL GUESTS

The average rental of a commercial campsite in 1985 was probably around $10 to $12, whereas the average hotel rate was about $63. If we assume that the average camper spent $15,000 on an RV, which has an average life of 10 years, we can depreciate the RV at a rate of $1500 per year. Assuming an average use, based on industry statistics, of 23 nights per year, the depreciation would come to about $65 per day of use. When we add a campground fee of $10 or $12, the cost of a night's sleep in an RV comes to around $75 or more. These are average figures, but the results suggest that many RV users spend as much or more than hotel guests do for their recreational lodging. An added economy for campers, of course, comes from preparing their own food instead of eating in restaurants. But any notion that campers are people who "can't afford" a hotel is dispelled by the rough calculation we have just made and the average retail price data in Table 12.4. Campers apparently choose camping because they find advantages in it, not because it saves them money.

TABLE 12.4 Summary of RV Sales by Type, 1985

	Average Retail Price	Number Sold (thousands)	Percentage of Total
Conventional travel trailer	$12,154	54.7	15.2%
Park trailer	16,750	7.5	2.0
Fifth-wheel travel trailer	16,034	20.7	5.8
Truck camper	6,709	6.9	1.9
Folding camping trailer	3,816	35.9	10.0
Conventional motor home (Type A)	48,809	33.6	9.4
Van camper (Type B)	23,131	6.7	1.9
Motor home (Type C)	31,281	28.4	7.9
Multiuse van conversion	18,769	164.8	45.9
Total—all RVs		359.2	100.0%

Source: Recreational Vehicle Industry Association.

Another study of the RV owner, by the Survey Research Center,[7] gives us further insights. The statistical profile of the RV owner closely resembles that of the population as a whole; that is, participation in RV use apparently is spread evenly across the country.

The peak ownership age is 35 to 44 years—the section of our population that will be growing most rapidly in the next decade. This suggests that the growth in ownership and use of RVs in that period may increase, offering a

[7]The data in the balance of this section are taken from a series of six articles that appeared in the magazine *RV Dealer* between August 1980 and January 1981.

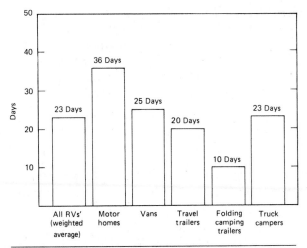

FIGURE 12.2   Average number of days used per vehicle (*Changing Times* magazine.)

significant market to those segments of the hospitality industry that have learned to cater to the RV community.

When ownership of RVs is examined by type of RV, some clear demographic trends emerge. The owners of motor homes and travel trailers are, on the average, older. In fact, 67 percent of motor home and travel trailer owners are over 44 years of age. Not surprisingly, the owners of the expensive motor homes (see Table 12.4) tend to have higher incomes. Owners of these two kinds of RVs are also less likely to have children at home, probably because so many of them are at the age at which their children have left home.

On the other hand, owners of vans, truck campers, and folding camping trailers tend to be younger—53 percent under 44 years of age for van owners, 56 percent for the truck camper owners, and 66 percent for the folding camping trailer owners. It may seem surprising that the least expensive RV (the folding camping trailer) attracts a significantly higher-income family until the statistics on average use shown in Figure 12.2 are examined. The pattern that emerges from this figure suggests that families who want to do a limited amount of camping purchase the relatively less expensive tent campers. Some 70 percent of these families have children at home.

On the other hand, older families who purchase an expensive motor home are able to and have made a definite life-style decision. These older, upper-income families have the vacation time—or the retirement income— to permit extended use of the RV. In fact, half of all motor home owners spend one to four months in their units.

What we appear to have in RV use is a flexible set of options that makes some kind of RV affordable to nearly all North American families. We noted that the peak ownership age category (35 to 44) will be growing rapidly in the near future. All the various RV users are served by the same kinds of businesses—campgrounds, fast food, camping outfitters, and the like—and those who learn to cater to this market should therefore prosper.

THE ECONOMICS OF CAMPING

From the standpoint of investment and operating costs, the campground is remarkably flexible. The cost per room for the construction of a budget motor hotel probably exceeds $25,000, and rooms in luxury downtown properties cost $100,000 or more. But campgrounds spend, on the average, between $1500 and $3500 per campsite. Obviously, the unit—a campsite with utility hookups—costs less than a hotel room. Moreover, the campground provides very little in the way of supporting services as lobbies, restaurants, and cocktail lounges.

Although a motor hotel's staff may run as high as one employee per guest room (including all departments), a commercial campground may employ no full-time people other than the couple who owns or operates the camp. Rather, it probably will hire only part-time employees for seasonal peaks. In the absence of an owner, campgrounds operated by state and national parks and the like tend to employ only a small number of year-round people, but their duties—park management, maintenance, and security, for example—tend to be spread out over an entire park. In most public parks, there are no full-time, year-round employees whose duties are devoted solely to dealing with the campground. Neither private nor public campgrounds are labor intensive.

Although hotels may be said to be both capital intensive (requiring large amounts of capital for construction) and labor intensive (requiring many employees for operation), campgrounds are neither. Interestingly enough, however, camping itself is both labor and capital intensive.

Recall the investment necessary for an RV and you can see what has happened: the investment has been shifted from the operator (as in a hotel) to the guest. The capital investment is made by the guest, who accommodates his or her own tastes and pocketbook at the time the RV is purchased. Like Disney World, the campground accepts all comers without regard to personal style; tent campers are accommodated right along with mobile Xanadus costing $50,000 and up.

Camping is, of course, labor intensive, and campers obviously supply their own labor. They cook the food, wash the dishes, and make the bed.

Camping offers travelers a wide range of places to visit where a short season or limited time will not support more traditional accommodations. (Photo courtesy of KOA.)

Because it's all part of a "fun" outing, much of this drudgery is treated as fun, and in any case, the work usually takes the form of chores that consume only a small part of the recreational time. Of course, if we added up all the minutes spent by all campers on campground chores, we would find that more work hours are consumed in a campground than in a hotel or motor hotel. But because nobody pays for these hours, they do not appear in the money rate charged. The shift is to that most egalitarian and uniquely American institution—self-service.

From the standpoint of consumers, the new hospitality institutions offer some distinct advantages in flexibility. Most motor hotels have an occupancy percentage break-even point somewhere in the range of 60 to 70 percent. Depending on its original cost, a campground can show an acceptable profit with an annual occupancy of just above 30 percent. A seasonal campground is thus probably easier to operate profitably than is a seasonal hotel or motor hotel. Furthermore, accommodations in campgrounds can be provided in seasonal areas when a short season or limited traffic would never support a hotel. A wider range of places to visit, therefore, becomes available to travelers, and this variety encourages tourism growth.

CAREERS IN CAMPING

According to KOA, the best preparation for operating a campground is actual working experience. From a management standpoint, campgrounds are bare-bones operations. The essentials of campground management fall within the area of hospitality management: accounting, managing people, dealing with guests, and the like. Only a few year-round jobs exist in camping (except for ownership). Seasonal employment is widely available, and so students with an interest in campground management have ample opportunities to become acquainted with the working side of the business. Career opportunities in commercial camping are limited largely to campground owners. The construction cost of a typical commercial campground facility ranges between $250,000 and $1,000,000. Of this total cost, 65 to 75 percent could be borrowed from a bank.

In addition to the option of operating as an independent, both chains discussed earlier, KOA and Yogi Bear, are heavily committed to franchising, and a number of other smaller, regional chains and franchise groups are growing, too. Thus, a brand name, operating expertise, and management training are readily available to those with the necessary capital.

THE FUTURE OF TOURISM

We began this chapter by observing that travel and tourism are established and growing parts of the American scene. The energy crisis of the early 1970s and a recession in the early 1980s temporarily retarded the development of tourism and probably altered the kinds of services offered. Although petroleum prices have stabilized at lower levels than the peaks they reached in the early 1980s, gasoline now costs much more than it did before the energy crisis, and consumers have adjusted their behavior accordingly. Though there has been a modest annual increase in the total number of passenger miles traveled by private auto, the *proportion* of intercity travel by auto has declined. According to studies by the Hertz Corporation, the average annual number of miles that an automobile is driven has fallen from about 9500 miles in the early 1970s to roughly 8500 miles in the mid-1980s.

Among common carriers (airline, bus, and rail companies), airline sales have shown considerable growth, probably as a result of deregulation and the slower rises—and some decreases—in fares that the deregulation brought. Train and bus mileage has remained fairly stable.

Business and consumers are responsive to price fluctuations. In times of rapid travel-cost increases, according to the U.S. Travel Data Center, they will use substitutes such as the telephone or destinations closer to home.[8] Changes in the price of petroleum—a major determinant of the cost of travel—are clearly a crucial consideration in looking at the future of tourism.

Because petroleum is both an economic resource and a political weapon, it is difficult to forecast its price at any point in the future. Barring a political catastrophe, however, it seems likely that although petroleum prices will fluctuate to some degree, they will not increase to anywhere near the dramatic degree they did during the energy crisis. Though many experts anticipate a rise in petroleum price levels beginning around the early 1990s, the big new factor on the tourism horizon is demographic. The move of the baby boomers into those age groups that have the highest propensity to travel suggests that tourism will continue to grow and change.

The tourism plant that is in place has largely been built to accommodate the baby boomers while they were growing up and then as young adults. But as these people enter middle age, their tastes are clearly changing. We have already seen how the motel business is adapting itself to those tastes. A shift in the kinds of services demanded is already apparent with the all-suite hotel, for instance.

Another likely possibility is the greater significance of rail passenger traffic in some high population areas of the United States such as the Northeast and the Upper Midwest, as well as between key population centers such as Seattle and Portland, San Francisco and Los Angeles, Dallas and Houston, and Miami and Tampa/Orlando.[9] The era of the grand North American hotels began with the expansion of railroads in the mid-1800s. A major shift to high-speed rail transportation could bring equally fundamental changes in some regions to the tourism plant of the mid- or late-1990s.

The kinds of attractions that will draw visitors in a better-educated, more affluent society are changing, too. Theme parks continue to be attractive, but educational and cultural interest are bringing North Americans back to the campus during summer sessions, and to museums and zoos. In the past, museums and classrooms were not seen as major tourist attractions, but that seems to be changing. Aspiring tourism entrepreneurs owe it to themselves to keep abreast—or, better, a little ahead—of developments on the local cultural and educational scene. On the other hand, to retain a balanced view, recall that the number-one tourist attraction in North America is Atlantic City and its casinos.

Another factor shaping tourism's offerings is the labor shortage, which suggests that the most likely attractions will be those that are not labor intensive. That is, the acceleration of a trend toward less personal service,

[8]*National Travel Survey,* p. 26.
[9]*The Economist,* September 14, 1985, p. 28.

Personal service is very much part of allied tourist businesses as it is in the hospitality industry. (Photo courtesy of Delta Airlines.)

already well established by fast food, is a distinct possibility in all mass-market tourism.

In tourism, as with upscale food service, the lure of the home entertainment center as an alternative "destination" can be expected to play a competitive role in tourism. Similarly, "big ticket" purchases—computers, video and VCR systems, sports cars, and boats—all constitute competitive alternatives for the potential tourist's dollar. The industry's growth, then, will not be automatic, but we can be reasonably sure that the folks who brought us Disneyland, John Portman's grand hotels, and Ronald McDonald—in a word, the very competitive tourism industry—will not rest on their laurels. Tourism will compete, and successfully, for the consumer's dollar.

SUMMARY

We began the chapter by discussing common carriers—airlines, bus companies, and railroads—and comparing their numbers of passenger miles traveled with that of private vehicles.

Next we turned to travel agents, both travel retailers and tour operators, and how they benefit travelers as well as the hospitality industry.

We moved on to camping in national and state parks and in private campgrounds and the advantages and disadvantages of all three. We also described the campers themselves: what kinds of people are most likely to camp and why. Then we considered the various kinds of camping vehicles, paying the most attention to recreational vehicles (RVs).

The business aspects of camping was our next topic. We compared campers with hotel guests and then running a campground with running a hotel. We found that camping may not always be much cheaper than staying in a hotel and that like running a hotel, camping itself may also be both capital and labor intensive.

We finished the chapter with a discussion about careers in camping and about the future of tourism in general.

KEY WORDS AND CONCEPTS

To help you review this chapter, keep in mind the following:

Common carriers
Passenger miles
Travel agents
Travel retailers

Tour operators
Campgrounds
Recreational vehicles

REVIEW QUESTIONS

1. What are common carriers? Passenger miles?

2. What is the difference between travel retailers and travel whole-salers?

3. Who benefits more from using a travel agency, a traveler or a hotel? Why?

4. Why would a hotel choose not to be represented by a travel agency?

5. What are the advantages of camping in a national park? A private campground?

6. What is the profile of the family most likely to go camping? Explain why this family might choose to camp.

7. Explain how recreational vehicles have managed to stay popular.

8. Is it cheaper to camp or to stay in a budget motel? Explain your choice.

9. Is camping itself labor intensive? Why?

10. Outline the prospects for tourism in general.

P A R T 5

MANAGING
HOSPITALITY

There is a real shortage of qualified managers and supervisors in the hospitality industry. This means that there are excellent career opportunities for those who are prepared by study and experience. The next eight chapters focus on management and management activities.

In Chapter 13 we consider how the development of modern management has shaped the present-day hospitality industry. In Chapters 14 through 18 we consider each of the functions of management: planning, organizing, staffing, controlling, and leading and directing.

In Chapter 19 we turn our attention to an all-important management activity and concern, marketing. The marketing mix—product, place, price, and promotion—is a concept that underlies the success of any hospitality operation. The significance of marketing will only increase as competition continues to heat up.

This section concludes with a chapter on franchising systems. We will look at franchising as a management system and as a marketing system. The strengths and weaknesses of franchising are different for the franchisee and the franchiser. They need to be understood by all hospitality managers—and will be of special interest to you if you are considering the franchise route to owning your own business.

C H A P T E R 13

Vernon and Gordon Stouffer (with a photo of their father, A. E. Stouffer, on the wall) as they appeared in *Time* magazine in 1935. (Photo courtesy of Stouffer Hotels.)

MANAGEMENT:
A NEW WAY OF THINKING

THE PURPOSE OF THIS CHAPTER

We modern North Americans are so management conscious that we often forget how new a field of thought and kind of work management actually is. Like any growing idea, management is even now moving rapidly toward maturity. As a student, therefore, you would be wise to be skeptical about any "eternal truths" or unchanging principles you may hear associated with the field of management. One useful way to develop a sense of management as a growing and changing field is to review its brief history. This chapter conducts that tour.

Management innovations have, of course, had a profound impact on the hospitality industry. In this chapter we examine closely two organizations that pioneered the application of modern management to the hospitality industry.

THIS CHAPTER SHOULD HELP YOU

1. Discuss the importance of the recent emergence of management as a field of work and study.

2. Describe the contributions of some of the early twentieth-century management thinkers and associate them with later management developments.

3. Discuss the significance of the contributions E. M. Statler and Vernon

and Gordon Stouffer made to the development of management in the hospitality industry.

4. Show how management is a set of rational, problem-solving techniques rather than a group of inborn abilities or traits.

5. Describe how the customer, not the operator, ultimately defines a business.

6. View management as supervisory and managerial work that uses a marketing approach and innovation to define the organization's purpose and the purpose of those it employs.

MANAGEMENT AND SUPERVISION

Students considering a career in hospitality supervision and management naturally want to understand the hospitality profession in general and the various kinds of opportunities it offers. It is equally important for them to understand the work that supervisors and managers do. We have devoted the last half of this text to discussions of this work.

Supervision is derived from two Latin words that, taken together, mean "to oversee." As such, supervision involves principally the direction and leadership functions of management. (These two functions will receive special attention in Chapter 18.) Supervisors are also involved in the other functions of management that we will soon be discussing. They must plan, and they must understand the plans made by senior management that they will follow in their operations. They must understand and come to function effectively within a complex organization. The staffing function that we will discuss in Chapter 16 is at the heart of a hospitality supervisor's work, and the control function simply cannot be carried out without supervisors' becoming sources of information and of the corrective action indicated by control systems.

There is some difference between supervision and management. The supervisor's work occurs at the operating level; that is, he or she works directly with the employees as they do their work. Management, on the other hand, is concerned with the totality of the organization's problems. But most hospitality managers also must do a good deal of supervision. Managers engaged in long-range planning may well discover a need, for example, to redesign the organization structure or the control system. Very often, especially in large organizations, managers direct the work of supervisors, who, in turn, direct the employees' actual tasks.

This distinction between management and supervision is not, however, of major importance early in a management career. In the hospitality industry, nearly all managers begin as supervisors, and able supervisors usually advance to more senior ranks. Moreover, "managers" often perform work that some might call supervisory—the actual direction of employees in productive tasks. As a practical matter, then, management and supervision are so closely intertwined as to make distinguishing them a theoretical exercise with little practical value for us. To be sure, we will often refer to *supervision and management,* but by itself the term *management* usually includes *supervision.*

In the next five chapters we will explore the work of managers and supervisors. In this chapter, we will define management and will address its development as a body of knowledge used by managers.

Although managing—both the overseeing and the designing and organizing of work—is as old as civilization, management as an organized body of thought is less than 100 years old. Indeed, until recent times, the way that society was organized made it unlikely (useless, really) to consider management as a field of study and thought.

In this and the following chapters, we will use the term *business.* In fact, modern management has been mainly a development of the private sector, the business community. But students whose interests lie in nonbusiness areas such as administrative dietetics or community food service programs should not feel at all left out, because nonprofit and government-funded food service programs now widely use these same techniques. In fact, minor adjustments make modern business management relevant to almost any managerial task.

THE ECONOMIZING SOCIETY

The economist Robert Heilbroner identified three means of organizing a society and dealing with its economic problems: tradition, command, and the market system.[1] The two means with the longest history are tradition and command, whereas the market system, by contrast, emerged from medieval Europe along with our modern age.

Tradition embodies the wisdom of experience, gained through trial and error, in a set of social customs regarded as nearly unchangeable. Primitive societies are traditional societies. Primitives regard the idea of change with fear, and so their whole society is based on the absence of change. For this reason, tradition offers only poor direction in the modern world.

Command, imposed authority, is a solution to society's problems often associated with traditional society. Command was the mode of social control of such ancient empires as the ones the Egyptians and Romans built, and it is the means by which modern dictatorships rule.

The market system, however, emphasizes the free choice of individuals. In theory, consumer decisions govern the allocation of resources, and competition sets the prices in the marketplace. In practice, critics point out,

[1]Robert L. Heilbroner, *The Making of Economic Society,* 4th ed. (Englewood Cliffs, N. J.: Prentice-Hall, 1972).

there are many imperfections in the market system, but we must recognize it as a system that offers consumers—and workers—more choice than does any other system that the world has ever seen.

One central idea of the market economy completely foreign to most other cultures (including that of medieval Europe, out of which our society developed) is the idea of individual gain or profit seeking as not just a legitimate activity but also as a cornerstone of our civilization. Traditional societies are based principally on community interests, but the market system encourages, indeed exalts, individual interest.

Management therefore focuses on the problems of large organizations, though it is used in smaller organizations as well. In premodern times the existing management thought served the church and the military. As royal power and ancient tradition were displaced by an economizing society and the market system, the creative energies of businesspeople began to occupy a more central place in Western civilization, and particularly in the United States. In the nineteenth century, large business organizations came into being, and with them came a need to develop theories to deal with the complex problems associated with those organizations. The field of management was born.

As we will see in the final chapter, some signs suggest that our society may be turning away from individual gain as the main basis of economic action toward a greater consciousness of community values. Because management's values derive from the changing values of the society in which it works, we can expect that a change in society's consensus on the importance of individual choice in the marketplace will have a major impact on management in the future. Management, still not 100 years old, has already passed through a number of changes. In the changing society out of which management arises, there is bound to be further development.

MANAGEMENT: A NEW VIEW OF PROBLEMS

The problems that management deals with weren't really problems at all in the traditional and command economies. People worked at what their parents had worked at; they did what they were told to do. The problem of motivation was largely solved by the fact that the worker's alternative to following orders was starvation. Even in early modern times, when democracy was still growing in the political realm and had little to do with our economic way of life, people worked for low wages. More applicants always were standing at the door if any employee wanted to leave.

Under these circumstances, work was accomplished by masses of poorly paid people using brute strength. They gathered for long hours in factories where they were treated pretty much as though they were machinery. Skilled artisans performed another kind of work. Their skills moved from parent to child—traditional means of dealing with traditional problems.

In the late 1800s, however, Frederick Taylor initiated a new way of thinking about work. It was called Scientific Management, and it focused on finding the best way to accomplish the task at hand. A few years later, a Frenchman, Henri Fayol, reflected on the problems of organizing large-scale enterprise. These two men set the directions that management thought was to follow for over a generation, focusing at one level on the task and, at a higher level of abstraction, on the organization of work in complex organizations. These concerns continue to be central to our studies today.

In the late 1920s the work of Elton Mayo brought a more conscious concern with workers as people. Thus, in not much more than 30 years, a whole new field of study began and moved from a concern with work to a preoccupation with the worker. A number of other points of view have developed within management since then, but these three original concerns— task, organizational design, and the worker—although considerably refined by later thinkers, remain at the heart of hospitality management today.

Management, then, is a very modern institution; indeed, it is a new way of viewing the problems of work in an expanding and increasingly wealthy society. This new way of viewing problems has become one of the strongest forces in the last 100 years of our civilization's development. Because its development has been so rapid, our view of management problems has changed dramatically during that period. Management continues to change with the dynamic society in which it lives, and those entering a career in management must prepare themselves for a constantly changing career. It is useful, therefore, for us to examine briefly the contributions of the early management theorists in order to see the power of their ideas and how this young field of ours grew.

THE MANAGERIAL REVOLUTION

The two thinkers generally credited with laying the foundation of modern management are Frederick Taylor and Henri Fayol. As we will learn, they were concerned with quite different problems. Taylor formulated industrial engineering principles and a wholly new way of organizing tasks. Fayol voiced the first ideas underlying what has come to be called organizational theory.

TAYLOR: THE WORK PROCESS FOCUS

Frederick Taylor founded the Scientific Management movement. He believed that "the most prominent single element in modern scientific management is the task idea." Taylor argued that instead of "herding men in large groups" and relying on brute strength of numbers, a careful study of the work to be done and the worker would result in greatly increased productivity (that is, more units of output per unit of labor input). Although the Industrial Revolution achieved a revolution in productivity through the use of machines, Taylor offered a further revolution through improved work planning. Here is Taylor's own summation:

> Scientific management consists of a certain philosophy which results in a combination of four underlying principles of management: first, the development of a true science; second, the scientific selection of the workman; third, his scientific education and development; and fourth, intimate, friendly cooperation between management and men.

Let us briefly consider each of Taylor's points. His "true science," based on time and motion studies, eventually became the new field of industrial engineering. His idea was to make management's study and planning of the work, rather than numbers and strength (or traditional skill), the controlling factor in work. It was a revolutionary proposal. His method of studying and planning the work meant analyzing each task and developing the "one best way" to do them.

Moreover, his approach replaced the artisan shop, based on traditional skills, with the *controlled shop,* a productive process in which management planning rather than worker skill or strength directs the enterprise.

This idea of management planning reappears in Taylor's second notion—the scientific (we might say "studied") selection of the worker. Rather than relying on the low wages of the time to offset low productivity, Taylor wanted employers to choose the right person for the job. Such an obvious idea hardly seems revolutionary to us, but most of the managers of his time resisted this approach.

The "scientific education" of the workers is a third factor in the controlled-shop notion. Having planned the work and hired someone qualified to do it, Taylor advocated training the worker in the one best way to accomplish each task. He also advocated supervising workers closely so that no other method inadvertently entered the process. Management and the methods it prescribed, rather than the worker's skill or brawn, controlled the productive process.

Finally, Taylor wanted to achieve "friendly cooperation between management and the men" principally through giving workers "what they most want, namely high wages." Taylor proposed to use some of the increased profitability of the now more productive business to improve the workers' wages.

Taylor's ideal worker was "Schmidt," a laborer whom he introduced to work and his foreman in this way: "When this man tells you to walk, you walk—and don't talk back to him." He called Schmidt a "high-priced man" because Schmidt would receive much more than the going wage if, by obedience to Taylor's methods, Schmidt achieved greater productivity.

It is easy to criticize Taylor for his extreme emphasis on pay as "what they want most" and for expecting unfailing obedience. What critics forget is the dramatic social change that has taken place in the world of work in the short time since the days of Schmidt, the "high-priced man."

In Taylor's time the work force was ill educated, largely immigrant, and in a poor bargaining position with their powerful employers. Today, social legislation such as unemployment insurance has removed the fear of starvation from the employer–employee equation. Most employers eagerly seek employees, and these employees are far better educated and more conscious of their own worth. Largely as a result of enormously improved productivity, the American employee works shorter hours for enormously improved pay. But at least two key ideas of Taylor's remain as centerpieces in the American work scene: the task idea and the controlled shop.

The Task Idea

We learned, through Frederick Taylor, that there is a one best way to do work. Thus, the study of layout and design in a hospitality curriculum usually involves finding the most efficient means of laying out the workplace. As we will see in the last chapter of this book, however, using outside experts to lay out the work and design the workplaces in a way that fails to take account of human social needs comes increasingly under challenge. Nevertheless, no one is ready to give up the central idea of work design through the close study of the task to achieve maximum productivity, for such a move would be costly to employer and employee alike.

The Controlled Shop

Taylor brought a shift away from achieving productivity through the skill of the artisan or unskilled brawn "herded in groups." The shift has been toward achieving productivity through work methods designed by management and work performance tightly controlled by supervision. As we will see shortly, Vernon and Gordon Stouffer, in developing the recipe kitchen, brought the controlled shop to food service. (McDonald's and other fast-food operators, through systems design and planning, have extended it even further.)

The notion of the controlled shop, too, is under challenge. Workers in some places now demand (and often receive) greater participation in the control of the workplace. Our discussion of this issue in Chapter 21 will reveal that no one challenges the notion that some agreed-upon system should be developed and followed. The discussion, rather, seems to focus on how the system should be designed and the amount of worker involvement in that design. Neither labor nor management wants to give up the high wages and profits that come from the high productivity bequeathed to us by Taylor and his successors.

Other Contributors

Our brief discussion may encourage you to explore further the development of management thought. Among other things, you would learn of the many contributions made to scientific management by Taylor's colleagues and those who came after. We note in passing two other pioneers. Frank and Lillian Gilbreth advanced the study of the task by developing the *therblig* ("Gilbreth" spelled backward), defined as the smallest unit of human movement that can be measured. Developing standardized therbligs for all work motions speeds and simplifies the task of the industrial engineer.

H. L. Gantt, like Frederick Taylor, insisted on the close supervision of the work and the worker. He developed a system of charting work operations that relies on the now-familiar Gantt charts. These charts have been adapted for use in hospitality employee scheduling. The discussion of staff planning in Chapter 16 includes a brief description of their use.

Clearly, although a changing world challenges and alters the early work of the Scientific Management movement, in many ways, the movement's contributions continue to have a lasting impact on our lives.

FAYOL: ADMINISTRATIVE MANAGEMENT

Whereas Taylor and his colleagues focused on the task and the shop, Henri Fayol focused on the organizational problems of departmental division and work coordination. The discussion in the next five chapters of this book is organized around management functions. This frame of analysis was originally advanced by Fayol in 1916, albeit in a somewhat different form. But his conceptual scheme for viewing the work of managers has had a profound, shaping effect on the development of management thought.

Fayol was French and his work, written in French, had limited circulation in English-speaking countries until 1929. It did not reach print in the United States until 1949. For this reason, it is difficult to trace Fayol's influence precisely. Doubtless, however, some scholars, students, and managers heard his work discussed. In any case, his ideas gained wide acceptance, which they still enjoy today.

Beyond describing management as a common set of activities—now called management functions—Fayol was among the first civilians to rationalize the staff role. He contrasted it with the role of line management and offered a clear statement of staff limitations. Our discussion of these topics in Chapter 15 owes a great debt to his early formulations of these issues.

Fayol first suggested two bases for dividing work into departments: functional and geographic. (An Englishman, L. H. Gulick, expanded this notion into four bases for departmentalization: function, process, clientele, and location.)

Fayol was concerned, too, with the number of people a manager could efficiently supervise, and his ideas on this subject were expanded by V. A. Graicunias into the notion of *span of control*. Departmentalization and span of control, too, are discussed in Chapter 15.

HUMAN RELATIONS: WORK AS A SOCIAL PROCESS

In the late 1920s, the Western Electric Company conducted a series of tests to study the effect of light levels on worker productivity. The researchers raised the level of light in the factory, and each time they did, productivity rose. Then, to test their results, they lowered the level of light—but productivity increased again. They lowered it still further, and again, productivity rose! Here was a puzzle. What was going on?

The researchers gradually formed a hypothesis that the way the workers felt about their work was significant. The experimental process, the attention that the researchers paid to the workers, seemed to stimulate their productivity. The research thus was expanded to include a close study of the human interaction in the work groups being observed. The researchers discovered that social pressures in the work group were at least as important as was pay in determining level of effort and output of workers.

This work was begun under the direction of Elton Mayo and carried out largely by Fritz Roethlisberger and W. J. Dickson, all famous names in management thought. It set in motion a process of research and controversy that continues to be a lively area of debate among management theorists as well as managers and supervisors. Although there is wide disagreement over exactly how to interpret and put into practice the findings of the human relations school (or as it has more recently been termed, *organizational behavior*), few would argue today that pay is all that counts. Most managers are much more sensitive to the human and social needs of workers than they were just a few years ago.

THE AGENDA FOR MANAGERS

We have noted the influence of the early theorists, Taylor, Fayol, and Mayo, and the practical uses to which their theories are put to this day. By way of a summary we should note that the basic issues in hospitality management for the foreseeable future are embodied in the work of these three men and those who followed them. From Taylor we get a concern with efficient production methods. Fayol set us to thinking about the design of the working organization. And Mayo and his followers alerted us to a concern for the worker as an individual and as a social being.

MANAGEMENT: A DYNAMIC FORCE IN A CHANGING INDUSTRY

The hospitality industry, too, has had its managerial pioneers. Although we cannot, in the space allotted here, discuss them all, a brief description of the work of E. M. Statler and Vernon and Gordon Stouffer will help demonstrate the impact of management ideas on the evolution of the hospitality industry.

STATLER: THE FIRST "NATIONAL" HOSPITALITY SYSTEM

Ideas, especially as textbooks present them, often appear neat and tidy. But they are usually the result of complicated development. The central perception of E. M. Statler—that a national market existed for quality accommodations for the growing American middle class—probably evolved from his experience in serving that market as his hotel holdings grew from the original Buffalo Statler to a chain serving many of the nation's major cities. After developing and operating two "temporary" hotels for the Pan American Exposition in Buffalo in 1901 and the World's Fair in St. Louis in 1904, Statler opened his first permanent hotel in Buffalo in 1908, where he had already made a name for himself with a successful, popular-priced restaurant. His hotel featured all the amenities of a luxury hotel, but both its plant and organization were designed for maximum efficiency. His slogan, "A Room with a Bath for a Dollar and a Half," shook an industry that associated the luxury of a bath with high prices. Statler's became the first popular-priced, full-service hotel. In the hotel business of that day, a substantial portion of the hotel rooms were *plain rooms,* that is, rooms without a bath. All of the popular-priced rooms were of this variety. Thus, "A Room with a Bath for a Dollar and a Half" represented a major social innovation.

As the size of the Statler organization grew, the company developed central staff services in control, architectural design, and personnel. Statler produced, then, the first centralized corporate staff (as opposed to line management, a concept we will discuss in Chapter 15) in the hospitality industry. The enforcement of uniform standards in all Statler hotels provided a guest with the assurance of a familiar quality level wherever he or she went. Moreover, Statler was the first hotelier to perceive the power of the American middle-class market, and his was probably the first true hospitality chain with common operating standards for all properties.

It would take a much fuller discussion of Statler's many contributions—including his important role as the first influential backer of hospitality education—to give full credit to this pioneer. Fortunately, such a discussion is available and has been listed among the suggested readings at the end of this chapter.

STOUFFER'S MODERN MANAGEMENT TECHNIQUES

Vernon and Gordon Stouffer were sons of the owners of a fairly successful family restaurant. In the early 1920s they attended the Wharton School of Finance, where they studied the ideas of Frederick Taylor and the other management pioneers. As a result of that experience, the Stouffers introduced ideas that transformed the artisan- and craft-based field of restaurateuring into a modern American restaurant industry. In short, the Stouffers adapted the thinking of Taylor and Fayol to the restaurant.

The Recipe Kitchen: A Controlled Shop

Their mother oversaw the original kitchen, but the Stouffer brothers obviously could not build a chain on the skills of one person approaching retirement age. On the other hand, they did not want a chef, because (they argued) when you lose the chef and replace him or her, your food could change and your organization might fall apart. With this insight into the weaknesses of the craft-based kitchen, the Stouffers sought to achieve management control over the kitchen by developing a set of recipes that would produce a standard product. For many years, the Stouffers hired only women for work in kitchen or pantry because (they argued) women were accustomed to following recipes, whereas men were inclined "to become chefs," making things their own way and destroying the uniformity of product for which Stouffers ultimately became famous.

The food production supervisor and her assistants were called managers: They planned the work; organized that work around stations; staffed the kitchens with the right people, properly trained for the right job; and controlled food costs through yield checks and portion control devices. Finally, the food production manager, while leading and directing her crew, placed great emphasis on following the recipes and methods specified by management.

The introduction of the management-controlled recipe kitchen greatly improved productivity over the traditional kitchens of the day. Closer management control also ensured remarkably low food costs. The result was a highly competitive price. As Statler had done with hotels, the Stouffers brought the amenities of fine dining within reach of the American middle-class mass market.

The organization of the traditional restaurant centered on the traditional roles associated with traditional work stations; the relations among workers and between work groups reflected the old chef–maitre d'–steward pecking order. Stouffers, however, adopted a modern system of departmentalization. Reporting to the general manager were the executive assistant manager and his or her assistants, a director of service, and the dietitian (or food production manager). Although these formally prescribed relationships have changed somewhat from time to time. Figure 13.1 is a reasonably accurate description of the way the typical Stouffers unit was arranged.

Within the organization, ranks with the rigidity and symbolic trappings of an almost military organization were developed, complete with titles of address (Mr., Miss, Mrs. for supervisors and managers; first names for workers) and uniforms that clearly differentiated management from worker.

The Stouffers pioneered, as well, in the area of personnel management. They offered fringe benefits such as paid vacations, paid holidays, and group insurance long before these practices became widespread. The Stouffers were among those who supported the pioneering work of William Foote Whyte, which finally took the form of his study, *Human Relations in the Restaurant Industry*.

Thus the three kinds of ideas that constituted then—and still do now—the agenda of management thought had a profound effect in shaping the Stouffer organization: the controlled shop focused on the task, a rational organization design, and concern for the worker as an individual human being.

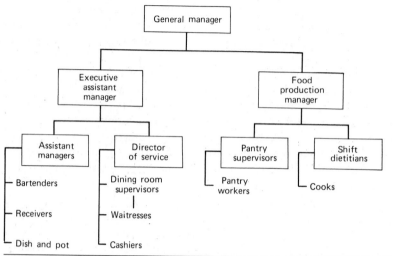

FIGURE 13.1   The Stouffer restaurant organization.

WHAT IS MANAGEMENT?

In the next five chapters we will examine the work of managers, and we will organize that examination around the five functions of management. Before we turn to that discussion, let us look at the basic work of a business (or any other organization, be it hospital, nursing home, or school lunch program). Peter Drucker, the economist and management consultant, stated that the basic purpose of business is to "create a customer"; that is, to determine unfulfilled consumer needs and find a way to fill them. Drucker argued that the customer determines what a business is and that the central functions of a business are *innovation* and *marketing*.[2]

Before discussing Drucker's theory, and applying it to our industry, we should pause for a moment to consider whether his line of reasoning applies to all of us in management and supervision. Some, for instance, would argue that marketing is activity for the sales department. Marketing, basically, is determining what the customer wants and then providing it in a way that makes it reasonably easy for the customer to obtain, while pricing it to recover the cost and make a profit. The specific work of marketing is usually handled by a separate department. But marketing also includes a way of thinking about problems that is often the hallmark of the successful manager. Drucker put it this way:

[2]Peter Drucker, *Management: Tasks, Responsibilities, Practices* (New York, Harper & Row, 1974), p. 61. The discussion in this section takes many of its ideas from Chapters 6 and 7 of Drucker's book.

> Marketing is so basic that it cannot be considered a separate function (i.e., a separate skill or work) within the business, on a par with others such as manufacturing or personnel. Marketing requires separate work and a distinct group of activities. But it is first a central dimension of the entire business. It is the whole business seen from its final result, that is from the customer's point of view. Concern and responsibility for marketing must, therefore, permeate all areas of the enterprise.[3]

This marketing viewpoint can actually guide us not only in dealing with guests but in dealing with employees as well. Employees are, after all, "customers" who "buy" jobs from employers with their time and effort.

We might also hear the argument that innovation is really a function of top management only. But surely opportunities for innovation exist on a smaller scale and at all levels of the organization. Indeed, it is almost "un-American" to attribute all the opportunity for creative work to some "top group." The supervisor or junior manager who does not try to develop his or her own solutions to problems will be less useful to an organization than if he or she sees innovation as part of the work.

Obviously, the marketing and innovation work of junior managers must take place on a smaller scale and lower level, and it will be subject to the policy of the organization. Nevertheless, thinking your work through in terms of the needs and wants of those you deal with—employees and guests—and trying to find a new solution when old ways seem ineffective will make your work more fulfilling for you and more valuable to your operation. Finally, an understanding of the significance of marketing and innovation should make you more ready to support the efforts of others in these areas.

Indeed, Drucker pointed to what he called "the fallacy of the *unterneymer*." (*Unterneymer* is German for "top man.") He noted that the definition of business purpose is most often thought of as the concern of the owner or, at most, a few people at the top of the organization. In the German tradition of the *unterneymer*, Drucker said,

> the top man and especially the owner-manager, alone, knows what the business is all about and alone makes all the entrepreneurial decisions. Everybody else is a technician who carries out prescribed tasks. . . .

> [T]his may have been adequate in the nineteenth century business in which a few men at the top who alone made decisions, with all the rest manual workers or low level clerks. It is a dangerous misconception of today's business enterprise.

> In sharp contrast to the organization of the past, today's business enterprise (also today's hospital or government agency) brings together a great many men of high knowledge and skill, at practically every level of the organization.

---

[3]Drucker, *Management: Tasks, Responsibilities, Practices*, p. 63.

But high knowledge and skill also means decision impact on how the work is to be done and on what work is actually tackled. They make, by necessity, risk-taking decisions, that is business decisions, whatever the official form of the organization.[4]

It is clear that the continuing definition of what a business is, is important to managers at all levels of an organization.

WHAT IS OUR BUSINESS?

To answer this question, Drucker posed a series of additional questions:

- Who is the customer?
- What is value to the customer?
- What will our business be?
- What *should* our business be?

We have seen how Statler and the Stouffer brothers, in different areas, thought through the needs of the emerging American middle-class mass market—a market that really constituted a "new" customer. Then they used the developing field of management to serve that market. Each saw that to that market, "value" comprised all the amenities of luxury standardized and produced so that they could be offered at popular prices. Kemmons Wilson, nearly 50 years after Statler, wrought a similar revolution in the lodging industry when he realized that the customers and their needs had changed and called for innovation. His answer to that call was the Holiday Inn.

Let's illustrate Drucker's frame of analysis with some examples from the hospitality industry: community nutrition programs, the community hotel, and the growth of franchised hospitality chains.

Who Is the Customer?

The answer to this question is complicated by the fact that there are usually at least two customers, and generally more. Recall that the school lunch program got its start as a national program not only to fill the needs of hungry students but also to use up surplus farm commodities and help solve the nation's unemployment problem during the Depression.

Although we can't trace the process exactly, we know from our discussion in Chapter 5 that the great expansion in the school lunch program was a response to the growing participation of women in the work force. Indeed, the development of preschool feeding and the school breakfast program are more recent innovative responses to the twin problems of working mothers and poor families. Although the customer is the child who eats and the par-

---

[4]Drucker, *Management: Tasks, Responsibilities, Practices*, p. 76.

ents who need no longer remain home to prepare a meal, the buying decision
is made by Congress, and the ultimate customer is the American people.
Much the same can be said for congregate feeding programs.

It is hardly possible to identify the single "entrepreneur" responsible
for the growth of community nutrition programs. They have resulted from
the work of many people, both within and outside the school lunch program
and other food service programs. This revolution in the way that social obligations are arranged to provide nutrition is still going on—a dramatic example of identifying customer needs and innovating to fill those needs with
people at all levels of many operations involved in the work. Clearly, neither
community nutrition programs nor any of its elements—school lunch, preschool feeding, congregate meals—is the work of an *unterneymer*!

On a smaller scale, community hotel promoters discover every generation or so that town leaders in smaller communities can benefit from a small
first-class hotel. The guest is also an important customer, but as the discussion in Chapter 6 suggested, many community hotels would never have been
built were it not for the positive influence (expected or real) of these hotels
on real estate values, employment, and community growth in a small town.
Thus, community leaders are important customers for community hotel developers, in many ways as important as are the guests the hotel is built to
serve.

The success of franchised businesses in the hospitality industry illustrates, once again, the notion of multiple levels of customers. When Colonel
Sanders developed his successful take-out chicken operation (in a restaurant, incidently, bypassed by an expressway and in need of innovation to
revive it); he recognized that if he could sell his *idea*—his system—to others,
they could, in turn, sell to the customer. Like other franchisors, the Colonel
was able to expand more rapidly through a franchise organization. Thus, in
addition to the Kentucky Fried Chicken guest, the franchisees were important customers of the Colonel's. The franchise company must design a product that fills the needs of guests; then it must develop a system that fills the
needs of local investors and entrepreneurs who want to run a successful
business in their communities.

What Is Value to the Customer?

Each customer has different values to be fulfilled. The guest at a Holiday
Inn values a standard level of product and service, conveniently located, and
priced within his or her means. (These means are defined by "the American
middle class," to which the guest almost invariably belongs.) The *franchise
holder,* on the other hand, buys a familiar hospitality brand name, national
advertising, and a referral system.

Value to the guest in a community hotel is clean comfortable accommodations. But value to the local investors results from factors such as im-

proved property values and a community that can more readily attract other employers with new local job opportunities.

The value of community nutrition programs to students, young children, and senior citizens is adequate nutrition and a palatable meal. Congress supports these programs for these reasons. But we can speculate that perhaps even more significant is the fact that these programs solve other problems. They fill the needs of families in which the mother works and can no longer serve a midday meal (or sometimes even breakfast). Congregate feeding for the elderly also supplies services that families no longer provide for their elderly. The obverse is true: congregate feeding often frees the elderly from a dependence on their children.

What Will Our Business Be?

This question recognizes the simple fact that "the only constant is change"—that for organizations to survive in a changing environment, they must change with it. Holiday Inns was originally and for many years a company of roadside inns located on the outer edges of cities, along expressways, or near airports. As urban renewal began to revitalize downtown, and as many downtown hotels continued to deteriorate or even closed their doors, a large new market began to emerge. Accordingly, Holiday Inns developed prototype properties to serve urban centers and changed from strictly a motel company to a hotel–motel company.

In the mid-1980s, as segmentation became more widespread, Holiday Corporation—its name changed to recognize the company's broadened commitments—has evolved into a multibrand company represented in nearly every significant area of lodging: Hampton Inns in the economy market, Holiday Inns in the conventional motor hotel market, and the Crown Plaza properties and the Embassy Suites in upscale markets. Holiday has recognized, as well, the significance of its destination activities in the casino business and has expanded to commitment there in its Harrah's Division.

What *Should* Our Business Be?

Drucker began his discussion of the question in this way:

> "What *will* our business be?" aims at adaptation to anticipated changes. It aims at modifying, extending, developing the existing, ongoing business.
>
> But there is a need also to ask "What *should* our business be?" What opportunities are opening up or can be created to fulfill the purpose and mission of the business by making it a different business?[5]

The school lunch program began by serving children in public schools. As public food service programs expanded to include preschool children and the elderly, however, many officials of the school lunch program started to

[5]Drucker, *Management: Tasks, Responsibilities, Practices*, p. 92.

wonder whether their organization can be expanded to embrace such other community food service programs as congregate meals for the elderly. The school lunch program in every community already has a production plant. Moreover, it maintains central service facilities in lunchrooms unused except during the noon recess (and, perhaps, the early morning). It also has skilled workers and managerial and nutritional savvy, and it is genuinely community based. Thus the question, "What *should* our business be?" is properly raised by school lunch leaders. It will be interesting to watch how food service answers these four questions in the next generation.

McDonald's began as a drive-in restaurant on the outskirts of a city, serving hamburgers, french fries, and shakes, principally at lunch and dinner. Because of its great success, McDonald's might have been content. Instead, management constantly asked what its business *should* be, and today's McDonald's features dining facilities attractively decorated where guests can sit and eat their meals rather than carrying them to the car. McDonald's has also moved aggressively and successfully into the breakfast market and has recently become a major factor in downtown food service. Instead of resting on its laurels as the country's most successful drive-in chain, McDonald's management continually looks for new opportunities. "What should our business be?" asks McDonald's. The answers account for McDonald's steady expansion and its place as our largest restaurant system (albeit a system of restaurants with very limited menus) serving all three meals and available in most market areas.

In Business for Yourself?

Some students certainly plan to enter business for themselves. Those who succeed will remember the key questions we have just reviewed. Students whose careers involve working as supervisors and managers for others must realize that they are also in business for themselves—selling their services and making a career based on their reputation for effectiveness. The analysis we have just offered serves them, too.

Who are your customers, and what is value to them? The patrons of your operation are obviously customers, and their needs and wants must be satisfied. The employer is your customer, and in an important way, especially for junior managers and supervisors, the employees you direct are also your customers. If they were not there, there would be no need for a supervisor. The balancing of the needs of all these "customers," properly done, will require creative marketing and innovation on your part.

What will your business be? And what should it be? Career change is so common in North America that we all should consider the possibilities together. Is there an area of the industry that might offer greater opportunities? Or shorter hours? Or higher pay? At some point in a career, you may want to change the nature of your business: for instance, from supervisor in a large operation to unit manager. As these changes arise, you should ask yourself questions about your ability to "change your business." Perhaps additional work in accounting, a human relations training program, or some other specialized work or study would help you supply value to your proposed new customers.

Success—defined as income, advancement, or more work satisfaction—will come from taking a creative approach to the work of management. In the next five chapters we will consider just what kind of work supervisors and managers do. We emphasize here, though, that even during that time when you prepare for managerial duties, by working as a waitress or a dishwasher, you can use an understanding of management functions. Waitresses, cooks, and bartenders are "in business for themselves," building knowledge through experience, building a reputation for effectiveness, and deriving personal satisfaction from work well done. This "business" is worth managing, and more success will come from having managed it well.

The functions of management summarized in the next five chapters are presented separately *for our convenience* in analyzing the work of managers. You should realize, as each of the next five chapters repeats, that *none* of these functions is *accomplished separately*. Management is really a continuous process involving, in varying degrees, all the functions nearly all the time.

SUGGESTIONS FOR FURTHER READING

Because we have covered so much ground so quickly in this chapter, you may want to explore in greater depth one or more of the areas we have discussed.

The emergence of the "economizing society":

Robert L. Heilbroner, *The Worldly Philosophers* (New York: Simon & Schuster, 1972), pp. 1–7.

For a fuller statement, see Heilbroner's *The Making of an Economic Society* (Englewood Cliffs, N.J.: Prentice-Hall, 1972), especially pp. 1–35.

Both are available in paperback.

The development of management thought:

Harold Koontz and Cyril O'Donnel, *Management—A Systems and Contingency Analysis of Managerial Functions* (New York: McGraw-Hill, 1976), pp. 25–54.

Joseph L. Massie, "Management Theory" in James G. March, ed., *Handbook of Organizations* (Chicago: Rand McNally, 1965).

Management leaders in the hospitality industry:

Floyd Miller, *Statler, America's Extraordinary Hotelman* (Buffalo: The Statler Foundation, 1968).

Donald E. Lundberg, *The Hotel and Restaurant Business* (Boston: Cahners Books, 1971), especially pp. 245–290.

What is a business?

> Peter Drucker, *Management: Tasks, Responsibilities, Practices* (New York: Harper & Row, 1974). This entire volume belongs in the library and on the reading list of every person who wants to understand American management in the last half of the twentieth century. The material that pertains to the discussion in this chapter is found particularly on pp. 58–94.

SUMMARY

This chapter began our discussion of management. First we defined management and supervision. Second we outlined the history of coping with economic problems: tradition, command, and the market system.

We turned then to three pioneers in management theory: Taylor and his work process focus, the task idea, and the controlled shop; Fayol and administrative management; and Mayo and his concern with the worker.

We moved to a discussion of two pioneers in the hospitality industry: Statler and the Stouffers. Statler introduced the idea of a popular-priced, full-service hotel as well as uniform standards in all his hotels. He was perhaps the first to recognize the power of the middle-class market in regard to the hospitality industry. The Stouffers adapted Taylor's and Fayol's ideas to their restaurants. They used a recipe kitchen—a controlled shop—which standardized the management and organization of their restaurants.

The last section of this chapter was devoted to a study of Drucker's theories of management and how they apply to the hospitality industry. We considered several questions: What is management? Who is the customer? What is value to the customer? What will our business be? and What *should* our business be?

KEY WORDS AND CONCEPTS

To help you review this chapter, keep in mind the following:

Management	High-priced man
Supervision	Span of control
Tradition	Administrative management
Command	Organizational behavior
Market system	Statler
Work process focus	Stouffer
The task idea	The recipe kitchen
Controlled shop	

REVIEW QUESTIONS

1. How do management and supervision differ?

2. Compare tradition, command, and the market system.

3. Describe Taylor's principal contributions to management theory.

4. What were Statler's main contributions to hospitality management? The Stouffers' contributions?

5. According to Drucker, what *should* our business—the hospitality industry—be?

Photo courtesy of the Flamingo Hilton.

THE PLANNING FUNCTION IN HOSPITALITY MANAGEMENT

THE PURPOSE OF THIS CHAPTER

Planning is a necessary everyday activity both in life and in managing. Planning *should* go on at every level of the organization, from dishwasher to the chairman of the board. Unfortunately, it often gets overlooked at all these levels. Planning for your life's work is as essential as planning today's menu. Accordingly, this chapter presents planning as an active process related to long-range organizational goals and to day-to-day work, as well. Although the concepts we present are most clearly related to planning in organizations, they need only be adapted to be useful to students considering their career goals.

THIS CHAPTER SHOULD HELP YOU

1. View planning as an organizational process that goes on at all levels.

2. View yourself as a supervisor or manager who plans and as an organization member who is affected by organizational plans.

3. Define and use the key planning concepts discussed in this chapter.

4. Explain how planning is related to and arises from goal setting that begins with a guest or client.

5. State the relationship between plans and evaluation.

6. Describe planning as a general management function (strategic planning), as an operation management function (tactical planning), and as work done by individuals for the organization and for themselves.

7. Explain the need for policy and long-range planning, and describe and use some selected tools developed in this chapter for this purpose.

WHY STUDY PLANNING

Planning is something that everybody agrees is important. But planning often is neglected, probably because it requires hard thinking and involves the uncomfortable work of dealing with uncertainty.

An absence of conscious planning leads to two related kinds of problems. First, because employees must know what their employers expect of them, an absence of management planning leads to confusion at work. Second, in order to settle that confusion, the employees often plan for themselves. Their plans may be aimed at goals completely unrelated to the organization's goals. For example, if management fails to develop a seating chart for the dining room, the waitresses will almost certainly work out their own system. Such a system may or may not be good for guest service, but you can bet it will suit the convenience of the waitresses.

Failure to plan invites trouble. Three different kinds of examples illustrate why planning is necessary at all levels of the organization. Consider, first of all, the waitress who does not plan her next trip to the dining room in the light of the needs of her entire station. She will probably have to run back and forth to get one or two items that she could have brought all at once. In this way, she wastes two of her most precious resources: time and energy. At the end of the day she has worked harder than her coworkers have and probably has earned less in tips from those customers who had to wait for her to complete those extra trips. Planning by individual workers, then, is important.

If you have ever been in a restaurant that ran out of eggs at breakfast or bread during a rush on the sandwich station, you have seen our second example—the results of poor operational planning. And you know its costs: dissatisfied guests, upset employees, the loss of some of those inconvenienced customers, and perhaps some of the people they talk to. In general, the operation's reputation suffers.

Notice in the third example that the higher the level of decision making is, the more widespread the effects of poor planning will become. For example, shortly after Walt Disney World opened, a wave of motel building in the surrounding communities produced an oversupply of motor hotel rooms that led to a series of bankruptcies.

Of course, the failure to plan entails serious risks at any level. Your own plans are most important to you. Just as the waitress wasted time and the restaurant that ran out of eggs lost profit opportunities, you may waste a good deal of effort and miss opportunities if you fail to plan in these two ways.

First, you need to plan for yourself at several levels:

1. Whatever work you do (desk clerking, college homework, or motel housekeeping), your work will be easier and quicker if you can plan it.

2. As a supervisor or manager, you must learn to plan the work of others. (Moreover, senior-level managers must not only plan work—*how* to do—but must also plan on the grander scale or organizational goals—*what* to do.)

3. In addition to planning the work you do for others, you must think of your own career as a business (because you sell services to your employer). Thus your career development means planning for the kinds of services you want to be selling at some future point—banquet manager, sales representative, food production supervisor, and so forth—and then planning how to achieve that position within a reasonable period.

Second, you will probably have to accept that as a member of an organization, you are part of somebody else's plans. The point is that understanding the planning process helps you understand the need of a well-managed company for carefully developed plans. As an understanding participant in planning, you should be a more effective employee and find greater meaning in your work.

The following discussion should help you work effectively by improving your readiness to plan your work and the work of others. Moreover, the basic approach to business can be applied to your own career planning.

PLANNING IN ORGANIZATIONS

> Planning is the work that managers (and workers) do to visualize the future in a concrete way and to determine courses of action that will achieve the organization's goals over a definite period.

As we have noted, planning at the different levels of the management hierarchy has different characteristics. The pyramid in Figure 14.1 provides a convenient way of symbolizing some of these characteristics. The higher in the organization the planning activity takes place, the fewer persons will be involved in the planning, and the more general the nature of the plan and commitment will be. At lower levels, the planning involves more people and more detail.

For example, the waitress's work plans might cover a period of one meal or, perhaps, just a *turn* on her station (the time it takes to serve a party—to "turn" her table). Purchasing at the operating level seldom covers a period of more than a week, and usually just a day or two. These are good examples of short-run planning.

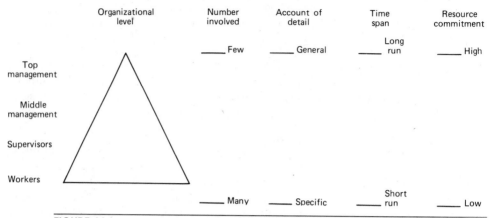

FIGURE 14.1 Dimensions of planning in organizations.

Although short-run planning is absolutely essential, it differs from long-run planning, in which resources are committed on a much larger scale. Not surprisingly, specialized tools for long-range planning have been developed to assist managers at that level. We will examine these long-range planning tools at the end of this chapter.

Formalized business planning is increasingly common in multiunit chains. A survey of chain food service executives revealed that nearly three-quarters of their companies made annual strategic plans (see Table 14.1) with five-year future projections.[1]

A full-fledged plan is complex. A marketing plan, for instance, will contain a research summary, a statement of marketing goals, a statement of both strategy and tactics for achieving the plan's goals, and provision for measuring progress toward the plan's goals and for revising the plan if conditions change.[2] It is important to remember, though, that the banquet manager's plan of how to serve tomorrow's banquets is no less a plan, if it is more straightforward.

SOME PLANNING CONCEPTS

The term *planning* denotes anticipating several different sets of circumstances for different purposes. Several other key terms will help you fill out the idea of the planning process.

Policies are general guides for dealing with the future. They don't tell what to do; they indicate how to reach a decision. Policies leave much to the

[1] Bryan G. Herron, "Strategic Planners or Restaurateurs . . . One and the Same?" *12th Annual Chain Operators Exchange* (Chicago: International Foodservice Manufacturers Association, 1985).

[2] *NRA News*, December 1985, pp. 37–39.

TABLE 14.1 Strategic Plan Data for S&A Restaurant Corporation

Economic
Government regulation
Real estate costs
Industry trends
Consumer
• Demographics
• Life-styles
• Attitudes
• Purchase behavior
Competitive
Internal
• Sales/counts
• Unit expansion
• Historical

Source: J. Michael Jenkins, "The S&A Evolution," *12th Annual Chain Operators Exchange* (Chicago: International Foodservice Manufacturers Association, 1985).

discretion of the decision maker. But they provide a predetermined, agreed-upon basis for decisions.

> The unit manager of a large chain of restaurants is approached every week for small contributions to local charities. The company's policy does not say what to give or whom to give to. Policy does say what general kinds of organizations can be considered and what the limits on the manager's discretion are. (The manager may be able to give, for instance, as much as $100 to a single organization without approval). It is still up to the unit manager to gauge the situation and decide whether to make any particular donation and how much to give up to the maximum set by the guidelines of policy.

A *plan* is a reasoned means of moving toward some selected goal. A plan reflects policy and may include rules, methods, procedures, standards, and budgets. A plan may have both strategic and tactical elements.

> The most comprehensive of plans may not be written down in one place. On the other hand, the operations manual of a well-run company is a useful example of a group of plans. Some companies, particularly larger ones, develop marketing plans over a long period; these plans elaborate goals, methods, budgets, and the like. Both these examples suggest that a full-fledged plan is complex. But the banquet manager's

plan of how to serve tomorrow's banquet is no less a plan, and it is straightforward.

Thus, a plan describes future events of whatever complexity in a way that shows how they will be ordered to achieve the organization's goals.

Rules state what must be done (or must not be done) in a given situation. Rules leave no discretion in their execution.

"Food production employees must wear hair nets in the kitchen" answers a question about one aspect of an employee's future behavior. Most companies have a rule that the "paperwork" must be done before a new employee can go to work, receive a paycheck, or take a vacation.

Methods and *procedures* resemble rules. Methods indicate how a standard job is to be done. Procedures are really a sequential set of rules.

The method for stripping a turkey carcass is determined by a food service operator with the help of industrial engineers. As a result of these studies, waste motions are minimized, and the time required is reduced to a minimum.

Most hotels have a procedure that specifies the process that a guest's records should go through during his or her stay—just as most health-care institutions have a similar procedure for patient records.

Standards specify not procedures but outcomes. Some standards pertain to cost control, and many relate to quality control.

Quality standards determine, for instance, how food should taste or what quantity of nutrition should be present, as in the approved plan school lunch. Standards might also specify how many seconds it should take for a phone operator to respond to a guest or to place an outside call; or the length of time a bellhop requires to room a guest.

Cost standards indicate an acceptable cost for some activity. Thus, the preceding method specifies a standard time for stripping a turkey. Similarly, most hotels have a standard number of rooms that should be cleaned per eight-hour maid-day (usually between 12 and 16).

A *budget* is a numerical plan, generally expressed in dollars, although sometimes units of weight or time may be used, as well. The budget specifies the dollar results expected from a plan of operation.

Most well-run operations prepare budgets that express in dollars the results they expect. Those budgets may be supported (in their estimates for housekeeping payroll, for instance) with a statement about hours budgeted at various levels of occupancy as a base for housekeeping payroll projections.

Strategy and *tactics* are terms borrowed from the military to denote level of importance and time dimensions in plans. *Strategy* implies large-scale, high-level, and long-term time commitment. In Figure 14.1, strategy would lie at the upper end of the pyramid. *Tactics* are often of great importance, but they generally imply a shorter period and a more localized plan.

A hotel chain may develop a marketing strategy that relates the hotel's services to the guests it seeks to serve and that prescribes, in general, how their patronage will be sought.

Each of the units of that chain must develop the tactics that best fit the individual property and its market. Strategies are concerned with overall goals and the general means of achieving them. Tactics are specific, relating methods to individual circumstances.

GOAL SETTING: MANAGEMENT BY OBJECTIVES

How do we go about setting goals in organizations? Some traditionalists insist that we should already know what our goals are. "A great hotel is . . ." and generally they fill in the blanks with a description of "the way we've always done it." If we press them, however, we find they really don't intend to offer the same level of service as the "great hotel" offered a generation or two ago. In most operations, anyway, this goal is just not possible. Costs, particularly labor costs, have risen astronomically, and the supply of labor for some jobs has decreased to the vanishing point. So, it turns out, what the traditionalist really proposes is for us to come as close as we can to "what we've always done."

The traditionalist's eyes, you see, are set firmly in the past. He or she defines what's to be done in terms of the standards derived from past experience. We, of course, do not argue that we can't learn from experience; we can and we must. But the past is not where one begins goal setting in a consumer-oriented society.

The logical place to begin goal setting is with the person who really sets the goals: the guest (or client). Accordingly, we should take a marketing approach to our operations.[3] If the needs and wants of the guests aren't met, they will take their business elsewhere. (If clients in a congregate meals pro-

---

[3]For the best statement of this point of view, see Peter Drucker's work, particularly *Management: Tasks, Responsibilities, Practices*.

gram, for instance, don't like what they are served, they will complain to the agency, to their congressperson, or to the newspaper.)

Examine these examples of goals and see how they relate to the guests' needs and wants: Elaborate service requires highly skilled waitresses and waiters, an attentive maitre d', and a large backup staff. This is "great" service, most restaurateurs would agree. But we would never put it in a truck stop. The reasons are obvious, but revealing.

Our guest at the truck stop wants a hearty meal of the kind of food he or she is used to. Correct classical service would seem "snooty." This guest wants friendly and fast service, simple food, and modest prices. Here is another example, not as extreme as it may appear:

> Not long ago my wife and I were talking to a professor in another field of study who had just came back from New York. He was describing in great detail a really "fine restaurant" he had eaten in. After he left, my wife turned to me and said "Do you realize what he was saying? He was describing as a 'fine restaurant' a place in which he doesn't like to eat!" As I thought about it, I realized he had intended to praise the restaurant but had, for the most part, been commenting on how snobbish he had found the place. Without saying so, he had indicated that the formality of the place made him uncomfortable.

Traditional forms of formal service are still effective in many operations, but we cannot assume uncritically that the traditional way is the only way. And we cannot uncritically accept traditional forms of service as goals to strive for.

Health care presents an unusually interesting example of shaping products and services to the guest's needs—and wishes. For example, most hospitals now realize that the meals they serve their patients can, to an extraordinary degree, raise or lower the morale of those patients. For some, the meal may be nearly the only pleasant thing that happens to them all day. For this reason, many hospitals have begun to spend more effort and money on food service than would ordinarily be necessary. Providing special diets is, of course, an even more obvious example of the guests' needs in determining service.

Guests' needs may, however, be only one of the goals to be met. As we saw in Chapter 5, our society has made the school systems largely responsible for feeding children their noon meal. In specifying the approved plan lunch requirements, the Food and Nutrition Service amplifies the young guest's goal (a good lunch) to include the need for the lunch to contain an adequate and balanced diet. The agency has yet a further goal mandated by Congress: nutrition education. A school must use the approved plan lunch to help teach young people what a balanced diet is. But the school lunch manager must still design a menu that will appeal to the students, or else he or she will face complaints from the students and their parents.

There is one more way to see the guest as the primary goal setter. Remember the motel-building boom outside Disney World we referred to earlier? Developers can build motels, but the guests must pay for them. Goods and services offered in the market, therefore, have to take account of how much a guest will buy as what he or she will buy.

CHARACTERISTICS OF WELL-THOUGHT-OUT GOALS

"Our goal is better service." That is the kind of statement to be wary of. Specifically, what does it mean? In the process of setting goals, we might better ask ourselves, "How will I know when I get there?"

Some people suggest a checklist nicknamed the 'Five *W*s and an *H*."

WHO
WHAT
WHERE
WHEN
WHY
HOW

This checklist can help a manager make sure that the issues have been examined from every angle.

Perhaps most important, though, is to set objective and measurable goals. "How will I know when I get there?"

The front-desk personnel of a motor hotel in the middle of a large city were criticized for being cold and impersonal. A number of unsuccessful "courtesy campaigns" were tried but had little effect. (This front desk was very busy, and the clerks felt themselves under pressure because of waiting lines, and the like.) Finally, a clerk suggested that everybody adopt a rule: *Always* smile at the guest during your first words. Then a "policeman" was appointed to remind those who forgot. Within a week, the smile had become habit and—just as that clerk thought—many of the guests responded with a smile and the interchange became much friendlier.

Goal. Be friendlier.

Objective Behavior. Smile.

Measure. Informal inspection.

A hotel that served mainly a business clientele felt that a fast breakfast service would attract guests. The guests at this hotel generally had appointments to keep and planes to catch. When management began to talk about "fast service," though, it specified what "fast enough" was:

- The guest gets a menu when he or she takes a seat.
- The guest gets water and is offered coffee within two minutes.
- The order is taken within three minutes (of seating) if he or she is in a hurry.

- A "jiffy breakfast" will be served within six minutes (of seating) if a guest orders it.

From this list of specific goals, the hotel established seating procedures that tried to ensure that a waitress would arrive on the station or one of the two adjoining stations at the time of seating. (If there was no waitress, the hostess would detail a busboy to get water or coffee or get it herself.) Waitresses were prepared to take orders on the station next to theirs and turn over those orders over to the appropriate person later. A special serving point (and procedure) was established in the kitchen for the jiffy breakfast.

Goal. Fast service.

Objective Behavior. Follow schedule.

Measure. Management could (and did) time the service.

It's worth noting that neither of these useful approaches would fit in every operation. In a small-town motor hotel with a fairly slow pace, the extreme effort on the part of employees to get a smile out of themselves wouldn't be needed. It might even make a nice friendly person look like a wind-up doll! In a resort hotel where guests come to relax, attentive service may be appropriate, but the hurry-up breakfast pattern would make them feel rushed. Our examples do not represent solutions; they represent goal setting procedures that solve problems in such a way that we can tell when we have, in fact, reached a solution.

GOAL CONGRUENCE

In setting its goals, an organization should be realistic. If a service goal requires a waitress to lose tip income, we can expect her, one way or another, to resist the goal. For example, restaurants sometimes promote their wine sales but then make it difficult for waitresses to find a bottle of wine quickly by inadequately stocking (and staffing) the bar where the wine is kept. Management reasons that the increased beverage check will increase the waitresses' tips. It urges them: "You really ought to want to sell wine." But the waitress finds she loses more in slow turnover and guest dissatisfaction because of delays. Management cannot understand why the waitresses don't try to sell wine—"they really ought to want to." When people don't do what they "ought to," though, management should look at the system design to see what went wrong, rather than urge compliance because "you ought to want to. . . ."[4]

Management scholars often use the term *goal congruence*. This term refers to the need to design and present an organization's goals in such a way that organizational goals and individual employee goals mesh rather than clash. Goals of different people in an organization should also fit the

---

[4]See Robert Mager and Peter Pipe for an excellent and witty discussion on this point: *Analyzing Performance Problems or You Really Oughta Wanna* (Belmont, Calif.: Fearon Publishers, 1970.)

goals of the organization if maximum harmony and efficiency are to be achieved.

GOALS AND POLICIES

Once an organization has established its goals, it is ready to develop policies to implement them. Policies, you may recall, are general guides for dealing with the future. They leave much to the decision maker's discretion while providing a basis for reaching decisions.

There are goals at all levels of the organization, of course, but policies address goals that affect the entire organization at once; they have, in short, a significantly broad effect. In the hospitality industry, one major policy issue centers on guest self-service, an idea that arises largely from the goal of holding down costs and rates on menu prices as much as possible in spite of rising wages, food costs, and utility bills. Eliminating or reducing the bell staff in motor hotels is one example of a policy decision; so is the increasing use of buffets and self-service salad bars. Once a company has established its policy in self-service, decisions on individual issues become clearer.

Companies often regard policies on unionization as especially important. Some companies set a goal of avoiding unionization and resist it by every legal means available, whereas others are indifferent to an organizing drive. A few companies actually encourage union representation. We take no position here on the pros and cons of a union. We merely point out that this illustrates policy as a guide for action. In the three instances just cited, an incipient union organizing drive would trigger three quite different reactions: a hurried and worried call to the home office, a yawn, or a friendly greeting.

As policies evolve, they call forth programs of action, strategies, and tactics to implement policy and achieve goals through action.

PLANNING IN OPERATIONS

When management establishes goals and thinks out policies, its planning work has only begun. It needs a plan of action to specify how the policy will be implemented. Those two terms borrowed from the military, *strategy* and *tactics,* distinguish between levels of plans. Strategy tells you *where* you want to go and *why* you want to get there. Tactics deal with *how* to get there.

STRATEGIC ISSUES

Strategy, as you remember, concerns long-term, basic plans. Our discussion will focus on three strategic areas out of many that could be chosen: product and service strategy, personnel strategy, and community relations. These three areas conveniently illustrate how policy guides decisions and is implemented by both planning and action.

Product and Service Strategies

In food service, a menu is a plan; the general pattern of an operation's menus represents a strategy; and the customer you intend to reach dictates the strategy you will develop. Consider a steak house such as Steak and Ale. The menu reflects a policy of limited selection. This limited selection simplifies production and service. A strategy of self-service for salads represents a decision to give up portion control in return for the advantage of having the guests serve themselves. The advantages of the self-service are (1) the waitress has one less course to serve, and (2) the guests get and eat salad while their steaks are being cooked. A waitress can carry a larger station; and so fewer waitresses are needed. Moreover, the guest begins to eat sooner; the wait between courses is shorter; consequently, table turns are more rapid. With faster turns, a restaurant can serve more guests during peak meal periods. The trade-off for portion control on salads is more than worth the advantages gained.

The recipe kitchen strategy that the Stouffers adopted years ago permitted them to dispense with highly skilled chefs. The rule at the Stouffers restaurants was that everything was prepared from a recipe. A recipe is, of course, a kind of procedure. This recipe kitchen strategy helped the Stouffers train unskilled cooks, and as long as precisely the same procedures were followed, it ensured constant quality in several cities. In much the same way, McDonald's and other fast-food operators have chosen a menu strategy that dictates much of the rest of what happens in their operation. Similarly, the economy motel's product and service strategy defines the market it will aim for, the kind of building it will construct, and the size of its staff.

Personnel Strategies

We will briefly examine two important personnel-related issues to suggest the policies and strategies they dictate. Many companies wishing to avoid unionization use a compensation strategy that offers pay and fringe benefits well above union scale. In other cases, an aggressive compensation strategy may be adopted by a company not because of unionization but simply to help it hire the cream of the crop in its labor market.

Such a strategy dictates the rule that whenever the wage level in the local labor market rises, the company raises its wages. To follow this strategy, the company must initiate a procedure of regular wage surveys in the area.

Community Relations Strategies

Not surprisingly, different sectors of the hospitality industry court community favor in different ways. Let us look briefly at policy—and resulting strategy—in the commercial restaurant business, in the hotel–motel business, in health care, and in school food service.

The traditional way to offer the goods and services of a fast-food chain is to buy advertising in the various media. Although a hotel or a local, independent, high-quality restaurant may also purchase advertising, many of these kinds of operations rely more on public relations activities. Thus, a local innkeeper may devote a great deal of time to public service activities in order, through such involvement, to build a favorable public image for the inn. This active public relations strategy may differ from that of a nearby fast-food operation dependent on advertising to bring the public through the door. The fast-food manager must spend his or her working time closely supervising operations; public relations may well be a minor part of the job.

In health care, only proprietary facilities advertise, and even then, that advertising tends to be low-keyed. On the other hand, community hospitals actively involve themselves in public relations. Although they do not seek sales per se, hospitals do rely on periodic fund drives to raise capital for expansion or improvements. Thus, a favorable image in the community is helpful to them, too.

In recent years, the school lunch program has discovered that an active, interested group of supporters in the community can help them obtain the financial and moral support of the school board and school administrators. Consequently, a strategy of community involvement for school lunch managers dictates their being active with parent groups and other influential groups, especially those interested in nutrition in the community.

Each of these institutions—fast food, restaurant, hotel, hospital, and school lunch—needs financial support from the community in the form of sales, donations, or appropriations. Each has a policy of seeking community support, but their strategies differ according to the operational circumstances of each and the guests or clients they serve.

FROM STRATEGY TO TACTICS

Tactical issues are generally concerned more with short-run and localized actions. But like strategies, tactics are plans, the means of implementing policy.

In one high-occupancy chain motor hotel in a busy city, the property's marketing strategy was dictated by its franchise affiliation. This affiliation attracted the middle-income traveler who wanted comfortable accommodations but could not afford a luxury hotel. The property's downtown location gave it a special appeal to businesspeople. The manager realized, however, that a very large number of hotel rooms were being built in this market area. It became apparent that when all the properties under construction opened, the area would have an oversupply of rooms for several years to come. To prepare for this future marketing problem, the manager developed what was dubbed "FIRM Service."

A list of the largest firms in the area was compiled, and the sales representative's work concentrated almost exclusively on these firms. At each of these firms, one or more contacts who placed rooms business was established and given a special number to call for reservations.

Furthermore, the manager instructed the front-office staff to hold a small number of rooms each day for FIRM Service accounts and to release them only as the house was filled. Only in exceptional circumstances was a FIRM Service request refused, and FIRM Service reservations were never "pulled" (canceled in the evening on the assumption the guest would not arrive).

The manager was too shrewd to assume that the property could keep business simply out of loyalty or gratitude; customers can be pretty fickle. What the manager did think—and rightly so—was that when the market became more competitive, the hotel's sales personnel would be in a good position to reach key people at important accounts in the community. This tactic cost practically nothing, and it dealt with the problem of heavy future competition by gaining an advantage in that local market the franchise group's strategy identified as its most promising.

LONG-TERM PLANNING TOOLS

You can often plan for today and tomorrow "in your head." The situation may be simple enough for you to grasp intuitively. But when you make decisions that will have an effect for months or years, you need more sophisticated planning tools. These tools are usually considered at some length in courses on management accounting and finance. Nevertheless, we provide a few related illustrations to acquaint you with this kind of analysis.

RETURN ON CAPITAL

When an organization makes an investment, it generally expects to earn that investment back within some definite period. Take the following simple situation: A new vacuum sweeper for use in public areas costs $2000. The larger machine is more efficient, and it reduces the number of hours required to vacuum the area from 100 a month to 90. If the operator's time costs $6 per hour, we can calculate two crude measures of value, and these measurements are common, simple decision aids. They are called the *payback period* and the *rate of return*. A useful formula is

$$
\begin{aligned}
P &= \text{Payback Period} \\
OS &= \text{Operating Savings} \qquad P = \frac{NI}{OS} \\
NI &= \text{Net Investment}
\end{aligned}
$$

For our problem:

$$
OS = 10 \text{ hours} \times \$6 = \$60
$$
and

$$P = \frac{\$2000}{\$\ 60} = 33.3 \text{ months}$$

Notice that we have specified the *monthly* saving, so the payback period is also expressed in months. The new machine will thus pay for itself in just under three years.

Another way of analyzing this problem is to determine the rate of return (ROR). Here we just invert our formula, but the results are usually expressed in annual terms, and so the monthly savings in the previous problem are multiplied by 12.

$$\text{ROR} = \frac{\text{OS}}{\text{NI}} \qquad \frac{720}{2000} = 0.36 \text{ or } 36\%$$

Such a short payback period indicates a very favorable rate of return.

In a business in which money to invest is at a premium and many departments require funds for new equipment, those techniques give us the means to establish investment priorities.

In more complex cases, a *time-adjusted* rate of return may be used. This tool recognizes that a dollar today is worth more, by the interest it can earn in a bank, than a dollar will be a year from now. The interest rate (called in these problems the *discount rate*) can be changed to reflect varying costs of capital and risk assumptions.

Another common tool is the *break-even point computation*. This technique is similar to the payback period method. Suppose a new banquet room is proposed. Management expects the banquet check average to be $9.00 and the banquet check food costs to be 33 percent. All other costs of the proposed banquet department are fixed. If the fixed costs (the monthly payroll; heat, light, and power; depreciation, and so forth) for this room amount to $15,000, how many banquet covers must be sold per month to *cover* the cost of the banquet room (in other words, to break even)? Our new formula follows:

$$
\begin{aligned}
\text{BEP} &= \text{Break-even Point} \\
\text{MR} &= \text{Marginal Revenue} \\
&\quad \text{(revenue less variable cost)} \\
\text{FC} &= \text{Fixed Costs} \\
&\quad \text{(the costs that will occur regardless of} \\
&\quad \text{volume of sales if the decision is} \\
&\quad \text{made to go ahead)} \\
\text{S} &= \text{Sales} \\
\text{VC} &= \text{Variable Cost} \\
\text{MR} &= \text{S} - \text{VC} = \$9.00 - \$3.00 = \$6.00 \\
\text{BEP} &= \frac{\text{FC}}{\text{MR}} = \frac{\$15,000}{\$6} = 2500 \text{ meals}
\end{aligned}
$$

Thus, 2500 meals per month will cover all costs for this room. Management can now decide whether or not to build this room on the basis of its judgment about the number of meals it will probably serve.

COST–BENEFIT ANALYSIS

In business, the measure of dollar profit earned is not just useful—it is the principal decision-making guide. In school lunch or congregate feeding, however, such a measure is not enough. To begin with, revenue from guests is not always a significant factor, because the cost of the program is covered by government funds. The program's purpose is not to earn a profit. Moreover, the decisions cannot always be measured in dollars. (In school lunch, how much is a hungry child worth?)

Although the variables cannot all be measured in dollars, a first step in cost–benefit (or cost–effectiveness) analysis is to make explicit those costs and savings that can be identified.

Suppose a congregate meals program is trying to decide whether to use 20 small feeding sites distributed throughout the county or to transport all its clients to a central point. The costs and savings to be specified would include the savings in food production and service staff in the central location and the reduction in food distribution expense (trucking food to 520 sites), in contrast with the cost of transporting clients to a central site.

Once this "homework" is done, however, it is still necessary to weigh the possibility that some aged clients might not feel up to the long trip and that others might feel uncomfortable in a strange neighborhood. For these reasons, participation might decline. These problems would actually reduce costs and subsidies, but that is hardly what the staff wants! Decisions in the public sector are sometimes more complicated than in private business, because not all costs and benefits have dollar values. Public programs, however, must still do their homework so they can report what cost effects result from program changes.

Goals and policies provide the basis for developing plans, both strategic and tactical. As the goals addressed relate to longer periods, however, those responsible for planning cannot rely on intuition. They must use more formal and often complex means of analysis.

THE INDIVIDUAL WORKER AS PLANNER

If an operation is to be successful, individual workers must begin to consider themselves as planners. Notice the planning that a waitress automatically engages in as she moves from kitchen to dining room and back. As she steps out of the kitchen, she quickly sums up the situation on her station: one of her three tables (Table A) has just been seated. A second party has finished its main course (Table B) since she left the dining room. A third party

(Table C) is waiting for the dessert she is carrying. She plans her next moves in order of priority.

1.	Serve dessert.	Table C
2.	Greet and assure return while serving water.	Table A
3.	Take dessert order.	Table B
4.	Take appetizer and main course orders.	Table A
5.	Return to kitchen.	

As she carries out this plan and heads back to the kitchen, she realizes that she also must plan her movements in the pantry to minimize wasted time and effort. On the way out of the dining room she asks the busboy if he can clear Table B. With his assurance on that, she plans her moves in the kitchen.

1.	Call dinner orders.	For Table A
2.	Pick up appetizer.	For Table A
3.	Pick up dessert.	For Table B
4.	Return to dining room.	

Her pattern is not necessarily the right way to handle a three-table station, and an actual situation would certainly not be this neat. The point is that a waitress relies heavily on planning, whether or not she is conscious of it.

When the head cook arrives at work at 8:00 A.M., she realizes that three meals confront her with immediate problems:

> Breakfast is now in progress and unusually busy. The short-order cook is in trouble because he's running out of his *setup* (raw food stored in a nearby refrigerator). The turkey on the menu for dinner needs to come out of the freezer right away. A roast round has to go in the oven immediately to be ready for an early banquet.

A great many different steps, the cook realizes, must be taken later in the day, but these are the matters of pressing concern. She takes these steps in order or priority and with a view to saving time and effort.

> She enters the walk-in with a cart, steps into the adjacent freezer (which can be reached only from the walk-in), and places the turkeys on the cart. Back in the walk-in, she places the round on her cart. These actions delay her only a minute. Now she loads the bacon, sausage, and eggs the short-order cook needs and proceeds to the kitchen, giving the supplies to the short-order cook first, . . . and so on.

Her solution here may not be absolutely correct, but the incident should illustrate how essential planning is for that cook. "Grab cart so you can carry everything. Take one minute while you're in the walk-in to get the two other things you need from there. While you are there, solve the breakfast cook's problem. It's going to be a busy day, so don't make three trips when one will do."

A good illustration of an employee engaged in planning appeared in Chapter 7. Remember the process of blocking reservations we described there? Clerks must determine the number of rooms they expect to be available and make increasingly difficult computations as the day goes on to determine whether or not to accept more reservations and, if so, how many. The essence of this task is planning. The increasing use of computers to manage hotel reservations discussed there is also a good example of how hospitality managers' planning tools are improving.

Not surprisingly, the hospitality industry rejects those management "experts" who assert that planning is exclusively a management function. Planning obviously pervades the well-run hospitality operation at all levels, from the maid who checks the stock on her cart to the general manager who orchestrates all the planners he or she works with.

PLANNING AS A PERSONAL PROCESS

In Chapter 1 we discussed the notion of knowledge as retained earnings. We suggested that someone interested in a hospitality career can begin to accumulate useful learning experiences in the earliest, least-skilled jobs. Now it is time to reinforce that concept with the conviction that personal career goals need to be identified as early as possible (without an artificial forcing).

These goals may well dictate a policy of putting skill learning first and income second in choosing jobs while in college and perhaps for those first years out of college as well. This "learn first, earn second" strategy ensures "practice." But if income is more important (or essential), you may have to alter your strategy. The point is, of course, that planning, policy, and strategy are not something somebody else does. No plan is more important to you than is your own plan for yourself.

SUMMARY

Planning in organizations was the principal topic of this chapter. We first explained the reasons for planning and its different levels.

We defined and described several planning concepts: policies, plans, rules, methods, procedures, standards, budgets, strategies, and tactics.

Next we discussed goal setting or management by objectives, and, after defining and illustrating it, turned to some of the subsets of goals. These included the characteristics of well-thought-out goals, goal congruence, and goals and policies.

Planning in operations requires strategy and tactics. We considered product and service strategies, personnel strategies, and community relations strategies. We then gave an example of successful tactics.

The long-term planning tools we explored were return on capital and cost–benefit analysis.

The last section covered the individual worker as a planner, which we illustrated with an example of a waitress. We ended with a short discussion of planning as part of career preparation.

KEY WORDS AND CONCEPTS

To help you review this chapter, keep in mind the following:

Policy	Tactic
Plan	Goal
Rule	Management by objectives
Method	Goal congruence
Procedure	Return of capital
Standards	Payback period
Budget	Rate of return
Strategy	Cost–benefit analysis

REVIEW QUESTIONS

1. Outline some of the reasons that you should study planning.

2. Define policies, plans, rules, methods, procedures, standards, budgets, strategies, and tactics.

3. What are the five questions that might be asked when setting goals?

4. What does goal congruence mean?

5. Is planning part of your study habits? Explain.

Courtesy of the Flamingo Hilton.

THE ORGANIZING FUNCTION IN HOSPITALITY MANAGEMENT

THE PURPOSE OF THIS CHAPTER

This chapter talks about the way people come together to work, an enjoyable and interesting subject. In a "society of institutions," knowing how institutions get "put together" can also help guide both work and life. Working relationships are rarely arbitrary. Moreover, an understanding of the limits of authority—and the limits on accepting authority—is essential to someone building a career in managing and supervising others. We are all on the receiving end of organizational decisions and the exercise of authority from time to time. So our feeling is that understanding how management organizes will help you polish your hospitality management skills.

THIS CHAPTER SHOULD HELP YOU

1. Describe organization as a problem that is often solved informally in small operations.
2. Distinguish between the various sources of authority and the limits of each in the workplace.
3. Explain how work is allocated among organizational units (departments, for instance).
4. Trace the line and staff functions and explain the differences in the kinds of authority each exercises.
5. Discuss the pros and cons of such organizational issues as the role of committees, the problems of bureaucracy, the "one boss" theory, and emerging approaches to organization in the modern hospitality industry.

What is a real emergency? Except in organizations set up specifically to deal with them (fire companies and ambulance crews, for example), emergencies are nonroutine, serious situations, in which nobody knows for certain what to do. Some people shout orders; others run toward the door; others do whatever seems best to deal with the problem. To try to achieve results without organization is to invite a permanent emergency.

Small food service operators often appear to have established no real organization. A small restaurant needs only the simplest of organizations. But you will recall from Chapter 4 that small restaurants have been declining in significance in the market. (The same is true of small motels.) Motor hotels, schools, colleges, and hospitals (even the small ones) are all, in reality, complex organizations. Your future, therefore, will probably involve work in an organization of some complexity.

Moreover, although we will discuss organizing principally from the perspective of the larger organizations in our industry, our discussion applies in a general way to the smallest organizations as well. When we feel special solutions to organizing problems are useful, we will identify and discuss these solutions.

Before we begin, here is a definition of the organizing function in management:

> Organizing is the work managers do to bring order to the relations between people and work as well as among the various people at work.

AUTHORITY: THE CEMENT OF ORGANIZATIONS

Organization charts sometimes give the impression that the company just fits together in that way. But in fact, for any group to function, it must have authority at several levels to make it come together and stay together.

THE BASES OF AUTHORITY

Formal authority has its basis in law, but there are limits placed on that authority by the way that people in the work group perceive the organization and their relation to it.

The Legal Basis for Authority

Laws and the legal system imply a community's potential use of force to maintain order. In our society, private property is a central social institution; in the business firm, the basic rationalization for management authority has been ownership. In the small firm, in effect, authority is often based on this notion: "I own this company and have the right to control my property. If you want to work here, you'll have to do as I say."

In the large corporation, the line of reasoning is more complex (stockholders elect a board, the board hires a top manager, the top manager delegates authority to subordinates). But the essence of it is simply "I represent ownership" instead of "I own."

In governmental activities such as school lunch programs and congregate feeding, the basis of authority is legislative activity exercised by the duly elected representatives of the people. The enabling legislation authorizes the activity, together with periodic appropriation legislation that specifies the amount of money available and how it can be spent.

In either the company or a public agency, there lies behind the manager's order the ultimate force of authority of the law. When the boss says "you're fired," he or she can call on public authority to back up this position. Although this is the ultimate basis of formal authority (and some such fundamental basis is undoubtedly necessary to give stability to social institutions), constant resort to the law is not an effective tool for getting people to do things on an everyday basis. A sure sign of a weak, inadequate manager is the repeated use of social force ("You do it or I'll fire you").

Acceptance As a Basis for Authority

Subordinates can undermine a manager's authority in all kinds of subtle ways. In a rich society, the simplest way is to quit and get another job. Of course, an employee can stay and simply ignore orders whenever the manager's back is turned. These two approaches are by no means rare in the hospitality industry. Thus to gain the employees' support, a supervisor or manager must win their acceptance of his or her authority and the employees' recognition that he or she is a person qualified for responsibility. In the hospitality industry this acceptance generally means, first of all, credibility as a person qualified in the work the employees themselves do. An illustration from personal experience may help:

> Unfortunately, I can't cook. This hasn't usually been a problem, as I've generally had a qualified food production supervisor to work with. I was once hired, however, as an innkeeper to replace a man who had been promoted. On arriving at work I learned that
>
> 1. The restaurant manager had just been fired.
> 2. The innkeeper was staying on "for a while."
> 3. I was the new restaurant manager.
> 4. I could take over as innkeeper as soon as the restaurant, which had been losing $8,000 on the average each month since it opened, became profitable.
>
> All of this came as a surprise, but I wasn't too concerned, as much of my experience had been in food service management. The problem I did have,

however, was that there was no kitchen organization—just some cooks, with no one in particular in charge! I knew there was no way I could supervise those cooks because I didn't know enough about their work to be credible to them. I'd have been laughed out of the kitchen.

Fortunately, I was able to find a retired chef willing to help me out for a few weeks. I could explain to him what results I wanted—hours of service, menus, price ranges, and so forth—and *he* could interpret this need into specific directions for the cooks. Without the necessary credibility, in short, I needed an intermediary.

Aside from being another good argument for wide professional experience, this story illustrates the need, in a complex organization, for supervisors whose authority is acceptable to the work group. It would be equally difficult to supervise a front-office staff's work without any understanding of the technical aspects of what clerks do. Supervisors don't have to be experts, but they do require a sufficient familiarity with the work to "speak the language" and understand what is happening.

This principle does not apply just to the skilled work stations. Anyone who has ever seen an executive housekeeper the maids thought of as "too good to get her hands dirty," or a restaurant manager who couldn't, in an emergency, help out in the dishroom or bus a few dishes, knows how difficult this detachment makes their work with their subordinates.

Informal Organizations

Sociologists who study work groups note that right alongside the formal organization established by management is an informal social organization that grows up within the work groups. This informal group usually has a leader consciously or unconsciously recognized by the group. The group develops its own expectations (norms) on what constitutes a fair days' work. And it develops an informal way of ranking its members (a status system). An insecure manager can feel threatened by an informal work group like this. The experienced manager or supervisor comes to accept the work group as a part of the natural order of things, like sunrise and sunset. He or she can usually establish working relations with this informal structure to ensure that the work at hand gets done. Most of all, the experienced manager realizes that the informal group constitutes a real limitation on his or her formal authority.

Authority and Responsibility

It is an axiom of organizational theory that the manager can be rightly held responsible for results only as far as his or her effective authority extends. For instance, you may recall from Chapter 7 that the Uniform System of

Accounts for Hotels records income and costs so that each manager is held responsible for results in the area that he or she controls. The innkeeper, for instance, is not responsible for capital costs because these costs reflect decisions made by the owners at the time of the construction or purchase of the property.

Authority: A Summary

The effective manager seeks to establish authority on the basis of competence acknowledged by the people he or she works with. The experienced manager accepts the social nature of a work group and learns to work effectively with its informal leaders. The ultimate basis of authority, however, lies in the legal reality of ownership or legislative authorization. The effective manager, though, has little need to rely on these fundamental sources of authority.

DEPARTMENTALIZATION

For work to be done in complex organizations, these organizations must divide authority according to some logical basis. One manager cannot, after all, do everything. This division of authority is called *delegation*. A discussion of delegation is necessary before we can properly understand departmentalization.

THE DELEGATION OF AUTHORITY

In formal organizations, authority must be shared. Management scholars assert, in the *scalar principle,* that authority must extend in an uninterrupted *scale,* or series of steps, from the top to the bottom of an organization. Responsibility is accepted at each level, and in turn, some authority is delegated to the next lower level. Although authority certainly can be delegated, most management scholars agree that responsibility cannot. That is, if something goes wrong because of a subordinate's error, the boss still must take responsibility along with the subordinate.

The scalar principle has been defined in one authoritative text as follows:

> The more clear the line of authority from the ultimate authority for management in an enterprise to every subordinate position, the more effective will be responsible decision making and organized communication.[1]

---

[1]Harold Koontz and Cyril O'Donnel, *Management: A Systems and Contingency Analysis of Managerial Functions,* 6th ed. (New York: McGraw-Hill, 1976), p. 379.

The delegation of authority may not be particularly important in small organizations in which management works closely with workers and can exercise control through actual participation. But in larger, more complex organizations such as a hotel or hospital, a large restaurant, or a school district made up of many lunch programs, delegation becomes necessary just to get the work done. For instance, each school lunch program spread out across a school district requires a manager. The district food service director simply cannot manage all these operations; nor can a hotel manager simultaneously direct housekeeping, the front office, and the kitchen. Thus, senior managers must delegate authority to subordinate managers, that is, managers below them in the scale.

A second, less obvious reason for delegating authority is to develop management talent in the organization. As people leave for other jobs or enter retirement, the organization must keep up with the turnover. Other organizations, of course, seek to expand, and most like to draw on their own employees to fill these openings. A third, related reason for maintaining subordinate management and supervisory jobs is to keep bright, eager employees engaged and excited about their work by assigning them increased responsibility.

Unfortunately, many people have trouble delegating authority. This is especially true of people, such as chefs or waitresses, who began as skilled workers. They are used to doing the job themselves, and they find it difficult to turn the work over to somebody else.

The fact is that when a manager delegates a task, it is sometimes done incorrectly. The newly promoted supervisor who is skilled in the work at hand becomes very frustrated. They feel "it's easier to do it myself." In the very short run—dealing with just one task—they're correct in that feeling. The reason for delegation, though, is the multiplicity of tasks that confront the work group for which the supervisor is responsible. Although any one task may be easier to do oneself, it's literally impossible for one person to do all of them. In order to get all the work done (with high average standards but probably some tolerance for error) this supervisor must delegate and concentrate his or her efforts on developing the competence of the work group.

Span of Control

You may recall from Chapter 13 that one of the early management scholars, V. A. Graicunias, attempted to develop a mathematical approach to determine how many people a manager can supervise directly. This *span of control,* Graicunias thought, was stretched taut by the increasing number of relationships between manager and subordinate; between subordinate and subordinate; and between the manager and the various combinations of subordinates. The number of relationships rises rapidly, as Table 15.1 shows.

Although the number of subordinates reporting to a manager cannot

TABLE 15.1 Increase in Relationships

Number of Subordinates	Number of Relationships
1	1
2	6
3	18
4	44
5	100
6	222
7	490
8	1080
9	2376
10	5210

really be stated precisely, some management scholars assert the ideal lies between three and eight subordinates. The exact number that a manager may supervise depends on the complexity of the work itself, the ability and training level of the subordinates, and the ability of the manager.

For instance, an industry analyst, after referring to Shoney's as "a very strong, operations driven company," described the company's span of control as follows: "A typical Shoney's is administered by a seven person management team including a store manager, assistant manager, relief manager, dining room supervisor, breakfast manager and kitchen manager. Area Supervisors (one for every three Shoney's) visit each unit twice daily."[2] Clearly, in his view, one strong characteristic of a "strong, operations driven company" is a well-thought-out span of control.

This concept of span of managerial responsibility is related to Graicunias's span of control, which refers to the number of people the manager supervises directly. The *span of managerial responsibility,* on the other hand, refers to the number of persons with whom the manager routinely interacts, that is, the number who have direct and unhindered access to the manager. For instance, a hotel manager may have a food and beverage manager, a rooms-department manager, a sales manager, a chief engineer, and a comptroller, all of whom report directly to him or her. In addition to these five, the manager may routinely consult with supervisors one or two levels below. For instance, he or she might discuss problems with a hostess, or the banquet chef, or one of the housekeeping inspectors. These people may feel

[2]Michael Culp, "Shoney's, Inc.," *Company Report,* Prudential–Bache Securities, March 25, 1985, pp. 2, 7.

quite free to consult with the general manager personally if a problem arises. For most hospitality organizations, span of managerial responsibility is a more important concept than is span of control. Span of control refers to formal reporting relationships, but hospitality organizations tend to develop important informal superior–subordinate relationships that don't fit the narrow span-of-control concept.

The principle of *unity of command* dictates that everyone has just one boss. This notion is generally sound, but as the discussion in the preceding paragraph indicates, reality is a good deal more complicated. In the hospitality industry, unity of command generally means that a manager does not routinely interfere in the workings of a subordinate's department. Rather, he or she discusses problems with the department head and lets that person take any remedial action necessary. When a serious problem of guest satisfaction or some other emergency arises, however, rules often are put aside, and the manager may intervene directly.

Bases for Departmentalization

There are five common bases for dividing the work (and the authority over the work) into departments: function, product or service, geography, customer, and process. The hospitality industry uses each of these departmental divisions. Function and product are the most common bases of departmentalization at the operating level, whereas territory and customer are the most common at the corporate level. A short discussion of each basis follows:

Function. The clearest example of functional departmentalization is found in food service, in which each functional department performs a different kind of work. Thus, the restaurant may be divided into service, food preparation, and sanitation. The kitchen may be further divided into such stations as meat, salads, and dessert. The organization of a Shoney's restaurant, which we mentioned a moment ago, is a good example of a functional organization at the store level.

Product and Service. Hotels are divided into quite different product–service units, each with its own expertise. The most obvious divisions are between rooms, food and beverage, telephone, and other departments (for instance, garage). Below that level, however, functional division is the rule.

Geographical. In school lunch, in which each lunch program is located in a separate school, geographic divisions make one manager responsible for each unit. In restaurant and hotel chains, it is common to assign supervisory responsibility for the operations in a particular region to a single officer. For example, Shoney's area supervisors have a geographic area of responsibility.

Customers. Some companies that operate in several different hospitality business areas divide their operations by customer type. For instance, Marriott has divisions devoted to lodging, contract food services, airline catering, and restaurants.

Process.   Many large hotels divide their food and beverage activities into a restaurant department and a banquet department because the preparation and service in these two areas involve such different processes.

No one of these departments represents the "best" means of division. What is important is that authority and responsibility be divided in a way that suits the particular needs of the market served and the organization doing the work. We should note, too, that smaller organizations may not identify formal departments at all. In a small motor hotel, for example, the manager may serve as sales manager and personnel manager and take operational responsibility in the rooms or food and beverage department as well. Nevertheless, as different functions are performed, the manager—and other "double duty" management people—realize the need to shift gears and call different skills and styles into play. Organizational people who serve in multiple roles sometimes lament their unpredictable existences. But they also tend to enjoy the recognition that attends their ability to get several different jobs done.

LINE AND STAFF

LINE MANAGEMENT

Line authority is closely related to the ideas inherent in the scalar principle. Line authority passes from one operations person to another in a direct line from the top to the bottom of the organization. The rooms manager reports to the general manager. In turn, the hostess, food production manager, and banquet manager report to the food and beverage manager and in turn oversee subordinate supervisors and workers, as shown in Figure 15.1. A direct, unbroken line of authority runs from, say, a banquet waiter to the general manager. The work of line people directly affects guest service at all levels. And line management is the preponderant managerial role in the hospitality industry.

STAFF ASSISTANCE

Staff roles were originally limited to providing specialized assistance to line managers. The staff person's special expertise is still important, but a number of related kinds of staff activities have also become common.

The Adviser

The personnel manager and comptroller are two good examples of advisory staff positions in the hospitality industry. They have specialized knowledge

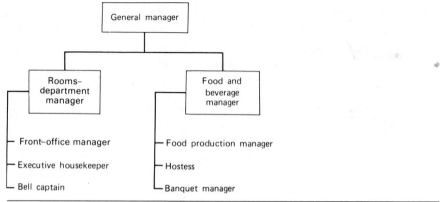

FIGURE 15.1 Line organization in a hotel.

about their area of work—wage-and-hour laws or accounting procedures, for instance—that the line manager they report to can and should call upon. Each of these persons also acts for the manager in their area of specialty: that is, these staff people not only give a manager their expert advice, but they also act for him or her and for other line people by interviewing and screening applicants or maintaining accounting records. In these acts, however, they function as *representatives* of the manager, and they amplify the manager's abilities in a specialized field.

Staff Service

The purchasing manager, like other staff people, renders a service to the line departments rather than directly to the guests. Similarly, the engineering department assists the line departments in maintaining the physical systems necessary to the guests' comfort.

The "Assistants to"

In large properties or at the corporate level, senior executives commonly designate a person as, for instance, the assistant to the manager. This person has no authority, but he or she assists the manager with any project requiring special attention. Persons in such jobs are not mere "errand runners." The "Assistant to" slot is often used to train rising young managers, and they are commonly given fairly wide-ranging (if temporary) authority for completing any project they are assigned to. Because people in this position are usually junior to those with whom they are working, while at the same time they represent high authority, the "Assistant to" position requires great tact. Its advantage is that it expands the capacity of the senior executive because it equips him or her with a trusted, able assistant who can pursue details closely and report back. And as we just implied, it can be a valuable training slot.

The Staff As Boss

A staff exercises authority in two kinds of situations. When the comptroller or chief engineer directs a subordinate in a task, the authority exercised is clearly identical with line authority. Beyond that, as we shall see shortly, staff people are sometimes given "functional authority" over line people. Thus, the comptroller may direct the dining room cashiers (who regularly report to the hostess) in how to complete a new form. Or the personnel manager may issue a directive to all departments laying out the procedures for handling grievances. This functional authority amplifies the competence of the line, but it sometimes creates confusion.

The Staff in the Small Organization

In a small organization, the staff work may consist of part-time jobs assigned to regular employees, or it may be handled by outside specialists who provide services as needed. For instance, a 100-room motor hotel probably cannot afford a comptroller, chief engineer, or personnel manager. That property will, however, probably retain a firm of auditors to inspect its books regularly and develop an internal controls manual. Maintenance may consist of routine work done by a handyman. The expert service of plumbers, refrigeration specialists, heating contractors, and so forth, will be called in as needed. Finally, the general manager, his or her secretary, or some other key person probably handles the personnel work.

ISSUES IN ORGANIZATION THEORY

Lest the student consider organization a cut-and-dried matter, we should examine some of the areas of organization theory that are, more than most, unsettled. Because each of these areas also sheds light on special problems in hospitality organizations, this section will serve the double purpose of explaining theory and increasing your understanding of practice.

FUNCTIONAL STAFF AUTHORITY

We mentioned that organizations sometimes authorize staff people to "give orders" across the entire organization within their special field of expertise. To illustrate the value—and some of the problems—of this practice, consider the problems of a chain hotel organization.

Figure 15.2 illustrates the organization of this chain at the corporate level and the organization of a typical unit within the chain at the operating level. As the figure shows, one vice-president is "in the line." The vice-president for operations is charged with overseeing all properties, and the

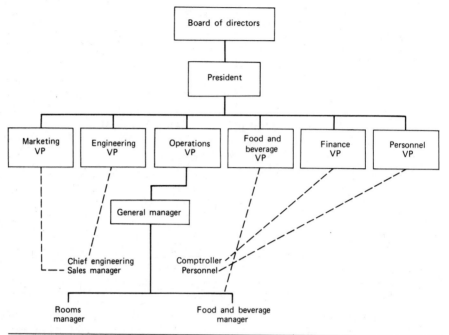

FIGURE 15.2   A hotel chain organizational chart.

general manager of each hotel reports to him or her directly. There are five other vice-presidents. These officers are specialists in the fields of marketing, engineering, food and beverage, finance, and personnel; each is responsible for developing programs in his or her respective area.

The work of the corporate marketing vice-president, for instance, includes developing the company's advertising program and directing its national sales office. The engineering vice-president develops energy conservation measures and commands a small, highly technical staff. The vice-president for food and beverage is an expert in that area of operation. He or she serves as a combination inspector, troubleshooter, and consultant in matters pertaining to foods and beverages. The financial vice-president oversees the company's accounting. The personnel officer is concerned with companywide compensation and fringe benefit policies and monitors changes in legislation affecting employment and work practices.

Notice that each of these staff vice-presidents is connected by a dotted line to a function of management at the unit level. This line indicates that each exercises staff supervision or functional staff authority over his or her special fields of work at the unit level. Now, who does the hotel's accountant work for? Does he or she have two bosses? The answer to this question for each of these "dotted line relationships," as they are sometimes called, depends on a number of factors.

First, the relationship is essentially technical. A new financial reporting procedure may be developed, and directions for implementing it may come from the vice-president. But notice that it is a fairly narrow, specialized exercise of authority.

Second, the staff supervisory activity varies in intensity both with the function and the circumstance. The engineering vice-president, for instance, probably interacts with the chief engineer at the property only infrequently, as, for example, when some new piece of equipment is installed or a new energy control procedure is developed. Most of the chief engineer's work in a hotel is routine, although the work of the vice-president is almost entirely specialized and technical. On the other hand, if a major renovation of the hotel is undertaken, the engineering vice-president would work much more closely with the property.

Obviously, the personnel vice-president does not tell the local personnel manager whom to interview or hire. That is the work of the line managers at the property. On the other hand, the vice-president will take an interest in the hiring process as it relates to complying with law, as in fair employment practices.

The possibilities of mixed loyalties on the general manager's staff and of clashes between general manager and staff vice-presidents are remote, but clearly these relationships call for tact. The disadvantages that accompany these blurred lines of authority are more than offset by the top-quality expertise made available. The hospitality industry is becoming too complex a business to do without such an expert staff.

One area in which staff supervision has proved uncommonly difficult is food and beverage. This area really involves a line function; therefore, a number of companies have eliminated staff supervision in this area, leaving it entirely in the hands of the general manager.

Independent operators avail themselves of various kinds of expert advice. We noted some of them earlier: an accountant, an attorney, specialized engineering people. The manager of the operation must often achieve the necessary expertise to act as a staff specialist in some areas, particularly marketing. Many an innkeeper has been heard to remark, "I'm wearing my sales manager's hat today." In fact, hotel general managers often join the Hotel Sales Managers' Association specifically for this reason.

COMMITTEES

Complex organizations that make decisions that involve several departments, or disciplines, need methods for communicating and involving different kinds of specialized expertise. Although "management by committee" is really a contradiction in terms, committees often serve as management devices in health care, education, and all kinds of governmental activities, such as congregate feeding and school lunch programs. Although the role of committees is not so prominent in the private sector, many companies find committees useful in a number of areas, particularly in energy conservation programs.

Committees allow a number of different interests to gain representation. In health care, the dietary department often prepares food that is delivered to the nursing care staff which, in turn, delivers the food to the patients. The food may be purchased for the dietary department by a separate purchasing office, which may also receive the deliveries and handle bulk product storage. The staff cafeteria is often intended as a fringe benefit to employees, providing subsidized meals to the staff below cost. This makes the dietary department important to the personnel officer, just as the need for cafeteria and other accounting procedures makes the dietary department important to the accounting office. The nature of dietary work may necessitate a committee, appointed by the hospital administrator, that advises the dietary department and reacts to proposed operating or policy changes in that area.

Such a committee offers all the advantages usually advanced for committees: it helps coordinate plans and transfer information. Junior management committee membership provides an opportunity for management development as the junior members come to learn how the organization functions. Occasionally the committee also builds morale: when everyone is consulted no one is offended, or so the argument goes.

The disadvantages of committees often equal their advantages. Committees tend to consume a great deal of time. A "short," one-hour meeting of six people consumes six labor hours. Moreover, committees often avoid action rather than take it, and they can be used to avoid or shift responsibility for unpopular or risky decisions. In addition, because committees are supposed to give a hearing to many views, they often encourage compromise.

In fact, the case for consultation in the hospital dietary department does not necessarily call for a committee. A committee will regularize consultation, but the same consultation could take place informally among the interested parties. This approach might take a little more time for the person seeking the consultation, but it would almost certainly take less time for all the participants.

Committees are unquestionably useful where the purpose served warrants their use. For example, in energy management, many hospitality organizations find the committee approach unusually effective in communicating technical information across the organization and in funneling practical suggestions to management. In these cases, committees also serve as a motivational tool by allowing all participants to be involved.

BUREAUCRACY

Bureaucracy is a bad word to most Americans. It is curious, therefore, to realize that Max Weber, the German sociologist who invented the term, developed his theory of bureaucracy as an ideal type of large organization and an ideal way of how it should be run. The following ideal characteristics are those that Weber identified as a part of large hierarchical organizations:

1. The organization's work is embodied in statements of fixed official duties.

2. Decisions are governed by abstract, rational rules which are the only proper basis for decision.

3. The bureaucratic official avoids emotionalism and is impersonal.

4. Technical qualification in the appropriate field is the basis for entry and advancement in a bureaucracy.

Weber's model of bureaucracy seeks the most efficient solution to problems on strictly impersonal, rational grounds. Bureaucracy is a means to avoid the arbitrary exercise of power as in an absolute monarchy, in which people exercise power because of their relationship to the king or some other person in power. It also seeks to avoid the problem of political organizations in which the "in" clique holds sway over everyone. In sum then, it seeks to replace personal relationships—with their possibility for favor and lack of fairness—with an impersonal, rational, efficient organization.

As large organizations have come to play a more and more important role in our society, we have discovered that *bureaucratic politics* (a notion that Weber would have abhorred) has become a problem and that bureaucrats can, in fact, be arbitrary and unfair, bending rules to their own purposes. Bureaucracies, moreover, can seek "efficient" solutions in ways that are wildly wasteful.[3]

Weber's contribution, however, remains. He asserted (and subsequent management scholars have confirmed) that large organizations have special problems. The special organizational rules along the lines Weber suggested, although far from perfect, clearly constitute a useful starting point for solutions to organizational design problems in an increasingly complicated society.

AD HOCRACY

In his book *Future Shock,* Alvin Toffler discovered a significant development in organizations that began in the aerospace industry and other science- and engineering-related activities. Toffler dubbed this new approach to management *ad hocracy.* The word is derived from the Latin phrase *ad hoc,* meaning "to this." The idea is that of an organization responding forcefully to particular situations in an environment that constantly changes. In these situations the work to be done, rather than a traditional organizational

[3]For a witty but telling analysis of the problems and "dysfunction" of bureaucracies, see C. Northcoat Parkinson's famous book, *Parkinson's Law* (Boston: Houghton Mifflin, 1957).

structure, dictates who is in charge. The structure can best be described as a team with changeable captains. If the problem to be solved involves engineering, the team leader will be an engineer with the skills necessary to the current need. If the problem lies in another area, the person with the necessary abilities will take the reins.

Although most hospitality organizations follow the traditional line or line-and-staff organization, operations whose problems resemble those of the aerospace industry are emerging, especially among the new, large resort operations.

The MGM Grand

In Las Vegas, the MGM Grand Hotel is an outstanding hotel in the country's number-one hotel city. The Grand is actually involved in five different businesses in a big way (and a few other businesses less closely connected to its operating format and organizational structure). First, the MGM Grand is one of the world's largest hotels, with over 2900 rooms. Second, it is one of the world's largest gambling centers. Third, it is a major factor in the convention business in North America, with 42 meeting and banquet rooms ranging in size from 75 to 3500 chairs. Fourth, it is a large center for entertaining and dining, boasting eight different restaurants, each with a distinctive menu and atmosphere. Finally, it has one of the world's largest and most extravagant stage shows, "Jubilee."

Operating these businesses for one common clientele would be challenge enough. But the Grand's situation is one complicated by the fact that it caters to three different markets: the casual visitor, who comes alone or with family for a Las Vegas vacation; the convention guest; and the junketeer.

The MGM Grand serves the first market, the traditional class of guest, with the traditional departments that operate according to an organization structure similar to that of any other hotel. The other two kinds of guests, however, present special cases, because each has been attracted by a specific marketing activity in a highly competitive area.

The national convention market receives the attention of literally hundreds of top hotel sales organizations. As a result, when the Grand sells a convention, its marketing department must follow up on the service. If, for instance, the sales department has promised a special registration procedure on arrival or has agreed to some special service for a banquet, that department must have the means of seeing to it that the special agreement is met. Moreover, if a problem develops for the convention group, the group's contact person will probably want to turn for help to the sales representative he or she first dealt with. That sales representative needs the organizational means to solve problems.

Junket guests are gamblers (with *good* credit ratings) who visit Las Vegas as guests of the hotel with all expenses paid, often including transpor-

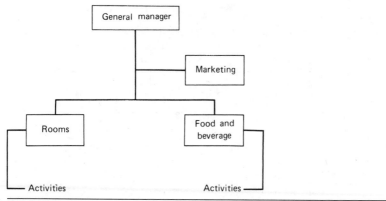

FIGURE 15.3   Traditional hotel organization.

tation both ways. Although some of these visitors win at the gambling tables, the perfectly legitimate casino percentages favor the house more than enough to cover the cost of visits. Many of Las Vegas's major hotels solicit junket business, and this solicitation at the Grand is principally directed by the marketing department. Once again, when junket guests get to the hotel, these "high rollers" must receive excellent treatment in order that the marketing department's efforts to secure return visits remain fruitful.

To solve the problem of these special markets, the Grand has evolved an unusual organization structure. In the typical hotel, a simple organization structure might look like the one in Figure 15.3. The marketing department sells, and the operating departments service the sale. The convention guest might have some contact with the sales representative, but this contact is probably just either a quick, friendly visit or some limited liaison with the operating department.

The MGM Grand has built a somewhat different structure. When an individual guest arrives, the organization functions much as it does in traditional hotels. But when a convention arrives, the marketing department stations a representative at the front desk during registration. This representative has the authority to intervene and settle any problems related to servicing the sale. Similarly, a representative of the marketing department is present at convention banquets, working right along with the food and beverage department's supervisors—again to guarantee the service sold by the marketing department. A similar, though less formalized system operates for junket guests.

For this reason we have to draw solid lines in Figure 15.4, indicating authority between the marketing department and the operating department activities. At the Grand, you see, marketing is actually a line department.

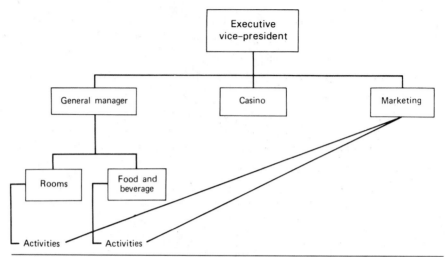

FIGURE 15.4 Ad hocracy at the MGM Grand Hotel.

Although confusion undoubtedly arises from time to time, this organization functions smoothly. People who work in complex organizations learn to live with more complex relationships. The MGM Grand Hotel determines authority by the task at hand.

Walt Disney World

Walt Disney World (WDW) is another highly complex resort organization comprising several distinct businesses, including the theme park, food service, hotel operations, outdoor camping, and sports. The problems at WDW are twofold. First, the park is constantly changing and growing, and will be for many years to come. This problem of growth and change is complicated by dramatic swings in volume which see the work force at WDW more than double during the summer's peak season.

During a recent visit to WDW, we were impressed by one small but interesting fact: the food service organization chart was drawn on a large metallic blackboard. Departments and organizational units were connected by chalk lines, and all the names on the board were on small magnetized plaques that could easily be moved around on the board. Conversation confirmed the impression suggested by the board: the organization structure changed so fast at WDW that the only way management could keep up with it was to use a medium on which changes could be made often and easily.

We do not intend to imply that blackboards are better than is paper for organization charts; rather, the point is that dynamic organization forms are increasingly required in growing, changing, complex hospitality firms.

SUMMARY

Our description of organization began with a discussion of authority, its legal basis and its acceptance by those supervised as a basis. The latter led us to touch on informal organization and then authority and responsibility.

We then turned to departmentalization and the delegation of authority. Span of control is an approach used to determine the number of people that a manager can supervise directly, and span of managerial responsibility refers to the number of people with whom a manager routinely interacts. The five bases for dividing work (and authority over it) are function, product or service, geography, customer, and process.

Authority also refers to line management and staff assistance, which we also described.

We considered some of the issues in organization theory: functional staff authority, committees, bureaucracy (as defined by Weber), and ad hocracy (as defined by Toffler).

We finished with two examples of flexible organizations, those of the MGM Grand Hotel in Las Vegas and of Walt Disney World in Orlando, Florida.

KEY WORDS AND CONCEPTS

To help you review this chapter, keep in mind the following:

Authority	Span of managerial responsibility
Legal basis for authority	Line management
Acceptance as a basis for authority	Staff assistance
Informal organizations	Functional staff authority
Departmentalization	Committees
Delegation	Bureaucracy
Span of control	Ad hocracy

REVIEW QUESTIONS

1. Does an effective manager often use his or her legal basis for authority? Explain.

2. Describe how informal organizations in work groups operate.

3. What is the scalar principle?

4. Differentiate between span of control and span of managerial respon-
    sibility.

5. What are the five common bases for dividing work? Briefly describe
    each in regard to the hospitality industry.

6. What are some of the advantages of committees?

7. Outline Weber's definition of bureaucracy.

8. What is an ad hocracy?

C H A P T E R **16**

THE STAFFING FUNCTION IN HOSPITALITY MANAGEMENT

THE PURPOSE OF THIS CHAPTER

One of the major contributions Taylor and the scientific management theory made was the principle of fitting the right person to the job rather than hiring just whoever came along. Accordingly, modern hospitality management has developed effective procedures for selecting its employees. This trend has been helpful because personal service—and personal interaction with a guest—are crucial to our field. Since a hospitality firm spends somewhere between 20 and 40 percent of its revenue on direct and indirect wage costs, an understanding of the management function known as *staffing* has become essential to the education of future supervisors and managers in our industry.

THIS CHAPTER SHOULD HELP YOU

1. Discuss the importance of job specifications and describe the bases on which they are prepared.

2. Name the major sources of employees and the advantages of each source.

3. Describe the selection and employment process and its major component activities of information gathering, induction, and training.

4. Outline the general procedure of staff planning, and identify and describe the major tools in that process.

Some management scholars argue that staffing is not a separate function but is actually part of organizing. But everyone in the hospitality industry believes that staffing at all levels is one of the major concerns of management.

In the 1970s when the hospitality industry was growing fastest, roughly 300,000 teenagers entered the work force every year. In the 1985, fewer than half as many teenagers entered the work force,[1] and that number will continue to fall into the early 1990s. In an industry so dependent on younger employees, these facts spell a crisis for many operators in staffing in the years ahead.

As early as 1985, more than 80 percent of fast-food managers surveyed by *Nation's Restaurant News* reported their operation to be understaffed. Fast food has felt the shortage of teenagers more severely than have some other hospitality businesses, but virtually all segments are significant employers of young people, and all draw from roughly the same total labor pool. When one part of that pool is in short supply, it doesn't take long for others to feel it too.

Friendly's Ice Cream Corporation, which operates family restaurants principally in the Northeast where labor shortages have been severe, found a labor shortage meant that "managers stopped being managers and became rotating crew members." Moreover, when not working to cover missing employees, they had to spend an excessive amount of time on recruiting.[2] We'll look at what they and others have done to address the labor shortage later in the chapter. Even if there wasn't a growing labor shortage, staffing would be a major concern for two good reasons.

First (and most important), in a field whose stock in trade is *personal service,* the success of the whole enterprise often rests on the kind of employee and how he or she performs a certain job. In particular, the public contact employee—the waiter or waitress, counterperson, or desk clerk—must be chosen with special care. The back-of-the-house employee must also have definite qualifications. If the cook that the waitress must deal with in the back of the house is a temperamental plate-thrower or a foul-mouthed grouch, it will be hard for her, regardless of how pleasant she may be, to show her good side in the dining room.

A second reason for the importance of staffing is the significance of its cost. Few hospitality firms spend less than 25 percent of their sales on payroll costs, and some hotel food service departments spend as much as 40 percent of food and beverage sales on payroll and related costs. But wages had been rising rapidly in the hospitality industry even before there was a labor shortage. With wages rising rapidly at all levels of operation, you can be sure that wage cost will be a major concern for the rest of your career.

Aside from wage rates, one of the major contributors to high cost of

[1]*Nation's Restaurant News,* November 12, 1985, p. 114.
[2]*Nation's Restaurant News,* June 4, 1984, p. 2.

labor is high turnover. There are definite costs associated with hiring and training an employee. If that employee leaves just when he or she is about to become productive, the turnover will be both expensive and wasteful. Reducing turnover, then, is a primary goal of the staffing function. This reduction involves some key ideas: matching the person to the job; giving the new employee a favorable first impression of the company; stressing the importance of the job; and providing enough training to make the new employee feel up to the work required.

Actually, staffing involves at one time or another all the other components of the management process. As you will see in the last section of this chapter, staff planning is crucial, and staffing reflects management's organizing efforts at controlling labor costs. The process of induction and training is closely tied to the function of directing and leading. Because of the importance of staffing in our industry, however, we must isolate the staffing work of managers for the purposes of study. This important management function called staffing can be defined in this way:

> Staffing is the work that managers and supervisors do to determine the specific personnel needs of their operations—to attract qualified applicants and to choose from these the best suited for employment and training. The manager accomplishes the staffing function by using specialized staff planning tools.

FITTING PEOPLE TO JOBS

Although some managers have always tried to choose the right person for the job, particularly in responsible positions, until Frederick Taylor's time, there was no general awareness of the importance of this practice. In some places, tradition determined who would take a job. Labor was often so poorly paid that people were chosen for the jobs on the basis of how little payment they would accept. Thus, although it may seem obvious to us, the modern practice of matching person to job has been the general practice for less than a hundred years.

We should note that some people in hospitality management still don't have an organized notion of the staffing function, and an even larger group sometimes appears not to understand it. Some managers are constantly surprised when work does not get done, even though they have not staffed their positions so that it will get done. Such people hire whoever comes in the door and puts him or her to work with little or no training. Either hospitality managers who proceed in this way fail or they succeed in spite of their staffing weaknesses because of some other special strengths. Just because some operators do not understand the principle of wise staffing, however, is no reason to follow their lead and ignore these principles.

A large group of successful, independent operators appear to follow no formal staffing procedures but achieve effective staffing results anyway. But if they ignore formal procedures, these operators generally follow informal procedures picked up through experience, in talking with competitors, at trade shows and industry meetings, and so forth. In practice, these informal procedures may come close to more formalized programs. These operators, by and large, are the "old pros." Although their results are good, beginners would probably do better to start with proven fundamentals.

JOB AND PERSON SPECIFICATIONS

If a company has no formal staffing procedure, the first step in adopting one will be to identify each job being done. For each job identified, the company prepares a job description. (Job descriptions for workers are often based on formal task analyses prepared by someone with industrial engineering training.) Figures 16.1 and 16.2 illustrate management job descriptions.

The logic of the job description should be obvious. We can hardly hire the right person for the job until we have a good idea of what the job is. Once a job is analyzed carefully, some minimum standards for an applicant should emerge. Sometimes these standards are broken down into physical requirements, mental ability, and emotional or attitudinal characteristics.

Physical Requirements

The person hired must be able to do the job. If a waitress must reach across a booth, the applicant may have to conform to some minimum height requirement (five feet is used by some companies). A receiver's job may require someone able to lift 100 pounds and generally be able to do heavy physical work. Many public contact jobs carry personal appearance requirements and personal hygiene habits. Cocktail waitresses, for instance, are often chosen for their attractiveness as well as their serving ability. Recent federal regulations have complicated this process, however, often making the hiring process more dependent on unwritten rules. An employer, however, still has the need to fit the person to the job, no matter what regulations are promulgated.

Mental or Intellectual Ability

Some jobs require specific intellectual abilities. Desk clerks and other public contact employees must speak reasonably clear English. (In Quebec, they will need English and also are required to be fluent in French.) Waitresses and waiters must have sufficient arithmetic ability to total a check. Cooks and bartenders must be able to convert recipes from one quantity to another.

Emotional and Attitudinal Characteristics

Once again, public contact employees should express by their manner a reasonably pleasant disposition. Those who are hired to work under pressure, such as waitresses and bartenders, should not project a nervous disposition.

NAME: _____ DATE: __/ __/ __ Page __ of __

POSITION TITLE: Food Service Manager	JOB CODE:	EFFECTIVE DATE:	
REPORTS TO: Food Service Director	LOCATION: East		
DIVISION: Educational	AREA GROUP	REGION/DEPT	DIST/SEC/UNIT

Basic Function:
   Handle all assigned responsibilities in a professional manner.

Scope:
   1. Responsible for all phases of unit as designated by FSD.
   2. Responsible for all phases of the cafeteria.
   3. Responsible for all catered events.
   4. Responsible for expanding business volume in the above listed areas.

Principal Duties (by Key Result Area):
   1. Train and develop staff to full potential.
   2. Ordering, using competitive bids and approved suppliers.
   3. Manning/pricing.
   4. Two specials per month as per schedule forwarded to FSD and DM; that is, "monotony breakers."
   5. Pre- and postcost to attain a financial success.
   6. Maintain records for following year reference.
   7. Attain financial goals.
   8. Maintain a high level of satisfaction.

Position Specifications:
   1. Must be able to work as an integral part of a management team.
   2. Must be able to maintain a rapport with superiors and subordinates.
   3. Must be able to cope with work pressures.
   4. Must be innovative and willing to take the initiative.
   5. Professional appearance as deemed necessary to satisfy the client.
   6. Must have the ability to plan and organize.

Where/How to Obtain Training:
   1. Second-Phase Management Development Program.
   2. On the job training.
   3. Company-initiated programs and films.
   4. Management meetings.

FIGURE 16.1   Job description—manager.

NAME: _____ DATE: __/ __/ __ Page __ of __

POSITION TITLE:	JOB CODE:	EFFECTIVE DATE:		
Chief Dietitian	FO 6			
REPORTS TO:	LOCATION:			
FSD	East			
DIVISION:	AREA GROUP	REGION/DEPT	DIST/SEC/UNIT	
Health Care				

Basic Function:
To obtain or improve nutritional status of patients.

Scope:
To be responsible for high-quality nutritional patient care and instruction.
To be responsible for overseeing the activities of one other dietitian.

Principal Duties (by Key Result Area):
1. Visiting and instructing patients and recording in medical charts.
2. Supervising diet-aides and insuring that all patients are visited within 24 hours of admission.
3. Working closely with in-service department orienting new hires and students to procedures of dietary department.
4. Operating an out-patient diet instruction clinic.
5. Supervising proper preparation and distribution of tube feedings and nourishments.

Position Specifications:
BS degree in Foods and Nutrition.
1 year ADA accredited internship.
ADA membership.
ADA registration.

Where/How to Obtain Training:
Local monthly Dietitians' Journal Club.
State and national Dietetic Association meetings.
Local and state Diabetes Association meetings.

FIGURE 16.2 Job description—dietitian.

Handicapped Employees

In some jobs, physical or mental disabilities are not a drawback. Many firms intentionally hire and train mentally handicapped people for dishwashing jobs. Persons with these disabilities often find personal satisfaction in the repetitive tasks that other employees don't enjoy. Although hiring handicapped employees may entail extra training and supervisory efforts, the lower turnover experienced with these employees more than offsets this extra effort.

RECRUITING

Once we know what kind of people we want for each job we've identified, we must try to attract a pool of applicants that permits us to select the best qualified. Indeed, we will shortly argue that in the face of labor shortages, it has become as necessary to segment the labor market as it has been to target the appropriate customer group. The major sources of prospective employees are the operation itself (the internal source) and various outside sources. Each has its special strengths and problems.

It is interesting to see what steps are taken in the search process in a crisis such as the severe problems we mentioned earlier at Friendly's. What that company did was to appoint a special task force of personnel and operations people to lead a crash recruiting program in the New England area. The task force compared Friendly's operating, pay, and personnel practices with those of its competitors. As a result, wages and benefits were adjusted as appropriate; an incentive program was introduced for suggestive selling; and the employee food discount and vacation programs were improved. Moreover, the task force used mobile recruiting vans and developed a reward program for referrals of new employees by those already on staff.

As you can see, "recruiting" for Friendly's involved thinking through the job it had to offer in much the same way it might have looked at a product for sale. Increasingly, employers are seeing themselves as having, in effect, "jobs for sale," with their prospective employees as their customers. Day in and day out, crisis or not, recruiting follows the same general pattern.

INTERNAL SOURCES

Employees often recommend their friends and relatives for work. Many employers, just like Friendly's, pay a bonus to employees who refer applicants who take a job and stay in it for a specified period of time. Hiring people who come with the recommendation of reliable employees increases the chances that the new employee will fit in with the existing organization. Because the person recommending the new employee has to go on record not only with the boss but also with fellow employees, he or she is likely to make recommendations cautiously.

A second internal source is the pool of former employees. Some may have left to raise children or pursue further schooling; others may have changed employers for what looked like a better opportunity. Because former employees are a known quantity—and because they know the company and its practices—they have an advantage over a new applicant. Many firms make a practice of using former employees, particularly waitresses, on a part-time basis for parties and banquets or for an extra busy day like Mother's Day or a football weekend.

Although internal sources offer the advantages of a known quantity, these sources may not supply enough people in a tight labor market. If an operation requires a major addition to its work force—for example, after expansion—these sources are often inadequate, and so the operation must look outside.

EXTERNAL SOURCES

The two major means of contacting employees are through advertisements and employment agencies. Also, some applicants occasionally "walk in" unsolicited. Finally, operations that are organized by a union can call the hiring hall and ask that members be referred for employment.

Advertising

The strengths and weaknesses of advertising lie in the number of applicants it generally yields. In a newspaper help wanted ad, you direct your request to a large readership. People who read help wanted ads are usually searching for a job or thinking of changing jobs. From this large number of readers, a goodly number of people are likely to apply. Thus the employer can choose those who appear to be best qualified from among a large pool of applicants. When several positions must be filled or when a new operation is being started, the large numbers of applicants offer obvious advantages.

On the other hand, those large numbers can be a disadvantage. Dealing with a great number of applicants is time-consuming. Each must be given an application and must be told how to complete it, and then each application must be processed. These clerical duties are compounded by management's time-consuming commitment to interview the applicants. Because applicants are members of the public—that is, members of the community from which the customers come—each applicant must receive courteous attention, or management risks losing their patronage or that of their relatives and acquaintances. Because of the time commitment necessary, many employers use newspaper advertising only if they have a number of positions to fill or if the labor market is especially tight.

Employment Agencies

Each state maintains employment offices in or accessible to all communities in the state. The agencies are operated with tax revenue; thus, they require no placement charge from either the employer or the employee. Because people must register with the employment service when they are out of work in order to qualify for unemployment compensation, this office remains constantly in touch with job seekers.

Many employers make it a point to become personally acquainted with the state employment office's manager and counselors. If the employment office staff knows an employer's applicant standards, the office can save a great deal of time by screening applicants for the employer. Then, too, these staff people are often contacted by people they have helped before who are considering a change of employer. The experienced counselor often helps employers make hiring choices, and the counselor's recommendation can also influence a capable employee's choice of employer.

Private employment agencies charge a fee, which is sometimes paid by the employer. Although some private agencies handle hourly personnel in the hospitality industry, the writer's experience suggests that the greatest users of private employment agencies in our field are supervisory and executive personnel.

SEGMENTING THE EMPLOYEE MARKET

Although the industry turnover is estimated at 300 percent or more, companies who go after particular groups of workers often report superior results. For instance, Naugles, a 24-hour drive-through operation that hires and trains both elderly employees and the handicapped, reports a turnover only one-quarter that of the industry as a whole. Best Western and Howard Johnson's train prison inmates for their central reservations offices and actually operate reservations centers within prison walls. They report low turnover after release, and some ex-inmates have even earned promotions.[3]

Each segment—teens, working mothers, or older workers—has special needs. For teens, part-time and weekend work is important. Many mothers are interested in working while their children are in school. Older workers have quite different perceptions of the hiring process and do not respond well to newspaper advertising. Rather, they are more likely to respond to specialized employment organizations and state, city, and local agencies. They, too, prefer part-time employment and flexible scheduling.[4]

In today's work force, an educated and often discriminating employee decides where to work: under the circumstances, recognizing recruiting as more like selling just makes sense.

[3]*Nation's Restaurant News*, March 11, 1985, p. 132.
[4]*Restaurants & Institutions*, January 23, 1985, p. 71.

SELECTION AND EMPLOYMENT

To this point we have explored ways to determine what kinds of employees we need and ways to contact potential employees. We turn our attention now to the process of selecting and "breaking in" new workers. The first step, *employee selection,* is followed by *induction* (which means *orientation*) and then by *training.* Each step is crucial to developing productive workers.

SELECTION

The selection process basically involves gathering, classifying, and analyzing information available from several sources. An application blank often tells more than an applicant realizes. For instance, if an applicant cannot follow the simple directions on the form, a manager is entitled to wonder if he or she will be able to learn the job. If an applicant does not bother to fill it out completely, he or she may be unwilling to do assigned work. If the open position—say, that of a desk clerk—involves writing, an application filled out in an illegible scrawl may disqualify the applicant.

A properly completed application should account for the applicant's work over the period specified on the application. Any "blanks" or "extended vacations" should be carefully checked. (The cashier you're about to hire may have spent some time in jail for embezzlement!)

The application form usually helps screen out applicants, retaining the ones that management is interested in interviewing. The application can also help start the interview. During the first part of the interview, an interviewer should clarify any ambiguous information on the application. The interviewer will also want to give the applicant information about the company and the job. This interchange helps most interviewers begin the process of sizing up the applicant, determining what kind of a person he or she is and how he or she would get along with the present employees. Interviewing should also focus on the applicant's background and indicate whether he or she is, in fact, qualified (or what is sometimes a bigger problem, overqualified) for the job and whether he or she would actually like the job and be likely to continue in it. A form that suggests one company's approach to summarizing an interview and an applicant evaluation is shown in Figures 16.3 and 16.4.

Applicants should list their references and former employers on the application blanks, and these entries should be checked. Most references are selected because the applicant thinks he or she will receive a good review, and so it is important to check with the employers to verify the employment history and, where possible, to learn how the applicant performed. At the end of the interview, the applicant should be told (if possible) whether or not he or she is to be hired. If several people are being considered, an applicant should be told when a decision is to be made. Those applicants who are not

INTERVIEW REPORT

TO: _____

FROM: _____

NAME OF APPLICANT: _____

ADDRESS _____   PHONE _____

CANDIDATE FOR: _____
(Job Title)

INTERVIEWER: _____   DATE OF THIS INTERVIEW: _____

PLEASE REPORT YOUR INTERVIEW IMPRESSIONS BY CHECKING THE ONE MOST APPROPRIATE BOX IN EACH AREA.

1. APPEARANCE	☐ Very untidy; poor taste in dress.	☐ Somewhat careless about personal appearance.	☐ Satisfactory personal appearance.	☐ Good taste in dress; better than average appearance.	☐ Unusually well groomed; very neat; excellent taste in dress.
2. FRIENDLINESS	☐ Appears very distant and aloof.	☐ Approachable; fairly friendly.	☐ Warm; friendly sociable.	☐ Very sociable and outgoing.	☐ Extremely friendly and sociable.
3. POISE-STABILITY	☐ Ill at ease; is "jumpy" and appears nervous.	☐ Somewhat tense; is easily irritated.	☐ About as poised as the average applicant.	☐ Sure of himself; appears to like crises more than average person.	☐ Extremely well composed; apparently thrives under pressure.
4. PERSONALITY	☐ Unsatisfactory for this job.	☐ Questionable for this job.	☐ Satisfactory for this job.	☐ Very desirable for this job.	☐ Outstanding for this job.

FIGURE 16.3   Analysis of requirements for a food service director.

5. CONVERSATIONAL ABILITY				
☐ Talks very little; Expresses himself poorly.	☐ Tries to express himself but does fair job at best.	☐ Average fluency and expression.	☐ Talks well and "to the point."	☐ Excellent expression; extremely fluent; forceful.
6. ALERTNESS				
☐ Slow to "catch on."	☐ Rather slow; requires more than average explanation.	☐ Grasps ideas with average ability.	☐ Quick to understand; perceives very well.	☐ Exceptionally keen and alert.
7. INFORMATION ABOUT GENERAL WORK FIELD				
☐ Poor knowledge of field.	☐ Fair knowledge of field.	☐ Is as informed as the average applicant.	☐ Fairly well informed; knows more than average applicant.	☐ Has excellent knowledge of the field.
8. EXPERIENCE				
☐ No relationship between applicant's background and job requirements.	☐ Fair relationship between applicant's background and job requirements.	☐ Average amount of meaningful background and experience.	☐ Background very good; considerable experience.	☐ Excellent background and experience.
9. DRIVE				
☐ Has poorly defined goals and appears to act without purpose.	☐ Appears to set goals too low and to put forth little effort to achieve these.	☐ Appears to have average goals; puts forth average effort to reach these.	☐ Appears to strive hard; has high desire to achieve.	☐ Appears to set high goals and to strive incessantly to achieve these.
10. OVERALL				
☐ Definitely unsatisfactory.	☐ Substandard.	☐ Average.	☐ Definitely above average.	☐ Outstanding.

THIS IS: 1st INTERVIEW ☐
          2nd INTERVIEW ☐
          3rd INTERVIEW ☐

FIGURE 16.3 continued

Applicant _____

Job considered for _____ Grade_____

Evaluated by: _____ Date_____

SUMMARY
APPLICANT EVALUATION
CONFIDENTIAL

Rating Overall	☐ Matches Requirements	☐ Exceeds Requirements	☐ Below Requirements	Recommend Hire? _____

Major Strong Characteristics _____

_____

_____

Major Weak Characteristics _____

_____

_____

FACTOR EVALUATIONS FOR THIS POSITION
See Management Employment Program for definitions.

	✔ Check	The Applicant in Relation to This Position		
SKILLS, KNOWLEDGE, ABILITIES	Matches	Almost Matches	Exceeds	Fails To Meet
Appearance and presentation				
Education				
Mental ability				
Mobility				
Experience				
Physical condition				
Special skills and knowledge				
Relationships background				

HABITS, AMBITIONS, DRIVES				
Leadership				
Perseverence				
Stability				
Self-reliance				
Energy				
Maturity				
Ability to get along with others				
Need for income				
Need for status and power				
Need to serve				

SFS 0121-0567

FIGURE 16.4   Applicant evaluation form.

hired should be notified promptly so they can continue their search for employment. Most employers maintain a file of applications from people who were not hired. Thus, a person not chosen at one time may be contacted later. (Incidentally, a file like this helps establish that management has followed fair employment practices.)

INDUCTION

It's an old saying—and a true one—that first impressions are lasting impressions. It is surprising, then, how often new employees are told to sign some papers, are given directions to the locker room, and are promptly forgotten! Such casual procedures destroy the golden opportunity to start a new employee off on the right foot. Common sense should suggest that the new employee be enthusiastically and cheerfully introduced to the operation, to fellow workers, and to the new job.

The Operation

Your restaurant or hotel or dietary department is old ground to established employees. But it is unmapped territory to a newcomer. For this reason, a guided tour by a member of management helps make an employee's first day comfortable. Basic information, such as where the employees enter the building, where and when smoking is permitted, and where personal belongings are kept, should be provided. Some employees report spending a very uncomfortable first day because they were too embarrassed to ask strangers directions to the restrooms.

Are you proud of your operation? Are there certain dining rooms that are especially nice, certain views especially attractive? Let the newcomer share in these high points, too.

Certainly, a part of this orientation should be a statement of the standards of the operation, with regard to both quality of product and service and personal conduct and hygiene. Such a statement should be made in a friendly way by a member of management, and it may also be presented to the new employee in the form of an orientation handbook. Such a "postinterview" conversation also gives management an opportunity to restate its policies on wages, fringe benefits and working conditions, days off, and so forth, as well as to make sure any questions the new employee may have are answered.

Fellow Workers

Don't assume a new worker is a gregarious person who quickly strikes up friendships. Introduce the new employee to the others in the work group and to others with whom he or she will come into contact. Thus, for instance, the hostess should introduce a new waitress not only to the other waitresses but to cooks, pantry workers, and dishwashers as well.

The Job

Finally, the new employee (1) should be shown exactly where he or she will work, (2) should receive a full description of the job and, if possible, (3) should get an opportunity to observe the work in action. Such an experience can be brief, but it gives the employee an overview of the work and lays a good foundation for training.

TRAINING

Some operations—especially independent operations that do not have the volume to justify a continuing training program—prefer to hire trained employees. Even when experienced workers take a new job, they must still receive enough training to orient them to the operation's special procedures. For the experienced, however, this training may amount to little more than an extended orientation.

Some companies prefer to hire people with no experience at all. These companies argue that it is easier to train from scratch than to hire someone who has to unlearn what the employer, at least, views as a satchel of bad habits. An employee who knows only one way to do the work is unlikely to stray from approved practice.

In any case, experienced employees are not always available, and so nearly every employer must offer some training. Training is unquestionably costly. Employees must be paid for the time when they are learning but not yet productive, and trainees also consume a good deal of the trainer's valuable time. This is why the selection process we discussed earlier is so important. There is no point in spending time, money, and effort on somebody who turns out to be unqualified for or uninterested in the job.

We ought to note, though, that the alternative to training—not training—may be even more expensive. Training does cost a lot; but the cost of not training is poor service and lost customers, and a lost customer may *never* return. Thus, the lost revenue from poor service far exceeds the cost of training a worker properly.

Not only does management lose customers by not training, but it is liable to lose the employee as well, at just about the time he or she becomes productive. An employee who is thrown into a job that he or she does not know is bound to feel inadequate, to say the least, and is likely to begin looking for other work.

Training and retraining can be the key to maintaining quality in products, and at the same time, reducing turnover. For example, one industry analyst attributed a large part of TGI Friday's success with a large menu prepared mostly from scratch to its very strong staff training program.[5]

[5]John J. Rohs, CFA, *The Restaurant Industry* (New York: Wertheim & Co., April 1985), p. 122.

MANAGEMENT TRAINING

Companies, particularly those planning to expand, often develop large entry-level training programs for new or promotable management employees. For example, Ponderosa stepped up its management training in 1985 in advance of opening new stores, with the goal of moving as many assistant managers as possible up to manager.[6] Morrison's Cafeterias leased space from a local college and centralized its management training in seven sessions per year, turning out 200 new managers annually.[7] And at Po Folks, a local athletic coach was brought in to help train managers as trainers because Po Folks's top management felt he had especially useful experience in dealing with young people.[8]

Because managers are responsible for the productivity of all their employees, it makes good sense for companies to concentrate their efforts on preparing productive managers. For the future hospitality manager, management training programs may offer a shortcut to acquiring practical management know-how. Looking into your prospective employer's training program is just enlightened self-interest.

PREOPENING TRAINING

An especially important training challenge is getting a new operation ready to open. Many companies have a training team especially developed for this purpose which draws on existing units for key workers during the preopening and immediate postopening training period. The preopening training at Casa Lupita, a Mexican dinner house, is typical of a well-thought-out program.

After very careful screening, which includes aptitude tests, personal interviews, and reference checks, the successful applicant is put into a two-week training program. The first week requires twice-daily classroom training sessions with groups of 20 to 30 employees. These classes cover the company's menu and its procedures and guidelines for cooking and serving food. The second week involves role playing: one-half the class serves the other half while managers critique their performance. Then there is a family night, and the employees' families are the company's guests for dinner—which does a great deal to build the employees' pride in their work. Finally, special VIP and benefit dinners are held as dress rehearsals. When the opening comes, the operation is successful in two ways: It is accepted well in the community, and it holds onto its employees, experiencing relatively low postopening turnover.[9]

[6]*Nation's Restaurant News,* August 12, 1985, p. 176.

[7]*Nation's Restaurant News,* June 4, 1984, p. 3.

[8]*Restaurants & Institutions,* May 29, 1985, p. 56.

[9]*Restaurants & Institutions,* May 15, 1985, pp. 169–170.

ON-THE-JOB TRAINING

The most common method of training in the hospitality industry is pairing the new employee with an experienced worker. Unfortunately, this pairing is often done haphazardly: a new worker is assigned to whichever experienced worker may be handy. Although the details of developing an actual training program extend beyond our concern here, we can note that the basic elements are developing trainers who (1) know—and will show—the approved way of doing the task and (2) are trained in training as well as in the job.

Task analyses that spell out in writing the steps necessary in each job greatly facilitate training. The learner can be given them to study, and the trainer can use them to be ready to give instruction.

During the first part of World War II, a huge number of war plant workers had to be trained for new jobs in a hurry. At that time, management experts identified a four-step procedure as the best way to go about this rapid training:

1. *Tell me.* Explain the task to the worker. Include why it needs to be done and why it must be done in just this way.

2. *Show me.* Demonstrate the job, explaining as you go along. Continue demonstrating until the worker is ready to try it.

3. *Let me do it.* Let the worker perform the task slowly, asking questions as needed. Not until trainer and trainee are comfortable with the trainee's independent performance should he or she be allowed to do it alone.

4. *Follow up.* Once the new employee achieves enough proficiency to be able to perform independently, he or she should receive close supervision to be sure that shortcuts or bad habits don't grow gradually to mar performance.

Notice that an employee is not generally trained in a job but in tasks. Thus, training for a new dishwasher might involve the following:

1. Scraping—removing garbage from plates.
2. Racking—putting dirty dishes in racks.
3. Feeding—feeding dirty dish racks into the dishwasher.
4. Catching—receiving dish racks from the "clean end" of the machine.
5. Stacking—removing clean dishes from the rack and stacking them in a temporary storage place.
6. Transporting—moving clean dishes back to where they are used, often in special carts or lowerators.

Each of these (and the list could be extended a great deal further) is a separate task; and for each, "one best way" will permit the greatest possible speed and the least breakage and injury. Teaching tasks separately, one at a time, may seem slow, but it is really the best way to prepare a new employee for the complete dishwasher job.

EVALUATING TRAINING

At Long John Silver's, the company sets training goals and then analyzes the results. It first defines the ideal results and then studies the actual results. The analysis then focuses on the gap between ideal and real. "Why don't people behave as they should?" management asks. If it's because the system doesn't work, the operational procedures will be changed. If the analysis indicates that there is not enough feedback, then rewards and punishments may need to be reviewed. Only if it is because the employees *don't know* is more training called for.[10]

EVERYBODY GETS TRAINED

A final point is worth noting here. Training goes on continually. When a new employee comes to work, management can take charge of that learning process or leave it to whatever influences come to hand. Either way, the employee will be trained. But clearly, common sense sides with a planned, management-controlled training effort.

RETAINING STAFF

Because so much effort goes into recruiting qualified staff, and so much time and trouble goes into training them, there is a clear need to hold onto good staff once they come on board. We can hardly solve so complex a problem here, but this may be a good place to review some key provisions that some companies are finding helpful. *NRA News,* a publication of the National Restaurant Association, points to several factors as crucial to retaining good employees. As we've already indicated, taking the effort to get the right people is an important first step.

Second, the way people are treated makes a great difference. Praise in public for a good job, but reprimand in private when things don't go right. Efforts to improve two-way flow of information are important, too. In smaller units, face-to face conversation may be enough. In larger companies, company newspapers can at least recognize employees' accomplishments. At the Chicago Claim Company, employees fill out every day an "employee comment slip" reporting what customers say, evaluating the food

---

[10]Doug Higden, "Setting Training Goals," *12th Annual Chain Operators Exchange* (Chicago: International Foodservice Manufacturers Association, 1985).

they served, and commenting on what was good or bad on their shift. Managers read these carefully.

Offering opportunities for advancement is important. Companies that promote from within, such as Magic Pan, which finds 40 percent of its management trainees in its own hourly ranks, offer an opportunity for advancement that is an added inducement to performance.

Many companies pride themselves on offering competitive pay and good benefits. Burger King, for instance, offers scholarships to college students who stay with the company. Others offer incentives: plaques, T shirts, or trips. A few even offer profit sharing. The NRA article concluded, "As fewer workers are available for restaurant work, keeping the good ones becomes more important. By treating employees with respect and consideration, the chances that they will grow with you increases."[11]

STAFF PLANNING

Hospitality managers concentrate on staff planning not only because of the high proportion of income they spend on salaries and wages but also because of the great importance they attach to adequate coverage—that is, always having sufficient staff in the appropriate jobs to meet the operation's needs. Anyone who has seen a hotel coffee shop flounder when the key breakfast cook failed to show up, or a kitchen where the pot washer walked out in the middle of a meal, knows the chaos caused by the absence of just one key person. On the other hand, you may have noticed some food service operations that both open at 7:00 A.M. and bring in a full dishroom crew at 7:00 A.M.. The crew then sits around with nothing to do until the dirty dishes gradually start to collect a half-hour or 45 minutes later. Proper staff planning ensures coverage, but it would avoid superfluous, wasteful coverage like this.

Because staff planning is so important, most hospitality curricula devote at least a large part of one course, and sometimes more than that, to it. In our brief discussions, we can only introduce this form of planning and some of its key tools.

JOB AND WORK NEEDS

Staff planning begins by identifying each working station in the operation. Next, a schedule showing the number of persons needed at these stations in the course of each day, by time period, is prepared. This analysis usually follows the graphic pattern shown in Figure 16.5. This kind of chart shows at a glance where there is double coverage for a job and what, if any, rest periods are provided.

[11]*NRA News,* October 1985, p. 25.

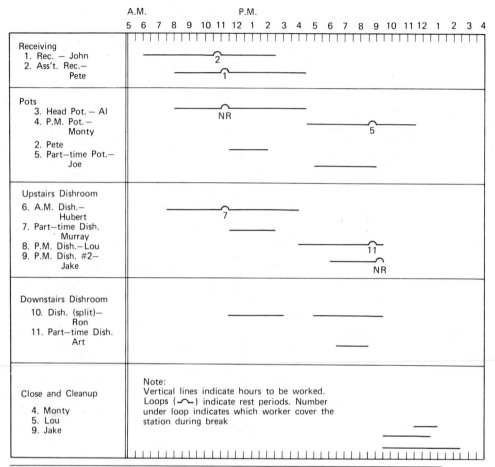

FIGURE 16.5 Typical daily schedule.

Because the volume of business may vary from one day to another, many operations prepare a separate schedule for each day of the week and sometimes separate sets for different seasons. Comparing actual coverage needs with staffing schedules results in a constant revision of these schedules. A dollar of unneeded labor cost at one station can, at a moment's notice, be moved to reinforce the coverage someplace else.

Once management prepares schedules of its operating needs for each day, and thereby ensures adequate coverage for each job, it can draw up a weekly schedule providing for day-off relief. The schedule for the dish, pot, and receiving crew shown in Figure 16.6 is primarily a management tool (1) to analyze seven-day schedule needs (the problem is simpler but similar in

	Mon.	Tues.	Wed.	Thurs.	Fri.	Sat.	Sun.
Receiver- 6-2:30 John						off \ N.R.	off \ N.R.
Yes't. Receiver- 8-4:30 Pete						off \ N.R.	off \ N.R.
Head Potwasher- 8-4:30 Al	off \ Hal	off \ Hal				off \ N.R.	off \ N.R.
P.M. Potwasher- 4:30-1:00 Monty							
Part-time Potwasher- 5-9:00 Joe					off \ Hal	off \ N.R.	off \ N.R.
A.M. Dishwasher 7:30-4:00 Hubert	off \ Mac	off \ Mac					
Part-time Dishwasher 11:30-2:30 Murray							
P.M. Dishwasher- 4:00-12:30 Lou			off \ Mac	off \ Mac		off \ Mac	
P.M. Dishwasher #2 5:30-2:00 Jake					off \ Mac	Mac	
Dish-(split) Ron 11:30-3:30 & 5:30-9:30			off \ Hal	off \ Hal			
Part-time Dish-P.M. 6:30-9:00 Art							
Dish. Relief- Mac	A.M. Dish 8-4:30	A.M. Dish 8-4:30	P.M. Dish 4-12:30	P.M. Dish 4-12:30	P.M. Dish #2 5:30-2:00	off \ N.R.	off \ N.R.
Pot.-Dish. Relief Hal	Head Pot. 8-4:30	Head Pot. 8-4:30	Dish. Split 11:30-3:30 & 5:30-9:30	Dish. Split 11:30-3:30 & 5:30-9:30	Part-time Pot 4:30-1:00	off \ N.R.	off \ N.R.
Pot.-Relief/ Part-time Noah						P.M. Pot. 4:30-1:00	P.M. Pot. 4:30-1:00
Dish. Relief Part-time Norm					P.M. Dish. 4:00-12:30		

FIGURE 16.6   Weekly posted schedule.

six- or five-day operations), (2) to ensure adequate coverage for each job each day, and (3) at the same time to be sure that each employee receives the appropriate time off.

A schedule like the one shown in Figure 16.6 is also a communication tool. When posted, this schedule shows employees which person works what job for which hours each day of the week. Managers who keep their schedules in their heads and rely on simply telling people when they are to work are almost bound occasionally to have two people showing up for the same job and no people on other days! The result is increased cost, inadequate coverage, poor service, and low morale.

PART-TIME EMPLOYEES

To complete our discussion of staff planning, we should offer a word about part-time employees. An operation often needs a position covered for only part of a shift, and it sometimes needs extra people on a job only on busy days. To hire a full-time person would obviously be an expensive solution; instead the hospitality industry is using more part-time employees to avoid overstaffing.

Some added costs and problems result from relying on part-time people. First, an operation that uses part-time help extensively carries more people on its payroll. The same (and often a lesser) number of labor-days can be worked, but more people will fill the jobs. This means more payroll records; and more recruiting, interviewing, hiring, and training. Moreover, a part-time employee usually works part-time because he or she has a main commitment elsewhere. (Part-timers are usually housewives, students, or "moonlighters" taking a part-time job in addition to their main employment.) Scheduling people with responsibilities outside your establishment creates special problems: to name only a few, a spouse's vacation; exams, semester breaks, or graduation; and fatigue.

Although part-time employees present some problems, greater flexibility and lower payroll costs often make them economically attractive. You can expect that the work of hospitality managers in future years will be even more involved with supervising and motivating part-time employees than it is today, as the industry's labor shortage grows more intense.

COMPUTERIZED SCHEDULING

Computer programs to schedule employees using a personal computer are now available. But people can schedule at least as well as computers can, and so scheduling programs don't generally seem to reduce payroll hours. Rather, their great advantage is their speed. By using a computer, managers can complete their scheduling work in roughly one-third the time that doing it by hand takes. Computerized scheduling is especially helpful when there is a change in managers in a unit. Much of the experience of the manager who has been there a while is programmed into the computer: work stations, staffing requirements, employee availability and work preferences, and peak and valley days and time periods. When the new manager comes in, he or she doesn't have to learn who everyone is and what their job is. Thus the computer offers a real convenience to managers and is a time-saver for them.[12]

This chapter, more than the other management function chapters, has focused on the "nuts and bolts" of hospitality management. Staffing in hospitality management is obviously a nuts-and-bolts function, but one that is vital to the success of an operation.

Our nuts-and-bolts approach in this chapter illustrates another important fact about hospitality management: the importance of attention to detail. It is important for management to develop sources of good employees, to look at the details found on an application, to pay special attention to a new employee's introduction to work, to base that employee's training on individual task analysis, and to undertake painstaking staff planning. As one of the earliest hospitality educators, Bernard R. Proulx, the first head of the School of Hotel, Restaurant and Institutional Management at Michigan State University, used to tell his students, "The secret to success in the service industry is attention to detail."

SUMMARY

In a service-oriented field such as the hospitality industry, staffing is especially important. Also because the hospitality industry usually spends so much of its income on wages, choosing the right employees is essential.

First, the right person must be chosen for the job, in terms of both physical and mental abilities. Second, those kinds of persons must be recruited for the job, using internal and external sources to find them. When a pool of applicants has been gathered, some must be selected, by means of the application, an interview, and a reference check. Then comes the employee's induction, or orientation, to the job and to fellow employees. Training is necessary, and generally involves on-the-job training.

Retaining staff and planning staff needs are also important. In regard to the latter, we talked about using part-time employees and computerized scheduling.

---

[12]*Nation's Restaurant News,* May 13, 1985, p. 157.

KEY WORDS AND CONCEPTS

To help you review this chapter, keep in mind the following:

Personal service
Wage cost
Job and person specifications
Recruiting
Internal sources
External sources
Advertising
Employment agencies
Selection

Application
Interview
Reference check
Induction/orientation
Training
Staff planning
Scheduling
Job and work needs
Part-time employees

REVIEW QUESTIONS

1. In the near future, will there be a labor surplus or shortage? Explain.

2. What kinds of qualifications should be considered when recruiting an employee for the dishroom? As a waitress? As a supervisor?

3. Describe some of the internal and external sources that employers use to find employees.

4. What does induction to job involve, and why is it important?

5. Why do some companies prefer to hire people with no experience?

6. Explain why training is especially important before opening a new operation?

7. What are the advantages of hiring part-time employees? The disadvantages?

Courtesy of W. R. Grace.

THE CONTROL FUNCTION IN HOSPITALITY MANAGEMENT

THE PURPOSE OF THIS CHAPTER

If you've ever found yourself working on too many projects at once and suddenly felt the need to sit down and "figure out just what I'm getting done," you will understand how important it is to control projects before they begin to control you. A hospitality system has so many varied activities that the control function is absolutely essential to their efficiency and success. In this chapter, therefore, we will explore the ways in which organizations measure their results against goals—how they appraise exactly what they are getting done.

Control is too often thought of as exclusively "something for the accountants to worry about." But nothing could be further from the truth! The information from control systems really exists first and foremost to guide management action. In fact, in hospitality operations, control information often does not even enter the accounting stream; it may not even be numerical. Although whole courses—indeed, entire curriculums, such as accounting—are devoted to a detailed study of control, our purpose here is more basic: we want you to see control as the heart of hospitality management.

THIS CHAPTER SHOULD HELP YOU

1. Explain the relationship control bears to the other functions of hospitality management.

2. See control *(a)* as future-oriented and *(b)* as a basis for management action.

3. Describe the characteristics of an effective control system.

4. Recognize the principal financial accounting statements and explain their managerial purpose.

5. Identify and describe the principal tools of managerial accounting used by the hospitality industry.

6. Explain the concept known as *decision accounting.*

Because specialized courses are taught in the area of control, hospitality students sometimes get the impression that control is separate, something located "over there" in the accounting office. But as we will see in this chapter, control is an integral part of every manager's and every supervisor's work.

> Control is the work that managers and supervisors do to measure performance against standards, detect and analyze variances from target performance, and initiate corrective action.

Control affects and is affected by all the other functions. For instance, the standards that result from planning are meaningless without some way of measuring performance, just as a set of numbers measuring performance are meaningless without some idea of the results desired (that is, some standard). Similarly, a major function of organizing is to fix responsibility for results. Once again, if we have a measure that can tell us something is wrong but no means of saying who takes responsibility for corrective action, the purpose of control will be stymied.

In Chapter 16, we saw that proper staffing is necessary to achieve the productivity that allows us to meet payroll cost targets and that staff planning is the basis for that control. As you read Chapter 18, on the directing and leading function, you will want to remember that control information is an important basis for management action. If control systems yield nothing but numbers, they will be useless. Perhaps an illustration from personal experience can demonstrate this point best:

> I once was hired to relieve a man—let's call him Mr. Brower—who was the food and beverage manager in a hotel whose food operation was losing money badly. Mr. Brower had received his early training in a well-established hotel company with several operations.

When I was introduced to Mr. Brower, he took me into his office and pulled out a set of ledger books. As he opened the first, he said, "We've got a terrific control system. All our food is issued from the storeroom only on requisitions, and the storeroom man sends the requisition slips up to me and I post them. As you can see, we have a daily food cost in 18 categories!"

As I talked further with Mr. Brower, I learned that most of his early experience had been as a "food controller"—someone responsible for maintaining the food cost accounting system for the hotel where he worked. What he had done was to come as close to duplicating the elaborate control system at the hotel where he used to work, and then he labored long and hard to maintain the system.

Unfortunately, he had produced a system that told him in great detail that his operation was going broke. He didn't know what to do about it, so he sat in his office and kept his records straight! The process of untangling the mess involved getting rid of the storeroom man who really wasn't needed in an operation of that size (and who had been regularly stealing the food), establishing food and payroll cost standards, and then correcting performances on specific work stations and food products.

CONTROL AND THE "CYBERNETIC LOOP"

The word *cybernetic* is derived from the ancient Greek word for the steersman on a ship. In early times the steersman would aim the ship toward some point on the horizon. If the ship's course varied to the left, he'd move the tiller to steer a bit to the right, and vice versa.

In modern management, control systems fill a similar function. As an operation progresses, various information about the progress is collected and presented to management in a usable form. If the report indicates that the food cost is on target, management can turn its attention elsewhere. But if the food cost is off, it's up to the manager to "move the tiller" and to take corrective action on the basis of the information, just as the steersman reacted when he saw the bow of the ship moving off the point to which he was steering. The term *loop* is used in conjunction with *cybernetic* because the process is continuous. Action constantly takes place, and information about that action must constantly pass through the loop to indicate either that the process is on course or that corrective action is required. This constant vigilance results in more information's being sent through the loop, and so on.

A simple diagram of the cybernetic loop appears in Figure 17.2. Here is a simple example of the cybernetic loop in action—a cashier's report (Figure 17.1).

Mary, a cashier, starts her shift with a $100 bank. Throughout her eight-hour shift she accepts from customers who are paying for their meals or making change. As necessary, Mary rings up each sale on a cash register. At the end of her shift, she prepares a report that shows

Cashier's Report

Shift: A.M.
Cashier: Mary

Sales	319.72
Cash Deposit	319.87
Over (Short)	.15

FIGURE 17.1 Cashier's report.

1.   The number and amount of sales rung up on the register.
2.   The amount of money she is depositing (which is always the amount of money in her cash drawer, less her $100 bank).
3.   The difference between the sales she has collected and her deposit, or the amount she is over or short.

Most cashiers make small errors, and so they may be over or short a few cents. But if the error is greater than 50 cents (or some other prescribed amount), management approval of the report may be required.

Notice what this procedure accomplishes. If Mary's report indicates she's "on course," no management action will be needed. If she makes an error over the prescribed amount, management must be informed. Depending on the circumstances, management can accept the error or initiate corrective action. The corrective action is not intended so much to correct an error that has already occurred as it is to find the cause of the error and take steps to avoid it in the future. Once management locates the error, that Mary has been making, they can help her avoid it. Thus, control is future oriented and forward looking. Control, in effect, records and studies what has happened, not principally to place the blame on someone, but to discover what went wrong so the error can be avoided in the future. We study the past not for itself but for what it can teach us for the future.

This example also provides a good illustration of a term we've already used a good deal: *information system.* An information system collects, transcribes, and summarizes information about transactions or other events, and provides management with a summary for analysis and action. Figure 17.2 shows a simple version of the information system as a cybernetic loop. An action is followed by some test against standards. If the performance is acceptable, the process will continue; if it is not, some corrective action or actions will be taken, and then we will try again.

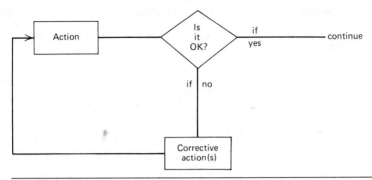

FIGURE 17.2   The cybernetic loop.

We should note that information systems are concerned with more than just financial data. For instance, some information systems involve personnel and marketing. Many states have developed nutritional audits for the custodial and health-care institutions they operate. These nutritional audits measure not so much the cost of food as the nutritional adequacy of the diets being served.

The key to designing an information system is to determine just what information is needed or, to use the language of the systems analyst, just what *information output* is required of the system. An information system, then, is any means of collecting information (cash register tapes, meat yields, guest counts) and translating the raw information into an intelligible, usable summary form. Examples shown in Figure 17.3 are a cashier's reports, a meat yield report, and a summary of guest arrivals per 10-minute time segment.[1]

The final element is that the report must go to the right management person to be useful. Figure 17.3 illustrates this simplified concept of a control system using the three examples cited.

Lest the term *information system* discourage a student with its apparent complexity, let us look at some examples of control through management action based on exceedingly simple information systems.

CONTROL THROUGH MANAGEMENT ACTION

Many food service operators have found that the recipe itself can be one key to controlling food quality and reducing waste. At Stouffer's Restaurants, the food production director and other members of the management taste samples of all the food that has been prepared to be sure that it has been

---

[1]In fact, in some fast-food operations, this report serves as the basis for advance preparation.

Data	Source	Report (Sample Format)	User (Person who Receives Report)
1 *Amount of Sales*	*Cash Register Tape*	*Cashier's Report*	*Restaurant Manager Accounting Department*

Date 7/1/79	Shift AM
Sales	252.00
Cash deposit	251.70
Over (short)	(.30)
Cashier	SW

Data	Source	Report	User
2 *Pounds of Meat and Price*	*Invoice*		*Food Production Manager Shift Supervisor*

Yield report

Product	Inside rd
Purveyor	Eastern
Raw weight	18
Cost	1.80/32.40
Cooked weight	16.5
Number of servings	
Cost/serving	.83

Data	Source		User
3 *Guest Count*	*Cash Register Tape (number of sales)*		*Store manager Shift supervisor*

Time/Sales Volume Report

Day of Week	Monday	Shift AM
Reading#	10AM	11AM
	Guest count	
1	2	7
2	3	12
3	7	18
4	6	
5	5	
		6PM
1	8PM	27
2	10	32
3	16	35
4	18	33
5	21	31

FIGURE 17.3 Illustrations of simple information systems.

prepared correctly. Because these managers are trained to taste (and have tasted the same recipe many times before), what better way to be sure that quality standards have been met?

Recipes also specify portion sizes, but it takes skill to portion correctly when carving a roast, for example, and errors are common. To aid a carver, many operations use the over-and-under portion scale. This scale is actually a simple information system that permits a carver to correct over- or under-portioning and to know when his or her carving hand has grown a little heavy or a little light. If the person portioning the meat keeps a simple record of how many portions are served from a cut of meat, at the end of the meal a supervisor can prepare a yield report and compare the results (portions served) with the standard that has been established for that product.

Indeed, some food production managers actually study the garbage can! By periodically raking through the garbage, they can see what kind of food and how much of it is being left on plates. If one item consistently becomes waste, it can indicate either poor quality or overportioning. Further study of the information serves as the basis for management action. In short, regular garbage inspection can be part of an information system!

In large- and medium-sized hotels, housekeeping supervisors below the executive housekeeper level are often called inspectors. Their supervisory duties include not only assigning work and issuing supplies but also physically inspecting each room as it is finished to be sure it has been made up to the hotel's standards and reporting the results to the housekeeper and front desk.

Many hospitals (and other hospitality institutions, as well) collect patient comments and tally them. If the dietary department complaint rate suddenly goes up, the dietitian knows there is a problem and can begin the necessary study to correct it. These complaints can become the focus, again, of an information system.

CHARACTERISTICS OF CONTROL SYSTEMS

We can conclude our discussion of control systems by identifying four of their common characteristics.

1. Control systems are *continuous*. Data are collected and stored on a continuing basis so that if something goes wrong, the data can be carefully analyzed to direct management's corrective action.

2. Reports must be *timely*. Data must be collected and reported so that management can act to correct a problem before there is too great a loss. Thus, many food service operators compute their food costs weekly or every 10 days, rather than monthly, in order to catch and correct promptly any unfavorable food cost patterns that develop.

3. Control is aimed at some *key point*, and no action is called for unless a problem is detected. This approach is sometimes called *management by*

exception. Thus, a food cost is computed periodically because it is a *key cost* in a food service operation. If the food cost is out of line, further study and action will be initiated. If no problem is detected in the routine report, no action will be taken.

4. Control is *action oriented.* At the risk of belaboring this point, we repeat that nothing really is controlled until somebody does something about the problem. Thus, control systems and information systems are similar, but a control system not only includes the information but also provides for corrective action, if it is required.

TOOLS FOR CONTROL

Managers use two somewhat different kinds of tools to achieve control: *financial accounting* and *managerial accounting.* Although each form of accounting has significant similarities, each is designed to meet particular needs.

FINANCIAL ACCOUNTING

Students will recognize financial accounting as the subject routinely taught in their first college accounting course. Financial accounting is based on a series of conventions adopted by the accounting profession to ensure a common basis of reporting the results of business operations. Financial accounting is principally designed for outsiders: for bankers who may be asked to lend money or for stockholders or potential investors who want to evaluate the firm's performance in comparison with other investments.

The principal financial reports used in financial accounting are the *balance sheet* and the *statement of income and expense.* The balance sheet is simply a statement prepared by a firm's ownership. On one side it lists the firm's assets, and on the other, the claims against those assets by those to whom the firm owes money and by the owners. Table 17.1 provides an example of a hospitality industry balance sheet. The balance sheet offers a great deal of information to financial analysts, but its use in day-to-day operation is limited.

The statement of income and expense, on the other hand, is used by operations people both to evaluate performance on a month-to-month basis and, as we shall see, to prepare budgets for future periods.

Each segment of the hospitality industry has a *Uniform System of Accounts* that tells accountants how to classify the various kinds of income and expense. The purpose of the uniform system is to present income and cost comparisons so that they reflect the effectiveness of each unit within the organization. In recent years the accounting profession has developed the term *responsibility accounting* to describe this means of classifying and

TABLE 17.1 Travel-On Motel Balance Sheet as of December 31, 19XX

Assets		
Current assets		
Cash	$ 10,000	
Accounts receivable	15,000	
Inventories	12,000	
		$ 37,000
Fixed assets		
Building	$1,000,000	
Less depreciation	250,000	
		750,000
Furniture and fixtures	$ 110,000	
Less depreciation	55,000	
		55,000
TOTAL ASSETS		$842,000
Liabilities and Capital		
Current liabilities		
Accounts payable	$ 15,000	
Accrued expenses	7,000	
Mortgage payable (within one year)	10,000	
		$ 32,000
Long-term liabilities		
Mortgage		600,000
Capital		
Common stock	$ 100,000	
Retained earnings	$ 110,000	
		210,000
TOTAL LIABILITIES AND CAPITAL		$842,000

reporting financial information. This form of accounting is not new to the hospitality industry, in which the hotel industry (with its own *Uniform System of Accounts*) has long pioneered responsibility accounting.

Income and expense are divided among departments—in hotels these departments include rooms, food and beverage, and telephone—and a departmental net income is derived by subtracting the department's expenses from the revenue it generates. Each departmental net income represents an accurate reflection of the department head's performance. The general manager's performance, you will recall, is assessed by total income before fixed charges (house profit), which is the total of all departments' net operating incomes less certain unallocated expense items. (See Chapter 7 for a fuller discussion of this point.)

Just as the American Hotel–Motel Association periodically updates and publishes a *Uniform System of Accounts for Hotels,* the National Restaurant Association publishes a *Uniform System of Accounts for Restaurants.* The American Hospital Association supplies similar guidance in health care, and the Food and Nutrition Service publishes guidelines for school lunch accounting.

One major purpose served by following the appropriate industry accounting system is that it permits your operation to compare its results with industry averages. For the hotel–motel industry, the accounting firms of Harris, Kerr, Forster, and Company and Laventhol & Horwath each publishes extensive studies of hotel industry performance based on the *Uniform System of Accounts.* Laventhol & Horwath, in cooperation with the National Restaurant Association, publishes a similar statistical study for restaurants called *Table Service Restaurants.* The American Hospital Association supplies similar data in health care.

MANAGERIAL ACCOUNTING

Whereas financial accounting is prepared according to accounting conventions that enable outsiders to evaluate performance, managerial accounting is prepared by and for insiders, that is, management. It uses, therefore, any form that is helpful to managers. The principal concerns of managerial accounting in the hospitality industry are food and beverage cost control and payroll control. Some operators pay fairly close attention to such miscellaneous direct operating costs as cleaning and guest supplies, but much less time and effort is generally spent on these operational aspects. The information these control systems yield, in turn, is used in the budgeting process.

Food and Beverage Cost Control

Food and beverage cost control can be divided, in turn, into two general areas: *precost* and *postcost control.* Precosting refers to the process of determining in advance the cost of a portion of food or drink (or of a whole meal). The best way to do this is to work from standard recipes and determine the cost of the recipe amount. Then, if standard portions are used, the recipe cost can be divided by the yield to determine the cost per portion. The cost developed in this process becomes an important selling price determinant. Once (1) the cost, (2) the selling price, and (3) the numbers of each item sold are known, an operator can predict food or beverage cost with reasonable accuracy—if nothing goes wrong!

Postcost control, sometimes called *historical control,* focuses on what has happened so that if something does go wrong, management will know about it at the earliest possible moment and will have the information necessary to find out specifically what did go wrong. The purpose of postcontrol, then, is not so much to remedy errors that have already taken place but, as we noted earlier, to take steps to prevent the same mistake from being repeated.

Payroll Control

Our discussion in Chapter 16 showed that the principal technique for controlling payroll costs is staff planning that includes a tight, analytical scheduling process to ensure adequate coverage for each station and to avoid wasted coverage. Scheduling may be likened to precost control. For each payroll period, the payroll cost (that is, the ratio of payroll cost to sales) is computed and compared with the target that management has established for that cost. When costs are out of line, management can institute special reporting systems for overtime hours (hours in excess of 40, for which time and a half must generally be paid) and for "extra" hours (hours in excess of those budgeted for the period).

Specialized Controls

Some operations develop special reporting procedures to control such other direct operating costs as cleaning supplies. These procedures generally take the form of issuing systems that permit management to monitor closely the use of supplies such as soap, cleanser, and paper towels.

Some restaurants control china, glass, and silver breakage costs by taking a periodic inventory to determine the number of pieces broken or lost. This figure is then related to sales in a ratio called "the number of guests per broken piece." This kind of information can be tabulated simply by noting breakage as it happens. If management notes who broke each piece (usually by sorting the broken pieces into bins for each worker group), it then becomes possible to categorize daily breakage by worker group. Management can then focus attention on those who are most responsible for the breakage.

Budgeting

The process of operating the controls described here yields a great deal of information about the business patterns that can be expected in the future. A budget is basically a plan of action spelled out in dollars, and it is usually based on information provided by the management accounting systems. Sales for some future period are estimated; then, applying the percentage for each expected cost (food cost, payroll cost, supplies cost, and the like), management can prepare an expense budget. Because cost patterns change, expense budgets may be based in part on past experience and in part on expected future cost trends.

The procedure for preparing budgets in many hospitality operations, especially at the unit level, is not especially complicated: On a copy of a current or recent statement of income and expense, write the estimate for the budget period alongside the figures for the past period. Base the new figures on experience and expected future trends (as shown in Table 17.2). These estimates may then be formalized after discussion with key department heads.

In multiunit companies, budgets are sometimes drawn up at the company's headquarters using computerized records of past performance and are then "rolled down" to the district and unit levels. At that point, the process reverses itself, with the units forwarding the revised unit budgets to the district level. Once approved at that level, the district totals its unit budgets and sends them to the control office as the district budget. As you can imagine, this process often involves a good deal of negotiation among the different levels of a multiunit firm.

Whereas business firms base their budgets on sales, public-sector food service operators (such as school lunch programs) must use appropriations as a basis for starting the budget process. Thus, the local school board, for instance, may supply some operating funds; the state is another source of funding; and the federal government supplies a certain amount for each lunch served, and an additional amount for each free and reduced-price lunch. Finally, most students pay a certain amount for each meal. The income portion of the budget is basically a reflection of the number of meals served (student payments and the federal subsidy) and thus is similar to the sales item in a commercial operation, but in some cases additional sources of revenue may also be identified.

In health care, sales (except in the pay cafeteria) are not the determining figure for budgeting. That figure is, rather, some budgeted amount based on (1) the number of patient days expected and (2) the budgeted cost per patient-day for food service. Although sales, as such, are not the key, the starting point in the budget is the number of physical units that management expects will be consumed—a concept fundamentally quite similar to the sales estimate of a commercial operation.

Expense items in nonprofit budgets are prepared in much the same way as in the commercial sector—that is, they are based on past experience and adjusted for expected change. In some cases the expenses themselves are different. For instance, public institutions may receive commodities donated by the federal government. These donations change the cost of some items, but the budgeting procedure remains basically the same.

A budget should be the basis for management's cybernetic action: actual results are compared with budgeted results; variances from budget target are analyzed to determine causes; and corrective action is initiated.

DECISION ACCOUNTING

Both financial accounting and management accounting are basically cyclical and repetitive. Budgets, for instance, can be prepared monthly, quarterly, and annually. As a month elapses, statements of results are reflected on

TABLE 17.2   Mid-Town Restaurant Statement of Income and Expenses Year Ending December 31, 19XX

	$	%	
Sales			
Food	757,251	77.0	*848,000*
Beverage	226,507	23.0	*252,700*
Total	983,758	100.0	*1,100,700*
Cost of Sales			
Food	326,375	43.1	*356,100*
Beverage	61,116	27.0	*66,000*
Total	387,491	39.4	*422,100*
Gross Profit	596,267	60.6	*678,600*
Other Income	14,756	1.5	*66,000*
Total Income	611,023	62.1	*695,600*
Controllable Expense			
Payroll	252,286	25.6	*290,600*
Employee Benefits	46,237	4.7	*53,900*
Direct Operating Expenses	54,107	5.5	*60,500*
Music and Entertainment	5,902	.6	*6,600*
Advertising and Promotion	15,740	1.6	*17,600*
Utilities	20,659	2.1	*23,100*
Administrative and General	59,025	6.0	*66,000*
Repairs and Maintenance	16,724	1.7	*18,700*
Total	470,680	47.8	*537,000*
Income before Occupation Costs	140,343	14.3	*158,100*
Occupation Costs			
Rent, Property Taxes, and Insurance	45,253	4.6	*48,000*
Interest	5,998	.6	*5,000*
Depreciation	19,651	2.0	*19,600*
Total	70,902	7.2	*72,600*
Net Income before Other Deductions	69,441	7.1	*85,500*
Other Deductions	4,918	.5	*5,000*
Net Income before Taxes	64,523	6.6	*80,500*

accounting statements and compared with the budget. Then the whole cycle begins again next month.

Financial accounting statements, moreover, embody the conventions accepted by the accounting profession. For instance, when an asset is acquired, a *useful life* for that kind of an asset is assumed, and the cost of the item is *written off* via an accounting entry reflecting its depreciation. Thus, a motor hotel valued at $1 million with a 20-year useful life will charge $50,000 a year to depreciation on its accounting statements. At the end of five years, following accounting conventions, the motor hotel will be valued at $750,000. Quite clearly, these conventions are convenient and permit standard treatment (or one of several standard treatments) to be applied in a way that helps make the resulting accounting statement understandable to insiders and outsiders alike. However, although accounting conventions are necessary, they often distort what is really happening. For instance, if the motel just described has been bypassed by an expressway, its value may have dropped far more than the depreciation entry indicates; by contrast, if a new office park has been built across the street, the motel's value may have doubled instead of depreciating.

Decision accounting, sometimes called *strategic planning*, differs from financial and management accounting in that it is not cyclical. The information for a decision is assembled in numerical form on a one-time basis. Also, the conventions of accounting play no part in decision accounting. The assumptions made are those deemed appropriate to the analysis of the particular decision in hand. For instance, decision accounting tends to focus on direct variable costs such as food cost and payroll. It tends to ignore bookkeeping entries such as depreciation. Some examples of decision accounting—the payback period, rate of return, and break-even point computation—were presented in Chapter 14.

SUMMARY

Control is the means by which management measures performance, detects and analyzes variances, and initiates corrective action. In this context, we defined a cybernetic loop and gave an example of it, a cashier's report.

Most control is enabled through an information system of some sort, and we also illustrated this with some examples: food portion sizes, inspections of cleaned rooms, and patients' comments on hospital service.

We then enumerated the characteristics of control systems and examined the principal tools to achieve control: financial accounting and management accounting. In regard to managerial accounting, we discussed food and beverage cost control, payroll control, specialized controls, and budgeting. Finally we considered decision accounting.

KEY WORDS AND CONCEPTS

To help you review this chapter, keep in mind the following.

Cybernetic loop	Statement of income and expense
Information systems	Responsibility accounting
Control systems	Precosting
Financial accounting	Postcost control
Management accounting	Specialized controls
Balance sheet	Decision accounting

REVIEW QUESTIONS

1. What is a cybernetic loop? How is it used in connection with cash control.

2. Give some examples of information systems in the hospitality industry.

3. What are the four characteristics of a control system?

4. How is managerial accounting used in food and beverage costs?

5. Describe decision accounting.

C H A P T E R 18

Edward L. Miller/Stock, Boston.

LEADERSHIP AND THE DIRECTING FUNCTION IN HOSPITALITY MANAGEMENT

THE PURPOSE OF THIS CHAPTER

The most visible work the manager does is to function as the leader of the work group: giving orders and instructions to employees, checking employee performance, and commending or correcting that performance. This chapter describes this work first as a *function of worker needs* and then as a *function of the manager and his or her abilities*. We intend this chapter to help you develop a style of leadership that suits your personality.

THIS CHAPTER SHOULD HELP YOU

1. Explain the relationship of leadership and directing to the other work that managers do.

2. Discuss the various incentives that motivate people to accept direction.

3. Associate your thinking about leadership and directing to a coherent body of action-oriented theory so that you can continue the process of learning this crucial subject *after* you finish this course.

4. List the factors discussed in this chapter that inhibit and support communication in the workplace.

5. Describe the factors that underlie management authority and the kinds of behavior managers engage in when directing.

6. Develop your management style in a way that is flexible enough to meet the variety of situations you will encounter as a manager.

THE "CONCLUSIONS" OF SOCIAL SCIENCE RESEARCH

Management scholars and other social scientists have devoted a great deal of attention to the study of leadership. This attention is appropriate because leadership is clearly an important activity in what Peter Drucker calls "a society of institutions." Unfortunately these scholars have raised more questions than they have been able to answer to everyone's satisfaction. Indeed, one sometimes gets the impression that those in the knowledge industry who concern themselves with management earn a living by disproving one another's theories.

In fact, social science research models itself on the kinds of definitive, quantitative proofs found in the physical sciences, but it may never reach definitive conclusions about such subjective concepts as leadership. Fortunately, our purpose is less ambitious than that of scholars. To be sure, we want a theory that will guide practice, but we can accept some ambiguity in both our analysis of this subject and the conclusions we draw from it. Because leadership remains an "open subject" we all have a great deal more to learn about it.

Management scholars differentiate between *direction*—a management function—and *leadership,* which they see as largely a social function. As Harold Koontz and Cyril O'Donnel put it, "Leadership is generally defined simply as influence, the art or process of influencing people so that they will strive willingly toward the achievement of group goals."[1] They have suggested that subordinates will respond to authority alone to do some bare minimum to maintain their jobs. But "to raise effort toward total capability, the manager must induce devoted response on the part of subordinates by exercising leadership."[2]

This distinction between authority and leadership is theoretically valid, but it does little to guide practice. Implicitly, managers lead when they simply direct. If the leadership is effective, the results will be raised above the minimum; if it is ineffective, the results will remain at some minimal norm or may even be pushed below a norm by personal antagonism.

As a practical matter, however, a manager's act of directing can never be separated from his or her leadership. Thus, we will use the terms interchangeably: when we use the word *direction,* we imply *leadership,* because, for better or worse, it is always present and in action.

[1]Harold Koontz and Cyril O'Donnel, *Management: A System and Contingency Analysis of Managerial Functions,* 6th ed. (New York: McGraw-Hill, 1976), p. 587.
[2]Koontz and O'Donnel, *Management,* p. 587.

Although social science research has not proved very much about leadership and directing, it has given us numerous insights into the process, and it has identified the key factors that managers must take into account as they go about building their leadership style. A brief review of some of these conclusions is useful in itself; moreover, it will help round out your understanding of the other management functions.

LEADERSHIP IS BASED ON THE OTHER MANAGEMENT FUNCTIONS

Perhaps the clearest way to show how closely the management functions are interrelated is to try to imagine leading without fulfilling the other functions. The results would be at once chaotic, dictatorial, and apathetic.

Without planning, work becomes chaotic. The order in which things are to be done, the quality of work deemed acceptable, and how much work must be done all would be determined by individual judgment and on the spur of the moment. The manager would be reduced to direction based on guess, and only the simplest or most stable operations would survive. Consider, as an example, the problems of staffing and staff planning: without a clear plan of the work to be done, and a plan that provides the right people to do it, an operation would be paralyzed.

Without organization—without some reasonable and coherent means of structuring authority relationships so that the work gets done—the authority of the strongest (power) becomes the only basis for directing. This is never the best approach to directing in any society, and it simply will not work in our affluent, educated society. In any case, only small and simple enterprises can operate on this authoritarian basis. We occasionally see operations in which direction is based solely on the authority of the owner ("Do it or I'll fire you"), but the employees rarely stay there for long.

Without control, employees begin to believe that nobody cares because nobody detects and corrects deviations from standards. Employees become apathetic about standards. Without feedback, no organism (let alone human employees) can learn. Once again, we are reduced to a chaos in which nobody really knows what to do or who is in charge.

Clearly then, your leadership must be informed by understanding the plans of your organization as well as the plans you make for yourself. Moreover, leadership must be exercised within the bounds of authority, implicit or explicit, in an organization. Finally, you must base your continuing acts of leadership on both measures of your own performance and the performance of the units and the people under your direction.

WHY PEOPLE FOLLOW

People enter an organization and perform their work, stipulated by a manager with definite plans, for several good reasons, all of them selfish. Un-

derstanding in a general way what people expect from their work will permit
you to base your directing activities on their needs and wants. This understanding is the essence of leadership. Our subject in this section, then, is
really *motivation*. You will come to understand employees' motives first
through study and observation and later, as a new manager, through practice. This growing understanding will permit you to shape your management
activities to reflect the motives of the people working with you.

NECESSITY AS WORK MOTIVATION

The time-honored and most basic reason that people work is to provide
themselves and their dependents with food, shelter, and clothing. When human labor was in excess supply and society's attitude was less protective of
the disadvantaged, this motive was indeed powerful. When the alternative
was between work and starvation, the threat of a job loss was terrifying, and
this fear maintained a society based on wages.

Economic and social policy in our society today has greatly eroded the
power of an employer. To be fired or laid off is certainly an inconvenience
and may often involve severe hardship. But economic policy in most Western countries is committed to maintaining high employment levels. Moreover, unemployment compensation provides sufficient income to stave off
disaster, and the government employment service facilitates placement in
another job. Thus, the manager's threat to fire (which would, in any case,
be a last resort, as Chapter 12 suggests) has much greater limitations as a
motivator than it did in earlier times.

ADVANTAGE AS WORK MOTIVATION

In a positive way, people seek not just enough money to live but also an
income to satisfy the many aspirations now taken for granted in an affluent
society. Thus people work not only for money but also for "more money."
Many employees are motivated to work harder to keep a good job, to gain a
raise, or to earn a bonus.

As ambitious people repeatedly demonstrate, workers will often put
forth extra effort to secure promotion in rank. They do this not only for the
increased income but often for the increased social status as well. We are
social animals, and once we have taken care of our basic life supports, we
begin to pursue socially recognized rewards other than money. Not everyone, however, chooses to pursue such goals at work. Rather, recognition in
their other reference groups—family, church, neighborhood, fraternal organizations—may be more important to them. Thus, personal ambition often,
but not universally, spurs increased effort at work.

PERSONAL SATISFACTION AS WORK MOTIVATION

We all know people who love their work, and work hard because they enjoy
what they do. Such people may include the chef whose whole life is centered

on preparing delicious food, the hostess or waitress who enjoys her contacts with people so much she seems to bubble, or (significantly) the mentally handicapped dishwasher who is devoted to his or her work. In some cases, the work itself may not be so interesting, but the job may provide other rewards of a social nature. For example, many people enjoy coming to work because that is where their friends are.

INDEPENDENCE AS WORK MOTIVATION

Many people are motivated toward self-direction and independence. The idea of "being your own boss" as a unit manager entices many managers and employees. Waitresses and cooks often find that an important part of their work satisfaction is that they are good enough at what they do to require almost no direct supervision. But this is by no means a universal motivation. Hardly anyone wants a work situation in which he or she is "hassled," but not everyone seeks independence. Some prefer or need clear company (or work group) norms and the frequent encouragement to achieve them. Indeed, for many employees, encouragement, praise, and personal recognition outweigh independence as motivation.

ENCOURAGEMENT, PRAISE, AND RECOGNITION AS WORK MOTIVATION

We have to recognize that many unskilled jobs in our industry are filled by people who find the work itself dull and unrewarding. But we can do a great deal to reduce that dullness by fostering a friendly climate at work, praising good performances, and recognizing the worker as a person who makes an important contribution. We set unrealistic goals, however, if we expect everyone to respond warmly to these managerial efforts. In the final analysis, people are hired to do a job, not to be cheerful. (Of course, being cheerful should be a part of public contact.) It is much more pleasant for everyone if workers are happy in their work, but the essential need is to have the work done according to the approved standards.

MONEY AS WORK MOTIVATION

Social science research has focused largely on the significance of nonmonetary rewards. But that research also provides ample evidence that pay is important. Money is, of course, an economic reward, but workers and managers often see it as a form of social recognition as well. For some people, a fancy title is important, whether a young manager is called "assistant vice-president" or the dishwashers are renamed "sanitation specialists." Most people, however, expect and want monetary rewards for superior effort.

COMPANY POLICY AS WORK MOTIVATION

Company policy regarding such important matters as fringe benefits and working conditions can be an extremely important motivator. Some social scientists maintain that these conditions are taken for granted by workers. They argue that their absence would cause dissatisfaction but that their presence is not positively motivating. In the hospitality companies I have studied, however, it seems clear that these factors are important positive forces for the long-term employees, for those who stay with the company. Because these loyal employees are especially valuable, we should view company policies as important motivators in our industry.

Fringe benefits include, among other things, vacation; sick leave; paid holidays; free or reduced-price employee meals; uniforms; group health, accident, and life insurance; educational benefits; and pension plans. Of course, some fringe benefits, such as social security and unemployment insurance, are required by law. Fringe benefits took their name originally from the fact that they were a minor part—only the "fringes"—of an employee's compensation. Today, however, fringe benefits account for up to one-third of some employers' wage bills. As they become a more significant part of compensation, employees consider them in choosing which jobs to take and, especially, in deciding whether to stay with an employer or to change jobs.

Working conditions is a term that refers to both the physical and the social aspects of the work place. One employer may offer an air-conditioned, clean, well-lighted kitchen, employee lockers and restrooms, and an adequate employee dining area. The employee who can choose will prefer this place (other things being equal) to a hot, dingy work place where the employee's personal belongings are unprotected and where he or she must take meal breaks in a remote corner or eat standing up.

Similarly, people prefer to work in a friendly environment in which they feel accepted and respected by their coworkers and by management. People generally like to work with other people much like themselves. This means that the employee selection process should take into account whether or not a prospective employee is likely to fit in and to accept the kind of work and interpersonal norms management and the work group expect.

Our discussion to this point suggests many different motives for working. An operation that recognizes that the motives for working vary from one worker to another will train its managers to respond to each worker as an individual. This means not only respecting the individuality of each worker but also shaping a manager's directing activities as much as possible to call forth the best effort from each worker.

DOES "HAPPINESS" LEAD TO PRODUCTIVITY?

Morale is the attitude a worker or work group feels or expresses toward the work. But young managers often assume, incorrectly, that if morale is high, the work will automatically go well. In fact, research results find little direct correlation between high morale in the workplace and productivity. People may be happy at work and spend a good deal of their effort visiting with one another and in other ways expressing their happiness instead of working.

Certainly, then, a manager's efforts to improve morale must include a clear expression of quality and quantity work standards. Just as we cannot expect every worker to be cheerful, we cannot settle for cheerfulness in place of adequate work.

In service organizations, however, employee morale (attitude and outlook) may be more important than it is in most other work. An employee with "guest contact" can hardly separate his or her attitude from the work, because work effectiveness depends on his or her manner toward the guests. The guests, in turn, do not recognize the physical service (a waitress brings the food) as separate from the way that service is performed (with a smile and a friendly word or with a frown and a snarl).

Moreover, employees in service systems are highly interdependent. Therefore, at least one criterion for acceptable employee performance has to be an ability to work with others. An irritable, unpleasant employee in a key position—whether or not the position deals with customers—can upset the other employees. If employees are irritated with one another, that irritation is bound to be sensed by the guest. So employee morale is especially important in service organizations.

LEADERSHIP THEORIES

THEORY X AND THEORY Y

Douglas MacGregor suggested that there are two different ways in which we can look at workers' attitudes toward work.[3] Each of these views, which MacGregor labeled *Theory X* and *Theory Y,* has implications for management.

Theory X

According to Theory X, people do not really like to work, and so they must be "coerced, controlled, directed, threatened with punishment" in order to get them to work. The average worker, this theory argues, avoids responsibility, is unambitious, and wants security more than anything else.

Management based on Theory X is paternalistic at best and, at the very least, authoritarian. Rewards and punishment, the "carrot and stick," are assumed in this theory to be the key to employee productivity.

Theory Y

In contrast with Theory X is a more generous view of human nature. It sees "physical and mental effort in work to be as natural as play or rest," and it

---

[3]Douglas MacGregor, *The Human Side of Enterprise* (New York: McGraw-Hill, 1960).

recognizes self-direction instead of external control as the principal means of securing effort. According to Theory Y, under the proper conditions people will, indeed, accept and even seek responsibility. Employees have (says Theory Y) a much greater capability for problem solving than most organizations realize.

Management based on Theory Y relies on a worker's achievement-oriented motives and his or her desire for self-fulfillment rather than on sheer managerial authority. Theory Y calls for developing organizations in which employees can best fulfill their goals by working toward the success of the organization.

Who's Right?

The best answers to the question, Who's right? are "both of them" or "it depends." The question addresses but does not answer the central problem of management in a democratic society. Although we don't have any absolute and final answers, we can identify and consider the issues better in the light of the two theories just discussed.

THREE IMPORTANT ELEMENTS OF MODERN LEADERSHIP

To exercise leadership in our modern society you must understand the nature of authority, both formal and informal, and the realistic limits on managers' use of authority. One of the most important limits on authority is the psychology of the individual worker, and an equally strong factor is that of informal group pressures. Leadership, then, is a result of the interaction of authority with the limits placed on management action by the psychology of the individual worker and the work group.

Authority

Authority in organizations is based on legal rights derived from business ownership and, in subsidized, governmental organizations, from legislative acts. A somewhat different kind of authority may be conferred on a leader by a group because through social effectiveness, this person impresses the group as an ideal leader.

We see, then, the crucial distinction between a *formal leader* and an *informal leader*. The formal leader is in charge because of legal rights. Nevertheless, the formal leader can and should seek to supplement this legal authority with recognition by the group of his or her professional competence. A formal leader may also win acceptance as the group's informal leader or, more commonly, establish a productive relationship with the informal group structure.

An informal leader exercises a more subtle but very real kind of influence. Effective managers strive to work whenever possible with the person or persons that a group chooses (more or less unconsciously) as leader.

Authority is accompanied by the right and ability to reward or punish.

Setting standards is an important part of leadership. (Photo courtesy of The National Restaurant Association.)

Although MacGregor and others see modern business relying less and less on formal authority, nobody expects it to disappear. But to get results, authority must be tempered, in a relatively affluent society, in both substance and style. Your directing must be as fair as you can make it, and you should issue your directions in a manner that does not offend. Workers these days have many options, and employee turnover is too expensive to permit indulgence in arbitrary or offensive directing behavior. Theory X may not be altogether wrong, but certainly it is no longer enough.

The Psychology of the Worker—and the Work

The strength of Theory Y is in recognizing that many workers attempt to achieve personal goals and to find self-fulfillment in their work. For these workers, a clear communication of the organization's standards and goals during their training period is the most welcome form of direction. Workers who perfectly fit this pattern are not as common in our industry as we could wish, but persons who come close and require a minimum of supervision are not hard to find. The manager who is secure in his or her own competence will avoid unnecessary supervision and the appearance of harassment without losing sight of the need to assert the organization's standards when necessary.

A word about praise may be in order here. Most people thrive on encouragement, but praise is difficult to bestow graciously and may be subject to inflation. If an employee is competent and hardworking, a pat on the back from the manager may look like condescension. When you say, "You're doing a good job, Jane," she may say (to herself), "I know that. Who asked you?" Moreover, just as too much money in an economic system can lead to inflation and devalued currency, praise given too often and too easily loses its value.

The best kind of praise is your respect for the worker and your appreciation of work well done. This respect and appreciation usually comes through in consulting with workers and in attending to their advice, solicited or unsolicited. This attention makes what *they do,* not what *you say,* important.

The work that people do may not really be important to them. For instance, a part-time waitress who sees herself principally as a wife, a mother, and a member of the PTA and her church group is unlikely to see her work as her principal means of self-fulfillment, even though she may take considerable pride in that work. Motivating her will thus require a different approach from, for instance, your boss's approach to motivating you, an ambitious, rising manager.

People in many unskilled jobs, such as dishwashers, simply do not find the satisfaction that Theory Y suggests they should be receiving. For that to happen we need to redesign our organizations—and society itself, for that matter. Although such a grand redesigning is an interesting subject, it goes beyond the scope of this chapter and, to be frank, the realistic limits of hospitality managers today.

The Work Group As a Social Unit

Leadership and directing must utilize the authority that a manager derives from the formal organization, and it must take into account the various individual motivations—from pay to praise to self-fulfillment—normally found within a work group made up of individual employees. A third significant force is the work group itself as a social unit. When people come together to work, they develop a social organization with its own leadership, its own norms of work and social conduct, and, very often, a cliquish structure.

In a waitress work group, for instance, managers find strong feelings about how work should be distributed (including the number of guests that should be seated in a station). Some restaurants actually use a *turn system* in which each waitress serves a party seated at her station in rotation. The object is to be sure each waitress gets a fair share of the business. Variations from the order of turns can create a great deal of trouble for a supervisor.

In practice, some waitresses can handle more parties than others can.

Following the turn system can, therefore, hold back the more able waitress and place some guests at stations in which a slower waitress is actually overloaded. The result is that the fast waitress may seek another employer and the guest who gets stuck with an overloaded, slow waitress may seek another restaurant. The turn system of seating, however, is most significant as an example of the power of a work group over a weak or indifferent management.

In responding to the norms that workers develop among themselves, no manager should surrender the formal authority inherent in the position. But neither can a manager afford to ignore a force as strong as social pressure. Perhaps the best way to deal with this force is exemplified by an incident from my experience as a manager dealing with an informal work group leader:

> When they encounter the person whom a work group has chosen (very informally, sometimes subconsciously) as their leader, many managers regard that person as a threat to their authority. But an alternative way to approach the situation is to view the informal group leader as a communication link to the work group. When I was a young manager, I met a waitress, Ethel, who was an unusually competent person and had the respect of all the other waitresses. At one point I wanted to fire her. But the man I worked for just laughed and said I could fire her "when you've learned what she knows." It took me a good deal of time to find out that if I *consulted* Ethel instead of ordering her, I could get not only her cooperation but often some good advice. Building on this realization, I found that instead of announcing "policy," I could discuss a problem or goal with Ethel, indicating what I thought but remaining open to her reactions. Generally, the results of our discussions would make the rounds and, in a few days, become adopted as policy both by the house *and* the waitresses—without any fuss. Moreover, the new policy carried force because it has been accepted voluntarily. Also, my own role as the formal leader was reinforced by my acceptance of the work group's social values.

Within the larger work groups, subgroups or cliques often form. Sometimes relations between these cliques are friendly or neutral; sometimes they become unfriendly or downright hostile. Management cannot do away with clique formation, but knowledgeable managers can arrange their directing activities so that they take these strong forces into consideration.

We do not present these few words on the informal group as a full discussion of this complex subject. Rather, we intend to offer only a few examples to illustrate the meaning of this third force bearing on the manager's directing and leading activities.[4] This discussion sets a useful background, too, for the subject of worker participation in management.

---

[4]An excellent discussion of this subject is found in George C. Homans, *The Human Group* (New York: Harcourt Brace & World, 1950).

PARTICIPATION

In a democratic society composed of educated and relatively affluent workers, the influence of the worker and the work group is increasing. But this increase in power need not be seen as a threat to management. A manager secure enough to invite and accept participation in decision making can harness strong forces for obtaining results. The level of worker participation, however, may vary with the circumstances.

Information

Keeping employees informed about matters that affect their work represents only the minimum level of consideration for a prudent manager. Employees whose assignments must be changed deserve an adequate explanation of what changes are to be made and why they must be made. When changes affect an entire group, the group should receive enough information to understand what is going on. Many managers use regular staff and department meetings to accomplish this function.

Consultation

Before a decision must be made, a manager can prevent hard feelings by consulting the workers who will be affected by that decision, as well as others who are knowledgeable in the area. Because of their familiarity with the activity in question, workers often see problems that managers may miss. Technical issues aside, this consultation often eases tensions associated with change and increases its chances of acceptance. As the previous section suggests, it is particularly important to consult workers who have the respect of their fellow workers and whose support may be crucial in gaining acceptance. Consultation in traditional management systems should not be viewed as relinquishing management's responsibility and authority for decisions based on the prerogatives of ownership or some other legally constituted authority.

Involvement

Managers often see a problem, develop a variety of solutions with the workers, and then present these alternatives to the employees themselves for *their* decision. If the first solution they choose does not work, further discussion and change are obviously in order. But often the best way to gain acceptance of change is to involve those affected in the decision. Moreover, the solution to some problems probably belongs to and should be undertaken by the work group.

Thus, for instance, a group of waitresses may be asked to help management develop the best means for assigning side work (housekeeping chores in the dining room such as stocking side stands or filling salt and pepper shakers). Management cannot really ask whether or not this work should be done; it must be done. The issue is how; and implicitly, if the solution offered does not work in practice, management must confer again with the affected workers and arrive at another solution.

COMMUNICATIONS

For directions to be followed, they must be understood. The best thought-out plan will fail if it is not communicated in a way that can be comprehended.

BARRIERS TO COMMUNICATIONS

Factors that inhibit clear communication pertain to the language we use, the differing backgrounds of the sender and the receiver, and the circumstances in which the communication takes place.

Semantic Barriers

Different people attach different meanings to words. The phrase *my work* may have quite a different meaning to a manager and to a busboy. To one, it refers to a life's work; to the other, a part-time job after school. The word *management* also conjures up different images for the manager and busboy. To the manager, it may mean "responsible execution of carefully studied company policy." By contrast, the busboy may think of the fact that "the boss docked my pay because I was late." A communicator must, therefore, choose words that convey the meaning of the sender in such a way that the receiver understands that meaning. *Loaded words* with strong emotional meanings—*free enterprise, the system, right to work*—may do more to confuse than to clarify discussion.

Social Background

Social background is closely related to the problem just considered. The values of the middle-class American, the background typical among managers, carry certain assumptions that may not strike the expected response among employees. A good example is the idea of ambition.

People brought up in middle-class families that encourage striving for success take ambition for granted. By contrast, people raised in poverty, who have acquired only limited schooling and who see themselves as "never having had a chance," may look at ambition quite differently. When the middle-class manager assumes, as he or she communicates, that the pot washer shares this enthusiasm for achievement, the manager may be in for some unpleasant surprises. It is important to consider exactly where (in the current vernacular) the other person "is coming from."

Immediate Environment

The place where communication occurs can have an important effect on what gets understood. If a worker has been late, calling that person into the office to discuss the tardiness may be taken as a signal of a serious offense. If that signal is appropriate, fine; but if the tardiness is a first offense, it may be better to mention the matter to the worker privately in the immediate work area at a time when he or she is not busy.

On the other hand, a reprimand in front of other workers has quite a powerful impact. (There's an old and good rule to remember: praise in public, reprimand in private.) Similarly, discussion of complicated matters at the wrong time results in confusion. Let's suppose the broiler operator asked you about a problem on his or her W-2 form at a time when you couldn't answer and you said, "I'll get back to you later." To try to answer that question in the middle of the rush hour when he or she is under considerable pressure will probably inhibit understanding and increase annoyance.

GATEWAYS TO COMMUNICATION

Listening

Curiously, one of the most important acts in telling somebody something is for *you* to listen. Communication is not a one-way street; it is an interchange. When you speak to people, they reply either in words or with *body language*—the way they hold themselves, the look on their faces, a shrug of the shoulders. Listening and observing these body language cues will tell you a great deal about how your message has been received.

Empathy

Your ability to put yourself in the other person's shoes in a conversation can be crucial to understanding and dealing with his or her reaction.

ELEMENTS OF LEADING AND DIRECTING

Leading and directing are really continuous processes, but we can break them down into some key activities in which managers typically engage. In fact, the actions (or elements) we discuss here portray the diversity of leading and directing and how they can vary from situation to situation. They include (1) telling someone what to do, (2) providing information on how to do it, (3) seeing that he or she has learned how to do it, (4) making the performance of the work as appealing and comfortable as possible, and (5) conferring specific rewards or punishments for performance. Now we will examine these elements of leading and directing in more detail.

Communication skills are the backbone of a manager's work. (Photo courtesy of W.R. Grace.)

1. Orders obviously tell someone to do something. They are acts of authority—authoritative directions.

2. Instruction provides information, for our purposes, about some food service work-related activity.

3. Training involves guiding employees toward the mastery of often complex activities. Thus, a manager may give new employees a week's training to qualify her or him to begin work as a waitress or waiter. Properly executed, training involves not only telling and showing the trainees how to do the work but also evaluating later—for the benefit of both the trainees and trainer—the quality of that learning. Trainees are permitted to do the work under supervision and to repeat the process until they achieve an adequate mastery.

4. Motivating moves beyond ensuring that the worker knows how to do something; motivating makes the employee eager, or at least willing, to do the work. A manager who motivates employees tailors the whole array of inducements—pay, recognition and status, self-fulfillment—in

a way appropriate to the needs and wants of each worker (within, of course, the limits of what is possible).

5. Sanctions may be either positive or negative, rewards or punishments. Although motivation generally may be thought of as continuous and positive, individual acts of sanction can be either a raise or promotion on the one hand, or a fine or reprimand on the other.

If a manager has done his or her job correctly, the employees will know what to do and how to do it, and they will have a sufficient mastery of the work to accomplish it properly. Managers must continually respond to the individual needs and wants of workers in order to gain their willing commitment to work. Finally, managers are expected to recognize outstanding performance and, when necessary, to penalize those who do not perform adequately.

DEVELOPING YOUR OWN LEADERSHIP STYLE

As we have seen, a manager's leadership role in directing the work ultimately stems from his or her formal authority. In this role, a manager takes account of the individual worker and work to be done and interacts productively with the informal social group structure that inevitably emerges in work groups. In fact, then, leadership is not an inflexible behavior pattern. Leadership styles will vary from situation to situation and place to place. If you are a junior manager just out of training and working with a group of senior workers, you will conduct yourself more tentatively than you might later as general manager dealing with a similar group. If your employees' work is exciting and highly profitable, as might be the case for a waitress group in a top-flight restaurant yielding generous tips, your leadership conduct might be different from what it would be toward the night cleanup crew that arrives as the restaurant is closing.

The dictionary provides several meanings for the word *style*. One of the meanings is a synonym for fashion—the way "everybody" is doing something. But when we speak of management style, we certainly do not mean the current fashion. The definition that suits our needs better is the manner or tone assumed in discourse. The way leadership is carried out reflects in important ways the person who does the leading. Some leaders are flamboyant and confident; others more reserved and (at least at first) unsure. The important point is that leadership in our industry is not some mysterious thing one is born with or without. Rather, it is a set of learned abilities. As people's personalities differ, so each person is likely to behave differently in directing the work of others. The difference, however, is usually in style, in manner and tone, not in substance. The basic goal of directing, as in all management functions, is achieving the desired results.

It will be up to you, finally, to determine how you best achieve results. But your success will depend not only on the strength of your formal position, on the workers and work you direct, and on the work group, but also on who you are and what manner and tone, what style, works best for you in the situations you face.

You can begin to form your leadership style now, and you should. In field experiences, summer jobs, and part-time employment, you can observe the management style of others, even though you may not at first be given managerial responsibility. You can analyze the situation that managers confront and the people in those situations. Then you can decide for yourself how well you think situations are handled; how they might be handled better; and how you might feel most comfortable in handling similar situations.

You should certainly consider the process of learning to act as a leader and directing the work of others as continuous and lifelong. The most accomplished artists, after years of practice, will still speak of how much they have left to learn. Management, as it is implemented by individual managers, is definitely an art based on understanding and practice. It is a fascinating art one can learn through both study and practice. The fascination can last a lifetime, and the process has already begun for you.

SUMMARY

First we defined leadership, differentiated it from direction, and explained the reasons that it is important.

Our second subject was people's motivations for working: necessity; advantage; personal satisfaction; independence; encouragement, praise, and recognition; money; and company policy. This led us to consider whether happiness, or high morale, results in high productivity.

There are many theories of leadership. We discussed MacGregor's Theory X and Theory Y, plus three elements of modern leadership: authority, psychology of the worker, and the work group. Worker participation was also described as important.

Good communication between managers and workers is important as well, and so we talked about possible barriers (semantic, social background, and immediate environment) and possible gateways (listening and empathy).

The last topic was an enumeration and description of the elements of leading and directing, as well as ways to develop your own leadership style.

KEY WORDS AND CONCEPTS

To help you review this chapter, keep in mind the following:

Direction
Leadership
Motivation
Fringe benefits
Working conditions
Morale
Theory X

Theory Y
Formal leader
Informal leader
Work group
Cliques
Leadership style

REVIEW QUESTIONS

1. What is the difference between leadership and direction?

2. Describe what would happen at a Burger King *without* leadership.

3. List and briefly discuss the motivations for working.

4. How do theory X and theory Y fit with *your* management style—or intended style? Would you lean toward X or Y or some other position.

5. Describe an informal work group to which you have belonged.

6. Describe a manager or boss you have admired, and explain why.

7. Do you think you would be a good leader? Why or why not?

"Courtesy of Holliday Inns, Inc."

MARKETING IN THE HOSPITALITY INDUSTRY

THE PURPOSE OF THIS CHAPTER

In Chapter 13 we explored marketing as a way of thought that has had a profound effect on how North Americans see management. Now we turn to a more detailed look at this subject as a management activity that will have even greater importance in the intensely competitive hospitality industry of the late 1980s and the 1990s. Although your career may not lead to responsibility for marketing planning or even for carrying out promotion activities, marketing in the hospitality industry is so closely allied to and dependent on operations management that every hospitality manager should have an understanding of the concepts of marketing. This chapter focuses heavily on a customer orientation of the hospitality industry and on an appropriate marketing mix.

THIS CHAPTER SHOULD HELP YOU

1. Identify the three most common points of view regarding marketing.
2. Describe in detail the elements of the marketing mix and tell how they are used in the hospitality industry.
3. Define the product–service mix and the benefit bundle.
4. Understand the importance of service strategy to hospitality marketing.
5. State the significance of location and physical plant layout in hospitality marketing.

6.   Identify the bases for a pricing policy.
7.   Define the three elements of promotion.

WHAT IS MARKETING?

There are at least three ways of thinking about the problem of getting a product to the consumer. First is the notion, popular early in this century, that the key to success in business is to build a good product. Sometimes referred to as a *product orientation,* this point of view is summed up in the maxim, "If you build a better mousetrap, the world will beat a pathway to your door." This way of thinking about business probably came down to us from the artisan tradition of preindustrial society, in which products were made in small numbers by highly skilled craftsmen. Many older restaurants have followed this approach—some of them successfully. The problem is, though, that these operators often base their definitions of the consumers' needs and wants on their own opinions and convictions. As consumers, food costs, product availability, labor costs, skilled labor availability, and other variables change, these restaurants' once-successful formulas are repeatedly put to the test in a market of exploding change.

A second way of approaching the problem is a *sales orientation.* This approach defines the business largely in terms of sales effort. The product available is "what we have," and the key is to "get out and sell." But in the hotel industry, many properties that adopt this approach, for all the competence of their sales staffs, ultimately change hands or close their doors. Selling, ultimately, is based on satisfying the guest.

As we saw in Chapter 13, the marketing concept entails defining our business in terms of the customers' needs and wants and reasoning from these to a product. We can restate our definition of marketing in this way:

> Marketing is determining the customers' needs and wants, providing product and service combinations that fill those needs, making the product and service available in a way that is convenient for the guests, pricing the offering in a way that makes it possible to recover both costs and a target profit, and communicating the offer to potential buyers in a way that motivates them to buy.

Boston's Copley Plaza seemed destined to suffer the fate of many other outmoded hotels, when the property changed hands and an enterprising management team began by asking themselves, "What kind of lodging customers do we have in Boston, and what do they want?" They looked at a variety of markets—tourists, airline crews, and cost-conscious government employees, to name three potential markets that management decided to

Boston's Copley Plaza has used its "grand hotel" style to pursue the high-income, free-spending guest. (Photo courtesy of the Copley Plaza.)

pass by. Instead of these, the Copley Plaza team decided to take advantage of the hotel's excellent location and its elegant, if badly faded, "Grand Hotel" style and to pursue the high-expense account and wealthy professional market.

With a fairly clear idea of who its customers were and what that clientele wanted, the Copley Plaza management plunged into a remodeling that recaptured the property's opulence in facilities and especially in food service. The result was increased occupancy, substantially higher rates, and, of course, much improved profits.

The moral of this story is pointed—and important. The customers' needs and wants are the starting point in the marketing process.

Marketing students quickly become familiar with the interrelated activities referred to as the *marketing mix*—often called the four *P*s. Figure 19.1 suggests a simplified application of the four *P*s to the hospitality industry.

A first observation about this mix is that it does (or should) also apply to nonprofit operations. Clients in congregate feeding or young people in

Product and Service	Dictated by guest needs and wants
Place	Make available through location and physical facility
Price	Recapture costs plus profit
Promotion	Communicate to consumers to motivate purchase

FIGURE 19.1   The four *P*s of the marketing mix in the hospitality industry.

school lunch—to take just two examples—deserve to be given products (and services) that are designed in terms of their needs and that are conveniently available to them.

Another observation we ought to make is that the word *mix* is used deliberately. The marketing mix requires blending the elements correctly. As with a recipe, if one of the ingredients is left out, used in the wrong proportion, or not combined properly with the others, the outcome will not be what we had sought.

Clearly, the development of a marketing mix requires all of the management disciplines we have already studied. The mix is basically a strategic operating *plan* that, among other things, must fix *organizational* responsibility for carrying out the operational aspects of the plan. Especially in regard to the service aspect of what we have to sell, *staffing* is a key factor in implementing a marketing plan. An important aspect of an ongoing marketing program is evaluation, for which the reports routinely developed as a part of the *management control* system are generally used. Finally, in executing the operational aspects of the program, the *leadership* provided to the staff by management is crucial at all levels. Thus, marketing involves all of the functions of management. It is a management process that is central to business success in our generation.

BEGIN WITH THE CONSUMER

If marketing begins with the consumer, that is the logical place for us to start looking at marketing in detail. We can look at the consumer collectively—that is, at the firm's social environment—and we can look at the consumer in individual terms.

THE ENVIRONMENT OF THE FIRM

Marketing is carried on in a social environment that really comprises a totality of all consumers. Aggregate measures of the consumer such as population trends or demographics are important. We noted in earlier chapters, for instance, the impact of the growing numbers of middle-aged people and people over 65 on the demand for both food service and lodging.

Another aspect of the consumer environment reflects the economy. When consumers lack confidence—for instance, when the country is in a recession that consumers fear is about to get worst—they will be in an exceptionally tight-fisted mood, and marketing planning must take account of that viewpoint. On the other hand, in good times when consumer confidence is strong, people are most willing to spend their money.

Two important measures of the economic environment that market planners (and everybody else!) will follow in the 1990s are income and inflation. When incomes were growing rapidly, that growth was widely credited as a major factor supporting hospitality industry growth, particularly in food service. On the other hand, recessionary periods are clearly associated with slow growth for eating out, or even a decline, together with a serious drop in lodging sales. Flat or negligible growth will make the hospitality marketer's job harder.

Inflation tends to distort relative prices. Food costs may rise sharply or labor rates may forge ahead, causing price rises in food service to exceed those of food at home and of other competitive leisure services. Moreover, inflation eats away at families' disposable incomes, thus reducing their *ability* to spend, and undermining their confidence, thus reducing their *willingness* to spend.

THE INDIVIDUAL CONSUMER

Professor Leo Renaghan of the Cornell Hotel School has suggested two major reasons that understanding individual consumer behavior is important:

1. If a firm does not know and understand the decision process that the consumer uses, it will not know where the efforts of the firm should be directed.
   a. Where should the advertising budget be spent?
   b. What information does the consumer need about a product and service?
   c. Who makes the buying decision?
   d. When should advertisements be placed?
2. You cannot modify a consumer's behavior unless you understand his decision process. This is especially important

a.   When the firm is entering a new market.

b.   When competition in an established market heats up.[1]

Problem Solving

Research on consumer behavior suggests that the consumer follows a problem-solving process such as the one illustrated in Figure 19.2. Consumers must first recognize a difference between their present situation and some other state. When they are aware of alternatives that they would prefer, they are likely to seek information so as to evaluate those alternatives. Significantly, consumers do not typically evaluate all alternatives. For instance, they do not choose among all the restaurants in town, but from a smaller group, called the *evoked set,* usually three to five restaurants.

In the final state, consumers decide on their choice. Interestingly, the period right after the decision is a crucial one, especially in regard to major purchases. The condition of the guest at that point is sometimes referred to as *postpurchase anxiety.* After paying a substantial deposit, for instance, a family may wonder whether they've chosen the right resort after all. This is a good time to offer a customer some reassurance, perhaps just a cheerful flyer from the resort detailing the activities for the week they will be there.

Information Sources

Market research often relies on highly sophisticated research design, but that is beyond our concern here. We should note, however, that much useful information can be obtained from the operation itself or from simple observation. For instance, in-house sales records should give information on typical party size (number of guests in a group), the average check, and the relative popularity of menu items. Guest comment cards can also yield useful information, especially if they are handed out at the cash desk rather than just left on the table to be used or not according to the guest's impulse.

FIGURE 19.2   Consumer problem-solving process.

[1]Adapted from Leo Renaghan, "Consumer Behavior: The Forgotten Variable in Marketing," in *Proceedings of the Hospitality Leaders Conference* (Guelph, Ont.: School of Hotel and Food Administration, 1981), p. 144. The material in the following section has been adapted from pp. 143–154.

Market segmentation relies on distinctive characteristics such as age, family, status, and ethnicity. Sometimes appeals are designed to reach multiple segments. (Photos courtesy of Wendy's.)

MARKET SEGMENTS

In the chapters on the restaurant and hotel business we discussed companies that identified particular segments and shaped their product and service to that segment of the market. Residence Inns, for instance, designed its inns to serve the long-stay market. We saw, too, how by means of salad bars, Wendy's sought more business from women. The key to customer-based marketing planning is to identify those segments of the market that the company wishes to serve and then to meet their particular requirements.

Bases for Segmentation

The particular needs and preferences of customers in target segments are used to develop marketing strategies in areas such as product design, pricing, and promotion. In actual practice, segmentation draws on very sophisticated market research tools. We will, however, confine our discussion to the most common bases for segmentation: geographic, demographic, psychographic, and behavioristic.

Geographic.   In the hospitality industry, because of the importance of location, geography, is an important variable. The needs of different areas can be quite different. Early in the development of the motor hotel in the southeastern United States, for instance, the use of exterior corridors offered important savings in construction that resulted in lower room rates. When this inexpensive construction format was brought north, however, the guests' reactions in the cold winters led most operators to change to the more comfortable interior corridor.

Demographic. Demographic variables are objective, measurable variables such as age, sex, and family size. Another variable, family life-cycle stage, has a substantial effect on recreational activities. For instance, recall our discussion of ownership of recreational vehicles, in which we noted that tent campers and truck-top campers predominate among younger families with children, whereas the more expensive RVs were preferred by older families who no longer had children at home and thus were freed of a major demand on their income. Allied with this example is another demographic variable, income. The families that had the most expensive RVs were, not surprisingly, from the upper income group. Other demographic variables include occupation, education, religion, nationality, race, and social class.

Psychographic. Psychographic dimensioning is based principally on life-style differences. Singles bars, for instance, target a group sometimes called *swingers*—reasonably affluent people, generally single, who seek the company of the opposite sex. On the other hand, some resorts, in requiring a coat and tie at dinner and enforcing dress rules in certain areas of the property, seek to cater to a more conservative group. Many currently popular table-service restaurants direct their marketing toward an audience that is "casual" and "youthful" in its outlook, whatever its actual age.

Behavioristic. One kind of behavioristic dimension is the benefit sought. For instance, restaurants offering salad bars and weight-watchers' specials lie at one end of a scale, and "all you can eat" restaurants can be thought of as lying at the other end. Shakey's Pizza offers guests a playful, entertaining atmosphere in which parents do not have to worry about their children running around or making noise. In contrast, Windows on the World, atop the World Trade Center in New York City, offers a dining experience related to luxury, status, and exclusiveness.

Another behavioristic dimension is user status. One pizza operation, for instance, offers speedy delivery service that can be personalized, because each guest order becomes part of a computerized guest history keyed to the caller's phone number. This personalized, speedy service is said to appeal to the heavy user, generally a 17-to-26-year-old male. Some marketers regard light users and nonusers as major potential markets.

Brand familiarity as a behavioristic dimension can also be important. Some years ago, for instance, Holiday Inns had become the dominant lodging chain in much of the United States and operated at a very high occupancy. When the chain expanded into the western United States, however, it found that potential guests were not familiar with the chain, and so the company had to adopt a much more aggressive marketing posture in that part of the country.

REACHING THE CUSTOMER: THE MARKETING MIX

Obviously, identifying the customer is not the end of marketing. We next must organize our thinking about how to secure these customers. The marketing mix is a useful way of thinking about and analyzing all of the variables that the operation can control. As opposed to environmental factors such as the economy or consumer behavior, which are beyond the control of the operation, the marketing mix is controlled by the operation. The elements of the mix are product and service, place, price, and promotion.

PRODUCT AND SERVICE

FROM PRODUCT TO PRODUCT–SERVICE MIX

There are three "levels" in the conventional product concept, as illustrated in Figure 19.3. At the core of the concept of product is not the physical product and service itself; rather, the *core product* is its function for the consumer. The *formal product* is "what the target market recognizes as the tangible offer"[2], that is, the physical and service amenities—in Figure 19.3, those of a motor hotel. The *augmented product* recognizes what has been called systems selling. In our example, the motor hotel chain offers not just food and lodging with a certain kind of amenity but also great convenience in getting to and using its properties, anywhere they are located. The Holiday Inn system, for instance, provides reservations service; printed directories that give information on location, facilities, and nearby attractions; and standard credit arrangement (i.e., acceptance of listed credit cards) worldwide. Moreover, the traveling family can be assured of the availability of a crib, bonded baby-sitters, and "kiddie" pools at any inn they visit.

The Benefit Bundle

At the core of the product, as we noted, is the consumer benefit. Ethnic foods, for instance, provide more than just a particular taste. One authority put it as follows:

---

[2]Philip Kotler and Ronald E. Turner, *Marketing Management*, 4th ed. (Scarborough, Ont.: Prentice-Hall Canada, 1981), p. 376.

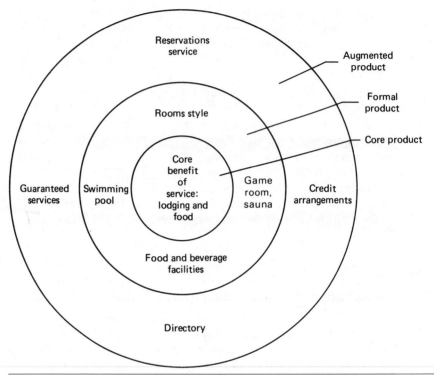

FIGURE 19.3   Three levels of product concept. [Adapted from Philip Kotler and Ronald E. Turner, *Marketing Management,* 4th ed. (Scarborough, Ont.: Prentice-Hall Canada, 1981), p. 316.]

> In the positive sense of the word I like to call ethnic foods "peasant" food because the ethnic interest not only adds variety but is perceived in the consumer's mind as wholesome, honest and all those other good things you can say about it.[3]

In fact, the benefit bundle concept is important in terms of both the core product and the formal and augmented aspects of product and service. Swimming pools mean fun or relaxation; saunas and game rooms suggest a feeling of affluence, as do luxuriously appointed guest rooms, dining rooms, and cocktail lounges. Holiday Inns' boast of "no surprises" offers the guest consistency and reliability, a feeling that is important to people away from home.

[3]John C. Hofer, "Marketing: Innovation, Analysis and Strategy Development," in *Proceedings of the Hospitality Leaders Conference* (Guelph, Ont.: School of Hotel and Food Administration, 1981), p. 132.

The "benefit bundle" offered by the Hawaiian Village includes all you could want in an oceanside vacation, according to this Hilton advertisement. (Courtesy of The Hilton Hawaiian Village)

The Product–Service Mix

Leo Renaghan offered us the term *product–service mix* to denote what we have for sale:

> The term "product–service mix" has been chosen because it explicitly reflects that hospitality firms offer a simultaneous blend of products and services. Consumers do not perceive the product and service elements of the mix separately; they perceive them instead as a unified whole.[4]

When guests come to dinner, as Renaghan pointed out, the whole dining experience—promptness and manner of service as well as food quality—is what they seek. If elegance of service is what we sell, then ritual and elaborateness may be important; if speed of service is what is offered, then Kentucky Fried Chicken or Harvey's or some other fast-food emporium will

[4]Leo M. Renaghan, "A New Marketing Mix for the Hospitality Industry," *Cornell Hotel and Restaurant Administration Quarterly,* August 1981, pp. 32–33.

have it. Ultimately, the product–service mix is the promise of the menu *and* the fact of the meal: product and service are inextricably mixed.

Service Strategy

Because service is an integral part of what we sell, decisions regarding service need to be made according to a coherent core product concept. It is important that service style and product type fit together logically. Haute cuisine served cafeteria style doesn't fit, any more than a Big Mac would fit on the menu of elegant restaurants such as Windows on the World or the Four Seasons. In addition to product–service coherence, we should consider three aspects of service strategy: service elements, service level, and service-form.[5]

Service element decisions for a food service involve choices such as that among self-service, table service only, and table service with salad bar (and/or dessert bar). In a hotel or motel, management must decide whether or not to offer bell service, whether to have automatic dialing or operator-serviced telephones, and whether or not to provide room service. Some hospitals, as we noted in an earlier chapter, in a desire to attract high-revenue medical examination business from large corporations, offer a formal dining room service at which patients can entertain their guests. All of these cases involve decisions about the elements of service to be offered.

Service level distinctions are at the heart of the differentiations among budget hotel/motel properties, upscale properties, and luxury properties. Similarly, the budget steak house in which guests order from a cafeteria line, but the dinner is delivered to the guest by a server is using a modest increment in service level to differentiate itself from its competitor.

Finally, *service form* in the hospitality industry has important distinctions. For instance, service might take the form of the efficient but somewhat mechanical service available in a family restaurant; service in a dinner house that offers a "fun atmosphere" and trains servers to exhibit a friendly personal style with guests but places no emphasis on elaborateness or particular expertise; or, finally, the elaborate service of an haute cuisine restaurant offering Russian service or tableside cookery. In each case, the product—cheeseburgers and french fries, steak and ale, or Tournedos Rossini and a fine burgundy—fits with the form of service to present a coherent dining experience designed to fit a particular set of guest needs and wants.

Because the product–service mix is so important, it is the subject of conscious policy decisions. As we have just looked at service strategy and policy, it will be useful here to give an example of management action that emphasizes product policy. Before examining this example, however, we

---

[5]Kotler and Turner, *Marketing Management*, pp. 400–414. We are using terms here somewhat differently from the way Kotler and Turner do.

The service level appropriate to fine dining requires elegance in appointment and service rituals. Clearly, it is difficult here to say whether product or service is more important to the product–service mix. (Photo courtesy of Caesar's Palace, Atlantic City.)

will define another product-related marketing term, *product line*. Several physical products and/or services may be combined to develop an effective marketing program. The product line at McDonald's originally comprised hamburgers (and variations of hamburgers) and french fries. After a period, management chose to broaden the line to include breakfast and desserts. In choosing to offer breakfast, management made a marketing decision to enter a whole new "day part" market—the breakfast period. The dessert decision moved the company's market stance more toward a full-meal position and away from its more limited sandwich menu. It is important to notice that these product line decisions were first marketing program decisions and then operations decisions. Clearly, *product policy* decisions will often be concerned with the product line.

FROM PLACE TO PRESENTATION MIX[6]

In the hospitality industry, three related variables define the element of place in the marketing mix: location, physical plant, and atmospherics. Some might argue that much of what we discuss involves product concerns, especially physical plant and atmospherics. The term *presentation mix*, however, suggests that this component of the hospitality marketing mix shares elements relating to the way in which the product–service mix is presented to the guest.

LOCATION

One of the great pioneers of the hotel industry, Mr. Statler, once said that the three main factors in the success of a hotel are "location, location, and location." Certainly, this piece of folklore has a strong element of truth. Though we do know of a few hotels that must pull their clientele to them by means of superior services and amenities, the discussion in Chapter 6 suggested that most hotels are located to serve travel patterns.

In many ways, a restaurant's menu and service style—that is, its product–service mix—are dictated by location. A high-traffic transient area might dictate a fast-food or family restaurant format. A location in or on the edge of an upper-income neighborhood, on the other hand, might suggest a fine dining restaurant. In each case, of course, the needs and wants of the prospective guests in a trading area fundamentally dictate the product–service combination that can be offered successfully.

Another aspect of location might be called *representation*. Because hospitality services are consumed where they are produced, it is necessary to have a unit in every market in which sales are sought. Thus, a fast-food chain seeks locations that will give it a market share judged to be in line with its goals in every market that it enters.

In the hotel business, representation by way of a location in every key market has another aspect. Recall the augmented product concept. In order to gain reservations for the total lodging system, it is important to have locations not only in destination areas but in major origination markets as well. Although a sales office in the origination area (i.e., the area where trips begin) will help, an actual operation located there gives the prospective traveler a much more concrete view of the distant hotel's offering—as the prospective traveler drives by an inn near home or stops in for dinner, a drink, or a call on a visitor staying there.

---

[6]The concept of presentation mix presented here is adapted from Renaghan, "A New Marketing Mix for the Hospitality Industry," but not all the elements he identifies are included here.

PHYSICAL PLANT

The exterior appearance of the physical plant is an important communications tool:

> If a physical plant has been designed successfully, the customer should be able to tell what is happening inside a building simply by viewing its exterior. The physical structure should reflect the intangible service elements that are part of the total offering. Trader Vic's, for instance, looks not only like a restaurant but a Polynesian restaurant. A hotel designed by John Portman is not only a hotel but also a specific type of environment.[7]

Notice, too, that fast-food restaurants give close attention to external appearance—at a McDonald's, the mansard roof and brick walls suggest a well-appointed, comfortable atmosphere within. Long John Silver's, on the other hand, uses a nautical theme to symbolize its fish specialty and attract the guest's attention.

Two aspects of physical plant that are important to the presentation mix are proximics and atmospherics.

Proximics refers to the way in which the interior of a property is arranged to communicate to the guest what services are available. For example, restaurants and bars are commonly arranged so they are visible from

From the exterior design of this building, El Pollo Loco lets passing customers know that it is a Mexican restaurant. (Photo courtesy of El Pollo Loco.)

[7]Renaghan, "A New Marketing Mix for the Hospitality Industry," pp. 33–34.

where the guest checks in, and gift shops are usually located just off the lobby.

Atmospherics relate to the way in which the design of the interior of a property is used to create or enhance a particular feeling in the guest. Thus, some Polynesian restaurants seek to offer the guest a source of adventure, whereas in its lobby, a luxurious hotel may seek to give an impression of exclusiveness.

PRICE

Few elements of the marketing mix are as poorly understood as price is. Not long ago, a motor hotel found itself faced with a new—indeed, shiny new—competitor. With the opening of the new property, the existing operator saw his occupancy fall. "I'll fix them," he said, and proceeded to cut his room rates, thinking to regain some of his lost guests. What happened, however, was that his occupancy fell even further. Instead of seeing his operation as a bargain, guests decided it was "cheap." In this section we will examine some customary bases for pricing and look at pricing from the guest's point of view.

BASES FOR PRICING

The three most common bases for pricing are cost, demand, and contribution. In each case, however, the price that the competition is charging is taken into account, although the exact weight given to competitive prices varies from one situation to another. We will next discuss cost, demand, and contribution as the bases for pricing.

Cost

The most common basis for pricing in the restaurant industry is the cost of the product. In general, management determines that it wants to maintain a certain product–cost ratio. When a product is considered for addition to the menu, the standard food cost percentage is applied, and then the price is assessed against the competition. For instance, if a fried-clam platter has a food cost of $1.50, and the operation's standard food cost is 28 percent, then the menu price yielded can be found by dividing the cost by the food cost target percent.:

$$\frac{\text{Food cost}}{\text{Food cost target \%}} = \frac{\$1.50}{0.28} = \$5.35$$

One of the reasons that cost pricing is so commonly used in the restaurant industry is that the industry is a highly competitive one in which market

Special prices offering savings in periods of low volume are effective off-season draws
in lodging. The reasoning, of course, is that the contribution from a discounted room
that is sold is greater than that from an empty room, no matter what it's price. (Courtesy
of Inter-continental Hotels)

share may be lost if an operation's price is out of line. For similar products, it is reasonable to assume that there will be similar costs. Thus cost, as a basis for price, is most likely to yield a price that is consistently in line with that of the competition.

Demand

In the hotel industry, new properties often base their prices on "what the traffic will bear"—that is, on demand. A new hotel has a kind of temporary monopoly, in that it probably has the latest location and the advantage of novelty, particularly in relation to atmospherics. As a result, although it cannot ignore competition, the new hotel can probably set its rate at or above the top of the market for its price category.

Contribution Pricing

Many in the industry would argue that cost-based pricing overlooks the most important element in the pricing equation—profit. Their case can be quickly summed up. Would you rather earn your target food cost of 28 percent on a chicken basket with a food cost of $1.25 or achieve a 35-percent cost on a steak platter with a food cost of $2.75? The analysis is as follows:

	Chicken Basket	Steak Platter
Food cost	$1.25	$2.75
Food cost percent	0.28%	0.35%
Selling price	$4.45	$7.85
Contribution (selling price minus food cost)	$3.20	$5.10

The general formula for our computation is selling price minus variable cost equals contribution to overhead and profits, or

$$SP - VC = \text{Contribution}$$

(our example treats food cost as the only variable cost, which is one reasonable way of proceeding.[8])

The argument for a contribution approach to pricing is clear from the example. The steak platter violates a 28-percent food cost target. But it yields almost twice the contribution to overhead and profit yielded by the chicken basket, although the latter doesn't violate the 28-percent target.

[8]This assumption treats labor cost as a fixed cost, assuming that a crew of a certain size is required to deal with a given level of sales volume. Some operators argue that the variable labor costs should be considered, but such a practice is rare.

The Red Lion Inn
Stockbridge, Massachusetts 01262

Drawing by Douglas McGregor
Figures by Norman Rockwell

Advertising creates and burnishes an image for places we haven't visited. (Courtesy of Red Lion Inn, Stockbridge, MA.)

Price Level and Inflation

One commonly hears it said among operators that "we've never cut a price," and yet their profit margins are shrinking. What has happened is that even though costs have increased, prices have been held back. In fact, what has happened in fast food has been a hidden price cutting across the industry in the form of only partial recovery of the inflationary cost rises.

FROM PRICE TO PRICE/VALUE

Price is a significant variable, but consumers do not consider it in isolation. Instead, consumers make a judgment about price in relationship to the *value* of the offering. For example, a generation ago, fast food offered consumers a fast meal at a very reasonable price. Gradually, however, as fast food became more competitive, efforts were made to enhance the value of the fast-food meal by improving the service offered, through adding a seating area for diners and, in time, through creating a pleasant and distinctive ambience. This could be accomplished without adding much to the cost of a meal, as the improvements could be amortized over hundreds of thousands of meals. The competitive tactic was to hold the line on prices (as much as possible given the rising food and labor costs) while taking steps to enhance the guest's perception of value.

To look at a somewhat different example, as hotel prices escalated to keep pace with rising land, building, and operating costs, many operators sought to enhance value through the addition of guest-room amenities that would help the guest accept the current price as warranted in the light of luxurious little extras.

PROMOTION

We have come now to that portion of the marketing mix that is sometimes thought of as the whole of marketing: promotion. The three major tools of promotion are advertising, personal selling, and sales promotion. Because each of these elements is concerned with communicating with the guest, promotion is often referred to as *marketing communications* or the *communication mix.*

ADVERTISING

Advertising is sometimes referred to as mass selling, and that sums up what it can achieve. Advertising reaches a mass audience at a modest cost per person reached—as opposed to personal selling, which is directed at individual buyers. But if the cost per individual reached is low, the cost of advertising to the firm is not. McDonald's, for instance, spent $686 million on advertising in 1985. Clearly, advertising is being used on a large scale in our history.

Whether large or small, advertisers face five decisions: target market identification, message, media, timing, and budget. (Additionally, they need to measure the effect of their advertising, but even an introduction to this subject goes beyond the scope of this text.)

Target

As we noted earlier, the firm's market is not the whole population but some segment or segments. Because we are reasoning from the consumer's viewpoint, an understanding of the target market is all-important to designing promotions to reach the appropriate target audience.

Message: Consumer Benefit

The message of the advertisement is basically "what we want to say." The consumer benefit, rather than the formal product, is commonly the focus of the message. Nobody expects McDonald's to say, "Hamburgers for sale!" In fact, in the recessionary times of the early 1980s, McDonald's reintroduced its "You deserve a break today" theme. The theme offered the consumer relief from tension and responsibility, under the assumption that

Joe Madden, spokesman for Ramada, is offering (to) guests in this series of ads good, prompt service. (Courtesy of Ramada Inns.)

guests are already familiar with the menu. Interestingly, there is evidence that the message is actually more important than is the number of dollars spent.[9]

On the other hand, when a company is not well known in a market, it may be better to stress specific product benefits. Wendy's of Canada, for instance, found that its product claims were not as well known there as they were in the United States. Accordingly, while Wendy's in the United States in the early 1980s was using "life-style" commercials emphasizing how well Wendy's fit in with its target market's way of life, in Canada a product-oriented campaign based on the theme "That's fresh, that's class, that's Wendy's" emphasized the fresh product appeal.

One of the problems that all advertisers share is the need to "cut through the clutter." North Americans are bombarded with literally hundreds of advertising messages daily, and we have developed a considerable tolerance, not to say indifference, to advertising. Wendy's use of the slogan "ain't no reason to go anyplace else" annoyed people who objected to the bad grammar, but it did gain people's attention.

Media

The selection of an advertising medium should be based on a judgment of the best way to reach the target audience. In general, media selection is based on goals related to *reach* (number of persons reached) and *frequency* (number of times that a typical listener, reader, or viewer is reached per time period). Additionally, an assessment of *impact*—that is, the consumer's perception of the reliability, importance, prestige, and general credibility of the medium—is significant. Reach and frequency are generally quantifiable, and numerical data based on readership, listenership, or viewership will likely be available from the media representatives. Any assessment of impact, however, will generally entail qualitative judgments.

The major media used by the hospitality industry are radio, television, newspapers, outdoor advertising, and direct mail.[10] Even a capsule summary of the merits of each of these media is beyond the scope of this text, but the following comments suggest some of the differences among them:

Television. Extremely expensive; generally limited to large independent and chain organizations. Television is expensive in terms of total cost, but it is often the lowest in terms of cost per thousand reached, with multiple units spreading the cost over many operations.

Radio. Less expensive and subject to considerable differentiation by choice of station type (i.e., progressive, contemporary, middle-of-the-road,

---

[9]Kotler and Turner, *Marketing Management*, p. 537.

[10]An emerging category, cable television advertising, is still in its infancy but is growing rapidly. Reportedly, it will offer the same power to segment markets that radio does, and it is presently competing most strongly with radio for advertising dollars.

news–information–sports, talk, good music, classical, country and western, or ethnic),[11] each of which has a distinctly different audience. Thus, radio offers frequency of exposure to selected target markets. It is especially useful for reaching travelers.

Newspapers. Broad-based readership helps build awareness of an establishment among key publics[12] and offers reach, but entails purchase of "waste circulation."[13] Specifying placement in a specific section—sports pages, women's pages, society news, travel section—improves targeting of message.

Outdoor Advertising. Only brief messages are possible. Very useful in conveying information to travelers. The government regulation of this medium is increasing, and there may be some unfavorable reaction to the medium among environmental enthusiasts.

Direct Mail. Highly targeted but expensive on a per-impression basis. "Waste circulation" is a problem here, too, if the secretary throws away the boss's "junk mail." Proportionately, this is the smallest medium of those discussed here.

In considering media selection, note that in addition to the media's time or space charges, production costs can be a significant factor, running up to 10 percent or more of an advertising budget. According to one authority, high production costs preclude the use of TV for smaller operations.[14]

Timing

Scheduling one commercial a week is largely a waste of time, because a single commercial is unlikely to "cut through the clutter." On the other hand, operators simply cannot place as many commercials as they think desirable for as long as they would like, because budgets are limited. The key is to choose the right balance between the frequency necessary to make an impression on the consumer during the planned duration of the advertising campaign, taking into account any seasonality that affects the operation and an affordable advertising budget.[15] As one authority, discussing radio advertising, noted:

---

[11]Harry A. Egbert, "Radio Advertising for Hotels," *Cornell Hotel and Restaurant Administration Quarterly,* May 1980, p. 32.

[12]Harry A. Egbert, "The Bread and Butter Medium for Hotel and Restaurant Advertising," *Cornell Hotel and Restaurant Administration Quarterly,* February 1981, pp. 34–35.

[13]The term *waste circulation* is based on the fact that an advertiser generally purchases on the basis of a cost per thousand impressions. To the degree that many newspaper readers (the same concept applies to radio and TV) are not potential customers, they are a part of the circulation that the advertising purchaser can think of as "wasted."

[14]Egbert, "The Bread and Butter Medium for Hotel and Restaurant Advertising," pp. 34–35.

[15]Ibid.

There are two basic kinds of advertising coverage: vertical and horizontal. *Vertical* coverage—where commercials are "bunched," all run in one or two days of a given week—is an effective technique for promoting special events, such as a Thanksgiving Dinner Special or an escape weekend. The horizontal approach is to spread the commercials evenly over the week, and to repeat that exposure week after week. Horizontal coverage is especially useful in building local image but requires greater dedication to the continuing use of the radio medium than the vertical technique does.[16]

The Advertising Budget

The most common means of setting advertising budgets in the hospitality industry is to determine, usually from industry averages or historical data, an appropriate percentage of sales and then to set spending targets based on estimated sales. Another method is to match the competition. Both these methods have the "advantage" of simplicity, but neither is goal directed.

More sophisticated firms determine their advertising objectives in terms of profits and/or sales and then construct a budget aimed at achieving the planned results. Firms large enough to afford market research to evaluate their promotional programs are likely to focus on measuring consumers' awareness of the firm's advertising, attitudes (i.e., favorable interest), consumer trial, and repeat business.

The marketing executive following goal-directed budgeting is less likely to be "right" than is one who follows the simpler methods. It is, after all, harder to produce an increase of, say, 10 percent of sales and 1 percent of profits than it is just to "spend 4 percent of sales." On the other hand, the planning process necessary to develop a goal-directed advertising budget is more likely to deliver favorable results, because it requires carefully reasoned judgments regarding message, media, and timing—as opposed to just needing to "spend X dollars." If you are tempted to opt for the "easier" approach of matching an industry or a competitive average, note two assumptions implicit in copying what others do: that the industry knows what its doing and that your operation has the same marketing challenge as does that of your competitors. Both assumptions are questionable, at best.

One aspect of advertising budget construction that is unique to the hospitality industry is the "trade out." Broadcasters and publishers are sometimes willing to trade advertising for services and food at a hotel or restaurant. This can result in an excellent bargain all around, provided that the arrangement is not seen as "free advertising for free rooms or food." The "free" notion can lead to casual treatment by both the media firm and the operator. Instead, trade outs should proceed on the basis of an exchange of valuable assets and should be planned just as carefully as if actual currency were changing hands.

[16]Egbert, "Radio Advertising for Hotels," p. 36.

PERSONAL SELLING

Personal selling is often thought of as the work done by sales representatives, such as those employed in hotel sales. Although this is true—and a point to which we will return—by far the largest amount of personal selling in the hospitality industry takes the form of the following three snippets of dialogue:

GUEST: I'd like a single room. What have you got?

DESK CLERK: I wonder if you'd like one of our executive sitting rooms. It would be just the right place to entertain your prospects, it has a good working area for a temporary office, and the couch pulls out into a comfortable three-quarter bed.

GUEST: That was a delicious dinner.

WAITRESS: For dessert, our cherries jubilee is delicious—and a lot of fun.

GUEST: I'd like a cheeseburger.

COUNTER SERVER: Would you like french fries and a beverage with that?

The point, of course, is obvious: that executive sitting room probably costs $10 or $15 more than a single does; and the cherries jubilee or, in another setting, french fries and a beverage, build the check average. Imaginative, marketing-oriented management's goal is to convert order takers into sales people who actively seek sales.

Two segments of the hospitality industry, however, rely especially on personal selling by salespeople whose job is selling and who, unlike waitresses or desk clerks, do not have another operational role. These segments are hotel companies and contract food service companies.

Hotel sales include group, rooms, and function (i.e., banquets, meetings, exhibitions) sales. Although personal selling is a very expensive form of promotion, the dollar level of the sale justifies the expense, and generally, the complexity of the arrangements requires it.

When a convention is booked, for instance, special room rates may be negotiated along with the provision of complimentary rooms for the executive and staff of the association (or other group) booking the function. Banquets, luncheons, coffee breaks, cocktail parties, and exhibition space might be required. For each of these, myriad details must be agreed upon and probably contracted for. The complexity of these arrangements requires a specialist with, on the one hand, the technical know-how necessary to spell out a realistic set of arrangements and to communicate and service them inside the organization and, on the other hand, the ability to persuade the potential customer that "ours *is* the right place."

The importance of technical know-how suggests that the best hotel sales representatives are people with an operations background and specialized sales training. Although there are many qualified sales representatives who join a hotel with sales experience and are then trained in operations, experience suggests that the best route to a successful career in hotel sales lies in sound operational training in rooms-department operations, and especially in banquet and food and beverage operations.

SALES PROMOTION

Sales promotion is often thought of as an "all other" category: that is, everything that is done as a part of the promotion element of the marketing mix other than advertising and personal selling. In the hospitality industry, however, sales promotion plays fairly well established roles.

Perhaps the most universally used role is in-house sales promotion. Another kind of promotion, that of *special events,* is used in hotels and table service restaurants. *Dealing* is used extensively in the fast-food and family restaurant segments. *Public relations* is used in all segments. We will examine each briefly.

In-House Sales Promotion

Most operations remind guests of where they are, and that service is rendered by *imprinted guest supplies:* matchbook covers, paper napkins, guest room supplies, stirrers, and the like. This is a very inexpensive form of promotion, because these products can be purchased in volume at very nearly the same cost as unimprinted products. Also, they are often used as souvenirs of a visit, thus publicizing the operation's name and encouraging repeat visits.

Other in-house promotion tools found most commonly in hotels and resorts include lobby signs, elevator cards, and "table tents" in guest rooms promoting such services-for-sale as pay TV movies, tennis, golf, and food and beverage facilities.

Point-of-purchase displays are another commonly used sales promotion tool. These displays usually have a more specific purpose. For instance, special posters and banners trumpeting the introduction of a new product in a fast-food restaurant encourage trial of that product. In a hotel dining room or other table-service restaurant, a wine display encourages guests to consider enhancing their meal—and the house's check average—with a bottle of wine. Many restaurants that specialize in seafood have lobster and trout tanks at the entrance to the dining room and encourage guests to pick out their own entree. At the table—which is itself a point of purchase—table tents, wine lists, dessert menus, and similar sales tools are also used to build the check average.

Special Events

Special-events promotion should be used for specific purposes. The appropriate goals are "to enhance awareness of the hotel in the local community,

Point-of-purchase materials include: posters, "bounce back" coupons, table tents and buttons for staff, which repeat or reinforce the advertized theme. (Courtesy of Skakey's, Inc.)

to generate renewed interest on the part of existing clients, to increase room revenues during a slack period, to contribute to the achievement of an overall image or to dispel an existing negative image." An example is a promotion for Dunfey's Berkshire Plaza Hotel, whose objective was to draw New York area residents into midtown over the weekend and encourage those working in the area to stay and have dinner in the hotel on weekdays. To encourage weekend patronage, the hotel sponsored a series of "culture brunches," which combined a champagne brunch with a walking tour of nearby galleries and museums, designed in conjunction with one of New York's most prestigious cultural organizations. The "culture brunch" was used in tandem with the hotel's "Classic Weekend" package to gain not only food and beverage but room revenue as well. The result was both increased sales and extensive publicity in the local and national media. To meet the weeknight dining challenge, Dunfey's started a dinner club, *La Cercle Rendez-Vous,* which offered "an exciting foray into food and wine for both novice and connoisseur offering a full *nouvelle cuisine* dinner with four different wines.[17]

[17]Jessica Dee Zive, "Solving Market Problems through Creative Promotions," *Cornell Hotel and Restaurant Quarterly,* November 1981, pp. 57–58.

In the quite different setting of the small, high-unemployment, rural community of Bloomsburg, Pennsylvania, Dick Benefield, manager of the Magee Hotel, offered a monthly dinner special, generally lasting for a week and featuring themes appropriate to the season, such as Oktoberfest or St. Patrick's Day, or regional favorites such as New Orleans or Polynesian menus. These dinners not only proved profitable in themselves but also succeeded in boosting food and beverage sales to a level many more favorably located restaurants would envy. They have also been successful in building rooms volume year-round in a hotel that was built just before the Civil War!

Dealing

An increasingly important aspect of sales promotion comprises what are called *deals*. These include inducements to patronize a restaurant such as BOGOs ("*B*uy *O*ne, *G*et *O*ne free") and other kinds of coupons, premium merchandise, and games. Deals are frequently used with advertising and serve as the focus of an advertising campaign. Some operations, however, do distribute coupons, called *bounce backs,* as a part of a point of sales promotion to encourage repeat patronage without advertising support outside the store.

The BOGO-and-coupon approach offers an actual reduction in price to the consumer. The first calculation that the operator must make is whether the cost of the promotion will be offset by the increased revenue. To use a somewhat simplified illustration, let us suppose that a company offers BOGO coupons in the newspaper. The cost of the campaign is the total of the advertising cost and the increase in cost related to the deal merchandise: If a local campaign costs $2000 for advertising and generates $10,000 in identified deal-related sales,[18] then an additional $10,000 worth of product was exchanged—as the "one free" for the "one bought"—for the BOGO coupons. If we assume that no additional labor costs were incurred and that variable costs were 35 percent, then the cost and revenue picture will be

Revenue (net of cost): $10,000 sales *less 35% variable cost*	*$6500*
Advertising cost:	$2000
Product cost ($10,000 × 35%):	$3500
	$5500
Deal contribution to overhead and profit:	$1000

The financial benefit of this particular example is $1000, but equally important is the degree to which new customers are attracted or old customers are persuaded to visit more often.

---

[18]Modern point-of-sales register systems make it possible to record deal-related sales separately. Reports giving sales and cost data are routinely summarized as a part of the daily report.

The real "trick" in the computation, then, is to estimate the degree to which the deal-related volume is actually increased volume, rather than just "giveaways" to regular customers. If your organization has a store not affected by the deal in a similar market, you can compare sales between the deal and nondeal stores and attribute the increased sales to the deal. The whole subject of measuring the effect of deals—or promotion generally—is an extraordinarily difficult one and well beyond the scope of our present effort. What we can say is that various estimating techniques that satisfy management's best judgment are used but that absolute certainty is rare.

Note that a coupon may offer any amount of discount and that not all discounts offer the customer the 50-percent savings of the BOGO. For instance, some coupons offer a certain amount off on specified items, whereas others offer a discount if a complete meal is purchased. A variant on coupons or a BOGO is that of increased portions and "all you can eat" specials.

Premium merchandise deals offer items for sale at cost, such as drinking glasses or T-shirts. Because the cost of the premium merchandise is recovered as a part of the transaction, these promotions are sometimes referred to as "self-liquidators," the revenue from the merchandise liquidates the cost.

Games comprise another relatively inexpensive promotional deal and offer "fun and excitement" to the customer. Games generally provide numerous inexpensive prizes in the form of free servings of a product and a few "big ticket" glamorous prizes, such as a trip to Europe for two, a new home, or a large sum of money. Games are relatively inexpensive, especially when compared with a reduction in price on all or a substantial part of a company's sales. Along with premium merchandise, they are often used to enhance consumers' price/value perception.

Table 19.1 shows the results of a National Restaurant Association study based on the responses of a consumer panel as to which "deals" consumers thought they would participate in. The popularity of deals that offer real savings to the consumer is clear and was confirmed by a study of actual behavior. The same consumer panel reported that nearly half the respondents had last used (48.2 percent) an incentive involving some form of price reduction, whereas only 9 percent had most recently used a premium. Games were last, used by 14 percent of the respondents.

Advantages and Problems of Deals. Deals provide a means of enhancing price/value perception. The premium offers a bargain and a souvenir, whereas the game offers, at least to some consumers, "fun and excitement." In a world in which one hamburger differs only moderately from another, deals offer a means of differentiating restaurants. The coupon offers an actual reduction in price with an obvious effect on price/value.

The coupon and other price reduction inducements run the danger, however, of cheapening the consumer's perception of the product and generating a hesitancy to purchase without a price reduction if the reduction becomes established—that is, if the deal is run too long or too often.

TABLE 19.1 Likelihood of Use of Various Types of Restaurant Promotions and Incentives

| | Percent Saying…[a] | | |
| | Very or Somewhat Likely to Use | Somewhat or Very Unlikely to Use | Mean Value |
Type of Promotion			
Two-for-one specials	60.3%	21.1%	3.7
Cents-off coupons	52.8%	28.0%	3.4
Complete meal specials	37.2%	32.9%	2.9
All-you-can-eat specials	38.3%	37.4%	2.9
Price reductions for midweek dining	28.1%	43.9%	2.5
Introductory menu item promotions	21.6%	44.7%	2.4
Early-bird specials	18.7%	53.8%	2.2
Games and sweepstakes	19.5%	54.3%	2.2
Premiums and nonfood merchandise	15.8%	58.7%	2.0
Special events in restaurants	13.5%	58.1%	2.0
Senior citizen discounts	11.1%	67.5%	1.6

Mean value: 5 = very likely to use,
  1 = very unlikely to use

Source: Consumer Attitude and Behavior Study (Chicago: National Restaurant Association, 1982).

[a]Totals do not add to 100 percent, because of exclusion of nonresponses and of those who answered that they were neither likely nor unlikely to use these promotions.

Marketers who use deals must balance the need to use the media to build the image of their restaurant—which, it is generally agreed, is best done by advertising—against the need to get immediate purchase response—an area in which dealing is highly effective. In an increasingly competitive market in which deals are of increasing importance, a further reason to use deals is simply to meet the competition.

PUBLIC RELATIONS

Most hospitality firms are aware that they can remain in the public eye and in a favorable light by keeping the news media informed of significant events, particularly positive achievements. The addition of a new dining room, the receipt of an award, the announcement of new staff appointments—all are newsworthy local events. Many firms are conscious, too, of the need for public relations to reach special publics via employee newsletters, the trade press, and (for large companies) the business and financial press.

In the hospitality industry, many executives choose to burnish their operation's public image through personal activity in public service work and local service clubs. Many firms present themselves favorably by sponsoring activities ranging from a little league team to Ronald McDonald House.

A somewhat negative task of public relations is dealing with unfavorable news. In general, experience indicates that dealing frankly and honestly with the media in case of a fire or other mishap is the best course.

The marketing mix is just that—a mix. Just as with a recipe, the key lies not in any single ingredient but in the proper combination and use of all the elements. We looked at some length at how the concepts of a total marketing program can be applied to restaurants and hotels and, more briefly, at how they can be used by contract companies in approaching the client and guest. The concepts are only a useful starting point, however, to the reasoning process. The marketing program, whether it be of large institutions, a restaurant chain, or an individual hotel, must be designed in the light of that operation's particular market, its competition, and the capabilities of the firm. As conditions change, the mix must be reviewed and updated or revised as different elements—such as pricing in a recession as compared with pricing in good times—change in order of importance and function. The marketing mix us a useful way of thinking about a firm's marketing problem, but an effective marketing program reflects the changing solution of the firm to the problems presented by a constantly evolving marketplace.

SUMMARY

We defined marketing by discussing some of the approaches that have been used in the past. Then we turned our attention to the consumer, the focus of marketing. We examined consumer behavior and then divided consumers into market segments according to their geographic, demographic, psychographic, and behavioristic characteristics.

Next we considered the market mix—a blend of product and service, place, price, and promotion. Within the product are the core product, the formal product, and the augmented product. And then there is the product—service mix, which includes a service strategy.

Place, or the presentation mix, is made up of location, physical plant, and atmospherics. Price is defined by the bases for pricing: cost, demand, and contribution. Consumers also weigh price in relation to value.

Promotion is carried out in a number of ways: through advertising, especially through the media; personal selling; sales promotion, including dealing; and, finally, public relations.

KEY WORDS AND CONCEPTS

To help you review this chapter, keep in mind the following:

Product orientation	Service strategy
Sales orientation	Presentation mix
Marketing mix	Atmospherics
Consumer behavior	Promotion
Market segments	Personal selling
Benefit bundle	Sales promotion
Product–service mix	Dealing

REVIEW QUESTIONS

1. Briefly explain product orientation and sales orientation.

2. What are the two reasons that understanding individual consumer behavior is important?

3. List and briefly describe the four bases for customer segmentation.

4. Differentiate the core product, the formal product, and the augmented product.

5. Give an example of the product–service mix in economy motels and all-suite hotels.

6. Give some examples of locations in which various kinds of hotels/motels might best be situated, and why.

7. What is the difference between proximics and atmospherics?

8. Describe a television commercial, and explain why you think it is effective.

9. What "deal" (or deals) do you find most attractive? Why?

Courtesy of Kentucky Fried Chicken.

FRANCHISE SYSTEMS IN THE HOSPITALITY INDUSTRY

THE PURPOSE OF THIS CHAPTER

Franchising is probably the most common way of doing business in the commercial hospitality industry, and it has important and growing applications in institutional services as well. Franchising offers significant advantages to the franchisor company like Holiday Inn or Burger King and major advantages to the individual franchisee. The system works so well for both parties because it brings large company expertise and local operator interest to every community of any size in North America. This is another way of saying that franchising works best of all for the consumer.

If you are interested in being in business for yourself, seeking a franchise is certainly an excellent way to pursue this goal. If you prefer to work for an established company, some of the best opportunities for growth, advancement, and income are with multiple-unit franchisees. All in all, it is in your interest to be well informed about franchising, which will almost certainly play some role in your career—if only that of an effective competitor.

THIS CHAPTER SHOULD HELP YOU

1. Distinguish between the major types of franchise.
2. Assess the significance of franchising in the North American economy.
3. Identify the principal characteristics of the franchise relationship and the franchise agreement.

517

4. Evaluate the advantages and disadvantages of a franchise for both franchisor and franchisee.

5. Enumerate the services provided to both new and established franchisees by franchisors.

6. Understand how franchising functions as a marketing system and a management system.

7. Appreciate the importance of and techniques for communication within the franchise system.

8. Recognize how the authority relationships and consequent management style of a franchise organization differ from those of a conventional line organization.

9. Identify the principal points of tension between franchisors and franchisees and how they are resolved by regulations and negotiation.

FRANCHISING: AN OVERVIEW

Probably the first firm to use franchising—at the end of the Civil War—was the Singer Sewing Machine Company. Later, near the turn of the century, the advent of the automobile and the franchised dealerships that it spawned helped franchising spread throughout the North American economy. Auto dealerships were followed closely by franchised petroleum service station networks. Then in the early 1900s, soft drink companies began to grow, by using franchised bottlers. The first franchises in the hospitality industry came in the 1920s with Howard Johnson's and A&W Root Beer.[1] The two basic types of franchise companies are those that use franchising to distribute a product or trade name and those that use business format franchising.

Product and trade name franchises were the earliest. Typical of these were the automobile and petroleum dealerships and soft drink–bottling organizations that gave franchising its real start. Although these kinds of franchise organizations are now declining in relative significance, they still account for nearly three-quarters of all sales by franchised companies.[2] That is, the number of product or trade name franchises is falling dramatically, but their average unit sales are more than offsetting the decline in units. Sales increases at product or trade name franchises are expected to level off at about 5 percent.[3]

[1] E. Patrick McGuire, *Franchised Distribution* (New York: The Conference Board, 1971), p. 2.

[2] Andrew Kostecka, *Franchising in the Economy, 1984–86* (Washington, D.C.: U.S. Government Printing Office, 1986), p. 1.

[3] The Naisbitt Group, *The Future of Franchising* (Washington, D.C.: International Franchise Association, 1986), p. 2.

Business format franchising, on the other hand, is growing by leaps and bounds. According to U.S. Department of Commerce estimates, the number of outlets using business format franchises grew by 48 percent between 1976 and 1986, and their sales more than tripled in the same period.[4]

A business format franchise, which is the kind we deal with in the hospitality industry, "includes not only the product, service and trademark, but the entire business format itself—a marketing strategy and plan, operating manuals and standards, quality control, and continuing two way communication."[5] One of the main reasons for the rapid growth of business format franchising, according to a study of the future of franchising by "futurologists" of the Naisbitt Group, is that more people have discovered that a franchise offers them the opportunity to be entrepreneurs without taking all the risks usually associated with starting a business. In addition, the shift in the economy from production to service has created an environment that encourages the growth of service franchise systems such as those found in the hospitality industry. One factor is the growth in service needs created by the greater number of working women.

THE ECONOMIC SIGNIFICANCE OF FRANCHISING

Franchised units are generally thought of as small businesses, but franchising itself is big business. Franchised sales accounted for 10 percent of the gross national product (GNP) in 1983. By 1985 that proportion had doubled to 20 percent of GNP, and franchised sales accounted for one-third of all retail sales. They are projected to reach half of all retail sales by the year 2000.[6] Large companies play a major role in business format franchising, with companies with 1000 or more units accounting for over half of format franchise sales in all businesses.

In 1983 within the hospitality industry, 13 restaurant chains with over 1000 units accounted for 52 percent of all franchised restaurants and 58 percent of all franchised restaurant sales, according to the U.S. Department of Commerce. Seventy-five percent of year-round–operated hotel and motel rooms in properties of over 25 units are in franchise systems. The proportion is still 50 percent even if seasonal and very small properties are included.[7]

Hospitality leads the way in the number of business format franchises. *Venture Magazine* reports that twenty-three of the one hundred fastest-growing franchise groups are restaurant chains. Table 20.1 shows the 10 fastest-growing business format areas. Two of the top three, restaurants and lodging, are exclusively hospitality firms, and hospitality and tourism play a major role in four out of the remaining eight (convenience stores, food retailing, auto rental, and travel).

[5]Kostecka, *Franchising in the Economy, 1984–86,* p. 3.
[6]The Naisbitt Group, *The Future of Franchising,* p. 1.
[7]The Naisbitt Group, *The Future of Franchising,* pp. 5–7.

A CONSULTANT'S VIEW OF FRANCHISING

What Is Franchising?

Franchising is a contractual arrangement between two parties where the franchisor grants the franchisee rights to market a product or service, including the right to use a trade mark and/or trade name.

A tested format or system is provided by the franchisor as well as know-how for the establishment and operation of the business by the franchisee. The franchisee is required to conform to the format or system, maintain quality standards and pay a set fee, usually by way of royalties, for a fixed period of time.

Why Franchise?

The benefits of franchising can include:

Franchisor

- Conservation of capital
- Ability to establish a reliable distribution network rapidly
- Reduced fixed overheads because outlets are owned and operated by franchisees
- Highly motivated and deeply committed owner-managers

Franchisee

- Opportunity to make a profit from the start of business
- Lower risk ownership with a proven operating business format and publicly accepted product or service
- Cost effective group purchasing and advertising in a larger organization which acts as a cushion against competition
- Better borrowing opportunities when backed by a solid franchisor

What Does the Franchisor Provide to the Franchisee?

The franchisee is provided with a comprehensive established operating system formulated from the franchisor's knowledge of the industry. It would embrace

- Selection of a suitable site, premises and equipment
- Production planning and control systems
- Market identification and penetration
- Volume purchasing
- Assistance with staff selection and training

- Co-operative advertising
- Finance and accounting packages
- Continuing consultation, research and development services

Source: "Franchising Services for the Franchiser," Pannell Kerr Forster.

TABLE 20.1   Business Format Franchise Growth Areas

	Estimated 1990 Sales ($ billions)	Annual Growth (percent)
Restaurants	$86.1	12.0%
Nonfood retailing	33.6	12.3
Hotels, motels, and campgrounds	22.5	9.0
Business aids and services	21.3	12.0
Convenience stores	19.4	9.5
Automotive products and services	15.9	8.5
Food retailing other than convenience stores (includes doughnut shops and ice-cream and yogurt stores)	15.9	7.0
Construction and home services	9.2	20.0
Auto and truck rental	8.9	11.0
Recreation, entertainment, and travel	6.6	29.0

Source: Adapted from the Naisbitt Group, *The Future of Franchising.*

THE FRANCHISE RELATIONSHIP

A conversation with a franchisee is likely to yield this contradiction: The franchisee clearly thinks of himself as an independent businessman but is likely to refer to the franchisor in the course of the conversation as "the parent company." "Many franchisees," one report suggested, "do not really wish to be independent at all but are tempted by the opportunity to be part of a large group, sharing in its success image, and yet also maintaining an "individual identity."[8]

This all-too-human tendency to "have your cake and eat it too" is probably heightened by the fact that the franchisee has many of the characteristics of an independent businessperson. The franchisee has a substantial in-

[8]McGuire, *Franchised Distribution*, p. 8.

investment, ownership (of the franchise and very possibly of land, building, furniture, and fixtures or a lease on them). Beyond that, he or she has full day-to-day operating control and responsibility. For instance, the franchisee is responsible for determining the need for hiring employees, supervising the daily operation (or managing those who do that supervision), and generally representing themselves in the community as independent businesspeople. The degree of franchisee control over key issues varies from one franchise group to another, but many franchisees shares considerable freedom of action in such significant business variables as pricing, placement of local advertising, choice of some suppliers, and additions to and renovations of physical plant. Although some aspects of the unit's budget are governed by the franchise agreement, the franchisee retains significant budgetary discretion under most agreements and, in practice, exercises even more.

On the other hand, the essence of almost all franchises in the hospitality industry is an agreement by the franchisee to follow the form of the franchisor's business system in order to gain the advantages of that business format. The franchisee has indeed relinquished a great deal of discretion in the management of his or her enterprise and is a part of a system that largely defines his or her operation. The franchisee's relationship is neither that of an employee nor that of an independent customer of the franchisor.

The most common characteristics of a franchise agreement are

1. A contractual relationship setting forth the rights and responsibilities of each party.

2. The purpose of the arrangement is the efficient distribution of a product, service, or entire business concept.

3. Both parties contribute resources to establish and maintain the franchise.

4. The contract describes the contribution of each party and the specific marketing and operating procedures.

5. The franchise is a business entity that requires the full-time business activity of the franchisee or his or her representative.

6. The franchisee and franchisor participate in a common public identity.

7. There is customarily a payment of an initial franchise fee, continuing royalties, and usually a required contribution to a common advertising fund.[9]

The Franchise System

We previously used the word *system* to describe an interactive whole, in which the totality of the system is more than just the sum of the parts. "One

[9]Adapted from McGuire, *Franchised Distribution;* and Kostecka, *Franchising in the Economy, 1984–86.*

thousand separate units plus a home office" is one way to describe a chain—the sum of the parts. But the *system* description would include factors related to the interactive way in which the system functions. The system achieves, for instance, impact and market identity through a common marketing program; economies through bulk purchasing; and operating impact in the marketplace through uniformity of menu, presentation of product, uniforms, and architecture and decor. Indeed, even the hospitality industry trade magazines' statistics generally treat the franchise group as if it were a chain that owns all the units. From the outside—and to a large degree, from the inside—the franchise group is seen as one organization.

Relationships within the system are more complex than those in wholly owned, multiple-unit systems. The franchisee is an independent businessperson, yet one who has given up a large measure of independence in return for access to a proven, successful format for doing business. The franchisor's representatives are not "the boss" in the same way as a district manager would be if the company owned all the units. Likewise, the franchisee is not an employee as a unit manager would be. Later we will discuss how leadership is maintained within the franchise system. For now, we should note that the franchisee is a member of a system and has accepted a set of obligations that he or she shares with others in the system.

Don N. Smith, President and Chief Executive Officer of SES Management and the 1985 Burton Shaw Lecturer at Washington State University, points to an important fact about franchising systems: "Successful relationships are always based on mutual benefits."[10] In the next section of this chapter we will discuss the advantages franchisors and franchisees take from their mutually agreed relationship. We will want to look at the costs and drawbacks to each party, as well. Next we will look at the functions of the franchise system and argue that franchising is both a marketing system and management system. Indeed, franchising illustrates well how interrelated are the management functions and activities we have discussed in the chapters on management and marketing.

THE FRANCHISEE'S DEAL

The franchisee has given up a good deal of autonomy, as we've just seen, in return for membership in a system. It is time now for us to look at the very real advantages that accrue to franchisees from the deal they have struck.

THE NEW FRANCHISEE

Franchising bridges the gap between an able, intelligent individual and an entrepreneurial opportunity. The business format franchise offers a proven

[10]Don N. Smith, Burton Shaw Lecture, Washington State University, Fall 1985.

Many franchisors seek new
franchisees through advertising.
(Courtesy of Arby's, Inc.)

way of doing business, including a proven product, or products, an operating
system, and a complete marketing program.

The franchise minimizes the entrepreneurial risk. Small Business
Administration studies indicate, for instance, that somewhere between one-
fourth and one-third of all businesses fail during their first year, and 65 percent fail within their first five years. On the other hand, the failure rate for
all franchised businesses is well under 5 percent, and the failed businesses
amount to less than a half-percent of total franchise sales.

In addition to a successful business format, the franchisor provides a
number of services that are especially important to the new franchisee.
These include screening, site selection, preopening training, and opening assistance.

Screening

Being screened to see whether you are the right person to be sold a franchise
may not seem like a service. A moment's reflection, however, will show that
careful franchisee selection is in the best interests not only of the company
and other, existing franchisees but of the new franchisee as well.

The initial contact may be in the form of a franchise marketing brochure, and more intensive screening begins after a prequalifying phase. The
potential franchisee's background and record of success—as well as financial position—are carefully reviewed. In preliminary interviews his or her

TABLE 20.2   Methods of Communication in Franchisee Recruitment

Communication Media	Percentage of Franchisors Using This Medium
Marketing brochure	92%
Telephone qualifying	87
Formal presentation	80
Meeting with existing franchisees	75
On-the-job training	37
Classroom session	31
Other	17

Source: International Franchise Association.

personal commitment will be probed; some franchisors even interview spouses to assure themselves of the family's commitment to the project if the prospective franchisee is expected to operate the new business. Some fast-food companies also ask the prospect to spend time in an operation—as much as a week—to ensure that they fully realize the nature of the business they are entering. The ways that contacts are made during the recruitment phase of the franchise relationship are summarized in Table 20.2. Curiously, in an International Franchise Association Survey, franchisors ranked the least-used medium, a classroom session, as the most effective.

Site Selection and Planning

Franchisors maintain a real estate department staffed with site selection experts. The franchise company also has its pooled experience to guide it. Given the importance of location to most hospitality operations, the availability of expert advice is important. Many companies actually select the site for the franchisee, and virtually all reputable franchisors insist on the right to approve a site. The physical layout of the operation, from the site plan to the building, equipment, and furnishing, and even a list of small wares and opening inventory, will be spelled out in detail.

Preopening Training

Virtually all franchise organizations have some means of training the franchisee and his or her key personnel. This service ranges from McDonald's Hamburger University and Holiday Inn University, which are extensive management training units, to simpler programs based on experience in an existing store. Table 20.3 summarizes the methods used during training and start-up. Many franchisors also provide an opening crew of lead people drawn from other units to help train the crew for the opening of a new unit.

Central training facilities emphasize management training (Photos courtesy of Holiday Inns, Inc.)

Operations Manuals

The backbone of the operating system is typically a set of comprehensive operations manuals that cover operating procedures from opening to closing and nearly everything in between. All major equipment operations and routine maintenance are described in the operations manual or in a separate equipment manual.

TABLE 20.3   Methods of Communication During Training and Start-Up

Communications Media	Percentage of Franchisors Using This Medium
On-the-job training	92.5%
Formal classroom training	91.0
Meetings with company management	91.0
Preopening checklist	83.0
Meetings with existing franchisees	61.0
Other	13.0

Source: International Franchise Association.

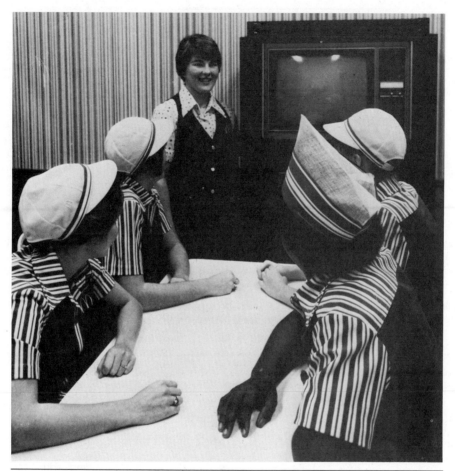

Crew training utilizes video cassettes to explain necessary unit level skills and operating procedures. (Photo, Courtesy of McDonald's Corp.)

CONTINUING FRANCHISE SERVICES

Once a unit is open and running, the first year or two of advice and assistance is the most crucial. Even once a franchisee is sufficiently experienced to manage his or her unit without close assistance, the advantages of a franchise are still impressive. We can group these under the general headings of operations and control and marketing.

OPERATIONS AND CONTROL

The franchisor needs continually to assess existing systems and design and introduce new ones as competition and technological developments dictate.

INTERESTED IN BECOMING A FRANCHISEE?

Here Are Seven Basic Questions for a Prospective Franchisee

1. Is the company itself reasonably secure financially, or is it selling franchises to get cash to cover ongoing expenses?
   - Is the company selective in choosing franchisees?
   - Is it in too big a hurry to get your money? Is this deal too good to be true?

   Today, sweetheart deals are few and far between.

2. Does the company have a solid base of company-owned units? If it does,
   - It is in the same business as are their franchisees.
   - It is in the company's interest to concentrate on improving marketing and operating systems.

   If *your* primary business is operations and *theirs* is selling franchises, the system is headed for trouble.

3. Is the system successful on a per-unit basis? To find out, you have to look at several numbers:
   - Comparable average sales of stores that have been open longer than one year (sometimes first-year sales are very high and then drop off).
   - Unit-level trends: What you really need is sales data adjusted for inflation or, better yet, customer counts at the unit level.

   A business is really only growing when it's serving more people.

4. Is the franchisor innovative across all parts of its business?
   - The company should be working on operating and equipment refinements.
   - Ask what it is doing in purchasing, recruiting, training, and labor scheduling. Is anyone working to make uniforms more attractive, durable, and comfortable, for instance?

   The best companies are consistently trying to upgrade every component of their business.

5. Does the company share sufficient support services with its franchisees?
   - In general, the company should provide guidance and strategic direction on marketing and excellent operations training. In addition, every franchisee should have contact with a company employee whose primary responsibility is a small group of franchised restaurants.
   - There are some services that a company can't provide, such as setting prices. And others are risky, such as getting involved in franchisee manager selection or outside financing.

   Support services must be shared in such a way that they respect the franchisee's independence.

6. Does the company respect its franchisees?
    *   In addition to formal publications, there should be regular informal forums or councils in which selected franchisees meet face to face with top management to discuss both problems and opportunities.
    *   Corporate staff should collect ideas, test them, and, if they look good, involve franchisees in expanded testing.

    Franchisees should actually participate in the development of any change that will affect their units.

7. Does the franchisor provide long-term leadership for the entire system?
    *   Franchisee participation is no excuse for franchisor abdication of its leadership responsibilities. Somebody has to make the formal decisions, and that must be the franchisee.
    *   A primary function of the franchisor is to protect the value of each franchise by actively and aggressively monitoring operations, demanding that each unit live up to system standards.

    Perhaps a necessary long-term decision is not popular. Making tough decisions and following through may be the best real test of leadership.

Source: Adapted from Don N. Smith, Burton Shaw Lecture, Washington State University, Fall 1985.

Franchisors develop and redevelop daily operating and control procedures, including information management systems. They are responsible for quality maintenance and inspection, training program and media development, and purchasing assistance.

Operating and Control Procedures

We often think of operation and control as separate functions, but ideally the franchisor strives to present operating methods that have control procedures designed into them. For instance, McDonald's not only specifies the portion sizes of its french fries but also has designed packages and serving devices that ensure that the portion size will be accurately maintained. Similarly, Long John Silver's specifies a procedure for portioning fish that, if followed, will minimize waste. In the hotel business, Holiday Inns provides numerous reports and analyses to its franchisees based on daily operating data transmitted by front-office and reservation transactions.

The essential ingredient in a successful franchisor's "proven way of doing business" is not just a great idea but an *operational concept*. The concept works and is accepted by customers, and its results can be tracked so that its continuing success is measured and assessed. We should note here, too, that the product and service that underlies the franchise must be continually redeveloped to remain current in the marketplace.

Information Management

Accounting systems furnished by franchisors normally integrate the individual sales transactions from the point-of-sales terminal with both daily management reports and the franchisee's books of account. This makes current management and marketing information available in a timely way and helps hold down the cost of accounting services. Given the rapidly changing state of information technology, information processing can be an especially helpful function to have a large organization carry out. For example, a large organization can achieve economies of scale in software design and equipment purchases.

Quality Control

Inspection systems help keep units on their toes and provide the franchisee with an expert—if sometimes annoying—outsider's view of the operation. Quality control staff use detailed inspection forms that ensure systemwide standards. Inspectors are trained by the franchisor, and their work is generally backed up by detailed written guidelines. In some companies, such as Kentucky Fried Chicken, the inspection is a part of the research and development organization rather than operations. This means that inspection is not a duty of the franchise district manager who is responsible for the daily working relationships with the franchisee. That is, it ensures a disinterested view.

Training

In addition to the opening training effort, franchisors prepare training materials such as videotapes for common tasks in a unit, training manuals, and other training aids. Most large franchisors have an expert training and audio-visual staff who are continually evaluating and updating programs.

Field Support

There is general agreement on the importance of field support:

> In the opinion of some long-term franchisees, it is the quality of field support that ultimately determines how good a franchise system is. One of them, who owns two restaurants from two different franchisors, states, "It is not so much a lack of knowledge as a lack of desire that separates the good franchises from the poor ones. I feel that I am with one of the best and one of the worst. The difference is how well they are staffed and how eager they are to assist."[11]

In the lodging industry, on the other hand, the unit generally operates without any franchisor field supervision beyond the regular inspection.

---

[11]McGuire, *Franchised Distribution*, p. 93.

Thus, the lodging franchisee is expected to hire more experienced people in the top jobs.

Field support often causes problems between the franchisee and the franchisor. One common complaint is that the field representative's visits are not frequent enough. For instance, the author visited with a motel manager who was getting ready to discontinue his franchise. He said that in the two and a half years he had been a franchisee, he had never had a visit from anyone connected with his franchisor's company!

Another complaint is the field supervisors' lack of expertise. One multiunit fast-food franchise operator told the writer that he found his own staff was generally more experienced than was the franchisor's field staff. "We end up spending a lot of time explaining things to the people who are supposed to be supervising us," he commented. Clearly, not all franchise organizations are of the same level of quality, and the field staff is one important differentiation.

Purchasing

Two quite different sets of practices are followed in providing purchasing services to franchisees. Some companies, particularly in lodging, have established supplier subsidiaries that are operated for profit. These subsidiaries supply materials appropriate for use in the operation, and they often carry a broad line of products that enables one-stop shopping. This range of products includes furniture, fixtures, and linens as well as cleaning and other supplies, but not foodstuffs.

On the other hand, many restaurant companies have purchasing cooperatives that often are nonprofit organizations. At KFC-USA, for instance, a separate corporation, the KFC National Purchasing Cooperative, Inc., has been established. The coop offers one-stop shopping for virtually all products required in a KFC operation: food, packaging, and equipment as well as a comprehensive insurance program. In addition, the coop periodically publishes a price list that the units can use in negotiating prices with local distributors. The coop also publishes a newsletter containing information on pricing and trends in equipment, food products, and supply.

A third approach in food service is found in companies that approve outside suppliers as exclusive purveyors at contracted prices.

Although attractive price and the convenience of one-stop shopping are important purchasing benefits, particularly with the coops, perhaps the most important advantage in the purchasing area is quality maintenance. The lengthy product development process includes careful attention to each product ingredient and the development of detailed product specifications. Often the franchisor will work with the research department of a supplier company to develop a product to meet these specifications and to anticipate market fluctuations. Moreover, it is common for franchisors to maintain a quality control staff in packing plants and maintain rigorous inspection systems that monitor the product from the fabrication plant to regional storage centers and then to the individual operating unit.[12]

There is another side to the purchasing coin, however. In some franchise systems, franchisees complain they have been overcharged for products sold to them by the franchisor or its supplier subsidiary. Tying agreements requiring the purchase of supplies from the franchisor, however, have been under concerted legal attack for some time and are not presently a major source of friction.

MARKETING

Second only in importance to providing franchisees with a unique way of doing business is the ongoing development and execution of the system's marketing plan. Although franchisees usually are consulted about the marketing program—in many companies quite extensively—the executive responsibility for developing and implementing the system's marketing program lies with the franchisor's top management and marketing staff.

The franchisor normally spends a significant part of its own marketing budget on national advertising. Moreover, most franchise contracts require the contribution of a certain percentage of sales by each franchised unit (including those owned and operated by the franchisor) to the system's advertising budget. Many franchise agreements also require the franchisee to spend an additional percentage of sales on local advertising which is commonly managed by a local or regional advertising cooperative.

By pooling advertising funds with other franchisees and the franchisor, the individual franchisee secures two kinds of advantages. First, the pooled resources make a much greater impact than each individual effort would. A single unit generally cannot afford television advertising, but 10 units can. Similarly, regional and national media purchases that single units couldn't even consider become feasible for franchise systems.

Creative and production costs for television are major stumbling blocks for individual operations. No "hamburger stand" could ever arrest the attention of a top agency, let alone fund the development of even one of McDonald's television commercials. A franchise group can, however, attract the best creative talent, and production costs can be shared by a large number of units. KFC's national advertising cooperative spends 12 percent or more of a multimillion-dollar budget on production costs such as preparing and shooting television commercials.

---

[12]For a fuller discussion of the significance of the logistical function in multiunit operations, see Thomas F. Powers, "Complex Food Service Systems," *Cornell Hotel and Restaurant Administration Quarterly,* November 1979, p. 55.

Advertising Cooperatives

Advertising co-ops typically provide copies of the company's television and radio commercials to franchisee members for a nominal price, as well as mats for both black-and-white and color newspaper ads at no charge. Co-ops also develop point-of-purchase promotional materials such as window banners and counter cards. Co-ops may also provide standardized material and know-how for local direct mail campaigns, develop national public relations programs, and give franchisees materials and advice to achieve local public relations tie-ins.

Many franchise systems have both national and regional or local advertising co-ops. The national co-op is charged with developing such material as just described and executing a national advertising program, often in conjunction with the franchising company's marketing department. Regional and local co-ops devote their efforts to media buying and to execution of the advertising program in their area. The pooling of media buys at the local level yields substantial savings, makes advertising dollars go further, and secures a frequency of advertising that heightens their effectiveness. Local and regional co-ops also often coordinate local promotional programs such as those using couponing, games, or premium merchandise.

Advice to franchisees and their local and regional co-ops is also available both on a personal basis and through marketing manuals, newsletters, and other written communications. The accumulation of experience in the franchisor's marketing department and advertising co-op makes it possible for an individual unit—on its own or through its local co-op—to have expert advice on specialized marketing topics such as coupons, ethnic marketing, newspaper inserts, media scheduling, and point-of-sale and local store marketing.

New Products

The marketplace changes constantly, and it is the franchisor's responsibility to monitor and respond to those changes. The company's marketing department carries out a program of continuing market research. When a need for a new product emerges, either from research or from suggestions from franchisees, the company develops a new product in its test kitchens and tests it for consumer acceptance with taste panels and for fit with the operating system in a pilot store or stores. If the product looks feasible, wider market research is undertaken on matters such as product acceptance, fit with the image of the company, cannibalization (loss of sales to the new product from their own existing products), and appropriate marketing tactics. More or less at the same time, the product will be market-tested in a few stores.

If the results to this point are favorable, the test will usually be broadened to several markets, and preparations will be made for a system-wide rollout. At the very least, this rollout involves "selling" the new product

Few individual restaurants can afford the production cost of a television commercial. The franchisor, of the national advertising co-op, provides first-class TV commercials to franchisees for use in their local market. (Courtesy of Hardee's and Ogilvy & Mather.)

internally, to franchisees, and preparing a promotional program including advertising media and point-of-purchase materials to sell it to consumers.

Although not all new products are successful—in fact, many are not—those that are keep the franchise system's image current and fresh. They are an important weapon in the fight to keep or improve the system's market share in the highly competitive hospitality marketplace.

ACCESS TO CAPITAL

Because of a franchise's record of success, it is much easier for franchisees to borrow money to start a new franchise or to expand or refurbish existing operations. The dramatically lower risk is also reflected in a lower interest rate, thus reducing an important capital cost.

Some franchise companies offer advice on finding debt financing, and some have established working relationships with lending companies. Franchise companies themselves, however, do not provide capital to franchisees.

A BIG COMPANY LOOKS AT BECOMING A FRANCHISEE

Greyhound Food Management has become a franchisee of Burger King. Its analysis of the advantages and disadvantages of this decision is instructive.

Advantages of Franchising

1. Franchising provides national exposure and a recognized national brand.
2. The franchisor offers proven operating systems, procedures, and standardized manuals.
3. Lower overhead and management costs translate into higher profits.
4. The franchisor provides management support.

Disadvantages of Franchising

1. The franchisor imposes operating restrictions.
2. The franchisor controls expansion and growth.
3. The franchisor can be inflexible.
4. We incur additional advertising expenses that do not directly benefit us.
5. The franchisor has its own complex organization and bureaucracy.

Source: Adapted from Joseph J. Fassler, president and chief operating officer, Greyhound Food Management, Inc., *12th Annual Chain Operators Exchange* (Chicago: International Foodservice Manufacturers Association, 1985).

DRAWBACKS FOR THE FRANCHISEE

Some of the more obvious drawbacks of obtaining a franchise have been implicit in our discussion: loss of independence and payment of substantial advertising assessments and franchise fees. If the franchisee has picked a weak franchising organization, field support and other management services may be inadequate.

Franchising is *not* risk free. The franchisee is generally completely dependent on the franchisor not only for marketing but often for purchasing and other operations-oriented assistance. If a franchise concept is not kept up-to-date—as many argue has been the case for Howard Johnson's Restaurants—or loses its focus—as, for instance, Kentucky Fried Chicken seemed to do for a time in the late 1970s—it is difficult for the franchisee to do much about it.

What happens when things really go bad is illustrated by the case of Arthur Treacher's Fish and Chips.[13] A successful and growing franchise of the mid-1970s, Treacher's then had serious difficulties ending in bankruptcy. Its national marketing efforts virtually ceased. Its product quality control system broke down, and yet the franchisees were contractually obligated to purchase only from approved suppliers. The franchisees also were required to pay both advertising fees and royalties but claimed they received little or no services in return. Many franchisees withheld payment of fees and royalties and then became involved in lengthy lawsuits which were expensive in both executive time and attorneys' fees. While some Treacher franchisees weathered the series of setbacks, virtually all suffered serious losses, and many left the field.

Don Smith, in his 1985 Burton Shaw Lecture at Washington State University, asserted that "franchising is the best single opportunity available to hedge your bet," but nevertheless pointed out, "No man and no management team can eliminate risks in any company."

THE FRANCHISOR'S DEAL

Just as the franchisee seeks benefits from the franchise arrangement, the franchisor stands to gain a number of advantages. These can be grouped under the heading of marketing, finance, operations, and entrepreneurship.

MARKETING

Franchising represents a solution to a company's marketing problem when "place" or representation in a geographically defined market is crucial. Clearly this is the case in the hospitality industry. If your restaurant com-

---

[13]The difficulties of a franchise system in trouble are told from the point of view of a successful multiunit franchisee in case-history form in Thomas F. Powers, "MIE Hospitality" (Guelph, Ont.: Advanced Management Program for the Hospitality Industry, 1983).

pany has no units in Iowa, you'll have no sales in Iowa, and so being "in place" is crucial to the marketing mix of the restaurant company with national or regional ambitions.

Don Smith pointed out that there is a level of distribution to be achieved in a market that causes sales to go up. First, the more units a company has in a market, the more advertising media it can buy. Second, the better coverage there is, the easier it will be for people to visit often; the restaurants are simply closer. Finally, continuous exposure of all kinds—seeing television commercials, driving past the sign and building, as well as actually visiting the restaurant—contribute to "top-of-mind awareness"; that is, being the first place that comes into people's minds when they think of a restaurant. Clearly, then, being in place in a market is a crucial advantage and one more readily secured quickly through franchising.

In the lodging industry, representation in major markets is important not only to get a share of the business in those markets but also to gain access to the business generated by those cities or areas for other markets. For example, travelers are more likely to stay in a hotel with which they are familiar at home, and one that can offer convenient reservation service near the trip's point of origination. Moreover, the lodging firm has a higher chance of retaining travelers as guests for the balance of a trip once they stay in one of their properties. Making forward reservations is easy and encouraged. This *system effect* reinforces the importance of representation in every major market.

Implicit in our earlier discussion of advertising from the franchisee's point of view is that the franchisor and its units, along with the system as a whole, gain from the large volume of local market advertising and promotion undertaken by the franchisees and their coops. Clearly, too, the franchisor gains from the franchisees' contribution to the national advertising fund. The pooling of resources, then, benefits franchisor at least as much as it does the franchisees.

FINANCE

Any company with a proven, successful format for doing business is likely to want to expand rapidly, preferably before its approach is copied. The first franchise in the North American hospitality industry was the result of Howard Johnson's financial inability to expand with his good idea during difficult economic times. The expansion that he and his company did undertake was financed largely by the capital provided by his franchisees.

When a franchise system begins to expand, one of its major advantages is that its need to expand its fixed asset base is much less than if the expansion were made up of owned units. In most companies, the franchisee acquires the fixed assets or a lease commitment to cover those assets. Although a company earns a higher total dollar profit on sales from owned units, the franchisor's return on investment is much higher for franchised units, just because its investment is so much lower.

This ad is provided by the franchisor to franchisees to run in their local newspapers. (Courtesy of Country Kitchen International, Inc.)

Not only do franchisees pay royalties on sales, they also commonly pay a franchise initiation fee. In a relatively younger franchise company, these initiation fees may help provide working capital during expansion. The major factor, however, in financing the expansion of the franchise system is the franchisee's assumption of the responsibility, through lease or ownership, of the fixed assets.

We ought to note that it is not only new companies that use franchising as a means of financing. Sometimes established companies increase their franchising activities, as Jack-in-the-Box and Denny's did to handle new debt they had taken on.[14]

[14]*Nation's Restaurant News* May 20, 1985, p. 3.

OPERATIONS

The franchisee is the owner of a business. As such, he or she can be expected to have a lively interest in how that business is run. The responsibility for the franchised operation's success is principally that of the franchisee. The franchisee's interest in his or her own operation also has important implications for the franchise company's organization. A district manager (DM) is likely to supervise somewhere between 4 and 8 company-owned units. A franchise district manager (FDM) is responsible for assisting franchisees with their operating problems and usually ensuring conformance with standards. The FDM's span of responsibility, in practice, ranges from 15 to 70 units, but Smith asserted that 30 is the maximum number of units that an FDM can reasonably handle.[15]

Clearly, a company like McDonald's, which owns about 25 percent of its units, would need a quite different organization to operate its 9000 or so restaurants if it owned all of them. The larger field staff of DMs (using the preceding figures, McDonald's might need something like 225 more DMs) plus additional layers of area supervisors to oversee the DMs would be unwieldy in size and necessarily more bureaucratic. Indeed, having ownership interest so significantly represented at the operating level in much of the system does wonders to simplify the company's organization.

Smith also pointed to the significance of the franchisees as a resource for know-how. Input from the grass-roots level "creates a check and balance that enables the corporate functional support groups to keep a proper perspective on the business."[16] Smith also stressed the value of practical ideas that franchisees running daily operations can bring to the solution of operating problems:

> A simple example is the sour cream gun at Taco Bell. Everyone in the Taco Bell system knew it was needed for better portion control and faster speed of service. After spending several years and several hundred thousand dollars with no practical solution in sight, the company gave up. Finally, a franchisee showed them how it should be done. On a much larger scale, breakfast at McDonald's had been tried without success until a franchisee came up with Egg McMuffin.[17]

ENTREPRENEURSHIP

The original idea developed by the franchisor constitutes the first and most important entrepreneurial contribution to the system. On the other hand, some franchisees also bring entrepreneurial ability to the local market. A particularly interesting aspect of the franchisee's entrepreneurial contribu-

[15]Smith, Burton Shaw Lecture. He calls what we have referred to as the FDM a Franchise Consultant, which may be a better way of thinking of the role. Field practice, however, tends toward titles like FDM.
[16]Smith, Burton Shaw Lecture.
[17]Smith, Burton Shaw Lecture.

tion was highlighted by a study of franchising that suggested that one of the major purposes of buybacks of franchised operations is simply to get a good franchisee to move on and open a new market.[18] The logic of this strategy is that the entrepreneurial skills needed to open a new territory for a franchise system are so rare that it is nearly impossible to find them. Thus by offering to the successful franchisee a substantial profit in a buyback, the franchisor frees that franchisee to move on to new territory and to use his or her skills to extend the franchise system's market penetration. Although this is likely to be significant mainly for younger, growing companies, it suggests the level of ability that most franchisees can bring to a franchise relationship.

FRANCHISING DISADVANTAGES

The bargain struck with franchisees has its costs to franchisors. Although their experience varies, many franchise companies find that their owned stores yield higher sales and profit margins. And if the company owned all its units—if it could overcome the organizational difficulties of a much larger, more complex organization—the profits earned from the same stores would be higher than the royalties received from a franchised store.

We should note, too, that not all franchise income is profit. Usually 2 percent of sales is needed to service a franchise system. And because of start-up costs for a new franchised unit *for the franchisor*, it may be three years before the royalties begin to contribute to the franchisor's profit.[19] In addition, the franchisor will already have made a considerable investment: The expenditures to establish a franchise system, including legal and accounting costs,[20] executives' time, and consultants' and managerial time, have been estimated at over $200,000.[21]

The international Franchise Association pointed out another paradox to which the franchisor is exposed:

> Although the success of a franchise system depends on the unique services and products sold through it, the United States Federal Trade Commission (FTC) and many states require the disclosure of so much information about the franchise, the franchisor's business operation, finances, franchisees, suppliers and the franchisor that few secrets remain for long.[22]

Perhaps the greatest drawback, however, is the loss of control. The management of an owned operation is much more straightforward. As Rick

---

[18]Professor R. M. Knight, School of Business of Administration, University of Western Ontario, personal communication.

[19]Smith, Burton Shaw Lecture.

[20]Robert & Kushell and Carl E. Zwisler III, *How to Be a Franchisor* (Washington, D.C.: International Franchise Association, 1984), p. 14.

[21]Smith, Burton Shaw Lecture.

[22]Kushell and Zwisler, *How to Be a Franchisor*, p. 10.

Duffy, former vice-president of Kentucky Fried Chicken and now one of its multiunit franchisees, put it in an interview, "When you own them, you run them. With a franchisee, you have to convince him to run them."[23] Sometimes a successful franchisee grows complacent, and the franchisor finds it difficult to motivate him or her to keep up with changes being encouraged system-wide or even just to maintain quality standards. Product line changes must be "sold" to franchisees, as must most capital additions such as drive-throughs or special joint marketing efforts like a national game promotion. (Note the almost-universal rider on "deal" advertisements: "Available from participating stores." Apparently not every store chooses to participate.) Management in a franchise system, then, requires somewhat different skills.

Difficulties with franchising do lead some companies to withdraw from franchising. When Stouffer's terminated its franchise contracts, it did so because it felt that it did not have adequate quality control in its franchised operations.[24]

FUNCTIONING OF THE FRANCHISE SYSTEM

We have seen that the franchise relationship is one of mutual interdependence. We have looked at how franchising affects operations and marketing. In the next section we will draw together some of those observations in order to see franchising as a marketing system. Following that we will discuss how franchising functions as a management system.

FRANCHISING AS A MARKETING SYSTEM

In marketing, the franchisor takes the lead, but both the company and its franchisees are essential to make the system work. One useful way to look at the functioning of marketing in a franchise system is to use the elements of the marketing mix (described in the previous chapter) as an organizing framework. We will arrange our discussion here, however, in order of the importance of each element to the franchise system: place, product and service, promotion, and price.

Place

The franchise system penetrates markets quickly and gives all members of the franchise system the advantages discussed earlier regarding representation. Covering a market fully makes it convenient for guests to patronize units, and convenience is a major selling appeal related to location.

Building exteriors are often identical. If not, the sign will use a known corporate logo to ensure recognition. Interiors are commonly much the same

[23]Richard L. Duffy, personal communication.
[24]*Restaurant Business*, July 20, 1986, p. 142.

STEP-BY-STEP GUIDE TO FRANCHISING

Launching a successful restaurant franchise is actually a three-step program. First, a restaurateur must have a well-managed, profitable restaurant or restaurants that have been in business for at least a year. Next, he can begin the actual preparation and marketing of the franchise system, and, finally, he must nurture the ongoing relationship with his franchisees.

Assuming the restaurateur has satisfied the first step, how does he get to the third step, the point where he could be declared a successful franchisor? The following is a brief guide to that second crucial step:

- Contract with an outside consultant to receive a second, objective opinion about the franchisability of the restaurant. Some criteria to consider: Is there a broad market potential for the restaurant or is it essentially a local phenomenon? Does the restaurateur have strong internal operations, accounting procedures, and financial and cash control systems that will enable the monitoring of franchisees from a distance? Can the restaurant, its systems and personality easily be duplicated?
- Develop a business plan, outlining goal of franchise, its marketing strategy, financial backing, expansion plans, training programs, management programs, and supply and revenue sources.
- Contract with an attorney specializing in franchising to draw up a franchise agreement and disclosure documents required by the Federal Trade Commission.
- Develop operations manual, training programs, franchise marketing and sales materials, bookkeeping and other franchise support systems.
  — if necessary, file registration documents. Fourteen states require registration before franchises can be sold.
- Hire an in-house salesman or salesmen to sell franchises. Franchises should not be sold so quickly that the franchisor does not have the resources to serve all his franchisees, nor should they be sold in a shotgun fashion around the country because they will be too hard to monitor and will not realize any economies of scale.

Source: Restaurants & Institutions, February 5, 1986, p. 105.

---

in food service. Ambience and decor—all of these things we referred to as the presentation mix in the last chapter—are manipulated to secure the establishment's identity. Uniformity is more pronounced in food service than in lodging. Even there, though, the guests are given numerous cues to remind them where they are: corporate logo, signs, and uniforms, for instance.

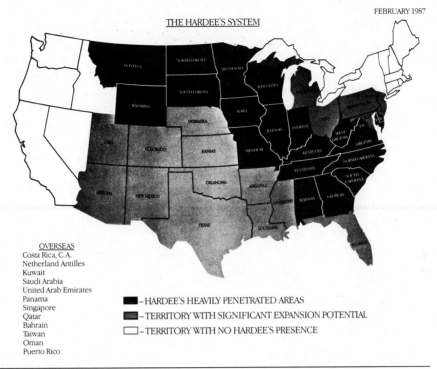

Hardee's system uses franchisees as an important means to expand into new territories, as well as to penetrate established territories. (Courtesy of Hardee's.)

Product and Service

"No surprises" is a tag line sometimes used in Holiday Inns' advertising, and it might be used by most franchise systems to sum up their product line. Most restaurant systems' menu offerings are identical, with minor variations. In lodging, there is more variety in individual menu offerings within a chain, and the details of decor differ, but the core product is essentially the same.

Franchisees are intelligent, independent businesspeople, and they often come up with new product ideas. Some, like Egg McMuffin, are highly successful and support the system's battle for market share. Moreover, the franchise system is a network for marketing intelligence on competitive products. Franchisees are concerned about new products in their local markets. It is the franchise company's function to meet those market trends with appropriate product innovations, but the information network is important to identifying and tracking trends, developing product ideas, and in testing and refining those ideas and products.

Promotion

At least two promotion advantages are available to franchise systems. First and most obvious is the pooling of financial resources that gives the system a large promotional war chest not only to mount a national advertising campaign (or a regional one for smaller systems) but also to develop first-rate media for local advertising efforts.

Less obvious but also important is the presence of decision makers in local markets who can respond to local trends. For instance, if couponing is used in a market, the local decision maker can assess the need to respond. For many decisions, then, the franchise organization is characterized by a very high degree of decentralization.

The local franchisee probably also becomes an affluent and influential citizen, likely to take part in local affairs in a way that benefits the company's image in that market. In a society as highly mobile as that in North America, this too is a significant advantage, because strength in many local markets adds up to significant advantages in the transient market.

Price

Although price regulation is not legal, system prices tend to be uniform, perhaps because of similar operating costs and common pricing rules of thumb. The general uniformity gives consumers an important piece of information when they are choosing where to eat or sleep. On the other hand, as with promotional practice, local decision makers can match local price trends and special conditions. In lodging, system directories provide information about price ranges, and reservation systems permit guests to secure a definite price in advance of their stay.

System Marketing

The franchise system functions across all variables of the marketing mix. Uniformity of product and presentation mix and aggregation of advertising funds are advantages of the system's centralization. Representation in many locations and flexibility in promotion and pricing decisions are advantages of the system's decentralization. As in any system, the whole is greater than the sum of the parts.

FRANCHISING AS A MANAGEMENT SYSTEM

The formal basis of authority in the franchise system is the franchise contract. The agreement between franchisor and franchisee should be structured

> to preserve the independence of both parties and to prevent each from being held liable for the other's acts, omissions and financial obligations. The contract must include enough control over image, product and service to

preserve exclusive trade marks and service mark rights and to ensure uniformity from outlet to outlet but must avoid unlawful controls over pricing, purchasing, territories or customers.[25]

Although the contract serves as the legal basis of the franchise relationship, the real key to the day-to-day working relationship is mutual interest. The recent history of franchise companies is marked by compromises between the interest of the franchisor and the franchisee. Pepsico, for instance, wanted to develop in the early 1980s a new, master franchise agreement for the Pizza Hut system, to replace the many individual agreements made under Pizza Hut's previous owner. The franchisor was generous on royalty rates for some existing franchisees. Balancing that, most of the franchisees agreed to join advertising coops, to increase mandatory central training of store management, and to require store remodeling every seven years. That is, they agreed to increases in costs and reductions in autonomy. The key appears to have been mutual interest: The franchisor was able to convince franchisees that what was good for the system was good for them.[26]

In operations, it often is necessary to enforce quality standards through the system's inspection program. It helps, however, if the franchisees have been consulted in developing those standards and if the maintenance of standards in one unit is in the interests of all the units. The best way to urge a franchisee who has quality deficiencies to "clean up his act" is peer pressure.[27] That is, other franchisees are urged to communicate to the recalcitrant one their commitment to standards and to persuade him or her to restore the operation to mutually agreed-upon standards.

Communications

In the early days of a franchise system's growth, personal contact between the franchisor's top management and the franchisees is generally the rule. And although personal contact remains important, as the company matures and increases in size, it appears that much of the contact is with a lower-level official of the franchise company such as the FDM, or that it takes place in group settings. Table 20.4 summarizes the most common forms of communication between the franchisor and the franchisee. Over twice as many franchisors evaluating communications rated field visits in first place. Meetings, conventions, and seminars were the second most highly valued for communication. Phone contacts were third, and newsletters were rated fourth. Franchisors also use special bulletins, toll-free lines, and even videocassettes and teleconferences. Meetings are held on both regional and national levels, and the franchisor is generally represented by senior manage-

---

[25]Kushell and Zwisler, *How to Be a Franchisor,* p. 9.
[26]*Restaurant Business,* February 1, 1982, p. 154.
[27]Richard L. Duffy, personal communication.

TABLE 20.4 Regular Methods of Communication with Franchisees

Method of Communication	Percentage of Franchisors Using
Phone contact	96%
Field calls	91
Meetings	89
Newsletters	87
Surveys and questionnaires	49
Other publications	42
Other methods	30

Source: International Franchise Association.

ment. Perhaps one of the most effective means of communication is the franchise association, which we will discuss in the next section.

Franchise Associations

Franchise associations are initiated by either the franchisees or the franchisor. Some councils are initiated and operated jointly by both. Their purpose is principally to facilitate communication within the system, but this purpose may be phrased as "discussing mutual problems," "disseminating information," "evaluating franchisor programs and policies," or "increased franchisor–franchisee teamwork in serving customers."[28]

The board of directors of a franchise association is generally made up of elected franchisee members. Franchisor representatives on the council are generally drawn from the highest levels of top management. (In some cases, members of the governing body may include franchisees appointed by the franchisor.) Commonly, the national franchise association will be made up mainly of elected regional franchisee representatives. The regional association is often the backbone of the franchisee network and is usually more active than the national association is, meeting several times a year, whereas most national associations meet only once a year. Franchise association meetings are generally concerned with the following kinds of topics:

Operations. Facilities, training, operating manuals, assistance with franchisees in house training programs, communications, and customer satisfaction.

Marketing. Advertising, promotion, sales training, long- and short-range market forecasting, competitive information, and current market position.

[28]*How to Organize a Franchisee Council* (Washington, D.C.: International Franchise Association, 1979, revised 1985), p. 8.

Finance and Management.   Financial operations and general franchisee management, standard accounting systems, capitalization, equipment financing, franchising, franchisee facilities and personnel, franchisee business continuity, and product liability.

Products and Services.   Product and services improvements and applications, and new product and service development.[29]

Persuasion, Compromise, and Negotiation

We began our discussion on managing the franchise system by remarking on how often compromise is the basis of settling disagreements in franchise systems, and that is a good note on which to conclude the section. Pizza Hut's relicensing negotiations referred to earlier required a year of face-to-face meetings of its franchisees and Pepsico's top management in which the franchise agreement was discussed on a clause-by-clause basis.

More recently, when Pillsbury acquired Godfather's Pizza, it took over a system in which franchisee relations had badly deteriorated. It promptly set about mending fences, consulting the franchisees in developing a marketing plan and support services as a means of securing their voluntary resumption of royalty payments.[30] The differences between Marriott and its Big Boy franchisees were settled similarly in all but two cases, by negotiations characterized by such give-and-take that in one territory, Marriott ended up as subfranchisee of one of its own franchisees!

As Smith put it, "Franchising isn't the place for someone who needs total control." The thing that draws together the franchisor and franchisee is mutual interest, and so franchisor management personnel must learn to appeal to that interest. It is the franchisee's own self-interest and acceptance of the rules of the game that enables the successful franchise relationship, rather than the letter of the franchise agreement. Persuasion and conciliation, rather than orders and directives, characterize the interpersonal exchange between franchisor and franchisee.

REGULATION

No one should think that all is rosy. When several parties' interests are at stake, there are bound to be different views. Many franchisees feel that the franchisors don't respect their independence. Even more importantly, there have been a number of cases of questionable and downright dishonest behavior by franchisors. For these reasons, franchisee lobbying has focused on the franchisees' rights and prevention of abuse and dishonesty by franchisors. As well, the growing economic significance of franchising and fran-

---

[29]*How to Organize a Franchisee Council,* p. 9.
[30]*Nation's Restaurant News,* December 2, 1985, p. 40.

chisee investing has drawn the lawmakers' attention to franchising. As a result, a considerable body of legislation has been passed regulating franchising at both the federal and the state levels.

A major focus of regulation has been on full disclosure and fair reporting of information to prospective franchisees. In 1971 the state of California adopted a law requiring, in effect, the franchisors to file a prospectus providing information on both the franchisor and the details of the franchise contract. Several other states have passed similar legislation. In 1979 the U.S. Fair Trade Commission (FTC) published a rule spelling out national disclosure requirements:

> Identification of the franchisor, including business experience and financial history of the company, its directors and officers, as well as the litigation and bankruptcy history for each.
>
> Description of the franchise, initial and recurring funds required to be paid to the franchisor as well as statistical information on franchised or owned units, site selection, and training assistance.
>
> Persons or companies with whom the franchisee is obligated or advised to do business, and financing arrangements.
>
> Degree of personal participation required of the franchisee, and termination, cancellation, and renewal arrangements.

The FTC also forbids publication of income forecasts unless they can be reasonably substantiated. Currently, over 36 states have disclosure rules, some of which are more stringent on some points than are those of the FTC.

Failure to follow FTC regulations can be expensive. One company, Philly Mignon, was fined $80,000 plus 5 percent of franchisee sales for five years for failing to provide complete and accurate information, misrepresenting key facts about the company's record, and failing to secure suitable sites for its franchisees. The penalties were deliberately stated to be "modest" because the firm's continuing in business would have been endangered—and thus its franchisees' livelihood—by a stiffer fine.[31]

FRANCHISE TERMINATION

A franchisor's failure to renew its agreement is naturally a matter of concern to its franchisees. In fact, however, over 90 percent of franchise agreements are renewed, and typically, fewer than 5 percent are refused renewal by the franchisor. Most of these are for failure to pay royalties or to comply with other financial obligations or quality control standards.[32] But this problem, despite its currently modest dimension, has attracted the attention of state

---

[31]*Nation's Restaurant News*, February 13, 1984, p. 6.
[32]Kostecka, *Franchising in the Economy, 1984–86*, p. 13.

lawmakers. In Wisconsin, for instance, the franchisor's power to terminate unilaterally or to refuse to renew without cause is sharply restricted. A number of other states are considering similar restrictions.[33]

In court, it seems, the franchisor is the "big guy" and the franchisee the "little guy." The International Franchise Association indicated, for instance, that "almost all ambiguities in the franchise contract will be construed against the franchisor in litigation."[34] A decision in a case between Dunkin Donuts and a franchisee is illustrative. The franchisee had intentionally and fraudulently underreported revenue on which his royalties were computed. While upholding the company's right to terminate under these circumstances, the court actually awarded a judgment of $115,000 to the franchisee, to offset his original investment and give him a decent sum to start a new enterprise.

TRANSFERRING A FRANCHISE

Another subject of concern to franchisees is the right to transfer ownership to a franchise. This is particularly significant when settling the estate of a deceased franchisee. Although they currently are not regulated, over 95 percent of franchise transfer applications are approved by the franchisor.

RECENT TRENDS

As franchise chains grow and franchisees' organizations mature, conditions change, and new problems emerge. Some of these are a shortage of locations for franchisors, expensive franchising renewal provisions for established franchisees, and a lack of opportunity for expanding established franchisees. We will close this chapter by considering how both parties are moving to meet these problems.

CONVERSION FRANCHISING

There are only so many desirable locations. Large franchisors have begun to acquire other smaller chains to secure their locations and to convert their properties into those of the acquiring chains in what is sometimes called *conversion franchising*. Another occasion for conversion that is particularly prominent in the lodging industry is presented by older properties whose owners determine that it is not economically feasible to meet expensive refranchising requirements. Franchise groups, as we noted in Chapter 9, have begun to spring up to offer conversion opportunities to other franchises.

---

[33]*Nation's Restaurant News*, May 21, 1984, p. 6.
[34]Kushell and Zwisler, *How to Be a Franchisor*, p. 11.

MULTIPLE-CONCEPT FRANCHISING

Once an energetic and able franchisee is successfully established in his or her franchise, that person is likely to seek opportunities for further growth. This can—and often does—mean using the successful franchise operation for expanding his or her business interests. This in turn can mean a division of interests and sometimes even a conflict of interests. To try to meet this problem by offering franchisees an opportunity within the system for further growth, some franchisors have turned to multiple-concept franchising. Pepsico, for instance, developed its rapidly growing chain of retail bakeries, La Petite Boulangerie, to offer additional opportunities to the company's successful Taco Bell franchisees.[35] Shoney's, another highly successful restaurant company, offers franchises for Shoney's, Captain D's, Fifth Quarter, and Famous Recipe.[36]

Multiple-concept franchising appears to be an effort by franchisors to keep alive the spirit of franchise systems—mutual interest—by offering to successful franchisees opportunities for continued growth.

THE SUCCESSFUL FRANCHISE: FOLLOW THE LEADER

The attitude of the successful franchisee to the business world is an interesting one. Dennis Reese, president of the Reese Organization, perhaps the largest multiple-franchisee organization in the United States, suggested there is no shame in playing follow the leader:

> I will be in business servicing whatever industry leaders decide are the trends of the times. We may change the looks of our business but people have to eat. I can't really tell you what my business is going to look like. I wish good luck to all the creative people. Keep pumping research and development, and marketing. I will hitch a ride.[37]

SUMMARY

In this chapter we examined more closely the subject of franchising as it applies to the hospitality industry. Business format franchising, as that is the kind found in restaurants and hotels, was our focus.

We looked first at the economic significance of franchising. The next section was devoted to franchising from the franchisee's point of view. Among the topics were the process of finding and being accepted by a franchisor, the training and preparation that the franchisor offers, the franchisor's services, marketing, and access to capital. Then we outlined some of the drawbacks of being a franchisee.

[35]*Nation's Restaurant News,* December 5, 1984, p. 74, and March 11, 1985, p. 56.
[36]John J. Rohs, *The Restaurant Industry* (New York, Wertheim & Co., 1985), p. 29.
[37]*Restaurant Business,* December 10, 1985, p. 194.

We shifted next to the franchisor's viewpoint, including a discussion of marketing, finance, operations, entrepreneurship, and, last, the disadvantages of being a franchisor.

The following section was on the franchisor's functions, as both a marketing system and a management system.

Regulation was discussed, as well as terminating a franchise and transferring a franchise.

The final section was a quick look at recent trends in franchising: conversion franchising and multiple-concept franchising.

KEY WORDS AND CONCEPTS

To help you review this chapter, keep in mind the following:

Product and trade name franchising	Franchisee
Business format franchising	Field support
Franchise relationship	Advertising cooperatives
Franchise agreement	Entrepreneurship
Franchise system	Franchise associations
Franchisor	Conversion franchising
	Multiple-concept franchising

REVIEW QUESTIONS

1. What is the difference between product and trade name franchises and business format franchises? Which is more common in the hospitality industry?

2. Briefly describe the franchise relationship.

3. What important services does a franchisor offer to a new franchisee?

4. What are the continuing services that a franchisor provides for a franchisee?

5. Do you think a franchise has more benefits for the franchisor or the franchisee? Explain.

6. What are the greatest disadvantages of franchising to a franchisor?

7. Describe how a product may be promoted in a local market and in the national market.

8. What is multiple-concept franchising, and why is it important to the franchise relationship?

P A R T 6

A LOOK
AHEAD

C H A P T E R 21

Courtesy of New York Convention and Visitors Center.

VIEWS OF THE FUTURE

THE PURPOSE OF THIS CHAPTER

As you now know, a field as broad as hospitality management has forced us to cover a good deal of territory in the last twenty chapters. Now we want you to see the interrelationships in the material and rediscover the fact that the hospitality industry, for all its different aspects, *is* one industry. All aspects of the industry share problems arising from shifting patterns of supply, demand, and technology.

A number of trends, however, appear to be cutting across all sectors of the industry, even though some may affect one area more than another. Management in the hospitality industry will—and must—change to meet new conditions. Because, as we have insisted throughout this book, we are all in business for ourselves, you must determine what your goals are in the context of a changing industry and the changing work of managers. Then you must develop a positive plan of action, a strategy for gaining those goals. This chapter, a summary that looks to the future, should help you form this positive plan of action.

THIS CHAPTER SHOULD HELP YOU

1.   List and discuss the *forces* currently shaping the future of the hospitality industry.

2.   Suggest the effects these forces are likely to have on the cost patterns in the industry.

3. Describe the three interacting elements of demand as they bear on the continuing need for managers and workers in the hospitality industry.

4. Discuss the impact of technology and automation on the industry.

5. Describe the market fragmentation of food service.

6. Appraise the advantages of the independent operation and the chain and the outlook for each.

7. List the management challenges of the 1990s coming from within the industry and from the more general forces of social change as we present them in this chapter.

8. Place *yourself* in some way in this growing field of work and outline the strategy and tactics of personal development appropriate to your vocational goals.

We study the future, to paraphrase the historian, to understand the present. Trying to look ahead forces us to think in an orderly way about the forces at work today that are likely to affect tomorrow. Thus, we are really not trying to prophesy in this chapter but, rather, to identify the forces visibly at work today that are important to our industry. Even if the pictures of the future that this chapter envisions may be off the mark here and there, the identification of significant trends will still be important to you. As you shape your own career plans, the forces we examine in this chapter will continue to command your attention in the years to come, when you will be making your own estimates of their likely effects.

THE FORCES THAT WILL SHAPE THE FUTURE

The most basic economic forces are, as always, supply and demand. But supply and demand operate in a changing social and technological environment. With so many variables at play, we can make no precise forecasts, but some general directions seem clear.

THE DEMAND FOR HOSPITALITY SERVICES

Ultimately, the hospitality industry is shaped by its consumers and the products and services they need and want. Demand is affected by factors such as consumer demographics and population trends, including age, sex, and marital status. Income and employment trends are also important shapers of consumer preferences. The education of the population and the changing culture we live in influence consumer tastes and interests. In the following sections we will look at both the quantitative and the qualitative aspects of demand from the point of view of demographics, employment and income, and education.

CONSUMER DEMOGRAPHICS

In Chapter 1 we looked at the trends in the population's ages. One conclusion we reached was that the middle-aged segment of our population is growing in significance. We noted that as people move into middle age, their incomes rise. By early middle age—say around 40—the expenses of starting a family such as furnishing a house and the adjustments and expenses that come with the birth of children are behind them. This is the age when guests are most likely to travel and when their spending on eating out reaches its highest point. The increase in the affluent middle-aged population, then, represents a major opportunity for the hospitality industry. The late middle years provide an even wealthier consumer. Dubbed the "Ultras," consumers aged 50 to 64 spend over 20 percent more of their income on nonessentials than does the average consumer.[1] Because the number of people choosing early retirement has been increasing, many in this age group are likely to have more leisure.

The senior citizen population segment, however, is where leisure really reigns. Although not as prosperous as middle-aged people, seniors on the average tend to be in comfortable economic circumstances and have lots of time to spend on eating out, travel, and recreation. In recent years, there has been a trend toward more part-time employment to supplement retirement income which increases the affluence of many in this group. In addition, the mandatory retirement age has been moved up, which means that a significant percentage of people in this age bracket are still employed, usually at the highest income they have had in their lifetimes.

EMPLOYMENT, INCOME, AND DEMAND FOR HOSPITALITY

Probably the most significant social development in the last generation has been the increasing number of working women and of two-income families. In Chapter 5 we saw that many of the "service functions" of the family, such as feeding children lunch (and sometimes breakfast) as well as caring for the elderly, have been moved to social agencies such as schools and congregate meal programs. The next decade will likely see the continuing expansion of day-care services as more mothers of young children move into the work force. Whenever another meal is eaten away from home, the hospitality industry grows.

Paralleling these developments, commercial food service has benefited as women and families are more inclined—and financially able—to eat out. The growth *rate* for working women is slowing somewhat, but female em-

---

[1]*Restaurants & Institutions,* January 7, 1987, p. 20.

ployment continues to rise. With more than half of North America's mothers already in the work force, food away from home has become a necessity rather than a luxury. This fact suggests that food service sales are likely to continue to grow slowly from their present stable base.

Lack of time is a fact of life for families with both parents working, which results in a greater tendency to eat out and in a demand for relatively fast service. Fast food, we can expect, is here to stay, but it has continually redefined itself and is likely to continue to evolve to serve the needs of a "middle-aging" population.

The two-income family has also meant growth in the number of those who can afford to travel. Although the number of hotel rooms sold has not grown appreciably in the last 40 years, there is a real possibility of an increase in some geographic markets as middle-aged prosperity and the senior "leisure class" hit the road. On the other hand, the campground and RV have been effective and growing competitors for the last generation and are likely to continue to be a strong market factor.

EDUCATION'S IMPACT ON HOSPITALITY

The North American population is the most highly educated in history in terms of its years of formal schooling. The average educational achievement is about 12 years, implying that at least half the population has somewhat more than a high school education.

But formal education is far from the only educational influence. If we include the pervasive effect of television and the increase in travel as educational, we can see why today's hospitality consumer is a sophisticate.

Attractions like Walt Disney World and other theme parks have done a great deal to raise consumers' entertainment expectations. A joint venture between George Lucas, the creator of *Star Wars,* and the Disney organization wed an aircraft simulator to movie projectors (outside the "windows") to create an impression of space flight. Indeed, the Disney organization has a whole division devoted to this kind of creative effort which it calls *imagineering.*[2]

In the business travel market, techniques such as videoconferencing are likely to become more widely accepted as a generation of businesspeople who take technology for granted come on the scene.

The educated consumer is, we argued in Chapter 3, a health-and nutrition-conscious consumer. Although younger consumers have shown a modest decline in nutrition concerns, over 65 percent of the "Ultras" (i.e., people aged 50 to 65) indicate that they are very concerned about their nutrition. Though consumers do appear less concerned about the whole question of processed foods than they did a few years ago, between 1983 and 1986 their

---

[2]*Wall Street Journal,* January 6, 1987, pp. 1, 16.

concern about the fat content and cholesterol in food roughly doubled.[3] Nutrition concerns, it seems, are a permanent part of the food service landscape.

Consumerism is a movement that educates the public. Consumerists want the guest to have a part in setting businesses' agendas, not just in deciding whether or not to patronize a business. Concern, for instance, about "passive smoking," that is, the smoke that nonsmokers inhale when there is smoking around them, continues to heat up as more data come in and the U.S. Surgeon General indicates a goal of a smoke-free society by 2000. Under the circumstances, no-smoking sections in restaurants will continue to grow in number, whether voluntarily or by law. Indeed, the greater demand for smoke-free guest rooms in hotels also suggests a trend that will continue to grow in importance in lodging.

Similarly, concerns over truth in menu will continue, and voluntary nutritional labeling to avoid legally mandated labeling may well spread.

Educated consumers are people who demand value in terms of quality of product, service, and entertainment. They value themselves, want to protect their health, and are responsive to consumer groups who seek to represent those kinds of interests. Educated consumers are in the driver's seat in our marketing oriented civilization.

SUPPLY CONDITIONS

Food and labor are the major factors of production that we will examine in this chapter.[4] Though the cost outlook is reasonably favorable for food itself, food service workers are likely to grow scarcer and more costly.

FOOD

The Reverend Thomas Malthus—an early nineteenth-century English economist and probably the man most responsible for earning for economics the title of "the dismal science"—offered some pessimistic conclusions about population growth and, the food supply. He predicted that as the population grew faster than the food supply did, worldwide famine would result. As it turned out, the crisis that Malthus foresaw did not materialize, but his ar-

---

[3] *Wall Street Journal,* November 3, 1986, p. 29.

[4] A discussion of trends in world and national capital markets is beyond the scope of this text. But the weight of expert opinion seems to be that we will continue to face an increasing scarcity of investment capital in the next generation. Interest rates that are historically high may persist, and smaller firms may have difficulty attracting debt or equity capital, if these predictions are accurate. This trend would mean that the substitution of capital-intensive technology for labor will be both more expensive and more difficult than in the past. Difficulties in raising capital will hit independents and smaller chains especially hard.

gument has been repeated ever since. Each time, however, the prophets of doom have been disproved by advances in agricultural technology.[5]

Barring a natural catastrophe, it appears likely that food supplies will continue in abundance to the point of posing a problem of surpluses. This should mean that raw foodstuffs such as grains will continue to be relatively inexpensive. (Of course, government intervention in the marketplace, which has been fairly common, could change the outlook. Intervention could take the form of restricting growing, artificially propping up prices, or both.)

Raw food prices have exhibited a long-term decline, but the price of meat has varied because of several factors that are beyond the scope of this text. We can say, however, that there is at least a reasonable possibility that the price of meat will fall somewhat by the early 1990s, after a significant lag, reflecting lower feed costs.

More expensive beef has been only one cause in the decline of beef sales. Perhaps more fundamentally, consumers' nutrition concerns have been a big factor in the marketplace. Concerns about fat and cholesterol have led to a greater consumption of chicken and, though to lesser degree, of pork. (Pork has less saturated fat—the source of cholesterol—than beef does.)

Despite the falling price of some foodstuffs—and the price of meat may join that trend—when significant labor is added, as with convenience foods, the price of labor is more likely to dominate, and prices may rise. These processed foods—and the grocer's freezer case, generally—are directly competitive with food service. Thus, any upward price trend in convenience foods is a help to the industry in maintaining its competitiveness.

LABOR

You will recall that the number of younger workers, on whom the hospitality industry normally draws, has been declining since the late 1970s. That decline will continue into the 1990s, and we can expect that even when the trend is reversed, the shortage of people that age is likely to continue through most of the decade. Under these circumstances, even as older workers are sought to fill the gaps, in many markets wage rates will continue to rise, and some companies may base their expansion plans on whether they can find the staff they need to operate. Most probably, labor costs will continue to rise; the use of part-time workers will grow; and the skills needed to motivate workers will become more important. So, too, will skills in scheduling, work simplification, and other measures aimed at alleviating labor costs.

We earlier noted the high average educational attainment of today's population. But we should also be aware that that poses some problems regarding the labor supply. Many people regard work in hospitality as too

---

[5]Earlier editions of this text, relying on expert testimony, expressed concern about possible food shortages.

demanding, too dull, or beneath them. Although students in hospitality programs are aware of the challenge and excitement of hospitality industry careers, many people do not share those values.

Two possible solutions to the labor supply problem should be noted briefly. Immigration, both legal and illegal, is projected to provide as much as 20 to 25 percent of the work force in the 1990s. Another source of labor for the hospitality industry may well be the continuing decline in manufacturing employment.

COMPETITION

The number of restaurants is expanding at the rate of 10 percent per year, whereas the population is growing by only 2 percent.[6] Beyond that, competition in the industry has changed in kind. In the 1960s and 1970s the competition that the new concepts faced was with outmoded smaller operators. Now, however, the competition is among large established companies. Though there will always be room for new concepts to grow, the presence of established dominant brand names in many markets makes it much more difficult to get started even when the concept is really new.

As the competition has heated up, advertising expenditures have risen as well. In 1985, food service spent over a billion dollars on television advertising alone. McDonald's spent $686 million on marketing and had "top-of-mind awareness" (the name that comes to mind first is top of mind), with 41 percent of consumers queried in 1986, compared with 15 percent for second-place Burger King.[7] The massive marketing expenditures of the market leaders present another set of difficulties to a new operation seeking a toehold in a crowded marketplace.

We noted in Chapter 4 the competition of restaurants with grocery stores and especially convenience stores. In 1986, convenience stores' fast-food volume was in the range of 8 to 10 percent of their sales, and the market leaders expect to increase their food service performance to the point that that proportion is doubled. As fast food upgrades and expands its menu, the cost advantages of low-labor convenience store operations increase. C stores obviously offer quick service and great convenience through their many locations, and so interindustry competition is likely to remain fierce.

TECHNOLOGY

The most significant technology in all segments of the hospitality industry is the computer. With the greater pressure on cost control, information systems will continue to be essential. Perhaps even more important, however, are the managers who have learned how to interpret and use the output of those systems.

[6]*Restaurants & Institutions*, October 29, 1986, p. 127.
[7]*Restaurants & Institutions*, July 23, 1986, p. 202.

As soon as you drive into Hershey you know you're supposed to enjoy yourself! After all, any place that has (Hershey) candy kisses for streetlights, such as those on Chocolate Avenue shown at left, must be meant for fun. The Hershey Hotel dining room is famous for fine food and the service of a classic luxury hotel.

DESTINATION CITY—HERSHEY

The emergence of "destination cities"—towns that present themselves as major tourist attractions—is already a fact of life in American tourism. In the future other towns are likely to emulate cities such as Hershey, Pennsylvania, where the local manufacturing plant (Hershey Chocolate) has been made into a tourist attraction and where even the city's streetlights follow

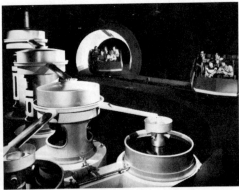

The local manufacturing plant tours became so popular that a special visitors' complex was developed to replace the former chocolate plant tour. The center includes a ride through a simulated world of chocolate, which realistically depicts the basic steps in the manufacture of chocolate.

Hersheypark, a large regional park that has themed areas such as Rhine Land (shown at right) and a variety of rides (such as "the comet," shown above), offers an exciting day's entertainment to the whole family.

the theme. Hershey boasts a large theme park, one of the country's finest luxury hotels, a sports complex offering a variety of indoor and outdoor sports, and a sizable convention center. The country's increasing affluence supports the growth of destination cities. (Photos courtesy of Hershey Foods Corp. and Hersheypark.)

Sports, indoor and outdoor, are a major attraction in Hershey. Spectator sports include basketball, hockey, and football. For those who want to be active themselves, Hershey's golf links beckon.

In lodging, the kinds of technology that make up the "smart hotel room" discussed in Chapter 8—technologies that improve guest services as well as control costs—can be expected to grow. Because of the competitive nature of lodging, an innovation such as using the guest-room television set as a terminal to check out guests is likely to be quickly matched by competing properties. Thus, technological advances, once successfully introduced, will spread rapidly through the appropriate segment or segments of the industry.

EMERGING TRENDS

The only thing certain about the future is that it hasn't happened yet. Still, we can hazard a look at trends that appear well established and speculate about some that seem reasonably likely to emerge from other established trends.

A FRAGMENTING INDUSTRY

Over the past generation, there have emerged pronounced specialized divisions in the industry. In food service we've seen a division along the lines of the eating and dining markets. In lodging, the economy chains have carved a kind of niche, while the luxury property at the other end has sought a quite different place. In between are a number of specialized products aimed at specific target markets: superfloors, all-suites, mid-range properties, and upscale properties, for instance.

This specialization is not a coincidence. Rather, it is part of a pattern of an increasingly sophisticated, marketing-oriented industry seeking to shape its products and services to fit specific consumer segments. As competition continues and marketing skills improve, we can expect to see an even greater degree of specialization in lodging resulting from tighter market segmentation.

COMPETING WITH THE HOME

As consumers invest more in home entertainment centers—VCRs, cable and satellite television, home computers, hot tubs, and the like—they become more difficult customers to reach in the away-from-home market. One tactic we examined in Chapter 4 is to offer foods for take-out and home delivery, a development occurring across all food segments from haute cuisine to fast food. And this trend is likely to accelerate as consumers become more and more accustomed to shopping from home or via interactive cable television.

For those operations committed to serving the guest away from home—and particularly those who specialize in the dinner market, which is not as convenience bound as lunch is—we can see opportunities for those who are able to develop an ambience and operating format that combines food with entertainment. Entertainment formats—such as talking, singing, and dancing robots in combination with video games—that proved so successful in the early 1980s can be copied quickly. Moreover, their concept life is often limited because they come into fashion but then quickly become yesterday's fad. Perhaps the concept of restaurants as stages—building a flexible shell that can be restyled every couple of years—will be one solution. Another possibility is suggested by the discussion in the previous section on fragmentation. Operators have successfully identified the preferences of specific segments of the market, often by developing a product–service mix that includes an entertainment component that tempts a particular segment of people out of their home. The strategy of segmentation is likely to continue to do well, but with continuing pressure on operators to keep up with a changing, fashion- and fad-conscious consumer.

What we have just said should not be taken to imply that food and service are irrelevant. Rather, they are the basics on top of which an "attraction" element needs to be erected.

THE AGE OF THE INDEPENDENT?

In this and the next section we will explore two seemingly contradictory trends related to organization and affiliation. Certainly, the continuing growth of franchise organizations seems likely. That trend offers opportunities to those who want the advantages of owning their own business and are prepared to give up a measure of independence. The decision to seek a franchise, if it is carried out with the caution that a major investment warrants, offers a relatively low risk entrepreneurial opportunity.

There also are opportunities for those who don't want to give up planning their own operation and having full control of it. This opportunity is presented by the surge in the upscale market that comes with the growing middle-aged population segment. These are, by and large, sophisticated, demanding customers who are accustomed to travel and eating out. The mass-market, "cookie cutter" operations that most chains offer are likely to pall for many in this age group. They will dine out less, or they will patronize the unique and new restaurants that catch their fancy.

One way that some entrepreneurs have taken advantage of the increasing primacy of the home is to enter the home-catering field. One of the main bars to owning one's own business is the large amount of capital needed to open the first operation. The catering business—a field that some students have entered while still in college—has minimum capital requirements and offers an opportunity to start on a small scale and grow.

CONGLOMERATES IN HOSPITALITY

Even though there are opportunities for franchisees and independents, the growth in mass-market tourism and hospitality continues to attract large companies like Marriott, with its airline and institutional food service division as well as restaurants and hotels. Such companies could be called "hospitality conglomerates." In recent years, however, conglomerates from outside the hospitality industry, seeing our growth, have been attracted to our field because of a particular fit with what they see as their main business.

In today's world, companies buy and sell business units and are themselves bought and sold. It is like a dance in which everyone keeps changing partners. The following portrait of four conglomerates illustrates how a major business interest outside what we think of as hospitality can see organizational advantages in entering the hospitality field to capitalize on its related knowledge, systems, or marketing clout. (During the life of this text, though, some companies may "change partners.")

We will now look briefly at a travel and tourism conglomerate, a leisure and recreation corporation, and two somewhat different food and beverage product companies—all of which have entered the hospitality industry in a big way.

Allegis

At the time UAL, Inc. changed its name to Allegis, it included one of North America's largest airlines, United Air Lines. It also owned the largest car rental agency in the United States, Hertz. In addition, the company had a travel wholesale operation, United Vacations, and owned the Appollo Reservation network.

What more logical development, then, than for Allegis to enter the hotel business, as it did with the purchase of Western International Hotels, now Westin Hotels. Then, to strengthen its presence in the international market, Allegis purchased Hilton International.

We should probably note that the integration of these businesses was more limited than at first we might have expected from their common ownership. Hertz reserved only cars and Westin only hotel rooms, and making a reservation at United would not lead to your being asked if you need a car or hotel room, nor did Hertz sell airline tickets or hotel rooms.

With a moment's reflection we are less surprised. These, really, are separate businesses each requiring a great deal of expertise and know-how. It just doesn't make sense to integrate them at the operating level because it would introduce mind-boggling complications. It is hard enough, for instance, to train a reservationist to the necessary level of competence in any one of those fields. Trying to develop that competence in all fields, then, would lead to very heavy training expense and reservation costs and raise the likelihood of error. Nevertheless, top management must have felt that the joint expertise of the related travel and tourism enterprises would give it an edge in each market. Finally, the corporate board decided to reverse the process and sold off many of these businesses. Never the less, the experience suggests the direction in which things can move.

Bally

The Bally Manufacturing Corporation sees itself as a major factor in the leisure-time industry. The company's original business was coin-operated gaming (slot machines) and entertainment (pinball games) machine manufacturing. Bally continues to be one of the leading manufacturers of those products and, as well, has three of the most popular video games—Pac Man, Mrs. Pac Man, and Space Invaders. In addition, Bally's Operations Division is the largest operation of what it calls "family amusement centers," with over 400 locations in the United States, offering between 50 and 60 amusement games.

Bally is also the largest operator of health and fitness centers. Their units use the names of Holiday Spa, Vic Tanny, and, in New York, Jack La Lanne. As well, another subsidiary, Bally Fitness Products, manufactures exercise equipment.

Bally is also the second largest operator of theme parks in the world, operating Six Flags parks in New Jersey, Chicago, Dallas, Los Angeles, Atlanta, St. Louis, and Hollywood, Florida. Bally also operates Astroworld and Waterworld in Houston.

Bally has become a major factor in casino gaming and the hotel business, first with Bally's Park Place in Atlantic City and more recently with the purchase of the MGM Grand hotels in Las Vegas and Reno, Nevada. Annual casino revenues were over $600 million in 1986. Bally is also involved in public lotteries through its subsidiary, Scientific Games, Inc. In its advertisements, Bally says "America's Fun is Our Business."

What is the future of fun?

In this institutional ad, aimed at investors, Bally stakes out their claim as the company that "makes America's fun their business." (Courtesy of Bally Manufacturing Corporation)

As with Allegis, the detailed logic of Bally's business definition isn't completely clear to an outsider. The link between its manufacturing arm and those using Bally's machines is clear. More generally, the company's ability to understand the leisure-time needs of Americans is probably heightened by the interaction of the units and the sharing of market research. Like Allegis, too, we might note, there have been persistent rumors that Bally might be reorganized or merge with another company. Among conglomerates, very little seems to stay the same.

Pepsico

Pepsico began, of course, as a soft drink manufacturer. Pepsico is also a major factor in the snack business through its Frito-Lay subsidiary. By purchasing several food service companies, it has clearly secured a large number of outlets for its soft drinks, but that is hardly the full or even the main reason for those acquisitions. Food service is a highly profitable business for Pepsico. Its operations are well known under their own names: Pizza Hut and Taco Bell are leaders in their respective segments, and La Petite Boulangerie is a rapidly growing chain of restaurants using a French bake-shop theme as an organizing concept.

Pillsbury

The Pillsbury Company is an old-line food manufacturing company with its earliest roots in flour and baking products. Its food service companies, however, have come to represent 45 percent of its sales and over half of its operating profit. These companies include the number-two fast-food company, Burger King, as well as the S&A Restaurant Corp., operators of Steak and Ale, and Bennigans. Pillsbury also owns Quick Wok, a Chinese fast-food chain, Haägen-Dazs Ice Cream Shoppes, and Godfather's Pizza. The company, at any time, has several new concepts in various stages of testing.

Pillsbury sees itself as "a diversified, international food company uniquely positioned to serve existing and emerging needs in the food at home and food away from home markets." It describes its restaurant group as "the largest multi concept restaurant organization in the world, and a quality leader in the fast food, casual dining and full service areas.[8]

Conglomerates in Review

Companies like Allegis, Bally, Pepsico, and Pillsbury bring enormous financial and marketing resources to the hospitality industry. In many cases, companies such as these first purchase a young company with a promising operating format and give it the financial depth and organizational muscle to expand as a major national chain. From the consumer's point of view, then, they bring successful innovations to the mass market. From the point of

---

[8]*Pillsbury 1986 Annual Report*, pp. 1, 14.

view of the hospitality industry, they are one of the factors leading to heightened competition. Given the prospects for growth in the hospitality, leisure, and tourism businesses, we can probably expect to see more such companies entering our industry and contributing to its fast pace of change, development, and growth.

THREATS

War, pestilence, and famine have been a threat to every civilization, and that continues to be true today. On the other hand, we have passed through one of the longest periods in modern history without a major war—over 40 years. Pestilence, or epidemic disease, becomes less of a problem with every advance in modern medicine. Famine is the unhappy lot of some, particularly in Africa, but it, too, seems unlikely as a major problem in North America.

On the other hand, there are problems we have been living with for some years that can't be dismissed readily. One of these is a possible resurgence of the energy crisis. Although the stocks of petroleum have been adequate in recent years, oil is not just a commodity but also a political weapon and hence unpredictable. Since the energy crisis has abated, the United States' consumption of foreign oil has increased substantially, and as prices have fallen, U.S. oil production and exploration have fallen as well.[9] Thus, the United States is vulnerable to another energy crisis.

Should a new crisis develop, we know from experience that in the short run, the hospitality industry would be badly disrupted. In the longer run, higher fuel prices seem to have resulted in a rearrangement of travel destinations that favors regional centers closer to home. But people still travel. We might expect another energy crunch to give further impetus to plans already under way to improve rail transportation which, to date, have been brought on largely by highway congestion.[10] As we noted in Chapter 12, any significant shift from highway to rail transportation would have major implications for restaurants serving travelers and especially for hotels.

Another threat whose outcome is less predictable is that of a major international or domestic monetary crisis. The economics of that danger—related to international debts in the Third World and to the trade deficit and the national debt in the United States—is well beyond our concern here. We will just say that such an event could create a panic that would be terribly disruptive for businesses and individuals alike. The possibility of such a crisis has loomed for several years, however, and money managers have managed to lead us through successfully so far. We can only hope their luck—and ours—will hold.

Perhaps these two possibilities are most useful to us, though, in raising the issue of uncertainty in any look at the future. In this chapter we have

[9]*Wall Street Journal,* November 3, 1986, p. 6.
[10]*Meeting News,* February 15, 1986, p. 30.

looked at what is called a "surprise-free projection." That is, we have assumed that there will be no major unforeseen developments, either good or bad. We've said that the future will probably be a continuation of trends already in place, and usually, it is. When presenting this kind of reasoning, however, it is incumbent on the writer to note that if there *is* a surprise, some bets may be off.

HOSPITALITY MANAGEMENT IN THE FUTURE

We have seen that management is an interrelated set of functions carried on more or less continuously by managers at all levels of the organization and, with respect to their own work, by workers as well. As a distinct way of thinking, management is relatively new; it has emerged as a field of study only in the last 100 years. As a separate practice, management grew up to meet the changing needs of our society, and it has in turn affected such social institutions in our society as the hospitality industry. Some of the central issues in management include the focus on the task idea and management's careful planning of work in the controlled shop; the organization and coordination of work outlined in Chapters 13 through 18 and first discussed by Fayol; and human relations and work—the social and individual needs of the worker.

In recent years, however, several social changes have challenged management's traditional assumptions. Although authority based on ownership or legal authority once held organizations together, the idea of private property as supreme is being challenged by organized community interest in such topics as the quality of the environment and product safety. As these currents gradually undermine the legitimizing authority of ownership, today's better-educated, more independent employees often seek a greater voice in decisions that affect their working lives. This movement is quite independent of organized labor; indeed some of those in organized labor resist it.

In both Europe and North America a small but significant movement called self-management is being put forward by management.[11] The assumptions that this movement makes about the workers differ radically from those propounded by Taylor at the turn of the century. They call for the full involvement of the workers in all decisions affecting the workplace. The concept of self-management assumes that workers are interested in doing a good job. It also accepts the notion that the workers often know more about their work than management or outside efficiency experts do. By reinvolving the workers in all elements of the job—including job design and quality con-

---

[11]In Yugoslavia, a form of self-management is almost universal. The practice also appears to be growing rapidly in Scandinavia.

trol—companies that use self-management seek to avoid the alienation associated with dull, routine jobs. In an industry with over 60 percent of its work force in unskilled jobs and a need to attract the workers to support its continuing growth, this new approach is bound to have great interest. As yet, not all the returns on self-management are in. Many observers will want to wait until it is clear whether this approach is just a fad or really a new stage in worker–management relations in an affluent, educated, choice-making society.

A related managerial development involves the breakdown of strictly hierarchical organizations. The process that Alvin Toffler dubbed *ad hocracy* sees task and team member expertise as the source of authority in work settings dominated by a flexible organization team. These new means of organizing work emerged first in the aerospace industry. Flexible organization forms have proved necessary, as we have seen, in complex resort organizations such as Walt Disney World and Las Vegas's MGM Grand Hotel. We can expect them to become more common in the industry as firms and cities offering planned play environments proliferate.

Management goals, as defined by the guest, will undoubtedly continue their rapid change, reflecting a dynamic society. A marketing approach that sees innovation as essential work for managers at all levels of the organization will undoubtedly be a useful asset for the hospitality managers of today and tomorrow.

THE FUTURE AND YOU

We began this volume with an exploration of your interests in the industry and some consideration of how you might make a place for yourself in it. This is also an appropriate note on which to end. From our consideration of career planning for managers and supervisors in the hospitality industry, three points particularly deserve summary consideration: an industrywide view, the notion of retained earnings, and the need to develop a personal strategy.

THE HOSPITALITY INDUSTRY

Your interests may lie today in a particular area of the industry. They will necessarily become specialized as you take your first job after completing your schooling. Although you certainly must specialize to do an excellent job at whatever you are doing then and concentrate your energies there, it will also help you keep a view of the whole industry in mind. As the industry changes and evolves, you may encounter opportunities that suit your goals better in, say, club work or institutions. The reverse might just as easily be true. The hospitality industry is, and will continue to be, characterized by a good deal of movement from one segment to another.

In charting a career, you should keep your goals clearly in view. If they involve advancing through supervision into senior management, your early jobs should probably be in areas that prepare you for the variety of opportunities in the hospitality industry now and in the future. Thus, experience in food service offers a background useful and often essential to practically all of the industry's components. Although front-office work (for example) is extremely rewarding, it offers limited opportunities for growth and little basis for a move to other sectors of the industry.

RETAINED EARNINGS

The notion that what you have learned is something no one can take from you is central to this text. The idea that you can learn a great deal more from every job than just the job itself is equally important. As anyone (whether as a student in a summer dishwashing job or as a graduate in a junior assistant manager's position) moves through a career, he or she occasionally finds a job that does not make the fullest use of his or her abilities. For these jobs to be profitable in the fullest sense, they must be explored from the perspective of what you can learn to make them really productive *for you*.

Consider the many changes that appear to be in store for the industry and the possibility of opportunities presenting themselves from unexpected quarters. This consideration should make clear the importance of a broad fund of knowledge of people, management techniques, and guest relations, to name just a few areas. Thus, what you learn through study and experience are the most important assets you can develop early in your career.

STRATEGIES AND GOALS

Career goals differ from person to person. Not everybody needs or wants to be a Henry Ford. Some people seek fame and fortune in a career; others want enjoyable work and an adequate income. To some, income is most important; to others helping other people is the key. The main thing to realize is that whatever your objectives are, you are more likely to attain them with consciously developed plans that move you toward definite goals.

Of course, setting goals is never easy and is always harder for some than others, so you must be patient. You may decide that, for now, your goal will be to form goals as soon as you can! If you cannot realistically set lifetime goals at the moment, you can adopt a policy of exploration and set intermediate goals that support that policy.

Although long-range goals are important, so are medium-range and short-range planning. These may even be more important for young people, because long-range goals have a way of evolving with experience and opportunity. Thus, it is important to ask yourself what you want to get done this week! What can you learn from your new job besides the job itself? How much should you be earning a year from now? What is the next job you want to seek with your current employer?

It is important to have goals, but it is equally important to develop the strategies and tactics for moving toward your goals. This notion invites you to see yourself as an active element in your career; not as someone who waits for things to happen but as someone who makes his or her own place in the world. Remember, no matter who your employer is, you are in business for yourself. It is your life!

SUMMARY

In our final chapter we looked at the principal forces shaping the future of the hospitality industry. The basic economic forces are demand and supply. Demand encompasses consumer demographics; employment, income, and demand for hospitality; and education's impact on hospitality. Supply includes the supply of food and labor, and competition. We also considered technology as a major force.

Then we looked at the emerging trends: the fragmentation of the hospitality industry, competition with the home, and the outlook for the independent and the conglomerate. We illustrated the hospitality conglomerate with four examples, Allegis, Bally, Pepsico, and Pillsbury.

We examined the possible threats to the future hospitality industry. And finally, we considered hospitality management in the future—and you.

KEY WORDS AND CONCEPTS

To help you review this chapter, keep in mind the following.

Consumer demographics   Leisure-time industry
Ultras   Self-management
Hospitality conglomerate

REVIEW QUESTIONS

1.   What are the two main economic forces? Describe briefly how each will affect the hospitality industry in the future.

2.   How will consumer demographics affect the hospitality industry?

3.   What are some of your ideas about solving the future labor shortage?

4. Which do you favor for the future—independents or conglomerates? Explain.

5. What do you consider the biggest threat to the hospitality industry, and why?

6. In what ways has this book changed your mind about entering hospitality management?

INDEX

NOTES

NOTES

NOTES

NOTES